THE
AMERICAN
ASTRONOMICAL
SOCIETY'S

FIRST
CENTURY

George Ellery Hale (right), the founder of the AAS and much of modern American astronomy, strolling with Andrew Carnegie (left) in Pasadena in March 1910. (This photograph is reproduced by permission of *The Huntington Library, San Marino, California*.)

THE
AMERICAN
ASTRONOMICAL
SOCIETY'S

FIRST
CENTURY

EDITOR

DAVID H. DEVORKIN

Smithsonian Institution,
Washington, D.C.

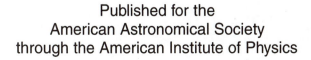
Published for the
American Astronomical Society
through the American Institute of Physics

The American Astronomical Society
Executive Office
2000 Florida Avenue, N.W.
Suite 400
Washington, DC 20009-1231

Front cover: Meetings of the Society (clockwise from top): 1897, 1919, 1950, 1953, 1963, 1979, 1956. Photographs courtesy of Richard Dreiser (Yerkes Observatory), Hugh Johnson, John Irwin collection, and the Emilio Segrè Visual Archives (American Institute of Physics).

Published for the American Astronomical Society through the American Institute of Physics.
Maya Flikop, Manager, Translations and Special Publications
Sabine Kessler and Michael Lynch, Production Editors

Library of Congress Cataloging-in-Publication Data
The American Astronomical Society's first century / editor, David H. DeVorkin.
    p. cm.
  Includes bibliographical references and index.
  ISBN 1-56396-683-2 (alk. paper)
  1. American Astronomical Society--History. I. DeVorkin, David H., 1944– .
QB1. A28593 1999   98-37594
520'.607--dc21   CIP

10 9 8 7 6 5 4 3 2 1

CONTENTS

8 Commentary by Recent AAS Presidents

EDITOR'S PREFACE

Centennials are times for celebration and reflection. The AAS centennial provides a chance to look back to take inventory of how the Society came into existence, how it grew, and the degree to which it met the demands of a growing and changing profession. Accordingly, the majority of the authors in this volume are astronomers who are interested enough in their Society to take the time to examine both it and their personal roles in its development. Several historians have contributed as well, but have done so knowing full well that their audience is composed mainly of American astronomers interested in gaining a better appreciation of how their Society reflects the profound changes that have taken place in their profession over the past century.

Indeed, the changes experienced by the profession are as radical and far reaching as the changes in our view of the universe since 1900. Organized astronomy in the United States began only in the latter half of the nineteenth century, and only a few hundred active workers were involved. Now, there are many thousands of diverse contributors, numerous societies, proliferating journals, and complex interdisciplinary and international networks. Astronomical institutions have multiplied to the point where astronomers can be found not only in academe but also in many branches of the government, both civilian and military, as well as in industry, performing a wide range of functions. Waves of physicists have entered the profession, some retaining their identity as physicists and forming subgroups within physics departments and national laboratories, and taking on the guise of astrophysicists as they apply their tools and techniques to astrophysical problems. Geophysicists and geologists have become planetologists, studying the worlds of our solar system opened up by space probes, and radio engineers have become radio astronomers, turning their craft to a reconnaissance of the most distant regions of the universe. Chemists and high-energy physicists have found the means to probe the depths of the sun, stars and supernovae, taking their temperatures by capturing the elusive neutrino. The universe, our galaxy in 1900, is now a universe of galaxies. What was originally a static universe, is now a dynamic, relativistic universe, whose origin and fate are perceived very differently than they were when the Society was young. Few people asked questions about the origin and structure of the universe when the Society was born. Now these are among the questions that drive the lives of most practitioners.

The essays written for this volume portray how the American Astronomical Society as an institution mirrors the changing nature of the profession. The Society was conceived at a time when astrophysics was challenging the traditional practices of positional and gravitational astronomy, and when the nation itself was establishing a separate identity in the world of science. The origins of the Society reflect both the need for national identity and the tension between the old and the new astronomies, just as the growth of the Society reflects the continuing expansion of the profession as it acquired new tools and techniques, and, as a discipline, asked new questions about the universe. New patterns of patronage after World War II, new technologies, and the growth of theory-driven practice all contributed to a broadening of the astronomical enterprise. What had existed largely as an elite academic profession nurtured by private philanthropy that had built the largest telescopes and astronomical institutions in the world, was revolutionized in the post World War II era, especially after Sputnik, by a vastly broadened funding base, by the rise of consortia and national observatories (on the ground, in the air, and now in space), and by the concomitant increase in expectations for continued growth that these changes engendered.

The astronomical enterprise has blossomed both in size and complexity. Diverse specialties devoted to the sun, the planets, dynamical astronomy, high-energy astrophysics and other areas within the profession reached critical mass in the 1960s and demanded either a separate identity, or more control of their fate within their parent organization. The Society coped and made adjustments in its structure to accommodate these pressures, but much remains to be done. Issues of gender and race, of inclusiveness and relevance in a rapidly changing world, of equitable access to large telescopes, of the need to maintain a robust infrastructure and the critical importance of an effective educational strategy, all have been raised, making the Society a platform for debate that has kept the professional community together, even though at times some felt it was at the breaking point. But as the millennium draws near, as each new funding cycle for NSF, NASA, DOE and DOD is debated in Washington and across the land, and as the membership of the Society continued to rise [it peaked a few years ago] through the last few decades at a rate that more than tasked the increase in light-gathering power per year, the pressures to perform and excel became immense, on the individual as well as on the many institutions which invested heavily in the astronomical enterprise.

All these matters are still on the table as the Society enters its second century. It is the editor's hope that the essays presented here will help air some of these concerns and will help demonstrate how the Society dealt with them in the past, and that this book will help to serve the needs of the profession as it faces an ever-more exciting and challenging future. Accordingly, we asked the four past presidents of the Society to provide topical essays that would illuminate contemporary issues and concerns that face the Society today and in the twenty-first century. Many of the other authors needed no encouragement to provide similar commentary.

With the exception of the reprint of Joel Stebbins' essay, all the essays presented here are by contemporary authors who either wrote specifically for this volume or modified existing commentary. Stebbins' chapter stands in marked contrast to all the others, for he represents the spirit of the Society when it was still a small body and where, as oral histories with many senior members attest, everyone knew everyone else. Stebbins' essay does overlap those discussing the early years of the Society. But his perspective was very different, such as his display of the generally accepted belief that the Society's origin should be dated from the 1897 meeting; hence his opening line that they were celebrating the fiftieth anniversary of the Society as well as the semi-centennial of the opening of the Yerkes Observatory. This may have been an act of convenience, or may have illustrated the centrality of the Yerkes Observatory to the profession in America in that day. More in tune with present-day views of how institutions are created, however, it is clear that the Society did not exist in 1897. The conscious process of forming a Society did start, but it took two years of gestation and negotiation before the actual Society existed, and, as we learn here, some 15 more years before it took on its present name, and decades more before it took on anything resembling its present form. What we celebrate in 1999, therefore, is the survival not of a tradition, but the continuation of a process.

Beyond the authors who have contributed chapters to this book, there are many people who have kindly aided and assisted the editor in meeting deadlines, stretching deadlines, and ignoring other deadlines in order to bring this project to completion. First, this centennial volume is but a part of a larger effort to celebrate the Society's first century. Leading that effort have been Don Osterbrock, Bob Milkey and Bob O'Dell, who have marshalled forces that have been instrumental in making this book a reality. The idea for a book, however, came first from Peter Boyce, always thinking ahead, who approached the editor several years ago asking if it might not be a good idea to put a bit of the Society's history on the World Wide Web. This effort was successful with the aid of Brant Sponberg, and led to the idea of a fuller volume to celebrate the centennial.

Most of the authors indicated to me that they had asked colleagues to read their drafts before submitting them to the editor. On behalf of the authors, I thank these readers as I thank those who read my early drafts. One person stands out for me: Paul Routly. Paul was the Society's first Executive Officer; he was my window on a critical time when the Society really began to change. Paul dug into the Society's history and helped me examine how the demographics of the Society changed. Working as a "Behind-the-Scenes" volunteer at the National Air and Space Museum, Paul was untiring as he gathered together an enormous amount of information about the Society and its leaders. The chapter we co-authored is but one example of his generous industry.

Members of the Historical Astronomy Division lent more than moral support. Some wrote chapters and many read chapters and offered solid advice and counsel: LeRoy Doggett, Steve Dick, Tom Williams, Marc Rothenberg, Richard Jarrell, Howard Plotkin, Richard Berendzen, Barbara Welther, Owen Gingerich, Ron Brashear, Katherine Bracher, Sara Schechner Genuth and Don Osterbrock stand out as especially helpful, filling a wide range of needs from photograph research to fact checking, to designing an advance brochure, to keeping the editor sane. Richard Dreiser, Hugh Johnson, Andy Fraknoi, Tom Williams, Mike Saladyga, Jay Pasachoff, Spencer Weart and others also provided photographic material. A great resource was John Irwin's incomparable photograph collection, housed in part at the Center for History of Physics of the American Institute of Physics (AIP) where Tracey Keifer and then Jack Scott were most helpful. Equally critical was access to the Council Minutes of the Society and to Society records provided by Caroline Moseley, also at the AIP. Dorothy Schaumberg of the Mary Lea Shane Archives located important documents and images for the authors, as did archivists at Harvard University and at the Dudley Observatory. Brenda Corbin and Greg Shelton of the U. S. Naval Observatory Library were, as always, terrific in making their incomparable resources available, sometimes on really short notice. Helping process many of the images, members of the NASM photographic department including Carolyn Russo and Marc Avino were especially kind in making our needs top priority. Mike Tuttle and Vicki Portway of the Center for Earth and Planetary Studies helped to process digital images, as did Kunie DeVorkin and Scott Custin. Joanne Bailey of the Department of Space History handled the many oral histories the editor took with astronomers during the process of preparing resource material for the book. Maya Flikop and Sabine Kessler of the American Institute of Physics calmly, with good humor, and with consummate skill, saw the book through the editing and production process. To all these good people, I offer thanks.

This book is dedicated to the memory of those who built and maintained the Society. Notable among those who died recently and who greatly aided the genesis of this book, both in substance and in spirit, were Martin Schwarzschild, Lyman Spitzer, Jr., and LeRoy Doggett.

David DeVorkin

PART 1

THE EARLY SOCIETY

AAS Meetings Before There Was an AAS: The Pre-History of the Society

Donald E. Osterbrock

INTRODUCTION

In June, 1999, the American Astronomical Society will hold its 194th meeting in Chicago, Illinois. The University of Chicago will be one of the host institutions, but the meeting will be much too large for its campus. Instead, this centennial meeting will take place in a large hotel in the Loop. More than 1,200 members will probably register for it, and some 800 scientific papers will be presented, mostly as posters. It will be a far cry from the first meeting of the Society, then called the Astronomical and Astrophysical Society of America, held at Yerkes Observatory in Williams Bay, Wisconsin, in September, 1899. That meeting, at which the Society officially came into existence, was attended by 50 astronomers, who presented 31 papers in all. At the time, it was called the Third Conference of Astronomers and Astrophysicists. It followed the Second Conference of Astronomers and Astrophysicists, held at Harvard College Observatory in 1898. There the sessions for papers were held in the drawing room of Director Edward C. Pickering's residence. That meeting, at which a committee was set up to organize the Society, can in turn be traced back to the scientific conferences held at the dedication of Yerkes Observatory in October, 1897. Those conferences represent the first national astronomy meetings in the United States, and these three meetings together may be called the pre-history of the American Astronomical Society. Yerkes Observatory was the Society's birthplace; it and the young director who raised the money to build it, and more than anyone else brought about the Society's formation, are essential elements of that pre-history.[1]

HALE AND YERKES OBSERVATORY

The first of the three conferences was organized by George Ellery Hale as part of the observatory's dedication. He was only 24 years old, two years past graduation from the Massachusetts Institute of Technology, when he and President William Rainey Harper, of the new University of Chicago, persuaded Charles T. Yerkes in 1892 to pledge the money to start the observatory. It was to include the "largest and best" telescope in the world, a 40-inch refractor. The Chicago street-railway tycoon would settle for nothing less. The newspapers held a field day, suggesting that Yerkes would use the telescope to find new right-of-ways on Mars, since he had already taken over all of them on Earth. This was intended as humor, but the editorialists were serious when they wrote that the Lick Observatory's 36-inch refractor, then the largest in the world, would "shortly be licked," and that the new 40-inch would confirm "Chicago's destiny to be great."[2]

At first everyone assumed the observatory would be located on the very new University of Chicago campus. A site in nearby Washington Park was seriously considered. However, professional astronomers knew the telescope would be wasted so near to the low, hazy, smoky Lake Michigan shoreline.[3] Harper heeded their advice and solicited information on better prospective sites. He and Hale received invitations or proposals for 27 possible locations. The furthest afield came from members of the Pasadena Board of Trade in California, urging that Yerkes Observatory be built in the Sierra Madre range just north of their town. They believed that "due to the steadiness of our atmosphere, the meteorological conditions would permit of better results being obtained from the location of the telescope in our Mountains than in any other part of the country." One of the board of trade members even pinpointed the exact location as "Observatory Peak" on Mount Wilson. Actually, the University of Chicago trustees never considered any site farther than a hundred miles from their city, but only a decade later Hale was to move to California and found Mount Wilson Observatory.[4]

Most of the proposed sites were in Illinois, including Elgin, Kankakee, Marengo, Peoria, Rockford, and Waukegan. Yerkes' private secretary particularly favored Eagle's Nest Bluff, in Oregon, on the Rock River, "one of the most picturesque locations in the State of Illinois."[5] Hale wanted to put the observatory at Lake Forest, north of Chicago, but that "deal" (Harper's word) fell through because the necessary land was not offered to the university. Highland Park, also on the North Shore, and Hinsdale, west of Chicago, were also considered very seriously.[6]

The only site proposed in Wisconsin was at Williams Bay, on Lake Geneva in Walworth County, approximately midway between Chicago and Madison. John Johnston, Jr., a wealthy Chicago real estate operator who owned large tracts of land around Williams Bay, offered to donate 50 acres for the observatory. As university property it would be completely free of taxes, he wrote Harper; and, as an additional advantage, "[i]t may be taken for granted that any legislation that may be desired from the legislature may be had easier & cheaper in Wis[consin] than in Illinois. And the placing of this great improvement in Wis[consin] will certainly appeal to state pride & be an advantage in that respect to the new university [of Chicago] in many ways."[7] George C. Walker, a University of Chicago trustee who had a home on Lake Geneva, strongly recommended the site, as did Thomas C. Chamberlin, the former state geologist of Wisconsin and former president of the University of Wisconsin, who had been lured to Chicago to head its Geology Department. Chamberlin favored Lake Geneva for the "delightful nature of the situation, the surrounding high hills, clear crisp atmosphere without fogs and vapor, absence of manufactories, no night or Sunday trains, easy access to Chicago,... resort for the choicest people of Chicago,... and the attention that will be directed to the University of Chicago because of that."[8]

Williams Bay met all the criteria recommended by the astronomers, and the only worry was whether the nearby lake would cause fog, clouds, or poor "seeing" conditions. Sherburne W. Burnham, the renowned double star observer who was to be a volunteer member of the Yerkes Observatory staff, had worked for a year at the University of Wisconsin's Washburn Observatory on Lake Mendota. Later he had tested the Mount Hamilton, California, site for Lick Observatory before its 36-inch refractor was erected there. Now Burnham gave his opinion, based on his experience at Madison, that Lake Geneva would not present a problem, and the last remaining objection was overcome. Hale and the president visited the proposed site in mid-March and considered it the "most beautiful" one they had seen. Within a few days, Harper and Martin A. Ryerson, president of the Board of Trustees, decided definitely on Williams Bay, partly because it was "essentially a Chicago location,"—the summer home of many wealthy Chicago families. Ryerson himself and Charles L. Hutchinson, another trustee, were to establish mansions there within the next few years.[9]

One cold December day in 1893, Harper, Walker, Johnston, Burnham, and university architect Henry Ives Cobb walked over the ground at Williams Bay with Edward E. Ayer, a wealthy Lake Geneva friend of the university, and picked the exact spot where the observatory would be built. The actual work went very slowly at first.[10] Money was hard to come by, and although Yerkes had committed to pay for the building and telescope, Hale and Harper had great difficulty raising additional funds for astronomers' salaries and auxiliary instruments for their research. Their appeals to the wealthy Chicago colony of businessmen with Lake Geneva summer homes went largely unanswered.[11]

Finally, toward the end of May, 1897, the 40-inch telescope was at last completed. The lens was delivered to Yerkes Observatory in the custody of Alvan G. Clark, its maker, and was mounted in the telescope the next day. That night was cloudy, but the following day Harper and a delegation of trustees, faculty members, and friends came out from Chicago to see the first light through the telescope. It was partly clear that evening, and they all marveled at the huge, bright image of Jupiter. After the guests left, Hale and astronomer Edward E. Barnard observed several other objects, giving the lens a more critical test. They found it fully up to specifications.[12]

However, just a few nights later, disaster struck. The financier Yerkes, fearful that some of his enemies or competitors would sabotage the telescope, had given strict orders that no one except the astronomers should ever be allowed anywhere near the telescope. He feared that "many persons—some of them high in the social scale—would even be pleased to see an accident happen to the telescope." It must be guarded "against either accident or malicious acts of anyone who might feel disposed to injure it," he demanded, and every precaution should be taken to keep visitors away from it.[13] His orders were fruitless, however, although it was a design failure rather than a saboteur that caused the crash. On the morning of May 29, just a few hours after Barnard and Ferdinand Ellerman, his assistant, had left the dome at the end of the night's work, the giant elevator-like wooden floor broke loose from some of the cables that supported it, came careening down, and smashed to pieces. The cables had not been securely fastened to the floor, and the weakened joints had parted. As they broke, half the floor, unsupported, had crashed to the ground. If the accident had happened a few hours earlier, Barnard and Ellerman would probably have been killed; had it happened a few nights earlier, Harper and half the University of Chicago high command might have died. As it was, the telescope was almost useless for months while the floor was rebuilt, this time with the cables securely fastened. Fortunately no damage had occurred to the telescope or lens.[14]

As the work progressed on the floor, Hale began planning the dedication ceremonies. For the scientists, they were to be built around a research conference; for the donor and the university bigwigs, they were to feature an academic procession and an oration by the most famous astronomer of his day. Since Yerkes planned to be away all summer for his usual vacation in Europe, the exercises were scheduled for the fall of 1897, soon after his return. Hale wrote literally hundreds of letters, inviting and cajoling the leading astronomers and pioneer astrophysicists to take part in the conference.[15]

FIRST CONFERENCE OF ASTRONOMERS AND ASTROPHYSICISTS

Finally, the third week in October arrived. America was at peace, and all was right with the world. In Chicago, Carson Pirie Scott and Company was selling a complete boy's "outfit" of clothes including a coat, two pairs of shorts, a cap, and suspenders for $4.10. Mandel Brothers was advertising a young man's three-piece suit for $10, the Fair had men's or ladies' bicycles for $13.95, and the National Dental Parlors were advertising sets of false teeth for $4. On Sunday, October 17, the popular Reverend Jenkin Lloyd Jones preached to his fashionable congregation at All Souls Unitarian Church on the Yerkes dedication. The title of his sermon was "Astronomy—Its Struggles and Triumphs," and he was quoted as saying that astronomical research "should inspire us with a new zeal for the quest, for such study releases us from the trammels of matter and carries us into the fellowship of the spirit... . The shackles of superstition fall off and the soul, unfettered, revels in the boundless universe of truth, beauty, and love."[16]

The conferences connected with the dedication began at the observatory on Monday. The imposing buff-colored brick building stood on a broad, level height overlooking Lake Geneva. A recent construction site, the ground was nearly bare, except for a few small, recently planted trees. One of the three domes still had not been put on the building, leaving an unfinished look. The 40-inch telescope and Hale's 12-inch telescope were in complete working order in the other two domes. In the surrounding woods, the maples were in brilliant autumn color, but the skies were gray and overcast. As the visiting astronomers arrived at Williams Bay, Hale met each train at the station with rented horse drawn hacks and buses and accompanied them directly to the observatory. There were no hotels in the little town, and although the most important guests were put up in faculty members' houses, the rest had to stay in nearby farmhouses or at the observatory itself. Many of them slept on cots which were set up at night in the library, then taken down before the scientific sessions began the next day.[17] Yerkes hired a chef and several waiters from one of his favorite restaurants in Chicago to come out to Williams Bay and cater the meals for the visiting scientists. The caterers brought a huge iron stove and several wagon loads of provisions with them; a local reporter inferred "that astronomers are good eaters, and indeed they look it." The stove was set up in the meridian-circle room at the Observatory, and the meals were served in one of the halls.[18]

No more than 30 astronomers were present for the first day, but the only scheduled events were the annual meeting of the board of editors of *The Astrophysical Journal* and informal scientific discussions. Several demonstrations were also set up in the laboratories and shops of the observatory building. Frank Wadsworth showed the

Figure 1. First Conference of Astronomers and Astrophysicists, Yerkes Observatory, October 1897. Edward C. Pickering, future second president of the AAS, is standing in center of group of three men in front right, wearing a soft, light hat; to left of him is James E. Keeler, the main invited speaker, wearing a derby; to right of them and slightly in front is Carl Runge, wearing a light hat. George Ellery Hale, wearing a soft, wide-brimmed hat, is at right end of second row from rear, and Edward E. Barnard, wearing a derby and with his hand partly in his pocket, is at left end of second row. Courtesy of Yerkes Observatory.

visitors a new interferometer (for measuring precision wavelengths), and George W. Ritchey demonstrated his methods of grinding the 60-inch mirror, which ten years later became the basis of the first large reflecting telescope at Mount Wilson. Carl Lundin, of the Clark firm that had made the 40-inch lens for the Yerkes telescope, demonstrated the method that had been used for testing its surface, and Henry Crew, of nearby Northwestern University, exhibited the operation of a new electric arc for spectroscopic research.[19]

Nearly 50 more visitors arrived that evening, and they had a chance to look through the 40-inch telescope, for the skies had temporarily cleared. Barnard and Burnham showed them close double stars, well resolved by the giant telescope. For the next two days there was a busy round of conferences, with the astronomers presenting papers describing their recent research results. James E. Keeler, of Allegheny Observatory, gave the most important paper on Tuesday morning. He described his photographic studies of the spectra of the "third-type" (cool) stars, showed lantern slides of his spectrograms of many of these stars (arranged in order of spectral features), and explained how the various lines and bands changed along the sequence. He and the other astrophysicists were searching for the meaning of these empirically discussed orderings, but too little was known of atomic physics, and success came only years later. Another important paper that day was by Simon Newcomb, who described his new method of finding the average distance of a group of stars, by comparing their apparent (proper) and linear (radial) motions. Only in that decade had astronomers begun to be able to measure "velocities in the line of sight" reasonably accurately. Still other papers were given by George C. Comstock, of the University of Wisconsin, on the visual observational work he was doing at its Washburn Observatory, and by Carl Runge, who had come from Hannover, Germany, to speak on his identification of oxygen in the solar spectrum.[20]

That afternoon, Hale led off with an address of welcome, coupled with a description of the observatory, its instruments, and especially the 40-inch refractor. He described its light-gathering power and resolution in scientific terms to the visiting astronomers, but the *Chicago Tribune* translated his talk into terms its readers could understand by saying that the Yerkes telescope was one-fifth more powerful than the only other telescope with which it could be compared, the Lick Observatory 36-inch telescope. The *Tribune* reporter had evidently been fed some background material by Hale or Burnham, for he added that the location of Yerkes Observatory was better than the Lick site on Mount Hamilton. This odd conclusion, attributed to "the opinion of practical men connected with both locations," is decidedly questionable, for there are many more clear nights at Lick than in southern Wisconsin. It was cloudy that night, so the visitors had to be content with a tour of the instrument and optical shops instead of the planned observing session with Barnard, who had hoped to show several stars, nebulae, and clusters with the 40-inch refractor.

Wednesday was a full day of scientific papers, the most interesting being Barnard's on his work of photographing nebulae, and Pickering's on the Harvard College Observatory research program. Yerkes himself arrived on the train that evening, and Hale met him at the station and took him directly to the observatory to meet the visitors. Then, after supper with Hale, Yerkes came back to observe stars with "his telescope," but it was cloudy again. Nevertheless, the big, florid magnate was pleased, and told the reporters, gesturing to Hale, that "the management could not be improved upon." He also predicted that, before long, a few comets and new stars would be discovered through "that tunnel," indicating the 40-inch refractor. He and Hale went into the library and listened for a few minutes to part of Barnard's talk, illustrated with lantern slides of his photographs, which was the substitute for the observing session that evening. Then Yerkes left for the night, no doubt spent as a guest of one of the trustees at a lake-shore mansion.

Thursday was the high point of the week's exercises. Two special trains left Chicago early that morning, bringing about 700 trustees, faculty members, and guests to Williams Bay. The crowd was so large that several lake steamers were engaged to take most of them from Williams Bay station, close to the shore, to the observatory pier. Only those too old or infirm to climb the steep hill from the landing to the observatory were conveyed directly to the door by horse-drawn buses. Entering the building, the spectators went into the 40-inch dome, where the floor was in its lowest position, supported on concrete blocks. Even so, as they seated themselves on the folding chairs that covered the newly rebuilt floor, some of them must have wondered just how strong it really was. The day was cold and gloomy, and the guests were advised to keep their hats and coats on in the unheated dome.

Shortly after the noon hour, the academic procession entered, everyone wearing caps and gowns, in the kind of pageantry that President Harper loved. First came the faculty members from Chicago, who made up the University Council and the University Senate. Following them, in pairs, were Hale and Newcomb, who was to be the speaker at the convocation in Chicago the following day, then Eri B. Hulbert, dean of the Divinity School at Chicago and the Reverend James D. Butler of Madison, Wisconsin, the two chaplains for the occasion, then Ryerson, the president of the Board of Trustees, and Keeler, the main speaker for the day. Bringing up the rear were Harper and Yerkes. They all marched to seats on a temporary rostrum that had been erected at one end of the floor.[21]

The ceremonies opened with a prayer by Hulbert, and then the Spiering String Quartet, a Chicago group which had volunteered its services, played an Andante by Tchaikovsky. The acoustics in the cavernous dome left a good deal to be desired, but at least the audience could hear well enough to know when the selection was over and applaud tumultuously. Then Keeler mounted the podium and delivered his address, "The Importance of Astrophysical Research, and the Relation of Astrophysics to Other Physical Sciences." He defined astrophysics as a subject closely allied to astronomy, chemistry, and physics, drawing material that could be profitably used from any science and concerned with the nature of the heavenly bodies—what they are, rather than where they are, which had been the task of the old astronomy. Mostly it depended upon the analysis of light. Although astrophysics had little practical, money-making value, its subject, like that of astronomy, was nothing less than understanding the universe. Thus it was of the deepest interest to scientists and to the general population alike. Astrophysical research was difficult and demanding, requiring the highest mental discipline, training, and insight. It also required complicated apparatus. Some traditionalists might look back with nostalgia to the good old days when the human eye was the only instrument an astronomer needed at the telescope, but those days were gone forever.

Keeler went on to describe the importance of photography and of spectroscopy in astrophysics, and to sketch out some of the problems they might be expected to solve—the motions of the stars, the abundances of the elements, the physical conditions in the stars, the detailed structure of the Sun, the surface of the Moon, the atmospheres and surfaces of the planets, the intrinsic differences between stars, their evolutionary histories, the properties of binary stars and their orbits, among other problems. It was a modern, forward-looking speech. The topics Keeler described were, in fact, the main problems of astrophysics for the next fifty years, and more than one of them is still under active investigation today. He closed with graceful tributes to the munificence of Yerkes and to the skill of the builders of the observatory. Its staff, he said, were masters of both astronomical and astrophysical research, and their work would throw light on the dark places in nature and thus advance true scientific progress.[22] He sat down to more tumultuous applause, but as he had spoken for slightly over an hour, many of the non-astronomical guests were probably clapping more to warm up than to express their appreciation of the fine points of his paper.

Next, the string quartet played the Largo from the "Quartet in F Major" by Dvorak, always a favorite composer in Chicago. Then Yerkes was introduced, and drew the most applause of all. According to the *Tribune*, the streetcar magnate "blushed like a bashful maiden." To an appreciative audience like this, Yerkes could be surprisingly modest. His short speech paid tribute to Harper, the university, and the builders of the telescope. He gave a capsule history of 5,000 years of astronomy, no doubt written for him by Hale, beginning with the Greeks and culminating in the spectroscope. Yerkes professed himself fully satisfied with the telescope, observatory, and staff, and with a flourish turned the structure over to the University of Chicago. Ryerson expressed the gratitude of the Board of Trustees, and Harper then delivered an address describing the building of the observatory and closed by thanking Yerkes fulsomely on behalf of the faculty and students.[23]

The benediction was given by James D. Butler, an 83-year-old retired minister who was the long-time curator of the State Historical Society of Wisconsin. He was substituting for President Charles Kendall Adams of the University of Wisconsin, who was ill. The small, wiry Butler, a well-known Madison character who signed his letters, "Superoctogenarianically yours," in closing his prayer spoke directly to Hale, saying, "You are happier that Plato. When Plato was asked 'Where will your ideal heaven be realized?' he looked upward and answered, 'in Heaven.' But your ideal you behold becoming actual here and now in the midst of your best years."[24]

After this, all the rest was anticlimactic. A gigantic luncheon was served to the guests in the halls of the observatory. Then they walked through the building and inspected the telescopes, instruments, and shops until the trains left for Chicago at 4 PM. The whole day had been a great success. The *Tribune* editorialized that "the dedication of the Yerkes telescope is another step toward that proud position of preeminence in science the culture to which Chicago is rapidly and surely advancing." It always considered southern Wisconsin a part of Chicagoland![25]

Finale in Chicago

Friday was given over to the dedication at the University of Chicago campus. In the morning, physicist Albert A. Michelson demonstrated some of his experimental work in light to the visiting scientists at Ryerson Laboratory. After a lunch hosted by Harper, they heard an address by Newcomb, the "rather grim dean of American astronomers."[26] Sixty-three years old, he had been in charge of the Nautical Almanac Office from 1877 until his retirement a few months before the dedication, and he represented the apotheosis of the old-time astronomy. Years earlier he had advised Barnard, then a keen-eyed amateur observer, to put aside his telescope until he had learned mathematics; during the Yerkes conference he had been a guest at the home of the now famous discoverer of Jupiter's fifth satellite. Newcomb was a master of gravitational theory, and had made many contributions to predicting mathematically the detailed motions of the planets and satellites in their orbits. His article on "Abstract Science in America," published in the *North American Review* in 1876, was one of the first appeals for support for pure science, as opposed to applied science, in this country, and according to one admiring biographer he had done more than any other person since Benjamin Franklin to make American science respected and honored abroad. Over the years he had given many lectures at commencements, dedications, and scientific congresses.[27]

When Newcomb rose and launched into his address at the Kent Lecture Theatre in the chemistry building, the audience saw a very distinguished, determined, patriarchal figure. He walked to the rostrum with a slight limp, but spoke slowly and forcefully. His address, "Aspects of American Astronomy," was a graceful, somewhat florid, but backward-looking speech. He paid many pleasant compliments to Chicago, and even cracked a joke at the expense of the reporters, who had "made known everything that occurred, and, in an emergency, requiring a heroic measure, what did not occur." The conferences on every aspect of astronomy had been inspiring, and the younger generation of astronomers would "reap the reward with which nature always bestows upon those who seek her acquaintance from unselfish motives." Newcomb then gave his version of the history of astronomy in the United States, beginning "in the middle of the last century" (just before the American Revolution). He tied it adroitly to the history of "the great metropolis of the West," Chicago, "just pride of its people and the wonder of the world." Nearly all the astronomical history he related had to do with celestial mechanics and astronomy of position; he referred to astrophysics only briefly. Newcomb paid indirect but graceful compliments to Burnham, Barnard, and Hale by describing their astronomical discoveries and emphasizing their fame in the scientific world. He ended with some extremely vague speculations about the future of astronomy — "it is important to us to keep in touch with the traditions of our race" — and closed with the words — "The public spirit of which this city is the focus has made the desert bloom as the rose, and benefited humanity by the diffusion of the material products of the earth. Should you ask me how it is in the future to use its influence for the benefit of humanity at large, I would say, look at the work now going on in these precincts, and study its spirit."[28] At the time, delivered in Newcomb's ringing orator's voice, his address probably made much more of an impression than Keeler's had the day before, but today it seems shallow and unprophetic.

That evening Yerkes hosted a banquet for the visiting scientists and the university officials at Kinsley's, a fashionable Chicago restaurant. Over 200 guests were present. They whetted their appetites with Blue Point oysters, consommé, and hors d'oeuvres, then dined on black bass, beef tenderloin, and breast of partridge, washed down with sherry, sauterne, champagne, and cognac. Eight rounds of toasts were proposed, and at the end Yerkes gave a speech expressing his gratitude to all concerned. He said that the visiting astronomers should regard Yerkes Observatory as a sister scientific center. He hoped that all rivalry would cease and that the 40-inch could be put to the use of all. On this high note, the banquet and the dedication ceremonies ended. A few details remained to be settled, as when Hale had to insist to the University comptroller that the bill submitted by Harley Williams of Williams Bay for his services at the dedication as a teamster should be paid. "Mr. Williams," Hale wrote, "is a real estate agent and notary public, it is true, but he adds to these public functions that of teamster, coal purveyor, etc, etc. The teaming was done by him."[29]

SECOND CONFERENCE OF ASTRONOMERS AND ASTROPHYSICISTS

The dedication, with its scientific conferences, was considered a great success by all the astronomers and physicists who participated. It combined a maximum efficiency of exchange of new research ideas and results with good fellowship and the chance to see old friends again.[30] Many of those present urged Hale to organize a second conference at Yerkes the following year. A tireless correspondent who burned to direct the research of others along productive lines, Hale tested the waters in his letters and found strong support for the idea. Joseph S. Ames, the young Johns Hopkins spectroscopist who had wanted to come to the 1897 conference to hear the stimulating speakers (except for Newcomb — "I feel sorry for you the hour he is to speak"), but could not afford the trip, had heard nothing but enthusiastic reports from those who had been there. Chamberlin was delighted by the plan for a second conference and planned to participate in it.[31]

Pickering, however, was less than enthusiastic. He would be too busy to leave Cambridge in the summer of 1898, and favored a longer interval between meetings. Besides, he thought that they should move around to different observatories, including his Harvard College Observatory, rather than always being held at Yerkes. If the conference were to be in summer, he favored holding it in the same city where the American Association for the Advancement of Science (AAAS) would be meeting.[32]

This provided Hale just the opening he wanted. Originally he had not wished to form a new society; he preferred holding a yearly research conference of all the active astronomers and astrophysicists, selected by himself. Already at the Yerkes First Conference in 1897, Newcomb had wanted to formalize it into a society which would meet annually in Washington. Now Hale joined forces with Pickering, his former mentor from whom he had learned photographic and observational techniques as a volunteer at Harvard College Observatory during his student days at the Massachusetts Institute of Technology (MIT), and fund raising as well. Hale was not at all positive about the AAAS, a large society of teachers and enthusiasts of science, rather than a small elite group of researchers of the type he preferred. But he recognized that the time was ripe to form a society. The *Physical Review* had already come into existence in 1895, and a new physical society would surely attract the budding astrophysicists unless he acted quickly. The AAAS was to meet at MIT that summer, and he allied himself with Pickering by proposing that the Second Conference be held at Cambridge from August 18 to 20, immediately before it. The astronomers could thus attend both meetings for the cost of only one (and the AAAS members got discounts on their railroad tickets to attend its meetings in those days). Hale publicized the change of plans through *The Astrophysical Journal*, and everyone fell into line.[33]

Hale had estimated that 30 or 40 astronomers would turn up for the Second Conference, but the eastern location (closer to the center of astronomical population than Wisconsin), the AAAS meeting, and the good reports of the previous conference combined to swell the advance registration to nearly 100. Harvard University had come into existence in 1636; its Harvard College Observatory (HCO) dated back to 1839, and Pickering was its fourth director. Its Great Refractor, a 15 1/2-inch, had gone into operation in 1847. Nevertheless, under Pickering, the HCO was a highly productive research center, its data secured with several smaller photographic telescopes and cameras and from its new Bruce photographic telescope, which had gone into operation in Arequipa, Peru only two years earlier. The HCO, in urbane Cambridge, Massachusetts, was almost the exact antithesis of Yerkes Observatory, 75 miles from raw Chicago.[34]

Over 130 people eventually attended the sessions. They were held in the drawing room of the Director's Residence, which must have been a spacious room indeed. Actually many of the participants were not working scientists, but friends of Pickering and financial supporters of the Harvard College Observatory; they probably only dropped in for tea at the breaks and occasionally to hear a few papers. Hale gave one on the spectra of stars of "Secchi's fourth type" (carbon stars), based on spectrograms he and Ferdinand Ellerman had obtained with the 40-inch refractor since the First Conference the previous year. George Washington Hough, of Northwestern University, presented a very good discussion of seeing effects in planetary visual observing, including what we now call "dome seeing," based on his comparative measurements with the Dearborn Observatory 18 1/2-inch refractor and a 6-inch refractor. Of the local Harvard astronomers, Williamina Fleming presented a paper on the classification of the spectra of long-period variable stars; Solon I. Bailey gave one on the light curves of variables in globular clusters; and Antonia C. Maury read a paper on spectroscopy of Beta Aurigae. Barnard, who had made the trip from Yerkes Observatory to participate in the AAAS meeting, as well as the Second Conference, presented a paper with many lantern slides, describing his wide-field astronomical photographs taken with a 6-inch aperture "portrait [Petzval] lens." He had exposed one photographic plate during a total lunar eclipse to search for possible satellites of the moon, but found none. Most of his photographs were striking pictures of Milky Way fields, in which the dark markings he was later to catalogue stood out. David P. Todd, of Amherst College, notorious for traveling to observe solar eclipses in distant, picturesque lands, gave three papers, one of them based on measurements of the 1896 eclipse in Japan he had made aboard the yacht of a friend, who had sailed there with him from New York. [35]

Everyone at the conference was invited to a lunch provided by Pickering and his wife in their house on the first day, and to another hosted by the president and fellows of Harvard University in University Hall on the second day. That afternoon, at a session at which Hale presided, the question of whether or not to form a permanent society was discussed. Everyone voted to continue the conferences on an annual basis; the only question was whether they should be meetings of a new society or not. The question was referred to a committee consisting of Pickering, Newcomb, Comstock, Edward W. Morley (of the Michelson-Morley experiment), and Hale. Evidently the power brokers had already reached their decision, for the committee was able to report the next day in favor of forming a new society and even presented a draft constitution for it. Comstock had legal training; a solid, conservative positional astronomer 13 years older than Hale, he was widely respected in the scientific community. No doubt he had drawn up a draft constitution in advance, at the suggestion of Hale. Pickering, Newcomb, and Morley joined them in recommending it. Hale had kept Newcomb and Pickering informed of his thinking in frequent, highly respectful letters. The committee recommended that a preliminary organizational meeting of the new astronomical society be held at the AAAS meeting the following week. Then, after a visit to the Blue Hill Meteorological Observatory outside Cambridge, the Second Conference came to an end.[36]

Move to Boston

On Monday of the following week, Barnard, who was a vice president of the AAAS, presented a more popular invited talk before its Section on Mathematics and Astronomy (the traditional grouping of earlier times) on "The Development of Photography in Astronomy." It was a historical treatment of the subject, going back to the first daguerreotypes of stars and to John Draper's first photograph of the Orion nebula with a telescope. It culminated in Barnard's own recent wide-field direct photographs. Like all his lectures, it was illustrated by numerous lantern slides of spectacular nebulae and Milky Way fields, and contained inspirational passages mixed in with the science.[37] On Tuesday, the astronomers and astrophysicists, nearly all still present in Boston, held their preliminary organizational meeting at MIT, and 61 signed up as charter members of the new society. Pickering, Newcomb, Comstock, Morley, and Hale, who had formed the organizing committee, were now named its interim Executive Council, with power to add four more members to it, and they were given the responsibility of calling the first meeting of the Society.[38]

The main, still unresolved, question was what to call the new Society. Newcomb and nearly all the traditional positional astronomers naturally favored the American Astronomical Society as its name. But Hale did not agree. He was the apostle of astrophysics, the "new astronomy," as Samuel P. Langley had named it in his book. Langley and Charles A. Young were its pioneers in America; Pickering, Keeler, and Hale were their immediate successors. Hale, in particular, was promoting it vigorously among physicists. He knew they would not join an American Astronomical Society, for he had polled them. Langley and Henry Rowland were particularly opposed to that name. The natural alternative, in the absence of other constraints, would therefore have been the American Astronomical and Astrophysical Society, but the large, powerful

Figure 2. Second Conference of Astronomers and Astrophysicists, Harvard College Observatory, August 1898. Edward C. Pickering is third from right, only his head visible, with short, pointed black beard; George Ellery Hale is ninth from left, also only his head (cocked slightly to left) visible, wearing a moustache; Antonia C. Maury is the left of the two women near the center of the first row; Williamina Fleming is the left of the group of three women to the left of the center, and Solon I. Bailey is the tall man second from left. Courtesy of Wellesley College Archives.

American Association for the Advancement of Science had preempted those initials years earlier. Two AAAS's would cause endless confusion.[39] So Hale decided on the Astronomical and Astrophysical Society of America, and that is what it became. He arranged for the Council to hold its first meeting in conjunction with the regular annual meeting of the Board of Editors of *The Astrophysical Journal*, which he had founded in 1895 with Keeler. The latter had played a role in it much like Comstock's in the new Society, and was now director of Lick Observatory in distant California.[40] The meeting would be held in Washington in February, 1899. Hale made sure Comstock would be there, and diplomatically discussed potential additional members whom they might add to the Executive Council. The Wisconsin director was more adventurous and open to change than Newcomb. Although Comstock suggested mostly positional astronomers like himself, in the end he went along with Hale's ideas.[41] Eventually Lewis Boss, Albert A. Michelson, Ames, and Langley, the latter three all physicists and members of *The Astrophysical Journal* Editorial Board, were named as the additional members. At the February meeting in Washington, this first, temporary Council made only minor modifications in the draft constitution of the previous summer, but wrote the "Astronomical and Astrophysical Society of America" as the name of the new organization. They also decided that the first meeting would be held back at Williams Bay that summer, and authorized Comstock and Hale to select the dates and make all arrangements for it.[42]

THIRD CONFERENCE AND FIRST AAS MEETING

This Third Conference of Astronomers and Astrophysicists, which the AASA (and the AAS, as it later became) has always counted as its first meeting, was a decided anticlimax. It was held September 6–8, 1899, the week just after Labor Day. By then additional charter members had signed up, and more did so at the meeting, bringing the total number to 114. Their names are published in the first volume of the *Publications of the Astronomical and Astrophysical Society of America*.[43] Only about 50 of them attended the meeting, a large percentage of them from Yerkes and the University of Chicago campus, plus essentially the entire astronomy departments from Madison and Northwestern University. William Harkness, the director of the Naval Observatory, presided over all the scientific sessions, as a sop to the older astronomy. Some 31 papers were presented, including five by the indefatigable Barnard, three by Hale, two each by Kurt Laves of the campus department, Forest R. Moulton (who had just received the first Ph.D. in astronomy given by the University of Chicago and joined its faculty), Edwin B. Frost, and one by Frank Schlesinger, all of the home team. Comstock, Hough, and Harkness gave papers on the old astronomy, which was better represented on the program than astrophysics at this meeting. Pickering did not attend, as he was too busy and too tired (the customary director's complaint), but he sent a paper on "The Revised Harvard Photometry," which was read for him. This was a standard procedure for many years for those members who wished to announce a discovery or simply demonstrate interest in the Society, as Pickering was doing.[44] From faraway Lick Observatory Keeler also sent a paper, on the Ring nebula in Lyra, and his younger colleague W. Wallace Campbell sent two, one on the measured wavelength of the green coronal emission line and the other on two spectroscopic binaries, Capella and Polaris.

On the first evening of the meeting, September 6, Hale and his wife Evelina entertained all the attendees at an informal reception at their home, and in the afternoon of the second day, Ryerson and Ayer, both wealthy friends of Yerkes Observatory, sent their steam yachts to take everyone for a boat ride around Lake Geneva. On both nights the 40-inch refractor was open for visual observing of nebulae and clusters, but the weather was mostly cloudy and few of the visitors saw much.[45]

On September 7 the members present adopted the constitution which had been recommended by the Executive Council; at the last session, on September 8, they elected the first officers and the first members of the permanent Council. These were Newcomb as president, Young and Hale as vice presidents, Comstock as secretary, C. L. Doolittle, of Flower Observatory of the University of Pennsylvania, as treasurer,

Figure 3. Simon Newcomb, first president of the Astronomical and Astrophysical Society of America (1899–1905), 1901. Photograph courtesy of Office of Smithsonian Institution Archives.

Pickering and Keeler for full two-year terms as councilors, and Morley and Ormond Stone with initial one-year terms, to get the rotation started. It seems practically certain that this vote was by acclamation, as a single, unopposed list of candidates had been nominated by the previous Executive Council. Certainly Hale played a very large part in preparing the slate, for it consisted largely of his allies. Newcomb, generally considered the greatest American astronomer of his time, and very well aware of his own importance, could not possibly have been ignored. Hale, who wrote deferentially to him constantly, was on as good terms with him as any American astronomer (or astrophysicist) was. Newcomb, Comstock, Doolittle, and Stone, a pleasant, cooperative, elderly professor of astronomy at the University of Virginia, were traditional astronomers; all the rest were astrophysicists. Comstock, who had been ill the previous year, apparently with a series of severe colds, had arranged for a year's leave from the University of Wisconsin to recuperate in southern California. In his place, Frost was designated acting secretary for the first year. The AASA was in business as a permanent, organized, scientific society.[46]

Over the years after 1899, the resistance of astrophysicists to being considered astronomers gradually declined, or perhaps they learned to grin and bear it. Nearly everyone agreed that the name of the Society was awkward and cumbersome, and finally at the tenth anniversary meeting, back at Yerkes Observatory, a vote was taken on a proposal to change it to simply the American Astronomical Society. The motion failed then, but not by a wide margin. Five years later at the Northwestern University meeting in August 1914 (at which Edwin Hubble, a beginning graduate student at Yerkes Observatory, heard Vesto M. Slipher report on the very high radial velocities of several spiral nebulae which he had measured at Lowell Observatory), changing the name of the Society was considered again. This time the motion passed nearly unanimously, and it has remained the American Astronomical Society ever since.[47]

CONCLUSION

The organization of the Society was one of the steps in the increasing professionalization of science. Professional research in astronomy and astrophysics was a growth industry, and its practitioners needed a society. The founding of *The Astrophysical Journal* in 1895, Hale's brainchild, was a first step in this direction, the founding of the AASA in 1899 was a second. The Society was a glint in the eye at the First Conference in 1897, conceived at the Second in 1898, and came to full-term birth at the Third in 1899. Hale played by far the major role at every stage of the process, just as he had in founding Yerkes Observatory and *The Astrophysical Journal*, and as he was to do in founding Mount Wilson Observatory and the National Research Council, revitalizing the National Academy of Sciences, and starting Palomar Observatory. Hale planned the dedication of Yerkes Observatory as a blockbuster research conference; he publicized it in *The Astrophysical Journal* as he promoted it in his correspondence with the movers and shakers in American astronomy and astrophysics. After that first conference he stimulated and encouraged the desire for a second one, diplomatically brought Newcomb's and Pickering's ideas into line with his own, and expended much of his energy in organizing many other scientists' unfocused ideas toward the Harvard conferences of 1898 and the organizing of a continuing, permanent society. He was a member of every committee, in most cases not the chair (he generally managed to put a sympathetic, older, better known scientist with less time and energy to spend on organizational matters in that post) but always pushed for action and for the "right" decisions. He succeeded, as he did in all his most important projects, although ultimately at a terrible cost to his own physical and mental well being. But the new society, first called the Astronomical and Astrophysical Society of America, later the American Astronomical Society, came into existence largely through his efforts.

The Society has met at least once a year (except 1907) ever since. Though the meetings have grown tenfold in size, with many parallel sessions in large halls for the presentation of papers, each repeats in essence the program of these first three conferences. Research discussions are the first priority. There are always research papers, invited lectures, working demonstrations, visits to telescopes, tributes to local benefactors, a reception, a banquet, and often even difficulty in getting the bills paid after the meeting, just as Hale experienced at Yerkes Observatory in 1897.

ACKNOWLEDGMENT

I am grateful to the State Historical Society of Wisconsin for permission to use as the basis of this article an earlier, shorter version of it which I published in the *Wisconsin Magazine of History* **68**, 108–118 (1985) under the title "The Minus First Meeting of the American Astronomical Society: Williams Bay, Wisconsin 1897."

THE PICKERING YEARS

David H. DeVorkin

INTRODUCTION

Edward Charles Pickering, Director of Harvard College Observatory, creator of the world's largest spectroscopic, photographic, and photometric programs in astronomy, and major champion of the profession, dominated the first two decades of the Society's life. He succeeded Newcomb as President in 1905 and held the post until his death in 1919. During his tenure, the Society remained very much an eastern and mid-western power block, centered on Pickering and his circle, although officers were elected from the mid-west and west coast to make it a truly national society. Here we examine the Pickering years to catch a flavor of the Society when it was still trying to find itself within a science whose centroid of activity was steadily marching westward and whose leadership was becoming more diverse.

Figure 1. E. C. Pickering. Photograph courtesy Dorrit Hoffleit, Yale University Observatory.

THE PRE-PICKERING YEARS

The fact that a society was voted into existence in 1898 did not guarantee its survival. Organizing is hard work. It does not come easily and requires coalition building and politicking ("horse-trading" as some astronomers, including Henry Norris Russell, put it). The effort involved can never be taken for granted in any historical account. In fact, as Rothenberg and Williams point out in their chapter elsewhere in this book, in its five years, the Society was hardly representative of the community of at–large astronomers. What made the difference eventually was that highly motivated people were at the core of the organizational effort. American astronomy's quintessential organizer, George Ellery Hale, may have created the Society, but he never really organized or controlled it. E. C. Pickering performed the latter functions, and they were extended by his successor, Frank Schlesinger. Here we retrace how the Society changed as it moved from the Newcomb to the Pickering eras, and beyond.

At the 1898 conference, the *ad hoc* Executive Council had to take various actions: it had to create a constitution and bylaws; it had to plan for the first meeting of the new Society; it was charged with soliciting and forwarding recommendations on the governance of the U.S. Naval Observatory; and it created a committee to plan for the 28 May 1900 solar eclipse. Control of the Naval Observatory and Nautical Almanac Office was Newcomb's deepest concern and he viewed the Society as a political vehicle to wrest control from the Navy.[1]

Even so, Newcomb did not show up for the Society's first official meeting at Yerkes. As Don Osterbrock has noted in the previous chapter, the first official meeting of the Society was something of an anti-climax. Indeed, Hale and George C. Comstock tried desperately to attract the luminaries to Yerkes for the meeting. The most prominent astronomers and physicists who had endorsed the new society — Newcomb, Young, Langley, and Michelson — were not coming, and Hale and Comstock's last hope was to convince Pickering that he had to make the trip. Comstock wrote, but to no avail. Hale weighed in: It was of the "highest importance to the new society" that Pickering make an appearance, he pleaded. He and Comstock agreed that Pickering needed to "give to the new society the advantage of your presence."[2] Pickering did not come.

Hale and Comstock were relieved when 50 people showed up, and in addition to papers hastily presented, the Society managed to elect its officers and plan for its next meeting in New York City in conjunction with the AAAS. The young Society frequently met with the AAAS, partly because the larger organization led the way in making local arrangements. Hale was deeply disappointed that Newcomb and Pickering were absent. Nevertheless, on the day preceding the last day of the meeting, the *ad hoc* Council created a nominating ballot for members to fill out. On the last day of the meeting, the top three names in each category vied for open election by those attending. Newcomb handily won the presidency, C. A. Young was elected the first vice-president, and Hale was elected the second vice-president. Comstock and Doolittle remained secretary and treasurer, respectively. Pickering and Keeler were

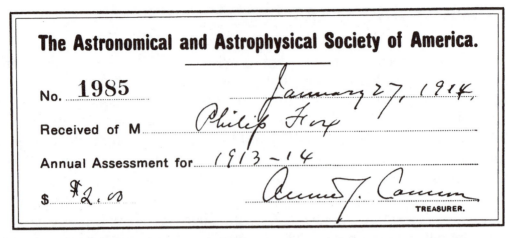

Figure 2. During Pickering's reign as President of the Society, Annie Jump Cannon maintained the books as Treasurer, filing copies from receipt books in administrative folders. Image from AAS Papers, II:8, Fox folder. AIP.

named councilors for two years, and Morley and Stone for one year, beginning the overlapping cycle the bylaws required.

In the first five years of the Society's existence, Newcomb, the elderly patriarch, managed his office without much flair. His one major passion was reforming the Naval Observatory, and he sought the support of the Society to this end.[3] As Young grew more feeble, Hale succeeded to the first vice-presidency and W. W. Campbell became his second, but Hale's and Campbell's energies and interests were in the west, and so the details of running the Society fell upon Comstock, who mainly worried about getting the Council to agree on where and when to meet next. In January 1903, Comstock laid out the options: A summer meeting at an observatory or at a resort (Comstock liked the Lake Erie resort island Put-in-Bay); a winter meeting in an eastern city; or a meeting in conjunction with the St. Louis World's Fair, again with the AAAS. Although Newcomb paid little attention at first, Campbell objected to St. Louis, which was Hale's choice and, eventually, the winner. To placate Pickering and Campbell, who preferred New York City, the 1905 meeting was held there, and soon after Pickering found that he had been elected President for 1906.[4] Newcomb could not attend the St. Louis meeting, although he did attend a special meeting of the Council in St. Louis in December 1903. During Newcomb's tenure, though offers came from places as far as Denver, five of the seven meetings of the Society were held in Washington, New York City, and Philadelphia. At the December 1905 meeting, reflecting its club-like nature and as a means of prompting members to pay their dues, the Council directed the Secretary to take roll call at the opening of each general session of the Society, "calling only upon such names as appear upon the register."[5]

On January 1, 1903, the Council accepted an invitation from the Permanent Secretary of the AAAS to have two of its members serve on the AAAS Council. C. L. Doolittle and George C. Comstock were elected as delegates, which strengthened ties that Pickering would find most useful during his long tenure as the second Society President.[6]

Figure 3. George Ellery Hale in the Monastery at Mount Wilson, circa 1908. Photograph courtesy of Yerkes Observatory, University of Chicago.

ESTABLISHING ORDER

Meetings

Within weeks of his notification of election in January 1906, Pickering directed Comstock to exert more control over the meetings of the Society. Frustrated at the months of time it required to get the entire Council to agree on anything, Comstock drew up "program rules" for meetings: From here on out the venue of the next meeting would be decided by a single mail ballot to the Council. Comstock created two types of contributed papers: communications (less than 10 minutes) and papers (less than 30 minutes). Some members had exhibited no concept of time limits, so these limitations were well received by the Council, especially since they now had the power to limit lengths of papers to make the proceedings fit into a pre-arranged schedule.

Comstock found, however, that the ballot idea did not work. Western members of the Council preferred winter meetings when the observing weather was poor, and eastern members, more involved with campus life, preferred summer meetings.[7] By 1908 he and Pickering led the Council to create a 3-member committee to worry over the site of future meetings, mainly to streamline the process. Hussey (Michigan), Frost (Yerkes), and Comstock (Wisconsin), not surprisingly chose Yerkes for their next meeting.

Decorum was always a concern. For the August 1908 meeting at Put-in-Bay, Pickering suggested that they dispense with "full dress" and Comstock agreed, although just to be safe he brought along "evening dress... as a matter of precaution... as we are to meet in a summer hotel." [8] But there were deeper concerns among Society members.

Under Pickering the Society began to create committees to deal with the professionalization of their science. Newcomb had focussed on the Naval Observatory, even though Hale had managed to convince him to endorse a committee on Solar Research in 1904, to prepare for the St. Louis Exposition and to ratify Hale's nascent International Union for Cooperation in Solar Research. However, Pickering had broader interests.

Committees[9]

At the ninth meeting in 1908, Pickering created two committees in consultation with the Council and with specialists. First was a Committee on Luminous Meteors, chaired by Cleveland Abbe and with W. Elkin of Yale and Peck as members. Elkin wanted to coordinate photographic meteor orbit research, and the committee recommended establishing a network of photographic stations 100 miles apart for meteor observation. His plan was endorsed, but only partially implemented.[10] Over the years the Committee continued to push for increased use of photography, adding C. P. Olivier, E. E. Barnard, and W. J. Humphreys to its ranks. F. R. Moulton, the dynamical astronomer and cosmogonist, was recruited, and the Committee began to oversee the work of the amateur American Meteor Society.

In 1908 Pickering also created a Committee on Comets in preparation for Halley's Comet in 1910. This was a high profile effort, chaired by Comstock with Pickering, Barnard, Perrine, and Frost as members. The Society sought direct funding to coordinate photographic and spectroscopic observations, the first time it did so, and raised $2200 from the Bache Fund of the National Academy of Sciences.

1910 was a watershed year for the Society. At Hale's urging, Pickering planned that the eleventh meeting of the Society be held in Cambridge in August so astronomers travelling from Europe to Hale's fourth International Solar Union meeting in Pasadena might attend the Society meetings as well. They hoped this would reinforce their mutual desire to further coordinate and standardize practice in the discipline. By that time, Pickering, Hale keenly knew, had devoted three decades to developing his spectroscopic and photometric systems, and he needed a platform to have them ratified (lest all his efforts be swallowed up by competing systems in Europe). The Cambridge meetings afforded him the opportunity to begin discussions with Europeans such as J. C. Kapteyn and Karl Schwarzschild, which eventually ended in the Harvard systems gaining tentative approval at Hale's conference in Pasadena.[11]

But in Cambridge, the Society also took steps to manage a broader range of astronomical practice. Pickering and Frank Schlesinger, Director of the Allegheny Observatory, convinced the Council to create two committees on radial velocities and astrometry. The "Committee on Co-operation in the Measurement of Stellar Radial Velocities" was headed by Campbell with Frost, J. S. Plaskett, and Schlesinger as members, along with foreign visitors H. F. Newell and Karl Schwarzschild as corresponding members. Although this combination held the potential of being a powerful alliance, over the

Figure 4. Astronomical and Astrophysical Society of America meeting at Harvard, 19 August 1910. Sitting in the front row, left to right, Leon Campbell (kneeling), Winslow Upton, Frank Very, W. J. Hussey, Joel Stebbins, Miss O'Reilly, Miss Carpenter, Miss Breslin, Solon Bailey, E. S. King. Among the rest: W. J. Humphreys, who campaigned to keep Hale's preferred name for the Society, is standing to the left of Leon Campbell, Annie J. Cannon is standing between Campbell and Humphreys, Mrs. H. N. Russell just to the right in a black hat, Russell is just to her right and R. S. Dugan is the face between them. E. C. Pickering is just left of center, and J. S. Plaskett is at the center. George Comstock is in the back row, center. Also in the photograph are visitors from Europe bound for Hale's Solar Union meeting, including Karl Schwarzschild, H. H. Turner, O. Backlund, A. Belopolsky, Alfred Fowler and Frank W. Dyson. Copy courtesy of Martin Schwarzschild. Photograph courtesy Yerkes Observatory.

next six years it accomplished little, discharging itself in 1916 after it decided that cooperation between observatories in standardizing radial velocity techniques was impossible.

The radial velocity committee failed to achieve the consensus that Schlesinger's photographic astrometry committee enjoyed. He headed the "Committee on the Determination of Absolute Positions of the Stars by Photography" which included Harold Jacoby of Columbia, Pickering, Frank Ross, and Henry Norris Russell, with H. H. Turner a corresponding member. It was soon renamed the "Committee on Photographic Astrometry," and Schlesinger used it as a platform to establish photographic techniques as standard means for determining stellar positions. Schlesinger convened an *ad hoc* meeting of the committee at the 1913 Astronomische Gesellschaft (AG) in Bonn to ratify their plan to make photography the primary tool of the astrometrist, and he received the endorsement of the AG. For the next decade he also led the Committee's deliberations over how best to refine and extend photographic techniques. Although he was less than successful in standardizing practice through a related "Committee on Stellar Parallaxes" before the war, Schlesinger eventually secured the Committee's endorsement of the *Yale Parallax Catalogue* in the 1920s.[12]

In August 1911, the Society created a "Committee on Cooperation in the Teaching of Astronomy" to assess astronomy courses in colleges and universities. C. L. Doolittle was the first chair, and members included Sarah F. Whiting of Wellesley, C. A. Chant of Toronto, and J. A. Miller of Swarthmore. They soon added more members and changed their name to the "Committee on Cooperation in Improvement of Teaching Elementary Astronomy," to reflect their growing concern for the lack of exposure young children were given to astronomy in schools. In fact, the results of a questionnaire that was returned by some 80 institutions was very disheartening, but the committee failed to enact any significant reforms and soon died out, to be reincarnated from time to time as the "Teachers' Committee" as members of the Society voiced their concerns (*see* the discussion by Wentzel and Franknoi elsewhere in this volume).

Other committees during Pickering's tenure were devoted to variable star nomenclature, to the determination of the Standard Equinox (epochs), and to coordinate work on asteroids, especially to secure more observations on asteroids on a consistent basis. The nomenclature committee was immediately bogged down because its members (Cannon, Russell, and Townley) could not agree on anything, and it soon was transformed into the more successful "Committee to Secure Variable Star Observations" in 1916 which, among its other actions, helped to oversee the American Association of Variable Star Observers, at Pickering's behest. The committee to standardize epochs eventually managed to report on a plan to replace the multiplicity of star catalog epochs with standard epochs.

Ad hoc committees formed when solar eclipses or comets were predicted, mainly to coordinate observations and to secure support for expeditions. Plans for the June 8, 1918 eclipse centered on testing Einstein's theory. Another *ad hoc* committee was formed to deliberate over the creation of an Associate Membership for amateur astronomers, which remained a stormy issue as many members did not like the idea of a two-tiered membership. In 1916, Frank Schlesinger pressed the issue as a means of expanding membership, but Pickering opposed the idea and dissolved the committee.

These committees reveal what types of astronomical practice were of concern to American astronomers at the time. The teaching and associate membership committees were concerned about the health of astronomy and its place in society, whereas the majority of the committees concerned themselves with means to standardize practice in the still young profession. All of the latter dealt with observational technique; there would be no committee devoted to celestial mechanics until the 1920s, and never a committee on theoretical astrophysics.

As war brewed in Europe, the Society was called upon by Hale's new National Research Council of the National Academy of Sciences to deliberate over the ways astronomy could aid the war effort, and also to plan astronomy's future in the wake of war. In a tripartite agreement between the NRC, AAS, and AAAS, the Society helped to form various wartime committees.[13] One committee investigated the efficacy of initiating a seasonal daylight savings plan. At first, 18 members favored the idea, 22 opposed it, and six were neutral. Astronomers made astronomical arguments to buttress both sides, but agreed that it was a useful expedient only after the country had already adopted the plan to accommodate wartime exigencies. When the Society failed to change the beginning of the astronomical day from noon to midnight, Pickering formed another *ad hoc* committee consisting of Eichelberger, Campbell, and Frost to look into the matter. At the August 1917 meeting in Albany, the committee deliberated over ways to contribute to optical and photographic technology, called for improved training in navigation, and deliberated over a French proposal on ways to reorganize international science after the war that would exclude the Central Powers and limit the status of neutral nations. Although many voiced sympathy with the French, Henry Norris Russell rejected any plan to limit the neutrals, "if there are any left," whereas Schlesinger considered the French proposal hysterical.[14] Pickering was less involved; he was more concerned about the discipline itself. He was a major player in the AAAS as chairman of the "Committee of 100" as he continued his decades-long search for ways to support science generally. Pickering had chaired a combined AAS/AAS/NRC committee on the "Needs of Astronomy" to create and manage funding in a way that had not changed since the 1880s and 1890s when he called for more support to manage the routine activities of observing and computing. Hale, who had a very different vision for the needs of astronomy, created a new organizational mechanism in the NRC after 1916 which eventually absorbed and transcended Pickering's efforts.[15]

NAMING THE SOCIETY[16]

As noted in the previous chapter, the Society did not choose its present name until 1914. The 15-year debate over the Society's name was in effect a reflection of a division between astronomers and astrophysicists that had existed for decades. The process through which the AAS acquired its present name reveals as well how astrophysics was regarded in its early years.[17]

In the late nineteenth century, many traditional astronomers viewed astrophysics as an upstart that would not endure. Astrophysics in Britain and the United States (save for the Astrophysical Observatory of the Smithsonian Institution) was the province of wealthy amateurs and private patronage. By the turn of the century, however, many professional astronomers were investigating astrophysical phenomena, utilizing new astrophysical techniques like spectroscopy. When their concerns for professionalization met those equally voiced by traditional astronomers at the end of the century, a myriad of possible titles for the future society were expressed that revealed a wide range of opinion over the relationship of astrophysics to astronomy.

Simon Newcomb represented the traditional view, whereas Hale championed the new view. Newcomb addressed the issue at a dinner meeting of the National Academy of Sciences on April 18, 1901: "The cultivators of the older astronomy have sometimes looked askance upon this youthful competitor as upon one that has not yet attained the dignity of the older science and have therefore been quite satisfied to make a distinction between the two classes, that of astronomers and that of astro-physicists. But it now seems impossible to keep the two sciences from merging together."[18] Newcomb, of course, did not subscribe to Hale's *The Astrophysical Journal*.[19]

The Society was formed at a time when traditional astronomers already enjoyed a strong disciplinary identity, but there was as yet no national professional organization devoted to astronomy alone. Astrophysicists, however, lacked both a strong disciplinary identity and a professional framework. Although astronomers and astrophysicists had convergent wishes to professionalize their disciplines through the formation of a society, they diverged greatly in their conception of the scope and purview of their profession just as their specialties and their leaders diverged in subject matter and age. In "Origins of the American Astronomical Society," Richard Berendzen provides an excellent discussion of the debate over the name of the Society.[20] Here we extend his discussion to explore in detail the arguments on all sides of the issue that will help to illuminate the relationship of astrophysics to astronomy.

As Osterbrock and Berendzen point out, at the outset Newcomb wished to call the body the "American Astronomical Society." But there had been an amateur society with the same name, which may have caused some confusion. Hale, as we have seen, had a very different society in mind — one that would include far more than astronomy. Hale did not want Newcomb to head the society, nor did he want to see Newcomb's title for the society to come into being. He wanted to establish a society that would attract physicists because he saw physics as central to the pursuit of astrophysics and, secondarily, because American physicists had not yet themselves formed a singular professional identity.[21] Hale was obviously excited by the possibility of fusing the analytical tools of physics with astronomical research in the field of astrophysics and wanted that fusion to become enshrined in the title and organization of a society.

Traditional astronomers of the 1880s and 1890s rejected astrophysics outright; now they tried to absorb astrophysics under the rubric of astronomy. In writing to Hale, Newcomb hoped that "astrophysicists [would] consider their science as a continuation of the ancient and honorable science of astronomy and allow the new body to be called the American Astronomical Society."[22] Newcomb and his cohorts did not think much of spectral classification, but they were hopeful that photography and spectroscopy, embodied in the new radial velocity techniques, would revitalize many traditional areas in astronomy. Thus, instead of directly confronting astrophysicists, astronomers like Newcomb, and later Campbell, attempted to co-opt the astrophysical profession under the title of the older astronomy. Hale resisted the co-option, viewing astrophysics as distinct territory.

By the late 1890s, Hale and other astrophysicists had taken the first steps to establish astrophysics as a discipline by standardizing practice through actions by the editorial board of *The Astrophysical Journal*, which included both physicists and astronomers. However, they had to go further to establish their new science as a profession, and here the title of the new society was all-important. Samuel P. Langley, the founder of the Astrophysical Observatory of the Smithsonian Institution, supported Hale's cause, as did physicists. Hale viewed astrophysics as a separate discipline that would be appealing to physicists. But Hale knew he had to compromise. The gulf was too large.

Hale was not alone in his attempts at last minute changes to the Society's name during the fateful meeting at the Smithsonian. Comstock keenly remembered the event: "My recollection goes back to the time at which the committee appointed to prepare a scheme of organization for this society sat around a table, I think there were 8 or 10 people present, and they found the most embarrassing proposition was to formulate a name. Finally, we were requested to write out on a piece of paper what we thought ought to be the name. No two papers had the same name."[23] Thus, as we have seen, the two factions reached a settlement which no one really liked: the "Astronomical and Astrophysical Society of America."

Hale's ambitions were boundless. His initial choice of a name, the Astronomical and *Physical* Society of America, may have been an attempt to grab American physicists as well. At the very least, he did not want to lose the allegiance of the prominent physicists he had gathered. Given Hale's success at realizing his ambitions, it is also quite possible that he might have succeeded in creating such an organization had the division between astronomy and astrophysics not existed.

RENAMING THE SOCIETY

During Pickering's tenure as President, the wrangling over the name of the Society continued. Pickering remained in the background for some time, knowing that feelings were strong on both sides. In 1908, Campbell proposed an amendment to the constitution that would have changed the name back to what Newcomb and Pickering originally wanted — "The American Astronomical Society." Although he was a spectroscopic astronomer, as was Pickering, Campbell gave what were very traditional reasons for wanting a name change:

> It has always seemed to me that the long name of the Society is unfortunate, for two or more reasons: first, because of its length and awkwardness; and, second, because Astrophysics is Astronomy. I greatly prefer a title like "The American Astronomical Society," — just as we have an American Mathematical Society. The latter is certainly broad enough to take in all branches of mathematical work, and the corresponding title should cover all who are doing good work in any phase of Astronomy. In my opinion, the sooner the name is simplified, the better.[24]

Campbell asked Comstock if it was a good idea to make such a proposal formally at the next meeting. As Joel Stebbins argues elsewhere in this volume in his retrospective 1947 essay, the original hybrid name gave "emphasis to the fact that many physicists had interests in common with the astronomers." But, he claimed, such an "artificial distinction between the older astronomy and the newer astrophysics was more important in the early years of the Society" than it was at mid-Century.[25] Equally likely, since Campbell's programs were centered on radial velocities, astrophysics for him was merely an extension of traditional astronomical practice.

Although the sympathies of the membership that met during the Society's tenth meeting may well have been with Campbell, the final vote was 16 to 9 against his proposal. Campbell's resolution failed, according to Stebbins, "out of deference to a few members who felt more at home under the old name."[26] Five years later, however, William J. Hussey, Director of the Detroit Observatory at the University of Michigan, reported to Campbell what really happened at the meeting:

> I believe you were not present at the meeting at the Yerkes Observatory, when this matter came up for consideration. Professor [William J.] Humphreys's fine flow of eloquence was able to turn the majority to the retention of the present awkward name.[27]

W. J. Humphreys was just the sort of person Hale had in mind when he pushed to include physics in the title of the Society. Trained under Rowland as a physicist at The Johns Hopkins University, he became a physical meteorologist with the U.S. Weather Bureau. Humphreys possessed sufficient presence and persuasiveness to overcome determined resistance. After Pickering read Campbell's proposal in Campbell's absence, Humphreys took the floor, filled with admiration for Campbell's, "great scientific attainments and his noble personal character." However, his proposal, Humphreys alleged, was based only on logic, and did not consider deeper issues.[28]

> The purpose of the name is simply to give a designation of some kind or another to the society. We plan to select the name that is helpful, rather than the name that is strictly logical. The name certainly has good parentage. There is good justification of the name astrophysical, on account of the dignity of *The Astrophysical Journal*, the Astrophysical Observatory of Potsdam, the Astrophysical Observatory at Mt. Wilson; so I think there is every good reason to think that the name astrophysical is one of dignity.[28]

The main function of the Society, Humphreys continued, "was to promote the work in astronomy, in every legitimate and possible way" and the best way to do that was by collegial contact:

> We go back inspired from these meetings, where every astronomer and physicist and others can get together. The astronomer will constantly and justly claim that physics is a branch of astronomy, the physicist that astronomy is a branch of physics, and the chemist that both are a branch of chemistry, etc.[28]

Humphreys believed that the old name was an invitation to anyone who could "throw any light whatever on astronomy to come and join hands, as an integral part of the society itself, and not as invited guests." The term 'physical' had to be in the title for Humphreys to feel welcome, to feel he had the same rights and privileges of any member. "I think that is the feeling of many physicists" he added, warning that "I have heard many physicists say that they would hate to see the invitation withdrawn." Among those he had spoken to, "whose feelings we can't afford to injure in the slightest way," were Henry Crew and Albert Michelson. Thus he called for Campbell to withdraw his proposal. "We do not like to decrease the kindly feeling, the desire to take an active part, on the part of such men as Crew and Michelson."[28]

Humphreys' impassioned defense of the old title, highlighting the consideration of physicists' interests, defeated Campbell's proposed amendment, especially since Campbell was not present and only Pickering and Ormond Stone spoke in support of Campbell's resolution (Pickering's support was only lukewarm). Comstock and Edwin B. Frost, both early Hale allies, threw their support behind Humphreys during the discussion, and it was enough to produce the 16 to 9 vote against Campbell's resolution.

Despite Campbell's defeat at Humphreys' hands, the issue remained alive. Many astronomers, including Pickering, referred to the Society as the 'Astronomical Society' in private, and clearly wished to make a clean break. With Hale distracted and distant from the Society in following years, the time finally seemed right in 1914, so Hussey made an anxious pitch to Campbell to revive his petition:

> I have talked with many members of the Society since, and their sentiment seems to be very generally in favor of the shorter name which you propose.... In the new volume of publications which we are just starting, on the new plan of publishing originally with *Popular Astronomy*, and using reprints from that journal for our own volumes, I am using with the consent of the President [Pickering] as a running head, the name "American Astronomical Society." I hope before the volume is finished, that we can have the change of name authorized, so as to appear on the title page. Will you not be willing to take this up? I shall be very glad to sign the petition for one.[29]

As he admitted, Hussey knew he was taking a calculated risk, but he was sufficiently confident that the Society would now agree with the new name to rename it in the draft of the second volume of the Society's *Publications*, which he hoped would set the right name in concrete. For a number of years, the Council mulled over the idea of publishing an "astronomical periodical" and a decennial volume and made plans to recommend these to the Society. In August 1909, the Council asked Edwin Frost to discuss the future of *The Astronomical Journal* with its editor, Seth Carlo Chandler. It was clearly looking for an official outlet. From its earliest years, notices of meetings had appeared in *Science* and then, more extensively, in *Popular Astronomy*. But these were not Society publications; the *Publications* only went part way to satisfy that need, but just as clearly, they had to be named in a consistent manner. The lingering debate over the Society's name was made all the more poignant by the pending *Publications*.[30]

Of course, Hussey knew that Pickering, now in his seventh year as President of the Society, had always supported the simpler title though at times he proved to be less than a valiant agent of change. Campbell was still miffed by the Council's original rebuff:

> I sympathize as strongly as ever with the proposal for changing the name of The Astronomical and Astrophysical Society of America. Surely a member whose astro-physical paper is eligible to use the prefix "astro" should not hesitate to read his paper before an astro-nomical society; and with logic absolutely identical we could refer to The Mathematical and Algebraic Society of America. However, I hesitate to father the proposal a second time.[31]

Campbell had only heard from a few members about changing the name, mainly from Hussey, Philip Fox, and Pickering, and he was not sure how others like Comstock and Schlesinger and the Yerkes astronomers felt about it, though he knew his own Lick staff was favorable. "If I know that the voting for the proposal would be in a large

Astronomical and Astrophysical
Society of America

PROPOSED AMENDMENT TO THE CONSTITUTION

Article I, Section 1

1. This Association shall be called the American Astronomical Society.

Article I, Section 1, of the Constitution as it now stands.

1. This Association shall be called the Astronomical
and Astrophysical Society of America.

———————

In compliance with Article VI, Section 2, of the Constitution, the Secretary forwards notice of the proposed
amendment upon a request of the following members of
the Society:

1. E. C. Pickering
2. S. I. Bailey
3. Annie J. Cannon
4. Frank C. Jordan
5. Charles J. Hudson
6. Frank Schlesinger
7. Henry Crew
8. Philip Fox
9. John F. Hayford
10. Frederick Slocum

Figure 5. The Society finally changed its name in August 1914. Among the proposers for the name change were the President, Second Vice-President (Comstock), Secretary (Fox) and Treasurer (Cannon) of the Society. Henry Crew was a physicist at Northwestern, the host for the meeting. The proposal "passed unanimously" according to the Council Minutes. The Northwestern meeting was the largest to date: 66 members attended, 27 new members admitted, and 48 papers were presented. It was the first where members were housed in campus dormitories. Image from AAS Papers, II:8, Fox folder. AIP.

majority, I should be willing to set the ball rolling."[32] Hussey and Pickering eventually convinced Campbell to lead the initiative after ten leading Society members and
the Council endorsed the proposed amendment to the membership at large. In 1914,
the amendment passed overwhelmingly and the Society became the *American Astronomical Society*.

What changed between 1909 and 1914? In particular, where was Hale in the
process? With but a few exceptions, not much had changed in astrophysics in America
during this period. Many of the pioneers were now gone, most notably Newcomb,

Figure 6. During the August 1914 meeting at Northwestern University, the Society formally approved its name as the American Astronomical Society. Standing in the center, first row, are Frank Schlesinger, E. C. Pickering, and George Comstock. Stebbins is directly behind Pickering, Edwin Hubble on the far right. AIP Emilio Segrè Visual Archives.

Langley, and C. A. Young, but the balance of power was definitely migrating toward astrophysics. One major change was Hale's acquisition of Carnegie money to build the Mount Wilson Solar Observatory in Southern California, which he used as a base to create the International Union for Cooperation in Solar Research and to further his vision for how physics and astronomy must cooperate to solve the deeper problems of physical reality, linking the atom to the stars. By 1914, however, Pickering's hold over the Society had strengthened while Hale's interests in the Society had waned in favor of other initiatives he was mounting to revitalize the National Academy of Sciences and further develop his International Union. If he took any role in resisting or advocating a name change, it has not been recovered.

The Society's name change in 1914 might be seen as a triumph for traditional practice. Few astronomers actually called themselves astrophysicists then, and even fewer held to Hale's view of the centrality of physics to astronomical practice. Despite the rhetoric of advocates, it would take several decades before astronomical practice in the United States would move decidedly in the direction of physics and when physicists would find the problems in astrophysics ripe for exploitation with their conceptual and instrumental tools. Thus the story of how the AAS got its name is not merely one of personal preferences, personal rivalries or ambitions to gain power. Although these factors certainly played a part, the question of a name had at its core a half-century-old struggle to build a new science and to give that science a visibility and credibility as a separate discipline. By the time astrophysics came wholly into its own, with a trickle starting in the 1930s and the rush not coming until the post-World War II years, astronomy itself had been co-opted by astrophysical practice. There was thus no need to reconsider a name change.

IN PICKERING'S WAKE[33]

Pickering died in February 1919 which threw open both the directorship of the Harvard College Observatory and the leadership of the AAS. Frank Schlesinger, who had been first Vice-President, assumed the presidency, and by the September meeting in Ann Arbor (held in conjunction with the American Mathematical Society), he and others started to initiate changes, once they paid tribute to their leader. "The Society will keenly feel the loss of his presence at its meetings. The members of the Society had every reason to regard him as a warm friend, and to them the sense of personal loss is very deep."[34]

Senior members of the Society, however, did not want to perpetuate a dynastic order. From the formation of the Society to Pickering's death, officers were elected on the last day of every annual meeting but there were no limits on the number of terms one could hold office. The process of nomination was rather haphazard until W. J. Hussey provided a coherent plan, which he presented at the Harvard meetings in August 1910. On the first day of the annual meeting members provided names to the Secretary for all the positions to be filled on the ballot. Members not in attendance could mail in ballots. Prior to the second day of the meeting, appointed tellers prepared a slate consisting of the most frequently nominated names. The top three names for each office were then distributed on a new ballot at the end of the second day and members voted on it, placing their ballot again with the Secretary who would again direct tellers to make the final count. If no one achieved a clear majority, then various contingencies were activated.[35] The system had a strong tendency to retain officers once they were elected the first time. Pickering was the best example; once elected after Newcomb retired, he gained great influence in the discipline, since in parallel to his presidency of the Society he also commanded high office in the AAAS. But there also was a general lack of turnover in the vice-presidencies and in the secretary and treasurer. For example, Campbell held one or the other of the vice-presidencies for a combined total of 15 years, Comstock served as Secretary for seven years, and Annie Jump Cannon was Treasurer for six.

Ernest W. Brown took the lead in reforming the Society's election system in 1919. He wanted a mechanism whereby the membership could get "good men into office but also make sure that they got out again."[36] Under Brown's new procedure, nominations were prepared by a committee that considered factors such as the institution, age, and astronomical specialization of the candidates. Continuity for fund-raising and committee work was a paramount concern but it did not override the need to limit terms of office, in order to broaden the Society's base. Thus it was decided that the President should serve for three years but could not be re-elected; vice-presidents were elected for one year and the Secretary and Treasurer for one year with the possibility for re-election assuming they had carried out their duties appropriately. Although the Secretary and Treasurer still tended to remain in office for long terms, the term limits produced a higher turnover in the Council.

This was a big year for Schlesinger. He had accepted a new post as director of Yale University Observatory, and along with Brown instituted a number of important changes in the constitution and bylaws. They also initiated membership drives through the early 1920s, and as a result the Society grew steadily. They already knew that more order had to be imposed on the meetings. No longer could members submit as many papers as they pleased. A resolution was accordingly passed at Ann Arbor in September 1919 that each member could read only one paper unless, after everyone had a chance to speak, there was still time available. The Society also voted to return dues collected during wartime to those members who were on active duty.[37]

The wartime connections established by Hale between the NRC and the AAS continued in the postwar era as the Society was asked to send representatives to the NRC as well as to aid in the formation of a national committee to help reorganize international astronomy. The Society's centrality in creating this representative body, which deliberated over the nature of the new International Astronomical Union (IAU), further established the AAS as the arbiter for astronomy in America; as the chronicler for the 24th meeting observed: "It is evident that the Society will, through its elected representatives, have virtual control of the American participation in the International Astronomical Union." The creation of the new IAU however, made many of the older AAS committees redundant, and they were soon abolished and replaced by committees whose focus was upon internal Society matters and on maintaining relations with other professional bodies.[38]

BEYOND THE PICKERING YEARS

Under the new election rules and other reforms, the elections were more stream-lined, sparing the meetings "of the time and effort which formerly was spent in what often amounted to a re-election of the same persons to office." The Society gradually became more representative of the general membership, but it was a very slow process. Schlesinger built up his own circle, partly through his formation of a 'Neighbors' group that met to deliberate not only over astronomical matters but over the governance of the profession. As one of the three "generals" (with Russell and Shapley) who exerted much control over the eastern portion of the community, Schlesinger's influence over the Society has yet to be properly assessed.[39]

From the beginning, membership in the Society was open to any recognized prac-ticing astronomer or teacher, regardless of gender. But the Council retained the right to decide on membership, often dealing with issues such as the election of foreign members, and, more sticky, the inclusion of amateurs or of those whose credentials were, for whatever reason, not respected. Women always constituted a small fraction of the membership. The first meeting to be held at a women's college was in September 1920 when Anne S. Young of Mount Holyoke and Harriet Bigelow of Smith acted as co-hosts. Seventy-two members attended, including at least 17 women, making it the largest meeting in the Society's history to that point. Four women were elected to membership at the meeting, and about one dozen women were admitted over the next 14 months.[40]

During the next two decades the Society grew steadily at about 4% per year, adding an average of 15 members each year until the Second World War. Attendance at meetings also increased steadily from an average of 60 in the early 1920s to the high 90s in the late 1930s, dropping off precipitously with the war. The most popular meeting before the war was the 65th, held in Philadelphia in December 1940, where 147 people attended and presented some 56 papers. The most important issues at hand at this time included the Society's involvement with *The Astronomical Journal* and *The Astrophysical Journal*. In the early 1940s, with a generous endowment from the estate of E. W. Brown, the Society agreed to take over publication of the former, with Dirk Brouwer of Yale as editor. It also agreed to provide collaborating editors for the latter, in cooperation with Otto Struve and the University of Chicago Press (*see* chapters on the *AJ* and *ApJ*). Thus the Society gained a new critical role in the discipline.

Reflecting the increased importance of specialist areas in modern astronomy and astrophysics, during the late 1930s the Society began to sponsor topical sessions; symposia on "Intrinsic Stellar Variation" and on astronomical spectra were organized for the Philadelphia and Yerkes meetings in December 1940 and September 1941. Symposia would become annual events after the war as specialties grew within the American astronomical community. But even as late as 1952, the Council refused to adopt a policy on symposia that would allow the rank-and-file to suggest and organize them. The Council retained the authority to sponsor symposia at the discretion of the President.[41] This decision was soon reversed as the Society continued to grow and diversify.

THE FIRST WEST COAST MEETING
OF THE AAS

Donald E. Osterbrock

In the early days of the American Astronomical Society, most astronomers and their telescopes were concentrated in the eastern part of the country, and it is not surprising that the first seventeen meetings of the Society were held there. Most had been along the eastern seaboard, fewer in the Midwest, the one furthest west in St. Louis in 1903. The first "Pacific Coast" meeting took place in the San Francisco Bay area in August 1915, held jointly with the Astronomical Society of the Pacific and the American Association for the Advancement of Science (also holding its first West Coast meeting). The occasion was the Panama-Pacific International Exposition, one of the gigantic World's Fairs which Americans of that era loved to visit. It celebrated the opening of the Panama Canal in 1914, and demonstrated to the world that San Francisco (and California) had recovered completely from the disastrous earthquake and fire of 1906.

Planning had begun in 1912, when W. W. Campbell, director of Lick Observatory, invited the AAS to meet on Mount Hamilton in 1915, and President Edward C. Pickering, director of Harvard College Observatory, accepted.[1] After the AAAS also decided to meet in San Francisco that summer, the astronomers scheduled their meeting with it, and added Berkeley and Stanford University as sites. In 1915, AAS Secretary Philip Fox came west from Northwestern University to survey the situation and found all in order.[2]

The meetings began on Monday, August 2, at an auditorium in San Francisco, with an address by Campbell, then president of the AAAS, to all the societies. Speaking on "Science and Civilization" he concluded that astronomy was one of the most important aspects of civilization.[3] Pickering had not made the long train journey from Cambridge, but First Vice President Frank Schlesinger of Allegheny Observatory took his place.[4] On Tuesday, at a joint session in Berkeley with the mathematicians and physicists, George Ellery Hale gave one of the three invited talks on "The Work of A Modern Observatory," meaning an astrophysical one like his Mount Wilson Solar Observatory, whose 60-inch reflector had gone into operation seven years earlier.[5] Armin O. Leuschner, head of the Berkeley Astronomical Department, chaired this session.

On Wednesday there was an excursion to Palo Alto, with a session on the Stanford campus, and on Friday to Lick Observatory for another session. In the evening there was viewing through the 36-inch refractor before a late return to a San Jose hotel. On Thursday there were two sessions at Berkeley; and then on Saturday an all-day excursion to La Hacienda, the magnificent Pleasanton estate of Phoebe Apperson Hearst, the fabulously wealthy University of California Regent. Her fleet of automobiles met the astronomers at the Pleasanton station, and after lunch and a stroll through her gardens, mansion, and art collection, she provided a special train to take them back to San Francisco.[6]

Forty-five members of the AAS attended this meeting, 20 of them from California, one each from Arizona, British Columbia, and Manila, three from the Great Plains, and the rest from "back east." Five women members were present, including Caroline E. Furness, of Vassar, and Margaret Harwood, of the Maria Mitchell Observatory. In all, 49 contributed papers were presented orally, including ten on stellar dynamical astronomy, seven on variable stars and photometry, six on astrometry, five on planets' and satellites' orbits, four on nebular spectroscopy and imagery, one on a theory of star formation, and none at all on galaxies, quasars, or cosmology. Two of these words had not been invented then, and the third was considered a subject for philosophical speculation, not scientific research. At a short business meeting on Mount Hamilton, Dutch astronomer Jacobus C. Kapteyn was unanimously elected an honorary member, and the AAS dues were fixed at $2 a year or $25 for life membership.[6]

Heber D. Curtis of the Lick staff had prepared a guide to the astronomical exhibits at the Exposition grounds; the most spectacular were a new 20-inch refractor built for Chabot Observatory in Oakland, and a replica of the 72-inch glass disk for the Dominion Astrophysical Observatory, which when completed in 1917 would briefly become the largest telescope in the world.[7] After the meeting ended, a number of the astronomers went south and visited Mount Wilson Observatory before their long train ride home from Los Angeles.

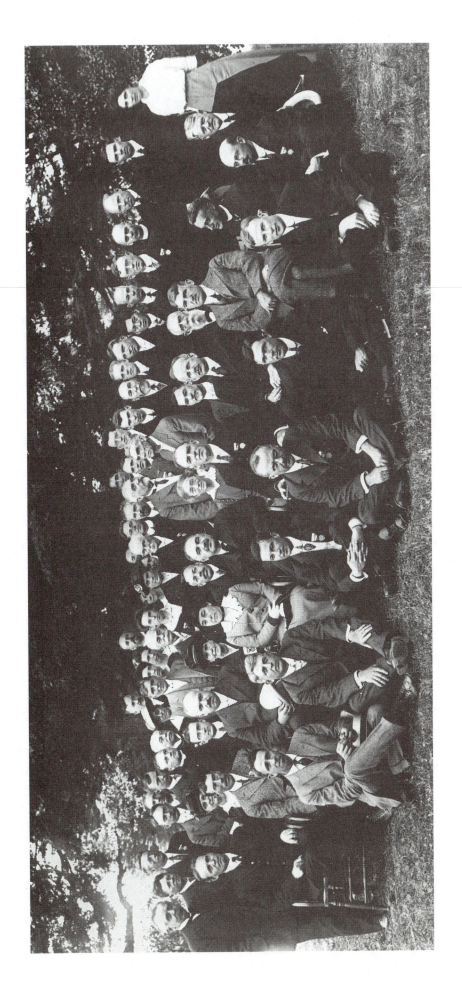

Figure 1. Joint AAS-ASP meeting, Berkeley, California, August 1915. Seated in the first row of chairs, the "power row," are, from left to right, Robert G. Aitken, Richard H. Tucker, Edward A. Fath, Elizabeth B. Campbell, Frank Schlesinger (first vice president of the AAS), William Wallace Campbell, George Ellery Hale, and Armin O. Leuschner. The bald-headed man at the right, seated on the ground, is Joel Stebbins, later at various times councilor, secretary, vice president and president of the AAS. Harlow Shapley, then at Mount Wilson, is in the back row, sixth from left. Courtesy of the Mary Lea Shane Archives of the Lick Observatory, UC-Santa Cruz.

Amateurs and the Society during the Formative Years

Marc Rothenberg and Thomas R. Williams

INTRODUCTION

The Society was founded at a time when American science was becoming more structured and much more a realm of professionals. In astronomy, unlike some of the laboratory-based sciences, the tradition of amateur contribution survived this period of professionalization and structuring. Thanks to the leadership of E. C. Pickering, American astronomy found a way to ensure a productive role for amateurs without endangering professional control of the discipline. By examining the issue of eligibility for membership in the Society, we can throw light on the larger issue of the relationship between amateur and professional astronomer at the turn of the twentieth century.

FUNDAMENTAL QUESTIONS

During the last quarter of the nineteenth century, and into the early years of the twentieth, American scientists went through a frenzy of creating disciplinary organizations. Starting with the American Chemical Society in 1876, and ending with the American Anthropological Association in 1902, American scientists established specialized forums for the discussion of scientific ideas and disciplinary problems. Among the issues each of these disciplinary societies faced was membership eligibility. In turn, membership eligibility raised two fundamental questions for each discipline: what were the intellectual boundaries of the discipline and to what extent was the society to be elitist?

American astronomy participated in this frenzy of society founding. The leadership of the astronomical community confronted both questions while establishing the Astronomical and Astrophysical Society of America; these questions arose again during the succeeding two decades. David DeVorkin's chapter discusses the problem of disciplinary boundaries. Here we examine the issue of elitism, especially as it pertains to the relationship between amateur and professional scientists.[1]

In the past few decades, at least four different ways to define professions have been suggested by social scientists, and it is helpful to consider them here in order to better understand that the distinction between amateur and professional is hardly a clear one. Some, like historian Konrad H. Jarausch, take the traditional or functionalist approach of enumerating traits or characteristics to define a profession. A second theory dismisses any effort to define a profession in static terms, describing such traits as largely self-justificatory rhetoric put forward by the professions themselves. Instead, as Margali S. Larson argues, one must examine and describe a monopolistic process and distribution of power within various occupations, defining the professions as only those occupations that have unique powers of control over both the supply and the market for their services. A third view, represented by Eliot Freidson, suggests that power is only another trait, and that all such definitions fail "in attempting to treat profession as if it were a generic rather than a changing historic concept, with particular roots in an industrial nation strongly influenced by Anglo-American institutions." Still, Freidson insists, some definition is needed as an analytical starting point, a conclusion supported by Robert A. Stebbins and Elliott A. Krause, as well. Krause, however, incorporates both these opposing viewpoints in a fourth model that envisions the professions, capitalism, and the state in a triangle of powers that are sometimes mutually supportive, and at other times in opposition. Krause uses this model to explain why, in his view, the guild-like power of the professions appears to be in decline at this time. Stebbins' view of the professions is much broader, as he divides occupations that may be viewed as professional into those which are client centered (medicine, law, etc.) and those that are public centered (arts, sports, etc.) and places science in the latter category. His perspective is one derived from his study of amateurs in a variety of avocational fields as well as other forms of serious leisure (collecting and volunteering) and is particularly useful in the present context.[2]

The history of the professions and professionalization of American science has not fared much better. Nathan Reingold's very suggestive tripartite division of scientists into researchers, practitioners, and cultivators works well for the mid-nineteenth century, but is less useful for the period of this paper. Other workers, like Robert V. Bruce, Nathan O. Hatch, and Daniel J. Kevles, looking at more recent times, have identified the generally exclusionary nature of the process of professionalization and the need for and means of legitimation, but they provided few specifics by discipline. Bruce A. Kimball has elaborated on the manner in which changes in the meaning of the word profession over several centuries reflected the changing views of the professions in America. He lumps scientists with the professorate in highlighting a brief period of glory for these professions during the late nineteenth and early twentieth centuries when science was, in his view, the reigning cultural ideal. Finally, John Lankford has dealt broadly with some of the questions related to professionalization in astronomy (education, exclusion from the market, and the reward system) but fails to deal explicitly with many other issues. Other histories of the professions have ignored or marginalized the sciences in their attempt to establish a usable understanding of the professionalization project. Thus, at least for science and certainly for astronomy, a definitive analysis of the process of professionalization has yet to emerge.[3]

Among late nineteenth-century American scientists, we can draw a distinction between those whose application of specialized scientific knowledge provided them with their main source of income and those whose income was from other, typically non-scientific, occupations. For the purposes of this chapter, the former are "professionals" and the latter are "amateurs" in their pursuit of their astronomical interests. In turn, the professionals can be divided into those who taught, those who carried out routine observations and/or calculations, and those who conducted research. Researchers fall along a continuum ranging qualitatively from the relatively prosaic to the cutting edge, and from the occasional to full-time. Amateurs fall along a similar continuum from routine observers to cutting-edge researchers.

THE YEARS OF UNCERTAINTY

Although there was no consensus among scientific disciplinary societies as to which professionals were worthy of membership and which were not, most of the disciplinary societies discouraged, if not barred, amateur participation. For example, the Geological Society of America (founded in 1888) restricted membership to those "engaged in geological work or in teaching geology." Although the American Chemical Society gradually modified its constitution, eliminating employment and educational requirements, so that in 1902 "any person interested in the promotion of chemistry" was eligible for membership, this liberalization is misleading. It was an effort by the industrial chemists to prevent domination of the society by academics — to ensure a broad definition of professional chemist — not an attempt to embrace avocational chemists. The American Physiological Society (1887) did initially in theory allow those who "promoted and encouraged" physiology to become members, but no one was ever elected a member under that criterion. The criterion was eventually eliminated, and membership eligibility was limited to those who have "conducted and published an original research," thus barring those who merely taught physiology.[4]

Given the history of astronomy and the state of the science in this country in the late nineteenth century, an American astronomical society might be expected to be one of the exceptions to the propensity of discouraging amateurs. Since the middle of the nineteenth century, amateur astronomers have contributed substantially to the progress of astronomy. In the United States, avocational astronomy became a realistic option when Henry Fitz, Alvan Clark and Sons, and others began manufacturing small-to-moderate aperture refracting telescopes at reasonable prices in the middle of the nineteenth century. The scientific contributions of amateurs have included: a) the discovery of many previously unknown celestial objects of astronomical importance; b) the evolution of instruments and development of observational methods that were vital to the eventual emergence of astrophysics as a separate discipline within astronomy; and c) routine observations of sun, moon and planets, comets, meteors, and variable stars that professional astronomers could not possibly monitor continuously. Studies of sunspots, double stars, variable stars, meteors, aurorae, and the zodiacal light constituted the main scientifically valuable observing programs of individual amateur astronomers though the second half of the nineteenth century.

Like other observational sciences, such as natural history, the collecting of data (or specimens) and the interpretation of that data could be done by different individuals, with very different levels of scientific knowledge.[5] In the United States, even the professional astronomical community contained many individuals with relatively limited formal training in astronomy and a number with access only to relatively small telescopes. The boundary between amateur and professional was not insurmountable. Edward Emerson Barnard, William Robert Brooks, Sherburne Wesley Burnham, Maria Mitchell, and Lewis Swift are all examples of nineteenth-century American amateurs who became so well known for their double star or comet discoveries that they were eventually employed as professional astronomers. Henry Draper and Lewis Morris

Rutherfurd were typical of the wealthy amateur astronomers who pioneered the use of photography in astronomy and made important contributions to the astronomical application of spectroscopy as well.[6]

As a result, the relationship of amateurs to the Society during the first two decades of its existence turned out to be relatively complex and was related to the larger issues of the role and status of the Society within the discipline of astronomy. Amateurs were never totally barred from membership in the Society. Charter membership was open to anyone "attending the second and third conferences who signed a statement of desire that a society be formed and of those who otherwise expressed to the committee or council their wish to join when the society should be organized."[7] This open policy towards membership and the wide publicity given the conferences resulted in a charter group which was 15% amateur.[8] These amateurs ranged from well-known and respected researchers like Henry M. Parkhurst, one of the more colorful and productive of American amateur astronomers of the late nineteenth century, to the extremely obscure, for whom there is little or no biographical information. The first American stenographer, Parkhurst (1825–1908) worked in the United States Senate and New York City Superior Court as their official recorder. He was one of the first astronomers to

Figure 1. Henry M. Parkhurst (1825–1908), court stenographer and an early amateur contributor to astronomical photometry. From: Popular Astronomy **16**, 231 (April 1908).

adopt the Pogson ratio that later became the standard in astronomical photometry. Parkhurst experimented with a number of designs for a stellar photometer, finally settling on what he called the deflecting photometer around 1883. With his deflecting photometer perfected, Parkhurst took up the study of the light curves of variable stars. Over the next 24 years Parkhurst published his observations of the maxima and minima of 96 variable stars, and he standardized photometry for some 3000 comparison stars. In addition, he developed a precise understanding of the changes in the brightness of 36 asteroids, correctly deriving the necessary photometric constants to compute a magnitude for each from orbital considerations. Parkhurst's work was regularly published in *The Astronomical Journal* and the *Harvard Annals*.[9]

The bylaws of the Society covering subsequent applications for membership were extremely flexible, stating only that "any person deemed capable of preparing an acceptable paper upon some subject of astronomy, astrophysics, or related branch of physics, may be elected by the Council to membership in the Society upon nomination by two or more members of the Society."[10] With the support of only two members necessary for nomination, being put forward for membership was not difficult. The real decision lay with the Council. It could restrict or open membership at will. That there was a trickle of new amateur members after 1899 demonstrates that professional status was not a prerequisite for membership.

This trickle is evidence that James Keeler's agitation in 1899 for a highly restrictive membership policy had been explicitly rejected. Keeler wanted astronomical society membership limited to researchers. In doing so, he contrasted his proposed selective membership of the new astronomical society with the very open membership policies of both the Astronomical Society of the Pacific and the British Astronomical Association.[11]

On the other hand, there are a number of indications that amateurs had only marginal status in the Society prior to 1909. Only 1% of the papers presented at meetings through 1909 were authored by amateurs. The number of amateurs in the Society slowly declined throughout the first decade of the Society's existence. By 1908, amateurs comprised fewer than 12% of the membership.[12]

It was not only the amateurs who were marginal to the Society. Apparently, so were many professionals. Or perhaps the Society was marginal to the lives and careers of many professionals. It is not clear which interpretation of the data is correct. What is clear is that although the founders of the Society — leaders in astronomical research like E. C. Pickering of the Harvard College Observatory and Simon Newcomb, newly-retired from the United States Navy — felt the need for the Society, many other American astronomers did not. By 1900 less than 62% of the potential membership pool of professional astronomers and astrophysicists had joined.[13] Subsequent membership figures indicate a continuing limited attraction. Professional astronomers in the United States did not believe that membership in the Society was a necessary prerequisite for complete professional status.

One of the characteristics of the Society during the first decade of its existence was the limited institutional base from which members were attracted. The Society was dominated by men and women employed at a relatively small number of institutions. Over one-third of the charter members were employed by only three universities and their affiliated observatories — Harvard, Chicago, and California — or the Federal government. Although this percentage dropped somewhat during the Society's first decade, it never fell below 28%. These same few institutions supplied 44% of the officers of the Society during 1899–1909 and 56% of the 285 papers presented at meetings.

Clearly, there were key questions still to be answered about the new Society. Was the Society open to anyone interested in the interchange of astronomical ideas, as the Astronomical Society of the Pacific was? Or was it to more closely resemble the American Physiological Society, limiting membership to individuals who could expand astronomical knowledge, and with the ultimate goal of shaping the discipline? To what extent was the Society going to recognize that amateur researchers could still contribute to the progress of the science?

ENTER THE AMATEUR

It was in this context of a narrow participatory base, disappointing membership figures, and unanswered questions about the ultimate nature of the Society that William J. Hussey, professor of astronomy at the University of Michigan and Secretary of the Society, solicited advice on January 16, 1909 on ways of increasing membership. President E. C. Pickering agreed on the need for new members and suggested that lists be drawn up of eligible individuals. These scientists would then be privately invited to accept membership. Pickering recognized that concrete inducements for joining the Society would be helpful, but he could only suggest offering a history of the Society, an annually revised membership list, and a hope that the Society would be doing work in the future of which astronomers would be proud.[14]

A more concrete response came from E. D. Roe, professor of mathematics at Syracuse University and a specialist in double stars. He answered Hussey's solicitation with a plea to make a special effort to attract amateurs. Not only would this solve the membership problem, but it would also lessen the possibility of the amateurs organizing a national society of their own free from oversight by the professionals. Roe took the opportunity to propose two amateurs for membership: W. R. Jewell, Jr., a lawyer, and J. A. Lawes, a mechanical engineer for the New York, Chicago, and St. Louis Railroad, who was a friend of Jewell's. Both men were experienced observers. Jewell owned a 15.5-inch reflector, while Lawes had erected an observatory with a 6.5-inch Clark refractor. Roe knew the men because he had purchased the Clark from Lawes. Such men, Roe felt, "should be taken under the protecting wing of the Society and inspired to do useful work for the science."[15]

Roe was responding to the need for increasing the membership rolls, the perceived marginal status of amateurs in the Society, and the larger question of the role of the amateur in American astronomy. His answer was one that the Society Council was comfortable with. Roe's two nominees were elected to membership by the Council, as were seven other amateurs during 1909–1910. Amateur representation in the Society reached 12.5%, reversing the earlier downward trend.

This growth was part of the larger growth of the American Astronomical Society (AAS), presumably as a result of Pickering's recruiting campaign among the professional community. In 1909 and 1910 more new members were obtained than in any other 2-year period since 1900. Senior faculty who had hitherto resisted joining the

AAS and young astronomers just starting their careers signed up. By 1910, perhaps as much as 80% of the professional pool were members of the Society.[16]

In the wake of increased membership came somewhat broader institutional participation. The percentage of members affiliated with Harvard, Chicago, California, and the Federal government declined steadily, reaching 21% in 1918. Between 1910 and 1918 only 37.5% of the officers of the Society came from those four institutions, as did only 36% of the 306 papers presented during the meetings of 1910 through 1915. Forty-two institutions were represented among the contributors, an increase of nearly 45% in the number of institutions.[17]

But what was at stake in 1909 and 1910 was more than simply increasing the number of Society members. These years marked the beginning of the era when the leadership of American astronomy tried to ensure that the Society was the central organization for all researchers within the discipline — a discipline which embraced both amateurs and professionals.

In his letter to Hussey, Roe had planted an important seed: the idea of actively integrating amateur astronomers into the research community and obtaining ''useful work for the science'' through inspiration and guidance. A corollary to Roe's attitude towards amateurs was the avoidance of a strictly amateur astronomical society. If amateurs only spoke to amateurs, how could the professional community supply guidance and direct the efforts of the amateurs in the path most beneficial for astronomy?

Roe did not specifically identify the cause of his unease, but there had been several efforts to organize amateur astronomers. For example, Frederick C. Leonard, a Chicago teenage amateur, organized a national or even international amateur society. Roe may have learned about this from his amateur acquaintances. Leonard owned a 3-inch refractor which he used to observe nebulae and planets. His Society for Practical Astronomy (SPA), founded in 1909, when Leonard was 13, had as its grandiose goal the binding ''together in one strong society all of the astronomical amateurs in America and elsewhere, and in this way encourage and help to promote amateur work in general.'' Leonard hoped to coordinate amateur observations through meetings and a journal to be published eight or nine times a year.[18]

After almost two years of effort, Leonard had four members and a typewritten journal. However, in the spring and summer of 1911 Leonard began a much more aggressive campaign to recruit members. This effort was marked by the actual printing of a first issue of his journal in March 1911. Copies were sent to leading astronomers, including Pickering. By June the SPA had 18 members, including John E. Mellish, a Wisconsin amateur who had joined the AAS in 1909. The next step in Leonard's campaign was to send a detailed announcement of his society to *Popular Astronomy*, a nontechnical journal edited by professional astronomers but aimed at amateurs, where he frequently published his observations.[19]

CONTROLLING THE AMATEUR

Leonard's suggestion that American astronomy should coordinate the activities of amateur observers resonated with some members of the professional community. One was Pickering, who had been using amateur observers for variable star work as far back as 1885. To ensure accurate and reliable data, Pickering spelled out in explicit detail the techniques these amateurs would use. Little was left to chance. They were given charts, told how to estimate magnitudes, and even forewarned not to look at earlier versions of the light curves of variables as it would prejudice subsequent observations. The data were then sent to Harvard College Observatory for reduction, analysis, and publication.[20] Pickering knew the advantages of using such observers, but he also knew the pitfalls. He and Henry Parkhurst had clashed over the use of universal time for Parkhurst's observations. As an amateur who worked for his own pleasure, Parkhurst claimed "individual sovereignty" over his observations and refused to adopt the standards established by Pickering.[21] Another was Herbert Wilson, director of the Goodsell Observatory and editor of *Popular Astronomy*. Wilson was "chary" of Leonard's organization and described Leonard as "only a boy with lots of enthusiasm but not very much knowledge of astronomical subjects." He wanted to "head him off."[22]

Wilson agreed to publish Leonard's announcement in the August issue of *Popular Astronomy*. Directly underneath it, however, Wilson published his own note, suggesting that what American astronomy needed was an astronomical society for amateurs with various specialized sections. He clearly had in mind the British Astronomical Association as a model. Members would concentrate on areas of research usually ignored by the professional and where the limited apparatus of the amateur would not be a handicap. Examples included variable star observations, systematic comet searches, the study of surface markings on planets, and observations of the Zodiacal light and gegenschein. To promote such research, Wilson offered to publish lists of objects, with suggestions for methods and forms of recording, in the pages of *Popular Astronomy*.[23]

In the next issue of *Popular Astronomy* there was a response by Pickering, who was not, however, responding directly to Wilson's article, but to a letter Wilson had sent him. In his reply, which Wilson quoted, Pickering expressed his opinion that the coordination of amateur observations required a "permanent organization... which can not be safely trusted to the amateur." Pickering stated that he would "be glad to do anything I can to secure a greater amount of useful work from amateurs."[24]

One of Pickering's amateur observers, William Tyler Olcott, agreed to take charge of a section of variable star observers within Wilson's proposed amateur astronomical society. Olcott (1873–1936) was the prototype of the professional astronomer's ideal amateur researcher, the "master" in Robert A. Stebbins' typology of modern amateur astronomers, who was willing to put up with regimentation, systematization, and discipline in exchange for the opportunity of contributing to astronomy,[25] and the complete opposite of Parkhurst's individual sovereign. He was introduced to the beauty of the night sky by a childhood friend of his wife in 1905. Within two years he authored the first of the six books he published on astronomy. His most successful book, *Field Book of the Skies*, attracted thousands of individuals to amateur astronomy and remained in print for over four decades. A passionate observer, with the amateur's usual interest in planets and deep-sky objects, he was attracted to variable stars by an exhibit Harvard had put up at the 1909 meeting of the American Association for the Advancement of Science describing its work in that area. Olcott contacted Harvard for advice and in response, Pickering sent Leon Campbell, of his staff, to train Olcott. A professional himself (law), Olcott accepted the hierarchical structure and intellectual

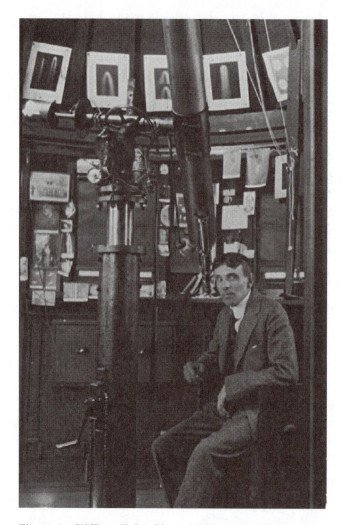

Figure 2. William Tyler Olcott (1873–1936), lawyer and a founder of the AAVSO, in his observatory at Norwich, Connecticut, c. 1927. AAVSO photograph courtesy Michael Saladyga.

control that Harvard College Observatory established over variable star observations. He acknowledged the superior knowledge of professional astronomers and seemed satisfied to be able to do his part to advance knowledge.

From the beginning, Pickering saw Olcott's group as under his control and integrated into the research community. First, Pickering explicitly advised Olcott to omit "or render less conspicuous," the word amateur from the name and descriptions of the proposed group. Pickering did not want to "deter some professional astronomers whose contributions would be of great value" from participating in the new organization.[26] (He had in mind, among others, David Todd of Amherst College, who assisted Pickering's variable star research.[27]) Pickering even went so far as to suggest that Olcott's organization become a section of the Society. Olcott rejected the latter suggestion, feeling unworthy to be part of the Society.[28]

By the end of the year Olcott's group had an independent existence, having evolved into the American Association of Variable Star Observers (AAVSO), with 15 active members. However, it was clearly under Pickering's control. Even though the

AAVSO officially incorporated in 1918 and was no longer simply an auxiliary activity of Harvard College Observatory, the action was more a symbolic than real demonstration of independence. Interpretation of variable star data still remained the province of the professional. Moreover, the AAVSO was dependent upon Harvard for office space and a considerable part of its budget for over 30 years after its incorporation.[29]

AMATEURS ARE WELCOME

The status of the Society as the central organization for the entire discipline, rather than just the profession, was confirmed time and again during the second decade of the twentieth century. Amateur authorship of papers presented at meetings between 1910 and 1915 totaled 3%, small, but triple the figure for the previous decade. Amateur membership climbed steadily, reaching 19% in 1918. Leading amateur researchers who were not members were actively recruited, just like their counterparts in the professional ranks.[30]

Within the restricted areas which the professional left for amateur research, the amateurs were eventually granted some semblance of power. Here the contrast with the pre-1909 era is clear. For example, in 1908 Pickering tried to name an amateur, Joel H. Metcalf (1866–1925), a Unitarian minister and astrophotographer, to the Society's comet committee. But he was opposed by George C. Comstock, the director of the Washburn Observatory of the University of Wisconsin. Metcalf was a prolific observer, and discovered six comets, 41 asteroids, and several variable stars. He also acquired superb skills as a self-taught lens designer and optical craftsman, and produced many fine astronomical lenses. Pickering so valued his abilities as an optician that he contracted with Metcalf to manufacture lenses for Harvard College Observatory's photographic survey cameras, including a 16-inch doublet and a 10-inch triplet. But Comstock wanted someone who was interested in the "interpretation of the phenomena," not "the search after comets and their observation." He asked Pickering to chose a mathematician or physicist instead of Metcalf. By 1918, in contrast, the majority of the Society's Committee on Variable Star Observations, astronomy's official coordinating body on this subject in the United States, established in 1916, was composed of amateur members of the AAVSO, including Olcott as chair, joined by Leon Campbell of Harvard College Observatory and Henry Norris Russell of Princeton University. Metcalf was ensconced as the only amateur on the Committee on Asteroids.[31]

A major factor in the Society's relative openness to amateurs was the attitude of its President, E. C. Pickering. Membership requirements were vague and flexible. When called upon to evaluate the credentials of apparently marginal amateurs he was generally extremely sympathetic, advocating a loose interpretation of the bylaws. His vision of the discipline of astronomy was broad and encompassing. For example, in 1914, when he was asked whether an architect with a 9-inch Clark mounted on his roof and a popular lecturer on astronomy with knowledge of descriptive astronomy were qualified for admission to the Society, Pickering responded by agreeing to support both men for membership.[32]

Pickering's enthusiastic support for amateur researchers was an acknowledgement that amateurs represented a cost-efficient way of doing astronomy, supplying professional astronomers with tremendous amounts of data at only a tiny fraction of the cost

Figure 3. The formal incorporation meeting of the American Association of Variable Stars Observers (AAVSO), Cambridge, MA, November 10, 1917. E. C. Pickering is in the back row at the left hand side of the door, Leon Campbell is kneeling at the far left; Professor Annie Sewell Young is standing just behind him. Annie J. Cannon is sitting third from left and Henrietta Swann Leavitt is fourth from left. William Tyler Olcott is in the middle row at the right side of the door. AAVSO photograph courtesy Michael Saladyga, identifications from Figure 15, p. 46 of D. Hoffleit, *Women in the History of Variable Stars Astronomy* (AAVSO, 1993).

of professional staff. Pickering was a master in exploiting resources. He had originated the concept of utilizing women, paid less than their male counterparts, as observatory assistants. Amateurs, like women, were an inexpensive but effective way of obtaining data.[33]

In 1913, and again in 1916, the Society formally discussed the issue of the status of amateurs in the context of considering proposals for the establishment of an associate membership.[34] The discussion in 1916, which is better documented, is quite expressive regarding the attitude of professional astronomers towards amateur members.

Frank Schlesinger of the Allegheny Observatory raised the issue of associate members in 1916 in hopes of enlarging the Society. His targets were those individuals who were interested in astronomy but unable to conduct significant research of any sort. They were the ''cultivators'' in Nathan Reingold's tripartite division of the nineteenth-century American scientific community — the lovers of science so evident in local societies. More narrowly, they were the ''armchair'' and ''apprentice'' astronomers in Stebbins' typology: amateurs who either did not observe, were satisfied with reading astronomy rather than doing it, or observed for recreational purposes only.[35]

The Council of the Society responded by appointing a committee to investigate the possibility and form of associate membership, with Schlesinger as chair and a representative of the amateur community (Olcott) as one of the five other members. The other three members were Roe, Comstock, and Clarence A. Chant, the University of

Figure 4. Joel Hastings Metcalf (1866–1925), Unitarian minister and a talented amateur astronomer and optical worker. From: Popular Astronomy **33**, 493 (October 1925).

Toronto astrophysicist. In establishing the committee, the Council made it clear that the status of amateur members had to be treated carefully. As Schlesinger informed the committee members:

> ...the Council expressed itself strongly in favor of some form of membership for amateur astronomers, especially as in recent years it has been shown that the cooperation of these with each other and with professional astronomers should be encouraged by our Society.[36]

The position of the Council was one that Schlesinger agreed with wholeheartedly. He did not want his proposal to be interpreted as an attempt to stratify the Society along vocational lines. Amateurs should not be excluded from regular membership.[37]

Schlesinger's initial draft proposed that "any person interested in Astronomy is eligible to Associate Membership." Associate members would have all the rights and privileges as regular members with the exception of voting and holding office, including the right to deliver papers at the meetings. Therefore, a corollary of establishing associate membership, explicitly stated by the Society Council, was the need for extremely careful screening of proposals for papers. Obviously, if these associate members had the ability and means to conduct research, they could have applied for membership under the usual provisions. In fact, Schlesinger's draft went on to define eligibility for regular membership as making "important contributions to Astronomy or a related branch of Science." The fact that associate members could only be allowed in under a special dispensation implied that any paper they offered the Society would be unacceptable.[38]

Strong opposition developed to Schlesinger's proposal, in no small part because, in the mind of some of the membership, he was dealing with nonexistent problems. As E. C. Pickering pointed out in an incisive critique of the proposal, if the Society wished to expand its membership, all it had to do was admit "to full privileges any person who has sufficient interest to wish to join." Nor was there any need to worry about such individuals delivering bad papers. The Royal Astronomical Society had relatively low barriers for admittance yet managed to keep the quality of their programs quite high by screening out incompetent papers. In fact, the Society had already followed the Royal Astronomical Society's example and rejected certain effusions. Pickering was not adverse to continue doing so "with other ambitious but ill-guided amateurs."[39]

Schlesinger's draft was circulated among the committee, revised, and recirculated. Ultimately, the committee could not come to a consensus on the specifics of a bifurcated membership, including the names of the two forms of membership.[40] With active opposition to even the advisability of any action in this regard, the committee concluded "that there seems to be no reason for trying to have two classes of members," and the committee was discharged.[41] Formal membership requirements were left as they had been. It may have been symbolic that at the Council meeting the day prior to that, at which the committee was discharged, two of the eleven new members elected were amateurs.[42] The issue of a bifurcated membership would come up again in four decades time (see DeVorkin and Routly this volume, page 122).

By the end of World War I, the AAS, under the leadership of E. C. Pickering, had found a place for amateurs both within the Society and within the discipline. Amateurs were welcome if they knew their place.

Popular Astronomy

Vol. LV, No. 8   OCTOBER, 1947   **Whole No. 548**

The American Astronomical Society, 1897-1947*

By JOEL STEBBINS

We are celebrating, as announced, the fiftieth anniversary of the founding of this Society at the time of the dedication of the Yerkes Observatory in October, 1897. Many of you do not know that several weeks ago we had a rehearsal for today by a celebration of the fiftieth birthday of the incumbent president of the Society, who is also the chancellor, or whatever you may call him, of the Yerkes Observatory; so there is occasion for congratulations all around. Mr. Struve will discuss the history of the Observatory, while the present paper will be confined to the activities of the Society. It would have been much better if we could have had with us today someone from that first meeting. I am thinking of Henry Crew of Northwestern, Charles Lane Poor of New York, and Frederick H. Seares of Mount Wilson—three known survivors of the sixty scientists who gathered fifty years ago.

As you will remember, the meeting of 1897 was called as a conference of astronomers and physicists; and it was so successful that a second such conference was held on the invitation of Professor Edward C. Pickering at the Harvard Observatory a year later; and then in September, 1899, the formal organization was accomplished in another meeting at the Yerkes Observatory. The name adopted was "Astronomical and Astrophysical Society of America," giving emphasis to the fact that many physicists had interests in common with the astronomers. The organization continued under that rather unwieldy name for ten years when, again at Yerkes, a vote was taken on the change of name to the "American Astronomical Society." Out of deference to a few members who felt more at home under the old name, the decision was against the change; but five years later at Evanston, the designation, "American Astronomical Society," was adopted by a practically unanimous vote. This artificial distinction between the older astronomy and the newer astrophysics was more important in the early years of the Society than it is now. The time is long past when astrophysics could be considered a separate science. For illustration, the contributed papers on the program of the present meeting include not more than ten per cent of titles in the old time astronomy, and several of these are based upon photography.

---

*Read at the fiftieth anniversary meeting of the Society held at the Yerkes Observatory, **September 6, 1947.**

The objects of the Society were first stated to be the advancement of astronomy, astrophysics, and related branches of physics; and the qualifications for membership were as follows: "Any person deemed capable of preparing an acceptable paper upon some subject of astronomy, astrophysics, or related branch of physics, may be elected by the Council to membership in the Society upon nomination by two or more members of the Society." With the change of the name of the organization, the scientific fields were defined as astronomy and related branches of science. The qualification that a candidate for membership be deemed capable of preparing an acceptable paper has been rather liberally interpreted. The Council once received a letter from an applicant stating that he was not a lawyer for nothing; and he pointed out that the rule does not state acceptable to whom. He himself could prepare a paper which would be quite acceptable to the janitor for starting a fire. I believe that the Council ruled that the candidate's own letter could be construed as an acceptable paper. In other cases, it has been suggested that a good-sized check on a bank might be considered an acceptable paper on astronomy.

Joking aside, while the rule for acceptance of new members has been liberally applied, the acceptance of papers for the program has always been a serious matter in the Council. The fundamental test has, of course, been that a paper be sound. At the risk of non-appreciation of some genius by his contemporaries, any doubtful title is usually held by the secretary and, if necessary, an abstract or the whole paper sent to a referee before acceptance. However, there are very few such cases, and usually it is easy to tell from the source what the nature of a paper will be. For instance, as far as I can remember, and I am pretty sure I am correct, we have never had any crank papers from the Yerkes Observatory. At the other extreme would be the papers which the secretary would know better than even to refer to the Council, such as the recent communication on the Flying Saucers.

In 1899, one hundred and thirteen persons expressed the intention of becoming charter members. You may be interested to hear the names of the eleven known survivors from that list. They are: Charles G. Abbot, Walter S. Adams, Henry Crew, W. S. Eichelberger, H. M. Goodwin, W. J. Humphreys, A. C. Lunn, Antonia C. Maury, F. R. Moulton, Charles D. Perrine, and Robert W. Wood. Messrs Poor and Seares joined shortly afterward. As you are aware, a goodly proportion of these are still active in astronomical work; they average seventy-nine years of age. By 1922, the membership had increased to 370, while the present number is about 625. Thus we can count on a gain of about ten members per year with no present prospect of the number leveling off at a saturation figure. A rough analysis of the membership shows that about one-half are actively working at observatories; one quarter are connected with colleges, universities, or scientific institutions; while another quarter are interested in astronomy without formal connection with institutions. Over the years, various suggestions have been made to have more than one class of membership; but all such movements have been voted down. We seem to be too happy a family to think of breaking up. We do have the class of Honorary Members under the rule that not more often than once each year the Council may elect one twenty-four foreign astronomer of distinction to such membership. Since 1910, twenty-four honorary members have been elected, of whom eleven are now living. A glance at the list of names will show the leaders in astronomy in different countries during the past generation.

The main activity of the Society has, of course, been in connection with the meetings, which were first held annually; but since 1920 we have met twice a year. The present is officially the seventy-seventh meeting which, with the first two conferences, makes a total of seventy-nine. The reports of the papers presented at these meetings give the record of the advance of American astronomy during the last half century. A count of the places where the Society has met gives the following: Harvard leads with eleven meetings; followed by Columbia with seven; and Yerkes six, counting today. Five meetings have been held at Washington and at Philadelphia; and three each at Yale, Northwestern, and Chicago; also there have been two meetings each at Ottawa, Cleveland, Swarthmore, Michigan, Wisconsin, and Ohio Wesleyan. Twenty-two places have had one meeting each, so we have had plenty of variety. The count also shows forty-eight meetings east and twenty-five meetings west of the Alleghenies, plus three in California and three in Canada. About half of the gatherings were in cities and half in what may be called college towns, though here the count is rather arbitrary. We have placed Harvard and Yale in the college town category—at least they are in academic surroundings—and Yerkes is left out in the country. The Society has met twenty-two times with the American Association for the Advancement of Science, usually at the winter meetings and especially at the four-year general meetings, which were formerly held in rotation in New York, Washington, and Chicago. Various advantages accrue to an observatory or institution in entertaining the Society. The approach of the meeting usually means a certain amount of house cleaning and fresh paint in addition to the stimulated local activity in astronomy.

We may note some possibilities for meetings which have been proposed but not held. Someone suggested a three-day reunion on one of the steamers of the Great Lakes. The housing accommodations would be take care of, and the social life would be even more intimate than on a college campus. Those of us who are poor sailors would want to know what the weather would be like for three days in advance. The nearest we came to such an excursion was at the meeting at Put-in-Bay on Lake Erie in 1908. Again, there has been a minority enthusiasm for

Florida or New Orleans in the winter time, but such suggestions have been squelched. The majority of members have preferred to remain in the North and run the risk of a blizzard rather than to visit the sunny South. Either an exposition or an eclipse has been necessary to draw us out to California, and the 200-inch will be the attraction in 1948. Another fine place for a meeting, if we can ever get that far, is Victoria where those of us who have been there know that the local arrangements would be ideal.

As the Society has grown in numbers, the attendance at meetings has also increased, but fortunately not in proportion. From sixty attendants at the original Yerkes meeting, the number increased to 130 at the second conference at Harvard, a good attendance for any meeting at the present time. The largest attendance up to date has also been at Harvard when last winter more than two hundred attended the Society dinner, but only 165 were able to crowd into the photograph, which was surpassed by that of Yerkes six years ago when the number was 170. But all these figures are small compared with the group that attended the dedication exercises at Yerkes in 1897. In two special trains from Chicago, trustees, faculty, students, and guests of the University of Chicago to the number of 700 came to be entertained, fed, and enlightened in this building.

One complaint about the meetings has always been that if it hadn't been for the papers, we should have had a good time! There seems to be no substitute for this evil. The evil has been lessened somewhat by limiting the papers to ten minutes and enforcing the rule of one author, one paper; though practically the question often comes up as to how many papers may be presented by several authors in cooperation. One suggestion which has been advanced in dead earnest is that the program be limited to only good papers. Just who would decide in advance which are to be the good papers has not been worked out; and there is something to be said for the training of the younger members in preparing any kind of papers—even poor ones. In recent years, we have had more invited contributions at symposia, though long ago one member said, "Why do we do it? Each symposium is worse than the one before." He had in mind the length of a program where every author went overtime by at least a factor of two. With the gradual training of the membership, not to say of the presiding officers, the time problem has been approximately solved, but it will require eternal vigilance to keep astronomers from talking too long.

Speaking of officers reminds one of the old method of elections. Formerly at the annual meeting each member was entitled personally or by mail to a vote on a nominating ballot for every vacancy to be filled. On the last day of the meeting, the votes were then taken in succession for the different officers, the selection to be limited to those nominated for the particular office or for some higher office. On one occasion the presiding officer pointed out that one good candidate, Mr. Frost of Yerkes, had been nominated for all the offices and that it would simplify the business of the Society if the members would proceed to elect him. Over the years the innocent phrase, "some higher office," had an unintended result. After the voting, which took considerable time, it almost always turned out that the same officers were elected as before; in fact, in the early years of the Society changes among the officers were very slow. In 1919, under the leadership of Ernest W. Brown, the new system was introduced. Brown had a hobby of reforming scientific societies; his idea being not only to devise the machinery for getting good men into office but also to make sure that they got out again. The procedure of having the nominations prepared by a committee insures that the officers and Council will be a representative group, taking into account such considerations as geography, age, and the different fields of astronomy. Under the present rules of limited terms more members of the Society are represented on the Council, and there is nothing like a feeling of possession to keep up the interest in an organization. Some criticism has been made of the three-year term of the president as being too long. The term is not long measured by the number of meetings—only six of them—but it means that two out of three of the annually elected vice presidents will be passed over. Perhaps the honoring of individuals should be subordinated to the best interests of the Society, and such matters as a campaign for funds and other important business of the Society could scarcely be directed by an officer in a term of one year. Since it is desirable to have continuity in the positions of secretary and treasurer, these officers are chosen annually with possibility of re-election pending good behavior.

It would be invidious to distinguish between officers and members who have contributed to the work of the Society, but there can be no objection to mentioning the presidents who have passed on. Simon Newcomb was elected as first president while he was absent abroad. He gave the Society the prestige of the foremost man of science of his time in America. I believe the record shows that he had between fifteen and twenty honorary doctor's degrees, evidence of the estimation in which he was held. Newcomb, himself, as you know, was largely self-trained; and he once expressed the doubt whether the next great student of celestial mechanics would come from a university or from the backwoods. He continued to serve as president for six years, when he retired at his own request. Following Newcomb was Edward C. Pickering, who dominated the meetings of the Society with his genial personality for fourteen years until his death in 1919. Pickering was an admirable presiding officer, and it was often remarked how he could bring out discussion of a paper, contributing himself with pertinent remarks in almost any field of astronomy. Frank Schlesinger was the first president to serve under the new rule of a three-year term. He

had long been active in the affairs of the Society, particularly as chairman of the Parallax Committee; and it was he who initiated the custom of two meetings per year. William Wallace Campbell was elected president of the Society just as he was taking over the duties of the presidency of the University of California. Despite the demands on his time, he did not hesitate to travel across the continent to preside at our meetings; and we remember how once, to be on time, he had to taxi fifty miles across New England, where trains run east and west on Sunday but not north or south. Campbell also headed the American delegation to the organization meeting of the International Astronomical Union in 1919 and was president of the Union at the Cambridge, England, meeting of 1925. George C. Comstock served as the first secretary of the Society for ten years and was chairman of the Committee on Comets at the time the Society sent an expedition to Hawaii for observations of Halley's comet. Comstock had legal training, and it was during his regime that the Society was incorporated. Ernest W. Brown introduced the reformed procedure for the election of officers, as we have mentioned before, and his interest in the Society was indicated by his bequest of two funds; one for the promotion of the Society's own journal when it should have one, and a fund for the Hollerith Computing Bureau. Brown's benevolent action led to some wag of a member saying that it should be a rule that every retiring president must leave a substantial bequest to the Society.

Although George E. Hale never held the office of president, it is no secret that the office was offered to him by a committee, but he had to decline on account of ill health. In addition to the observatories which Hale established, we name some of the scientific societies he was instrumental either in founding or reforming. Besides our own Society, they are the National Academy of Sciences; the National Research Council; the International Union for Cooperation in Solar Research, afterwards reorganized as the International Astronomical Union; and the International Research Council, since changed to the International Council of Scientific Unions. Lest Hale's other activities be overlooked, we must add his influence in the Huntington Library, the California Institute of Technology, and the planning of the city of Pasadena. As someone remarked, those of us who had the privilege of coming under Hale's influence will be telling our children and grandchildren that we knew such a man.

Many other members have, of course, rendered great service to the Society, but we must mention the donors of the different endowments. For a long time it looked as though the amateurs would get all the money around the country, but this situation is gradually being rectified. Besides the Life Membership Fund, to which we have contributed ourselves, there are the Annie J. Cannon Fund, the two Ernest W. Brown funds, the Isaac Roberts Fund, the Jessie Stevenson Kovalenko Fund, and finally the Henry Norris Russell Lectureship Fund. In round figures the Life Membership Fund amounts to $5,000 while the others add up to $27,000, making a total of $32,000, which even at present day interest rates gives a substantial amount for the activities of the Society. There is no reason why we should not keep on and bring up our endowment to something like what outsiders expect of astronomers. One slight move in this direction would be to persuade more individuals to take out life memberships. The first life members got in at a bargain—only twenty-five dollars. When the rate for this privilege was placed on an actuarial basis, we understand that at least two of the former life members were so conscience-stricken that they made up the difference between what they had paid and what the current life membership would cost. The same opportunity is always open to the rest of us who feel likewise.

The Society is incorporated under the laws of the state of Illinois, with the Dearborn Observatory designated as the legal home of the Society. Several years ago when the Collector of Internal Revenue was trying to locate the Society to see about a tax on one of the bequests, the Dearborn Observatory was actually being moved two hundred yards or so on the campus at Evanston. I believe we managed to evade the collector. The Yerkes Observatory has been designated as the depository for the archives of the Society; and before this day is over, some of us should prowl around in the attic and see what the archives look like. In 1915 the Society received an official bronze medal or plaque commemorating the meeting at the San Francisco Exposition. Since that time, the medal has served as a paper weight in an office at Madison, Wisconsin; and to ease a guilty conscience, I am now turning over this plaque to the secretary with the recommendation that the Washburn Observatory be made the official keeper of all such trophies of the Society.

From the beginning, some of the main contributions of the Society to our science were through various committees. About 1920, the rule was adopted that ordinarily all committees are discharged at each annual meeting; but in the early days, a number of standing committees continued over many years. Among these may be mentioned the committees on asteroids, comets, eclipses, meteors, photographic astrometry, radial velocities, stellar parallaxes, and variable stars. The reports of these committees will be found in the *Publications*. Still continuing we have, of course, the Finance Committee and the increasingly active Teachers' Committee. One or two of the many committees appointed for special purposes bring up recollections of interesting episodes. The Committee on Variable-Star Nomenclature reported that because each of the three members was in favor of a different system of naming variable stars, little progress could be made in the work of the committee, and they asked to be discharged. There was a Committee on

Daylight Saving. President Pickering considered daylight saving merely a device to make children think they were staying up later before going to bed. I have forgotten about this committee's report, but owing to the fact that daylight saving is illegal in Wisconsin we gained one hour for this meeting today. The Committee on the Beginning of the Astronomical Day recommended the change to the beginning of the day at midnight, and this recommendation was endorsed by the Society with one dissenting vote, which vote happened to be cast by your present speaker. I am still unreconciled but I can take refuge in the Julian Day which begins then, now, and forever at Greenwich Mean Noon.

The *Publications* of the Society have had an interesting history. At first the reports of the meetings were scattered in different journals like *Science* and Popular Astronomy, but after ten years these reports were all gathered together into Volume 1 by the secretary, William J. Hussey. From then on the reports of meetings, abstracts of papers, and the valuable reports of observatories were reprinted, largely from Popular Astronomy, and distributed to the members and libraries. So far as I know, ours was the only organization which got out a publication at its own expense and distributed it free everywhere. After the first World War, the cost of printing increased so much that this liberal policy had to be changed; and whereas similar societies nearly became bankrupt on account of their journals, we managed to come through unscathed simply because the *Astronomical Journal* and the *Astrophysical Journal* had support from other sources. As you know, the *Publications* in their first form came to an end with Volume 10 in 1943; and since then the abstracts and reports of observatories have been published in the *Astronomical Journal*. The Society was able to take over the publication of the *Astronomical Journal* only because Dirk Brouwer was willing to serve as editor, with Louise Jenkins as assistant editor. Three associate editors are appointed by the Society, and another by the directors of the Gould Fund who have continued a substantial subsidy in support of that journal. The Society now has also a closer connection with the *Astrophysical Journal*, since the nine collaborating editors are designated by the Society. But the important connections with these journals are the reduced rates of subscription to members. Up till now there has been no compulsion about such subscriptions, but perhaps we can look forward to the time when our Society will be on the same basis as others: membership in the Society to mean subscription to a journal.

The Society has had the usual relations with similar societies, such as joint meetings, joint committees, and so on. Astronomy is now represented in the National Research Council by two members who are chosen at our annual elections. The American Section of the International Astronomical Union is officially organized under the Division of Physical Sciences of the National Research Council. The executive committee of this Section, which serves between meetings of the Union, is composed of the president and secretary of the Society, the two members of the Division, and the American vice-president of the Union. Thus, the international relations are effectively in the hands of our national Society.

Ultimately someone will undertake to write the history of the Society during the next fifty years. By noting the tendencies in the past, we can extrapolate some predictions. The membership has certainly become younger. In the photograph of that first meeting at Yerkes, if we look at the faces of the men and the dresses of the ladies, we can see how we have changed. Probably we are now as young as we can get. The steady increase in numbers is a cause for mixed feelings. Surely when we get very much larger our best days will be behind us. The mere problem of finding a place to meet will be a serious one. We already have a number of local groups like the Midwestern Group, the Ohio-Michigan-Indiana Group, the New England Neighbors, and the larger Astronomical Society of the Pacific, not to mention the many strictly amateur societies who all have our best wishes. Our national meetings are large enough; and, to my mind, it would be bad to divide the scientific sessions into separate sections. Members of other organizations have often noted that the atmosphere around the astronomical meetings is like that of a club while that of larger societies is much like a market. We should hate to lose the intimate contacts which we get in the small Society. The friendships which one makes with his professional colleagues are the lasting ones; and let us continue as President Simon Newcomb said in his letter declining further election: "Through the Society we share the advantages enjoyed by the promoters of other branches of pure and applied science, which flow from mutual help, counsel, criticism, and friendly interest."

The present is a rather late date to discuss what our profession would be in this country without the Astronomical Society; astronomers must have been a group of lonely individuals in the eighties and nineties when they had little opportunity to get together. Those doing research were pretty far apart with few personal contacts. One thing which the Society has done has been to eliminate various controversies which otherwise might have appeared in print. I remember a case of two individuals who were at sword's points before they came to a meeting; but it was arranged for them to sit next to each other at the dinner; and at the end it was gratifying to see them shaking hands and saying how glad they were to have had the opportunity to talk things over.

I must apologize for the levity of some of my remarks. They certainly would have been out of place fifty years ago; but, as I told you, we have grown younger. What we have lost in dignity we may have gained a little in the way of a good time. For addresses appropriate to an occasion like this we can refer to those at the dedication: by

James E. Keeler on "The Importance of Astrophysical Research and the Relation of Astrophysics to other Physical Sciences," by George E. Hale on "The Aim of the Yerkes Observatory," and by Simon Newcomb on "Some Aspects of American Astronomy." These addresses were published in the *Astrophysical Journal* for November, 1897; they make as good reading now as when they were delivered, and they could well be required reading for astronomers fifty years hence.

The American Astronomical Society and the Yerkes Observatory are of the same age and parentage. Unlike many twins on their fiftieth anniversary, we can be proud of our lives as we have lived them thus far, and we can promise still better careers in the half century to come. In all human probability we shall be able to celebrate, again together, our first centennial with even better prospects for the future.

Joel Stebbins and his photoelectric circle at a meeting of the AAS circa 1940. (L to r) J. S. Hall, G. E. Kron, J. Stebbins, A. E. Whitford, and C. S. Beals. Photograph by John Hall (with an automatic timer) and provided by him.

PART 2

BEYOND THE BORDERS

HONORARY AMERICAN ASTRONOMERS: CANADA AND THE AMERICAN ASTRONOMICAL SOCIETY

Richard A. Jarrell

INTRODUCTION

While the American Astronomical Society has enrolled foreign members for most of its history, it remains a fundamentally American scientific organization. The majority of its members live and work in the United States, its meetings are typically held in U.S. cities, and its institutional and political interests are, naturally, focused upon national concerns. Among its foreign members, however, Canadians became increasingly visible and active over time. Their presence in the Society reflects an ambivalent kind of relationship. Canadians are not quite "foreign," but they are not truly American. They have always formed a distinct scientific community, with its own perspectives, goals, and, until relatively recently, a narrower range of disciplinary interests.[1] Yet, the U.S.-Canada border has been porous. Although the flow has been typically north-to-south, a certain reciprocity in positions and education has long existed. Numerous Canadians have been prominent in the AAS over the past century, being, in many ways, "honorary American astronomers." This chapter will examine various facets of this relationship and its change over the past eighty years.

EARLY CANADIAN PARTICIPATION

When the Astronomical and Astrophysical Society of America (*I will refer to it throughout as the AAS*) met officially the first time in 1899, electing as its president Canadian-born Simon Newcomb, it had no Canadian members. Two Canadians, radio physicist R. A. Fessenden and McGill University meteorologist and astronomer C. H. McLeod, attended the preliminary Harvard meeting of 1898, though neither signed the list of prospective members.[2] McLeod joined soon thereafter, remaining a member at least until 1911,[3] but he does not seem to have attended any meetings. At that time, in the Dominion of Canada, probably no more than six men earned their living as professional astronomers. Canada was a very small country, with a population of 5 million people, with a tiny scientific community. As the few professionals were primarily involved in surveying, geodesy or meteorology, almost none paid attention to the new American organization.

John Stanley Plaskett and Clarence Augustus Chant, the co-founders of modern Canadian astronomy, were the key figures to open communication. Plaskett, hired by the new Dominion Observatory as its mechanical superintendent, soon envisioned a

Figure 1. Detail from a group photograph taken during a Dominion Observatory eclipse expedition to North West River, Labrador, 1905. J. S. Plaskett is sitting front row center with C. A. Chant sitting to his right. W. F. King is standing behind them. From [1]. National Archives of Canada.

program of stellar and solar spectroscopy.[4] To that end, he toured American observatories in 1906 and forged lasting friendships with important American figures, such as E. C. Pickering, W. W. Campbell, George Ellery Hale, and Frank Schlesinger. With the acquiescence of his chief, William F. King, Plaskett organized a small team of young graduates. At the same time, Chant, a physics lecturer at Toronto, desired to create a degree program in astrophysics. He contacted Campbell in 1906 to arrange a summer's study at Lick Observatory to learn spectroscopic techniques. With their newly-cultivated connections, it was natural both Plaskett and Chant would soon travel to AAS meetings.

Chant was the first to appear, at Columbia, in December 1906. His account of the meeting appeared in the pages of Volume 1 of the *Journal of the Royal Astronomical Society of Canada* (RASC),[5] a new publication which he edited. This inaugurated a 50-year tradition of reporting on the meetings in the journal's pages. Plaskett made his first foray to the Put-in-Bay meeting in August 1907, reading three of the 33 papers presented. His research was sufficiently prized to garner him membership on the Society's new Committee on Co-operation in the Measurement of Stellar Radial Velocities, struck at the 1910 Harvard meeting. This associated him with men of the first rank. Before setting out with other astronomers on the cross-country rail trek to Pasadena for Hale's Solar Union meeting, Plaskett, with King's blessing, invited the Society to hold its next meeting in Ottawa the following summer. Council agreed, and in August 1911, Americans travelled north for their first extra-territorial meeting.

THE 1911 DOMINION OBSERVATORY MEETING

By meeting outside the United States, the Society was following a convention pioneered by two larger organizations, the American Association for the Advancement of Science, which had met in Montreal as early as 1857, and the British Association, which visited Montreal (twice), Toronto, and Winnipeg. Extra-territorial meetings had several functions. One was to showcase national science in another setting; another was to attract new membership in the host country.[6] No doubt a third was to provide a pleasant junket for scientists and their families. But the host benefitted equally, thanks to the publicity of these events, which provided ammunition for lobbying efforts for more funding. In this instance, the Society had received invitations from St. Louis, Colorado Springs, and Chicago, but Ottawa was reasonably close and had a new national observatory to inspect.

By early August, Ralph Curtiss, acting as secretary in Hussey's absence, noted to Joel Stebbins that, "Papers are coming in very slowly though the rush may come later. However all will agree that papers are only incidental. The Ottawa people are planning to treat us royally."[7] The meeting took place August 23–25, with the sessions at the observatory.[8] It was not a large gathering by recent standards, with only 33 members in attendance and 30 papers read, including four by observatory staff. Pickering presided, and several prominent Americans, including Stebbins, Annie J. Cannon, H. N. Russell, E. S. King, Henrietta Leavitt, E. E. Barnard, E. B. Frost, Solon Bailey, and Sebastian Albrecht, read papers. Five new Canadian members joined the ranks, while Plaskett became a councilor and Chant joined the new Committee on Cooperation in the Teaching of Astronomy, chaired by C. L. Doolittle. Chant also later joined the Committee on Associate Membership in 1916.

Pleasant weather and the beautiful observatory grounds, within the Central Experimental Farm, added to the meeting's enjoyment. The Council Minutes refer to the "sumptuous luncheon" at the Observatory.[9] An excursion by rail into the Gatineau River Valley, with luncheon on a bluff overlooking the river and a paper session al fresco in a pine grove added, one supposes, a peculiarly Canadian flavor to the proceedings. The final day ended with a three-hour drive (by car or by carriage is not stated) to see the sights of this "foreign" capital city.

The meeting also played a pivotal role in Plaskett's campaign to obtain a large reflecting telescope for the observatory. Having exhausted the research potential of the observatory's modest 15-inch refractor, Plaskett's desire for something larger was whetted by his attendance at Hale's 1910 Pasadena meeting. Seeing G. W. Ritchey's 60-inch telescope on Mount Wilson sparked his desire to possess a similar instrument. Enlisting King, he began soliciting influential American astronomers for letters of support to show his deputy minister. During the Ottawa meeting, Plaskett engineered the passing of a resolution — which he drafted — praising the observatory for its astrophysical work and supporting its desire for a larger instrument.

Although the campaign faltered when the Liberal government went down to defeat in November 1911, a renewed campaign, employing the Ottawa resolution and new letters from friends, succeeded in the spring of 1913. It must have been gratifying for Plaskett to deliver an evening talk on the new instrument at the 1914 Evanston meeting. Four years later, Plaskett directed operations of the world's largest telescope at the Dominion Astrophysical Observatory (DAO) in Victoria, British Columbia. The Ottawa resolution of the Society was a crucial element in his campaign. It would be no exaggeration to claim that had Plaskett not been successful, Canadians would have taken much longer to become important players in the new field. The importance of American support at this critical juncture cannot be minimized: Canada was a very small country, in terms of people, financial resources, and scientific abilities. But Plaskett's vision, and it was largely his alone, carried the day. He desired to be part of a larger international effort, but that effort itself was centered upon American astronomy. In another way, the Society's Ottawa meeting was critically important for Canada as it gave exposure to Canadian work and attracted its astronomers to the AAS. Only six Canadians were members before the meeting, a dozen afterwards.[10]

THE INTERWAR YEARS

During the war years, three or four Canadian members went south annually for Society meetings. At war's end, participation increased. At the 1918 Harvard meeting, nine members of the Dominion Observatory staff attended, contributing 13 papers among them and seeing Otto J. Klotz elected to Council.[11] This level of participation remained into the early 1920s.

An important factor in strengthening relations between the two astronomical communities was American graduate education. Until the early 1950s, no Canadian university offered a Ph.D. in astronomy. This meant that Canadian graduates—almost entirely Chant's students from Toronto — proceeded south for post-graduate instruction at California, Harvard, Chicago, Michigan, and Princeton. The first two were most important because Chant's own Ph.D. was from Harvard, and his primary professional link was with Lick Observatory. These connections ensured that young Canadian astronomers became intimately involved in the American professional community.

The Society returned to Canada twice more before World War II. The 42nd meeting took place at the Dominion Observatory in August 1929.[12] Tea on the observatory lawn, luncheons at the Geodetic Survey, bridge games at the Director's house, drives, and a final dinner at the Chateau Laurier Hotel leavened the paper sessions. Like the 1911 meeting, this one attracted fewer Americans north, but a home-based

Figure 2. The first meeting of the Astronomical and Astrophysical Society outside the continental United States took place in Ottawa on 23–25 August 1911. Prominent in the center is Pickering. W. F. King and Otto Klotz (long white beard) are standing to Pickering's right. J. S. Plaskett (black mustache) is on the right side of the portico. To the far right standing on the grass is C. A. Chant eclipsing Joel Stebbins. Frank Schlesinger (holding hat) is sitting in the front row to Annie Cannon's left. Henry Norris Russell is in the doorway, wearing a light suit. W. E. Harper, Plaskett's associate, is standing next to the left column. Photograph courtesy Yerkes Observatory.

meeting brought out considerably more Canadian astronomers than usual: of 45 papers presented, 22 were by Canadians. Virtually all the Ottawa and Victoria staffs contributed. Four new Canadian members joined the fold.[13]

The next foray came only six years later, when the University of Toronto wished to commemorate the opening of the David Dunlap Observatory — with the world's second-largest reflector — with a Society meeting at the university in September 1935. Chant, who was just retiring, invited RASC members to hear the sessions, swelling the numbers. It was not a large meeting, with some 30 papers, but the attraction was the new telescope.

> President Russell opened the meeting, and after a brief but hearty welcome by Dr. Chant, the sober business of hearing papers was begun. At about four o'clock it was unanimously decided that we had had enough of sobriety for the time being and the meeting was adjourned. For the rest of the afternoon the astronomers made themselves at home in and about the observatory buildings and inspected and praised and criticized our equipment as only astronomers can. In the midst of it all, a very informal supper was served by the ladies of the observatory staff; and when darkness came the visiting astronomers had a busman's holiday doing some stargazing with the "74-inch."[14]

These three meetings were the first of nine held north of the border (see Table 1). Most were summer meetings. The Department of Mines invited the Society to Ottawa for its summer 1938 meeting but was declined due to the impending IAU General Assembly.[15] Ottawa was again host to the summer 1949 meeting, with the National Research Council of Canada (NRC) jointly hosting events with the observatory.[16] With air travel more common, and good highways connecting with the eastern U.S., the attendance was about the normal level of an American-based meeting. Canadian participation was substantial, with 16 of 54 papers read.[17] The meeting provided a chance to describe new lines of Canadian research: Peter Millman organized a symposium on meteoritics, and the NRC organized a post-meeting excursion to its radio astronomy facilities. The Ottawa meeting saw the largest gathering of radio astronomers at the AAS to date. The summer 1959 meeting at the University of Toronto was the largest in AAS history to that time, with one-fifth of the 70 papers by Canadians.[18] The June 1952 Victoria meeting, held jointly with the Astronomical Society of the Pacific, was the first in western Canada, with west-coast astronomers predominating.[19] Curiously, it was the last meeting reported in depth by the RASC Journal.

TABLE 1. *Canadian Meetings of the AAS.*

Meeting	Date	City	Institution
12th	23–25 Aug 1911	Ottawa	DO
42nd	27–29 Aug 1929	Ottawa	DO
54th	10–12 Sept 1935	Toronto	U. Toronto
81st	19–23 June 1949	Ottawa	DO
87th	25–28 June 1952	Victoria	DAO
103rd	30 Aug–2 Sept 1959	Toronto	U. Toronto
117th	28–31 Dec 1964	Montreal	U. de Montreal
124th	21–23 Aug 1968	Victoria	U. Victoria
189th	1–16 Jan 1997	Toronto	U. Toronto/York U.

Figure 3. Helen Hogg at the 74-inch reflector at David Dunlap, using a novel way to lower photographic plates to the night assistant, circa 1940s. From [1]. University of Toronto Archives.

CANADIANS IN OFFICE AND AT THE MEETINGS

When Canadian astronomers began joining the Society in larger numbers, they took an active part in the operation of the organization. Plaskett and Chant were naturally the first, both serving as Vice-Presidents. W. F. King took little interest, but his administrative duties were onerous and his health deteriorated towards the end of his regime. His eventual successor, Klotz, became active until his death in 1923. Canadian office-holders tended to come from either the University of Toronto or the DAO, the two primary research centers after 1920. Table 2 lists Canadian office-holders.[20]

In addition to the senior offices, Canadians also contributed to a number of committees over the years. Chant and Helen Hogg were members of various incarnations of the Education Committee; the Nominating Committee had, at one time or another, Frank and Helen Hogg, J. A. Pearce, Peter Millman, Andrew McKellar, and Donald MacRae. Others sat on the Russell Lecture and Helen Warner Prize Committees. More important, Pearce, C. S. Beals, McKellar, Gerhard Herzberg and Anne Underhill were Society designates to *The Astrophysical Journal* editorial board. However, Canadians were conspicuously absent from the list of awards: Helen Hogg won the Annie J. Cannon Prize in 1949 after several years of being nominated. Pierre Demarque won the Warner Prize in 1967.

TABLE 2. *Canadian Officers of the AAS.*

C. S. Beals	Vice-President 1950–52; President 1962–64
C. A. Chant	Vice President 1934–36
R. H. Hardie	Councilor 1964–67
J. F. Heard	Councilor 1957–60
G. Herzberg	Councilor 1958–61
H. S. Hogg	Councilor 1965–68
O. J. Klotz	Councilor 1918–20; 2nd VP 1920; 1st VP 1921
A. McKellar	Councilor 1949–52
D. A. MacRae	Councilor 1963–66
P. M. Millman	Councilor 1947–50
R. M. Petrie	Councilor 1945–48; Vice-President 1954–56
H. H. Plaskett	Councilor 1931–34
J. S. Plaskett	Councilor 1911–13, 1914–16, 1916–18; VP 1927–29
K. O. Wright	Councilor 1952–56

In reviewing the records of AAS meetings between 1908 and 1970 — records of a dozen meetings are missing — we find 153 Canadians participating by reading papers. This counts Canadians working at home, expatriates and foreigners after they came to Canada. Together they read a total of 724 papers at meetings over six decades. Nearly half the total was contributed by just 15 Canadian astronomers who read at least 15 papers apiece, with a total of 342 papers (see Table 3). Most striking is the participation by the DAO staff (R. M. Petrie, Harper, Pearce, Beals, Underhill, K. O. Wright, and McKellar), following Plaskett's lead. They account for over 60% of the highly-visible Canadians at American meetings.

The number of papers read remained remarkably stable through much of this period. Despite year-to-year fluctuations, Canadians read on average about seven papers a year from 1911 to 1950.[21] During this time, the astronomical community did not grow significantly. When growth came, it was reflected at the AAS: 12 papers/year for 1951–1960 and 15 papers/year for 1961—1970. This was a sizeable contribution, as meetings through most of the 1950s and 1960s rarely attracted more than 100 members. The second-last foray into Canada, the August 1968 meeting at the University of Victoria, attracted a large local contingent, with 22 of 166 papers read.[22] By the 1970s, however, meeting sizes jumped, and Canadian participation began to recede, both in percentage and absolute numbers. A check of selected winter meetings shows this clearly: in 1975, of 259 abstracts, only eight papers were Canadian;[23] in January 1981, 16 of 421 papers were Canadian;[24] by January 1997, on home turf, 84 papers had Canadian authors or co-authors among some 859 contributions.[25] Given between 200

TABLE 3. *Canadians Reading 15+ Papers at AAS Meetings.*

R. M. Petrie	40	Anne Underhill	21
W. E. Harper	31	K. O. Wright	19
J. A. Pearce	30	Helen S. Hogg	18
J. S. Plaskett	27	A. G. W. Cameron	17
C. S. Beals	23	Francois Henroteau	17
Sydney v. d. Bergh	23	Andrew McKellar	16
Ralph De Lury	23	Robert Hardie	15
Peter Millman	22		

and 300 professionals in Canada during the past two decades, this was not strong representation. The reasons for this decline may have to do with organizational changes in Canada.

SOCIETAL SCHIZOPHRENIA: THE ROYAL ASTRONOMICAL SOCIETY OF CANADA AND THE PROFESSIONALS

It is a curious fact that Canada, with its much smaller population and professional astronomical community, could boast a national society with a longer history than the AAS. The Royal Astronomical Society of Canada (RASC) had its roots in a Toronto-based amateur group founded in 1867.[26] After several name changes and shifting — and always limited — membership, it incorporated in 1890 as the Toronto Astronomical and Physical Society. Despite its name, it enrolled members from other parts of the country and elected honorary fellows from among important American astronomers, including Hale, Campbell, Frost, and Pickering. The society was accorded the title "Royal" in 1907. From the outset, the RASC differed from sister societies in other countries. It embraced both amateurs and professionals like the Royal Astronomical Society in the United Kingdom, but membership was open and not restricted by an election process. It was not as exclusively professional as the AAS. Its organization was not centralized, but regional: when sufficient numbers enrolled in a city, a group petitioned the national council for recognition as a "Centre." After Toronto, the first urban Center admitted was Ottawa, which was naturally dominated by the professionals of the Dominion Observatory, where the group met.

For seven decades, the RASC served the dual functions of professional and amateur society. Its Journal served both constituencies, although the professionals always had the upper hand. Chant edited the Journal from 1907 until 1956, and all his successors have been professionals. However given the split personality of the journal, and its Canadian orientation, it never commanded the attention of the professional community as *The Astrophysical Journal* did. That the RASC and its Journal could maintain their unique characters owed itself to at least two factors: the professional community was never very large, and a strong desire to maintain a Canadian identity. Almost every distinguished Canadian astronomer participated in RASC affairs at some point, and many published in the pages of the Journal, even if their most important work appeared elsewhere. This was typically a matter of community loyalty, for they certainly understood that their Journal was not a front-rank international astronomical publication in terms of readership or citation.

If the best of Canadian astronomical papers did not appear in the *Journal of the RASC*, where did they appear? A few notable workers, such as Plaskett and Beals, published in the *Monthly Notices* because they were fellows of the Royal Astronomical Society. But the RAS was not an important venue for Canadian astronomers. Until relatively recent times, most Canadian astronomers were government employees, and their work appeared in the *Publications* of the Dominion and the Dominion Astrophysical Observatories. Sporadic papers did appear in foreign sources such as *The Astrophysical Journal*, *The Astronomical Journal*, or the *Publications of the Astronomical Society of the Pacific*. Only when the university community began expanding rapidly in the 1960s, and new fields in government astronomy, such as radio astronomy, appeared, did the menu broaden to include journals such as *Astronomy and Astrophysics*, *Solar Physics*, *Icarus*, *Meteoritics* or the *Proceedings of the IRE*. From the late 1950s, Canadian astronomers' choices for publication outlets began to resemble those of larger communities elsewhere.

THE AAS AS A MODEL FOR CANADIAN ASTRONOMERS?

So long as the Canadian professional community remained small, the RASC was sufficient for their national organizational needs. There were other possibilities.[27] Some became fellows of the Royal Society of Canada, founded in 1882 as an honorific society, including both scientists and humanists. Its annual meetings in Ottawa allowed the few astronomical fellows to read papers and have them published in the Society's annual *Transactions*. As timely publication became important, the Royal Society became increasingly irrelevant. Being an honorific society with a fixed number of fellowships in any discipline, it could not provide a meeting place for the wider community. One organizational alternative after World War II was the Canadian Association of Physicists (CAP), but it appealed to few astronomers.

Canadian astronomers were early supporters of the International Astronomical Union (IAU), likely because of Plaskett's regard for G. E. Hale. For many years, Canada's IAU National Committee dealt strictly with matters relating to international congresses and commissions. Not surprisingly, government scientists dominated its proceedings. In the post-World War II era, however, with increasing numbers of faculty and graduate students in universities, the need for closer interaction grew. By the late 1950s, the Canadian National Committee's (CNC) meetings, by now peripatetic, began to feature a few scientific papers — though rarely more than a half-dozen — and a talk by a visiting astronomer, often an American.

One other important institution was the National Research Council of Canada, founded by the government in 1916. In the interwar years, the NRC struck a number of "Associate Committees" to tackle specific scientific problem areas. These committees brought together NRC personnel with university and industrial scientists to coordinate research. Until the 1950s, the NRC did not involve itself in astronomy and did not strike an associate committee. Given that most Canadian work was under the direction of the Department of Mines and Technical Surveys, the NRC could not impinge upon another federal agency. However, this began to change when the NRC embraced astronomy-oriented work in meteoritics, laboratory astrophysics, and radio astronomy. By 1970, the Trudeau government, responding to earlier studies suggesting the amalgamation of government astronomy, closed the Dominion Observatory and transferred all its astronomical activities to the NRC, which then created an "Astrophysics Branch" within the Radio and Electrical Engineering Division, home of its radio astronomy program.

Now that the NRC was the dominant player in Canadian astronomy, the need to coordinate national astronomical programs — NRC was also the funding agent for facilities, research grants, fellowships, and scholarships in universities — led to the formation of an Associate Committee for Astronomy (ACA) in 1971. This body, meeting twice yearly around the country, included both NRC and university members.

As an efficiency measure, the Associate Committee became identical to the IAU National Committee; its meetings dealt with the affairs of both. The earlier National Committee meetings, with related paper sessions, had been rather informal. Because the new ACA/CNC was an appointed body, the association of a paper session became more problematic. The solution was to form a national professional astronomical society, and in May 1971 an organizational meeting was held. The first regular meeting of the Canadian Astronomical Society/Société Canadienne d'Astronomie (CASCA) followed in November. Apart from the obvious similarity in name to the AAS, CASCA also limited its membership to professionals (i.e., those who published scientific papers) and to graduate students. Its meeting style developed a superficially similar character, with scientific paper and poster sessions, invited speakers, awards, and the typical social events. Like the AAS divisions, CASCA maintains committees devoted to sub-disciplines, along with education and history. Several of these committees in fact pre-date CASCA, having being subcommittees of the ACA/CNC.

The relations between the ACA/CNC and CASCA remained intimate, with an officer of the latter always appointed to the former, although in practice virtually everyone active on the official committee was a CASCA member. Formal representation from CASCA on various matters filtered through the ACA/CNC. Such a structure was very different from the American system, but such were the intimate links between university and government astronomy: the NRC was the official adhering body to the IAU and was also the banker to the university sector. This cozy arrangement came partly unstuck when the government moved the granting function from the NRC to the newly-formed Natural Sciences and Engineering Research Council in 1978. With financial stringency, the NRC began to fold up its associate committees, the ACA meeting its demise among them.

There are other significant differences. In the U.S., some professionals remain active in amateur groups, but the former have had their own organization for 100 years and the AAS dwarfs most popular societies. CASCA has just more than 400 members (compared with more than 6500 in the AAS); the RASC, now with a strongly amateur orientation, remains an order of magnitude larger than CASCA. The latter has no link with a professional journal. The *Journal of the RASC* has attracted few professional articles in recent years, although it continues to publish the abstracts of CASCA papers after its annual meetings. Both the RASC and its journal have recently undergone an identity crisis; it is still not clear what its final direction will be. Its appeal to the professional community is increasingly limited.

CASCA's annual meetings have a flavor quite distinct from the semi-annual conferences of the AAS. My discussions and interviews with individual astronomers leads me to believe that, while the AAS meetings remain important venues for Canadians to announce research results, CASCA meetings, despite their outward appearance, are really devoted more to politics and networking. Although these activities are a feature of AAS meetings, given the small community, the smaller (relative) science budget and the greater proximity of scientists to law-makers and civil servants in Canada, the politics of science are more immediate and palpable. It seems entirely likely that the example of the AAS, and Canadians' experience in it, were stimuli for Canadian professionals to organize a similar association. What Canada lacked, until the early 1970s, were sufficient numbers to create a smaller, local version of the AAS. The reorganization of Canadian government astronomy was the catalyst.

CANADA AND THE AAS TODAY

Although the Society is "American," and that term seems to be interpreted broadly to include the three largest North American nations, it has a substantial international membership. In 1997, among the 6500 members, astronomers from just over 50 nations subscribed.[28] The Canadian contingent is the largest single group from outside the U.S., with 206 members. This represents most of the professional astronomers, active or retired, and a substantial number of graduate students. At the same time, CASCA enrolled 407 members,[29] of whom 255 were also AAS members (not all Canadian citizens or residents), representing a 63% overlap.

Yet Canadians account for only 3% of the Society's membership, which overwhelmingly is based in the U.S.. This is scarcely an identifiable minority. Although Canadians have distinguished themselves as AAS officers over the years, none are involved at present. Once CASCA was in place, the AAS could have become irrelevant, but it has remained important to most Canadian astronomers' organizational culture. The advantage to continued participation by Canadians in the AAS is its neutrality: one can go simply to discuss science and to meet colleagues. The political baggage, forever evident at CASCA meetings, can be forgotten momentarily. From the viewpoint of a graduate student, an AAS meeting offers contacts for a wider range of employment opportunities than at home.

The programs of recent Society meetings indicate that Canadian astronomers continue to participate by giving papers and posters (more in the winter meetings than in the summer meetings) but not at the percentage levels of the 1960s. Still, there is an immense advantage, both to hear and to be heard, at the largest regular professional astronomical meetings in the world outside of IAU assemblies. The added attraction is proximity: given that the two greatest concentrations of Canadian astronomers lie nearly a continent apart, it can be cheaper and quicker to attend an American meeting than one at the opposite end of Canada.

CONCLUSIONS

It was to the credit of the Society's founders to welcome Canadians early and to include them as equals. For their part, Canadians seem to have treated this connection as a family affair. Yet they knew they were not part of the American community. As K. O. Wright commented after the 1948 Pasadena meeting, "In astronomy, international co-operation has always been of the highest order and, in particular, Canadians have always been warmly welcomed at gatherings of American astronomers."[30] For Canadians, AAS meetings were not as international in flavor as IAU assemblies, for the former united the two communities with bonds of language and intertwined education. They used the same equipment, published in the same journals, and cooperated in research programs. Although Canada was part of the British Empire and then Commonwealth throughout the history of the AAS, Canadian astronomers very early forged their strongest scientific links with their colleagues south of the border, and the American Astronomical Society has remained an essential element in this relationship.

ACKNOWLEDGMENT

This study was supported, in part, through a grant-in-aid from the Friends of the Center for History of Physics, American Institute of Physics, which is gratefully acknowledged.

Figure 4. At the 81st meeting of the Society in Ottawa, host Peter Millman (l) shakes hands with Gerald Kron (r) of Lick Observatory. Katherine Kron is at the far right, Delia and George Herbig stand at the far left. Newton Studio photograph, courtesy the Mary Lea Shane Archives of the Lick Observatory, University of California-Santa Cruz.

A Century of Astronomy in México: Collaboration with American Astronomers

Silvia Torres-Peimbert

INTRODUCTION

The astronomical situation in México during the last century is briefly described. The conditions during this period have been far from stable as a consequence of the economic and social changes in the country. The origins and modifications of the two main astronomical institutions in México: the Instituto de Astronomía of the Universidad Nacional Autónoma de México and the Instituto Nacional de Astrofísica, Optica y Electrónica are presented. Special attention is given to the influence of American astronomers.

ASTRONOMY IN MÉXICO PRIOR TO 1940

In 1874 Francisco Díaz Covarrubias headed the Mexican expedition to observe the transit of Venus across the solar disk from Yokohama in Japan, that occurred on December 8, 1874, to obtain a better estimate of the solar parallax. This expedition was commissioned by President Sebastian Lerdo de Tejada, and it represented the greatest scientific effort for the country. The expedition was successful and the results were published earlier than the other American and European expeditions.[1] To assess this effort it should be recalled that México had recently undergone internal war and two foreign invasions. Figure 1 depicts one of the Mexican camps in Bluff Hill near Yokohama.

The Observatorio Astronómico Nacional, OAN, was inaugurated in Chapultepec Castle in 1878. Its first activities were the observation of the transit of Mercury across the solar disk on May 6, 1878, the determination of the geographic location of the observatory, and meteorological observations. The activities of the observatory were firmly established by 1881; it was possible to start the publication of the *Anuario* (yearly astronomical almanac). This publication has continued to the present day. In 1883 the observatory was moved to a temporary location in Tacubaya (8 km SW of México City) and later to its permanent site, also in Tacubaya. Construction started in 1884 and finished in 1908.

The activities from 1885 to 1890 were varied. Some meridian observations of reference stars, asteroids, comets, solar activity, and the solar eclipse expedition to Aguascalientes were carried out. The first photographic images of the moon were taken.

Figure 1. A drawing of the Mexican camp in Nogue-no-yama near Yokohama in Japan to observe the transit of Venus on December 8, 1874 (drawing from Díaz Covarrubias 1876).

In 1887, the International Meeting of the Carte du Ciel (Astrographic Catalogue) was convened in Paris. Mexican participation was invited. The OAN was assigned a zone of the sky from −9 to −17 declination. The project included the publication of charts and the determination of magnitudes and positions of stars brighter than 11th magnitude; it required 1260 photographic plates to determine the coordinates for 5000 reference stars. Grubb-Parsons, Ltd., in Dublin, were commissioned to build a 33-cm photographic refractor for this purpose.

From this time on, and for many years to come, great effort was devoted by the observatory to the completion of its section of the Astrographic Catalogue. Initially, the project was carried out relatively smoothly until the Civil War curtailed economic support for all observatory endeavors. The publication *Boletin del Observatorio Astronómico Nacional* was started in 1891, in which all the astronomical activities of the observatory were reported. Some translations into Spanish of current topics of astronomical interest were also included. Financial support was not constant, however, so its publication was irregular during several periods.[2]

As part of a major overhaul of the Universidad Nacional Autonoma de México (UNAM), in 1929 the Observatorio Astronómico Nacional was transformed from a government institution to a department of UNAM.

By 1940, the activity of the OAN was quite limited; most of its efforts were on the Astrographic Catalogue project. It also conducted other projects in positional astronomy, such as double star measurements and minor planet orbit determinations. Spectroscopic observations were also conducted but never published. J. Gallo provided his objective-prism plates for W. W. Morgan's *Atlas*.[3]

THE PERIOD FROM 1940 TO 1960

The Beginning of the Observatorio Astrofísico de Tonantzintla

Mr. Luis Enrique Erro, a very enthusiastic amateur astronomer, was First Secretary of the Mexican Embassy in Washington for several years; from there he established contact with the AAVSO, and through it he also became acquainted with the Harvard College Observatory. Erro persuaded President Manuel Avila Camacho to provide funds for establishing a modern astrophysical observatory in México.

The construction of the Observatorio Astrofísico de Tonantzintla, OAT, in Puebla was started in 1941 in very close cooperation with Harvard College Observatory astronomers, in particular with the Director, Harlow Shapley, and the Chief of the Milky Way Bureau, Bart Bok. The plans for this southern observatory drew the interest of various astronomers, who reported on it, as well as on the dedication of the observatory itself.[4] The first major telescope planned was a 24–31 inch Schmidt camera very similar to Harvard's new Jewett telescope.

> The optical parts were made by the Perkin-Elmer Company, of Glenbrook, Connecticut, with their chief optician Halley Mogey supervising and doing the work on Sundays and at night, owing to the pressure of defense work already undertaken by the firm ... . It was not possible, however, to find a firm willing to undertake the construction of the telescope mounting and tube, and this obstacle was overcome only by Dr. Shapley's offer to have the work done in the shops of the Harvard College Observatory, under the supervision of Dr. G. Z. Dimitroff...[5]

The mechanical work was supervised by E. A. Guertin and Walter A. Locke. "In spite of the war difficulties, six months saw the entire construction of the telescope."[6] The images cover a field of 5° on a side on 8-inch square plates. Later it was found that the telescope could be effectively used over the complete size of the components; hence, it was mounted as a 27–31 inch instrument.

Since the latitude of Tonantzintla is +19°, some of the rich southern sky, inaccessible to observation by instruments farther north, became accessible for study. The telescopes were planned mainly for starcounts, colors, magnitudes, and spectra in the southern hemisphere. The program for the new observatory was outlined by Erro and Escalante following recommendations by Shapley and Bok. The program of research included the study of southern variables (Erro's original interest) and Milky Way studies, the main interest of the HCO. The Milky Way program included the regions of Puppis and Vela and the regions around the south galactic plane to complete Harvard's program. An extension of the Mt. Wilson Catalog of Selected Areas to include the areas at declinations −30° was also planned. To facilitate these plans, Tonantzintla and Harvard would continuously exchange staff.

The formal dedication of the OAT took place on February 17, 1942. For this occasion, 27 distinguished astronomers, physicists, and geologists from the U.S. and Canada traveled to México. Since this was a time when the U.S. and Canada were deeply involved in the war, the effort made by American and Canadian scientists to attend the dedication made clear that the project included not only the scientific results but an interest in maintaining close ties with México, at a time when definitions were very important.

Figure 2. Luis Enrique Erro, on the left and Joaquín Gallo, on the right, during the inauguration of the Observatorio Astrofísico de Tonantzintla. Gallo (1882–1965) was the director of the Observatorio de Tacubaya and Erro (1897–1955) was the director of the new observatory in Tonantzintla (picture from the IA-UNAM photograph collection).

Following the dedication of the new observatory, an Inter-American Scientific Congress was held at the Universidad Autónoma de Puebla, in Puebla, at the UNAM in México City, and at the new observatory itself. The delegation of scientists were honored by being personally invited by the President of México and were guests of the Mexican government. In the letters of invitation it was written, "The purpose of the Mexican government is to contribute to the maintenance, in the American continent, of the progress of science and culture, and thus counteract as much as possible the paralyzation of scientific and cultural activities in the countries devastated by war."[7] Three of the visiting scientists and a Mexican scientist, Walter S. Adams, Henry N. Russell, Harlow Shapley, and Manuel Sandoval Vallarta, received honorary degrees from the University de Michoacan.

The theme of the Congress was the structure and constitution of the galaxy and its relationship to other galactic systems. Descriptions of the meeting were given by Payne-Gaposhkin and Russell.[8] The topics ranged widely and covered most of the major questions in stellar astronomy and galactic structure. As a result, Menzel declared that, "There is no question but that the conference is among the most important in the history of science.... . The international situation, however, laid a dramatic setting that deepened the significance of the congress."[9]

FROM 1948 TO 1970

The Tonantzintla Schmidt telescope was a relatively large and modern instrument, and after its mirror was completed and corrected, it became a very powerful data gathering system. Gradually the astronomers of the Observatorio Astrofísico de Tonantzintla (OAT) developed their own projects, not all of them following the original ideas from Harvard. They included detection of flare stars, detection of emission line objects in the plane of the galaxy, open cluster research, etc. In 1950, Erro retired and Guillermo Haro became director of the OAT.

In 1948, Haro was designated director of the Observatorio Astronómico Nacional, and Paris Pishmish became part of its staff. A program to teach astronomy and astrophysics was started in UNAM. Within a short period, Haro discovered, independently of George Herbig, a new class of variable star now known as Herbig-Haro objects. Haro also discovered flare stars in Orion, and Pishmish described and analyzed the infrared cluster in this same nebula.

Figure 3. Guillermo Haro (1913–1986). He was director of OAN from 1948 to 1968, and of Tonantzintla from 1950 to 1975 (picture from the IA-UNAM photograph collection).

Figure 4. Paris Pishmish (1911–). She was born in Turkey and has lived in México since 1942 (picture from the IA-UNAM photograph collection).

Although in principle there were two independent institutions present in México, in practice for several years starting in 1950, both observatories worked in very close contact, as both institutions had the same director. By 1951, the OAN also moved its instruments, previously in Tacubaya, to Tonantzintla, on a site immediately next to the original OAT site. The publication *Boletín de los Observatorios de Tonantzintla y Tacubaya* started in 1952 and lasted until 1972. A picture of the staff of the observatories in 1945 is shown in Figure 5.

From 1948 on, for many years, most of the astronomical development in México took place on the OAN-UNAM axis. In 1961 an f/15 1-m Cassegrain reflector was installed at Tonantzintla. The mechanical structure was made by Rademakers in Rotterdam and was designed and supervised by Houghout. The mirrors were made in California, under the supervision of Don O. Hendrix, of Hale telescope fame. The economic support was from the Rockefeller Foundation, Fundación Mary Jenkins (in Puebla), and the Mexican government.

Young students from UNAM were attracted into astronomy, and the most promising ones were sent, with scholarships, for graduate training to the U.S., to be hired later as staff. Foreign training was important to continually diversify and modernize astronomical studies in México and this tradition lasted for several decades. There has always been considerable influence from U.S. and European astronomy in México.

FROM 1970 TO THE PRESENT DAY

UNAM

By the mid-1960s, it was clear that Tonantzintla was not an adequate site for a larger telescope; its skies were not of photometric quality, and it had been overcome by the surrounding towns. An astronomical site was established in San Pedro Mártir, Baja California in 1968.[10] For that purpose, it was necessary to establish a scientific office in Ensenada, Baja, California. Both the Observatorio Astronómico Nacional (OAN/SPM) and the offices are now part of the Instituto de Astronomía, IA-UNAM. Among many collective efforts, UNAM founded the *Revista Mexicana de Astronomía y Astrofísica* in 1974. It continues publication and has started a new "Serie de Conferencias" that contains proceedings of astronomical conferences in Latin-America. Graduate training in astronomy within México also started at UNAM in the graduate program in physics, and in 1989 an astronomy graduate program was opened.

By 1979 OAN/SPM managed three large telescopes: a 2.1-m telescope with interchangeable secondaries (f/7.5, f/13, and f/27); an f/13.5 1.5-m telescope (the H. L. Johnson Telescope); and an f/13.5 0.84-m telescope. At present, the 2.1-m telescope has several instruments, including an echelle spectrograph, a near infrared camera, and a Fabry-Perot interferometer. The 1.5-m telescope is used for photometry and direct imaging, and the 0.84-m telescope is used for photometry and spectroscopy. The San Pedro Mártir site has extremely good conditions regarding seeing and dark skies. In

Figure 5. Staff of Tacubaya and Tonantzintla Observatories in 1945. In the bottom row are Paris Pishmish, Manuel Sandoval Vallarta and Joaquin Gallo. Standing are: Fernando Alba, Carlos Graef, Luis Enrique Erro, Felix Recillas, Guillermo Haro, Guido Münch and Luis Zubieta, among others. The picture was taken at Tonantzintla Observatory.

1990 IA-UNAM started a project to build an optical telescope of much larger size in San Pedro Mártir. At present it is in the design phase.

Currently the scientific offices in IA-UNAM are located in three cities: in the main university campus in México City, in Ensenada (3000 km from México City), and in Morelia (300 km from México City). There are 70 astronomers, 30 graduate students, and 50 technicians as support staff working in astronomical projects.

Observatorio Astrofísico de Tonantzintla

In 1971 the Observatorio Astrofísico de Tonantzintla was transformed into a new institution, Instituto Nacional de Astrofísica Optica y Electrónica, INAOE. It developed an astronomical site at Cananea, Sonora (40 km south of the México–U.S. border) where there is a 2.1-m telescope (the G. Haro Telescope). It is equipped with a direct camera and a multislit spectrograph. At present, INAOE has started a project to construct, in collaboration with the University of Massachusetts, a 50-m millimeter telescope in Puebla.[11] The present staff of the institution includes 23 astronomers. INAOE has also developed a graduate program in astronomy.

Astronomical work also takes place elsewhere in México, for example, in Puebla and Jalapa. Also a new astronomy department of the Universidad de Guanajuato was started in 1994, and it has plans for moderate growth in the near future.

INTERACTIONS WITH AMERICAN ASTRONOMY

Personal Interaction

Felipe Valle from OAN traveled to the U.S. to observe the eclipse of January 1, 1889 in California. He further extended this trip to visit several observatories, including Lick, Dearborn, Dudley, Yale, and the U.S. Naval Observatories. In his report, it is clear that his American colleagues were very informative and helpful, and he was able to learn modern observing techniques. From this visit he was able to establish very valuable personal scientific contacts with U.S. astronomers. Also Joaquín Gallo visited Yerkes Observatory in 1905 to get acquainted with the spectroheliograph, and in 1908 and 1909 he visited Lick and Mt. Wilson Observatories.[12]

In 1939, and the several years that followed, interaction with the U.S. was very strong, and there were not many other influences. Most Méxican astronomers in the 1940s were trained in American universities or American observatories. In 1941, Bart Bok reported that Harvard was very active: "Sr. E. Erro and Dr. C. Graef both spent about a year working at Harvard College Observatory and Prof. F. Recillas has now been our guest for almost a year."[13] Very shortly afterward, Haro spent several months at the Harvard observing station as an assistant, where he published a study of spectral classification. Later, he was guest investigator at Case Institute of Technology in Cleveland (with J. Nassau), at Yerkes Observatory, and the McDonald Observatory (with O. Struve).[14]

The development of the site at San Pedro Mártir in Baja, California was aided by collaborations with different observatories that installed equipment for measuring the insolation, humidity, and other sky conditions. In 1970 a formal collaboration was established with the University of Arizona to install a 60-inch aluminum mirror photo-metric telescope on the site. H. L. Johnson was critical to the development of the photometric equipment. Later Johnson became part of the UNAM staff.[15] Similarly, the selection of the site in Cananea for INAOE was aided greatly by G. P. Kuiper, of the University of Arizona.

In addition to the many fruitful individual collaborations with American astronomers, there are many continuing collaborations with university departments and observatories. For example, the continuing series "Texan-Mexican Conference in Astrophysics" has been organized jointly by the University of Texas at Austin, the Rice Institute, and UNAM. Also there is the joint millimeter telescope project between INAOE and the University of Massachusetts. Mexican astronomers also have the opportunity to apply as principal investigators for observing projects (without funding) at U.S. national facilities (like NOAO, CTIO, IUE, NRAO, VLA, and HST). From these projects there has been mutual enrichment. Even more important, the training of Mexican astronomers in the U.S. has continued. Thus far, 32 of the 96 astronomers at UNAM and INAOE have had graduate training in the U.S. and in Canada.

THE AAS

The first Mexican to become a member of the AAS was Joaquín Gallo, in 1920, at the 24th AAS Meeting. He was interested in establishing contact with American astronomers and attended two meetings, the 24th and 30th, which required great determination on his part. In 1925, Miguel Chávez Orozco and Rosendo O. Sandoval were also accepted as members, although they remained in the Society only briefly. A collaboration was established by the AAS Eclipse Committee for September 10, 1923, and some equipment was loaned to OAN to reinforce their existing instruments. From 1922 to 1936 the report of the Observatorio de Tacubaya was prepared and included in the section 'Reports of Observatories' in the *Publications of the AAS*.

The new impulse in astronomy in the 1940s was felt also in the AAS membership. In 1942, Graef became a member of the AAS; by May 1945, five Mexican astronomers were included: Erro, Gallo, Graef, Haro, and Pishmish (she was a member since 1939, although at that time she had no connection to Mexican astronomy).

In February 1946, a group of Mexican astronomers (Erro, Pishmish, González, and Graef) attended the 74th AAS meeting hosted by Columbia University in New York. At that time the first formal links with Mexican astronomy were recognized by the AAS.

In August 1960, the 106th Meeting of the American Astronomical Society took place in México City. There were 80 technical papers presented. A highlight of the meeting was the Russell Memorial lecture, given by Martin Schwarzschild, who spoke on convection in stars. A public lecture was given in Spanish by Donald H. Menzel, director of Harvard Observatory. He showed pictures of prominences on the sun. Among the social activities were the banquet at Chapultepec Castle and a visit to Tonantzintla Observatory.[16] The influence of this meeting on the local students that attended was very significant, providing strong motivation for several of them to pursue astronomical studies. Some participants to this meeting are shown in Figure 6.

Figure 6. Aspect of the conference during the 106th Meeting of the AAS. Some of the participants in the picture are, in the front row: E. Mendoza, C. Mendoza, A. Poveda; in the second row: A. Cox, G. Herbig, R. Minkowski; in the fourth row: H. Weaver.

In January 1979, the 153th Meeting of the American Astronomical Society was hosted again by UNAM in México City.

Altogether, the interaction with the officers of the Society has been rich, and several Méxican astronomers have been members of the AAS Council: G. Haro was council member for 1956–1959 and Vice President for 1960–1962. Other council members have been A. Poveda for 1970–1973, M. Peimbert for 1975–1978, and S. Torres-Peimbert for 1988–1991.

It is interesting to note that, in spite of the fast growth of Mexican astronomy in the last decade, the fraction of Mexican astronomers in the AAS has not varied significantly from 1945, from 0.75%, (5 out of 660) to 0.4% in 1997 (29 out of 7,250).

CONCLUSIONS

Mexican astronomy has developed only in the last century but it is growing fast in this century. It should continue to grow at a faster rate since the proportion of astronomers to general population lags behind that of the U.S. by a factor of 30 (1 per million inhabitants in México compared to 30 in the U.S.). Mexico has had very rich interactions with American astronomers, and at present there are significant projects that suggest that these will continue.

I am grateful for conversations with P. Pishmish, A. Poveda, and M. Peimbert as I prepared this review, and to J. C. Yustis for photographic reproductions.

PART 3

RECOLLECTIONS OF THE SOCIETY

Personal Reminiscences of Being AAS Treasurer and Other Stories

Frank K. Edmondson

I served the AAS as its Treasurer for one-fifth of its first 100 years (1954–1975), and I have attended meetings over a span of 66 years (1931–1997). I was not yet a member when I attended my first AAS meeting at the beginning of my junior year at Indiana University. It was held at the new Perkins Observatory in September 1931. My teacher, Professor W. A. Cogshall, took me to the meeting and paid for my dormitory room and meals. My memory of that meeting, 66 years later, is pretty dim. I do recall being with a small group in the dormitory parlor one evening and listening to Ed Carpenter (later a very good friend) and Lois Slocum reminiscing about their time as fellow graduate students at Berkeley and at the Lick Observatory.

I was still not a member when I attended my second AAS meeting in June 1933. It was held in Chicago at the new Adler Planetarium, located inside the Chicago World's Fairgrounds at the time of the meeting. AAS members had special passes to get in without paying the admission fee to the Fair. My only memory of this AAS meeting is the lecture by Niels Bohr. The cord for the lapel microphone gave him a lot of trouble, and his heavy accent gave his listeners a problem. Dean B. McLaughlin wrote in *Popular Astronomy* that he "... alternately understood the Physics and the English, but never both simultaneously."[1]

Following graduation from Indiana University in 1933, I went to the Lowell Observatory as Lawrence Fellow, and continued as a staff member in 1934. Henry Norris Russell and his family spent their third summer at the Lowell Observatory in 1934. This and my job provided the opportunity that led to my marriage to Margaret, the youngest of the four Russell children, on November 24, 1934.

V. M. Slipher and C. O. Lampland nominated me for membership in the Astronomical Society of the Pacific in 1934, and I assume they nominated me for membership in the AAS at the same time.[2] My third AAS meeting, and my first as a member, was the December 1935 meeting in Princeton, at the end of my first semester as a graduate student at Harvard. We enjoyed a fine family Christmas before the AAS meeting began. Again, my memory is dim, except that Einstein played the violin at the AAS banquet. He played it very well and received an ovation from his audience. My fourth AAS meeting was the very next one, in September 1936, held in Cambridge at the time of the Harvard Tercentenary Celebration. Sir Arthur Eddington gave an impressive public lecture, and Serge Koussevitsky conducted a concert by the Boston Symphony Orchestra in Harvard Yard. I have no memory of the AAS meeting itself!

After graduation from Harvard, I was appointed instructor in Astronomy at Indiana University in 1937 by President William Lowe Bryan, who took a course in Analytic Geometry from Daniel Kirkwood in 1880. I did not have to leave home to attend my fifth AAS meeting because it was held in Bloomington in December 1937, during the customary time between Christmas and New Year's Day. Professor Cogshall had made the arrangements for this before I was appointed, so I had very little to do. The attendance was at about 100, and I think this was a record. Fifty-three papers were presented. The sessions for papers were held in a lounge in the Union Building, and Professor Cogshall had arranged for overstuffed furniture to be brought in from other parts of the building. Nearly everybody was sitting in a soft, comfortable chair or sofa. Professor Cogshall also brought a dark-room timer to the meeting, and it was used to regulate the length of the papers. I think this was the first meeting when a mechanical timer was used.

The next Bloomington meeting was in June 1950, and celebrated the 50th anniversary of the construction of the Kirkwood Observatory. The Annie J. Cannon Award was presented to Helen S. Hogg at the Society Banquet, and Dr. Goethe Link was elected a Patron of the Society by the Council. I became a member of the Office of Naval Research Astronomy Panel, following my nomination by the Council at this meeting.

Shortly before this meeting, I had been elected to a four-year term as Secretary of Section D (Astronomy) of the AAAS, and I was re-elected in 1954 for a second term. At the same time, Otto Struve nominated me to be Treasurer of the AAS for a three-year term. The duties of the AAAS position were very light, so I decided to wear two hats because my first priority would be to serve the AAS if I were making a choice. I was re-elected by the AAS Council for a second three-year term in 1957, and terminated my AAAS position when that term ended in 1958. I was still wearing two hats when the AAS met with the AAAS in Indianapolis in December 1957. I was a member of the AAAS Newcomb Cleveland Prize Committee, and my nomination of Martin Schwarzschild's first report on Project Stratoscope as the outstanding paper was successful. My appearance in a wheelchair at the meeting of the Committee probably helped.

I told the AAS Nominating Committee I was not a candidate for re-election as Treasurer in 1960. When the deadline for nominations arrived, the Committee told me they had not been able to find anyone who wanted the job, and they asked me to accept another term. This scenario was repeated in 1963, 1966, 1969, and 1972.

The third Bloomington meeting was in March 1975, to celebrate the 75th anniversary of the construction of the Kirkwood Observatory. By that time the bylaws had been amended to limit the Secretary and the Treasurer to two consecutive terms, and my 21 years as Treasurer ended in August 1975 at the San Diego meeting. I attended every meeting during those 21 years, except the Greenbrier Hotel meeting at White Sulpher Springs, West Virginia in December 1962. I was the newly elected President of AAAS Section D, and had to be in Philadelphia to preside at Bert Petrie's Retiring Presidential Address.

What do I consider to be my most useful contributions during my 21 years as Treasurer? First, I put the AAS accounts on double entry bookkeeping by employing an accounting major in the School of Business to keep the AAS books. Second, I found an outstanding person, Joseph M. Chamberlain, to be the first Chairman of the new AAS Committee on Education in Astronomy. This came about because I was NSF Program Director for Astronomy in 1956–1957, and we had received a research proposal from the Hayden Planetarium to support Ken Franklin's work. I visited the Planetarium to check this out, and I discovered that the Director, Joe Chamberlain, was the person we were looking for. Third, I suggested that the Perkin Gift that was given to the Society

Figure 1. Left to right—Margaret Russell Edmondson, Frank Edmondson, and Margaret Edmondson (now Olson). AAS meeting, Butler University, December 1957. *Sky & Telescope* photograph.

in honor of Harlow Shapley should be used to continue the program of Visiting Astronomers. This program had been supported by NSF, which had recently decided that it could not continue to fund what had become a most worthy and constructive service of the Society. President Bok wrote to me, "Priscilla says this is the best idea Frank ever had."[3] I also participated in making arrangements for the AAS to be a member of the American Institute of Physics and helped to hire Paul Routly as the first Executive Officer. Gerald Clemence and Lyman Spitzer were the prime movers; Spitzer got a start-up grant from the Ford Foundation to help pay for the first two years of operation of the Executive Office. I was also involved in the transfer of *The Astrophysical Journal* funds from the University of Chicago to the AAS. This was my last action as Treasurer.

Recollections after Fifty Years: Haverford AAS Meeting, December 1950

Vera C. Rubin

Fifty years is a long time in a professional career, yet recollections of my first AAS meeting have not faded. And now, remembering that meeting almost 50 years ago, I recall clearly the question that troubled me then, "Will I ever be a real astronomer?" To be a real astronomer was to study at Harvard, or Yerkes, or Berkeley, and to travel in the world of astronomers. Instead, I was a student at Cornell, where the entire astronomy department consisted of a chairman and one assistant professor, Dr. Martha Stahr. I, at 22, had a B.A. and was a candidate for an M.A. in astronomy; my husband was a Ph.D. candidate in physical chemistry.

For my M.A. thesis, I posed the following question. If you remove the expansion component from the known radial velocities of galaxies, are the residual velocities coherent; that is, are there large regions of the sky with positive or with negative residuals? With velocities known for only 108 galaxies, this question had never previously been examined. Indeed, in a more establishment environment, I would likely have been dissuaded from completing it. To examine the question, I applied to these 108 galaxies the only large-scale pattern I knew, the Oort theory for a rotating galaxy. Distances were found from magnitudes, velocity residuals were plotted on a globe to search for patterns, and parameters were fit following the identification of a principle plane (to be named the Supergalactic Plane a few years later by G. de Vaucouleurs).[1]

With the enthusiasm of youth, I (not yet a member of the AAS but introduced by my adviser, Dr. Stahr) submitted the paper, "Rotation of the Universe," for inclusion in the AAS December 1950 meeting. In those days, the program stated, "Subject to the approval of the Council, the following papers are placed on the program: (time limit, 10 minutes)." The paper was accepted, to be presented on the morning of December 29, 1950. Fifty years ago, programs were simple. There were no competing sessions, but instead a sequential listing of all the papers to be given. Coffee or lunch breaks were inserted by the chair at appropriate times.

There were two major problems involved in getting to Haverford. Barely self-supporting graduate students, we had no car, and little money. We solved this problem by asking my parents to drive from Washington to Ithaca, and transport us to Philadelphia, their home town. The second problem was especially major; we had a four-week old son. So on a snowy winter day, my father drove us, plus his first grandchild, to my grandmother's home (thereby aging 20 years, he later told me).

The next day my father drove me and my husband Bob to Haverford College. I was wearing a new, properly professional dark blue dress that my mother and aunt had given me as a gift the day before. I had prepared the ten-minute presentation

Figure 1. Vera Rubin, 1947, at a Vassar College telescope.

enormously carefully, and I spent the drive rehearsing it in my mind. We entered the hall during the session, but I knew not a single astronomer there; indeed, I knew few astronomers anywhere. I can still visualize the arrangements of the chairs — perhaps eight on each side with a center aisle, and a low raised platform with the speaker to the left.

Shortly after arriving, I presented my talk ("smoothly and confidently"; Figure 2), and then a sea of unknown faces rose one by one to ask questions and raise objections. I can still picture their faces and the location of their seats in the hall. I was not unfamiliar with tough questions, coming from physics classes with Hans Bethe, Philip Morrison, and Richard Feynman. In fact Feynman, a member of my Masters' committee, was a skeptic, continually asking "What's moving it around?" Whether the discussion following my talk was actually more acrimonious than usual, I cannot say, but the astronomers seemed to me to be unusually cross. All except one, a small man who spoke in a high-pitched voice, and said those wonderful things that one says to a very young graduate student, "This is a very interesting work, but perhaps we must wait for more data until we can make a study which is more believable." Later, of course, I could identify him as Martin Schwarzschild. Following the questions, the chairman called a coffee break, hoping perhaps to calm the audience.

As I rose to leave, an astronomer approached me, introduced himself as the editor of *The Astronomical Journal*, and said, "We can't publish an abstract called 'Rotation of

THE ITHACA JOURNAL, ITHACA, N.Y.

SATURDAY EVENING, DECEMBER 30, 1950

Student Says Stars May Show Creation's Center

By HOWARD BLAKESLEE
Associated Press Science Editor

Haverford, Pa.—(AP)—A young mother, in her early 20s, startled the American Astronomical Society today with a daring report —so daring, in fact, that most astronomers think her theories are not yet possible.

Mrs. Vera Cooper Rubin of Cornell University reported that it is possible to figure out the center of creation and how far away it is.

Mrs. Rubin is a graduate student at Cornell, and today's astronomy report is her thesis for which she hopes to get the degree of doctor of philosophy. She came here with her husband, Robert J. Rubin, who is a Cornell graduate in chemistry also trying for a doctor's degree, and their month-old son. They live in Trumansburg.

Her demonstration of the great mystery was mathematical, given smoothly and confidently. She based it on some mathematical assumptions that you can find evidence for the center of creation in the motions of 108 galaxies

of stars each a collection of hundreds of millions, like our Milky Way.

Her results showed that creation — that is, all the stars that exist—covers a sort of cart-wheel area whose distance from rim to rim is seven billion light-years. A light-year is the distance light travels in a year at 186,000 miles a second.

This outer edge of creation is about three times farther away than the world's greatest telescope can see.

She said the center is about 35 million light-years distance from earth, that the mass of all the stars is that of the sun multiplied by the one followed by 21 zeroes.

And that in this great cart wheel the Milky Way, carrying earth along with it, is moving at about 500 miles a second.

The astronomers were not complimentary. They politely and persistently questioned her figures, because there are not enough sure observations to substantiate them. She replied that it was worth while to try.

Figure 2. An article from the *Ithaca Journal*, December 30, 1950, describing my talk at the 1950 AAS meeting at Haverford College.

the Universe', so I have renamed it 'Rotation of the Metagalaxy'." This is surely the only time that the word metagalaxy has appeared in my work. I think a newspaper reporter also talked to me, but I am less certain about that. Thus, my participation in the meeting having ended, we exited rapidly to return to the young son I had to nurse.

One year later, Schwarzschild wrote to me, saying he had heard from George Gamow, my Ph.D. advisor, that I was having trouble getting the Masters' work published. "Could I help?," he asked.

Surprisingly, I felt rather upbeat about the experience. I had given a paper before the AAS, and thought I had done pretty well. I recognized the difficulties in the study: limited data, questionable distances, lack of statistical tidiness, which in response to a question I attributed to the "nebulousness" of the study, thereby ending the questions amidst much laughter. And when I walked back into my Grandmother's house, my first words (according to those present) were "Was he happy?"

The newspaper reports of the talk were totally unexpected, but fun. Even a respected science editor of that day, Howard Blakeslee, had confused stars, galaxies, and universes. And the headline in the *Washington Post*, "Young Mother Figures Center of Creation by Star Motions" was to amuse me for many years. Of course, the word creation had not been mentioned nor inferred in my talk. When in 1993 I was awarded the National Medal of Science by President Clinton, long-time Washington physicist friends printed a mock newspaper with the headline, "Old Grandmother Gets Medal of Science." They knew I would recognize the phrase.

Periodically, astronomer friends reminded me of that meeting. Edwin Carpenter wrote me a long letter on his train ride back to Arizona following the meeting, outlining his ideas about large-scale structure in the universe. Frank Kerr has stated, "I was present at the AAS meeting in late 1950 (this was my first AAS meeting). I happened to hear by chance three prestigious council members discussing whether Vera Rubin's paper should be allowed. They seemed to be shocked by this brash young outsider (and a female at that) making such an outrageous and impossible sugges-tion."[2] And my long friendship with Gerard de Vaucouleurs dates from his interest in my early work. In 1963, on my first observing run at Kitt Peak National Observatory, Art Hoag came into the 36-inch building, and I introduced myself. "I remember you," he said, "I was running to your talk at the Haverford meeting, slipped on the ice, and hurt my back."

In retrospect, my attendance at the meeting was very brief, and my informal interactions with AAS members there were nonexistent. Perhaps even then it was unusual to 'attend' a meeting in this fashion. My attendance at my second AAS meeting, April 1955 in Princeton, took place under different circumstances. I had an astronomy Ph.D. The paper I was presenting there, "The form of the Galactic Spiral Arms from a Modified Oort Theory," was more establishment, as judged by the fact that Frank Edmondson too was presenting a paper on a similar subject. Only shortly before had I identified him as the man with the beard who had seemed so fierce at the Haverford meeting.

By 1955, many astronomers had become friends, some from the 1953 Michigan astronomy summer school. [3] At the Princeton meeting, interactions were numerous; I recall long conversations with Walter Baade. I was on my way toward becoming a real astronomer.

THE AAS AS A NETWORK

Arlo U. Landolt

THE IMPORTANCE OF GENERAL MEETINGS

The greatest reward from being involved with the AAS is the opportunity to meet and work with individuals from across the astronomical spectrum. E. C. Pickering, the second President of the AAS, thought that an especially important function of the new Society was to bring together in a social setting older and younger astronomers:

> [T]he latter may think the work of the older men out of date, but they may find the experience of the older men and their personal acquaintance with the eminent men of still earlier date of great assistance. The older men have much to learn regarding new methods, and the extensive appliances at their command often may be employed to much greater advantage if they keep themselves personally in touch with the most recent developments of astronomical research.[1]

Personal networking remains of immense value 100 years later — it is a form of social and professional interaction which should be fostered universally. In order to facilitate such interactions, at the meeting where Pickering made this remark, he also suggested that abstracts of papers should be made available prior to their presentation to permit more lengthy and thoughtful discussion.

Our forefathers thought it important that astronomers congregate at locations far removed from city influences, preferably meeting at a large hotel capable of accommodating everyone under one roof, where they could meet, eat, and sleep, and where all sessions (unparalleled) could be held in the same building. Perhaps the most exotic location chosen early was Put-in-Bay, Ohio, an island in Lake Erie. Most astronomers today claim to prefer a "cozy-feeling" meeting where all astronomical and gastronomical events are within an easy stroll. This has become difficult, of course, because the meetings have become very large, but the winter meetings still provide the best opportunity to reap the advantages of networking on a professional level since they are the most heavily attended. Winter meetings are also the time when the search for staff and jobs peak. Also, during the summer small topical symposia take place scattered across the globe, which distract individuals from more encompassing fare.

Meetings play more than a professional role in an astronomer's life. They can stimulate life-long friendships. I recall my first AAS meeting (Columbus, Ohio, March, 1956) when Martin Schwarzschild laughingly presented the 1956 "solar model," making allusions to the yearly appearance of a new model automobile. I also remember Lyman Spitzer wondering whether there might be an interstellar galactic corona.[2] Again, I remember vividly that at the same meeting, where I was still a wide-eyed graduate student, a real professional astronomer took the time to sit beside me and talk. Thus a friendship began with Hugh M. Johnson which has lasted more than four decades. Such thoughtfulness needs to be continued through the generations; it's an effective mode of tying together the community, which in the long run not only is fun socially but enhances and invigorates the research product.

Frank K. Edmondson, chair of the Indiana University astronomy department when I was a graduate student, was an excellent example then of a man who devoted himself to service for the astronomical community. He was very active in Section D (Astronomy) of the AAAS and was long-time Treasurer of the AAS. The whole department encouraged contacts. My advisor, John B. Irwin, made sure that I came to know Frank Bradshaw Wood because I had an interest in binary stars. Later I succeeded Brad as Secretary of Section D of the AAAS. Similarly, conversations with Laurence Fredrick over a period of time about service in the AAS may have influenced my becoming the AAS Secretary. My introduction to Robert Fleischer at the Christmas 1958 AAS/AAAS meeting led to an opportunity 20 years later to work at the National Science Foundation as a program manager.

Interactions at meetings are extremely important. Broad meetings, those covering many topics, probably are more important for the overall health of a science than are single-topic symposia. However, many AAS members feel that AAAS meetings are too broad in scope, as are AAS meetings or the International Astronomical Union (IAU)

Figure 1. John Irwin, who was responsible for preserving the likenesses of so many AAS members, as he appeared before the camera. Courtesy AIP E. Segrè Visual Archives.

General Assembly. Many turn up their noses because they say, "You know, I don't do that kind of work. I don't want to go hear that stuff." Sadly, such attitudes may cause those individuals to miss out on chances of networking and of meeting many interesting and diverse scholars. One never knows. Someday down the road you might meet one of them and find that you may have something in common. The sole reason for recalling these interactions is to emphasize that the Society, meeting, and association activities are crucial over the long haul — the broader the organization, the more likely one will meet individuals who may play an interesting role farther on in life. One should note that this kind of networking is not premeditated. It is a social function or process, the execution of which is quite necessary for the maintenance of the health of a discipline.

Astronomers continue to specialize despite the sense today that breadth is what is needed in the modern world. More popular gatherings include specialized symposia, whereas at general AAS or IAU meetings one can meet professionals from across the spectrum of the discipline. While one can meet an immediate goal through participation in one-dimensional (topical) meetings, it is the cornucopia of a large Society or IAU meeting that exposes one to the wealth of ideas and opportunities that modern astronomy has become. And it is the breadth acquirable from large meetings that most of us need in our professional lives, since the majority of us are educators. Certainly as important, if not more, are the contacts and friendships that develop and endure through the meeting process. Astronomy as a subject traditionally has required broad collaborations, and it is an international network that must be nurtured and appreciated.

The apparent narrowness of interest of so many professionals today and the lack of willingness of many astronomers to attend anything other than the most specialized symposia is lamentable when one reviews the efforts of our forebears. They worked hard to put together meetings to broaden and enhance the knowledge and efforts in astronomy, and to create a real community. They helped to make astronomy what it is today.

PARTICIPATION IN ELECTIONS

Certain aspects of Society life appear to track national trends. It seems that even AAS members are not immune to a growing indifference. A characteristic of the AAS members from the United States that follows a trend throughout the country has been a tendency over the last decade or so for ever fewer members to participate in Society elections. Those voting percentages found in documents available to the Secretary are presented in Table 1. As one can see from the Table, turnout is greater in elections, marked with an asterisk, when an AAS President is to be elected. It is also a fact that many of our foreign members take the elections more seriously than the average American member. Each year the Secretary receives from a few to several ballots express mailed from overseas because the sender is concerned to meet the election deadline.

TABLE 1. *AAS Election Summary Statistics.*

Year	Percentage Voting	Year	Percentage Voting	Year	Percentage Voting
1930	38.7	1981*	40.8	1989*	35.7
1931	31.3	1982	46.7	1990	30.2
1932	40.6	1983*	46.4	1991*	32.5
1933	36.3	1984	39.2	1992	25.3
1935	35.4	1985*	49.8	1993*	31.0
1936	34.5	1986	37.6	1995*	28.3
1937	26.7	1987*	42.4	1996	18.9
		1988	34.0	1997*	25.6

INTERNATIONAL RELATIONS

The IAU, dating from July 28, 1919, was the first of the international scientific unions to be formed under the auspices of the International Research Council (IRC).[3] The purpose of the IAU was twofold: (1) to facilitate the relations between astronomers of different countries where international cooperation is necessary or useful; and (2) to promote the study of astronomy in all of its departments.[4] Perusal of the *Publications of the American Astronomical Society* volumes, Blaauw's (1994) history of the IAU, etc., reveal the leading role played by United States' astronomers in the formation and definition of the IAU. As evident from Table 2, U.S. astronomers historically have comprised 25–30% of the IAU membership.

Prior to 1955, there were no individual IAU members; only national committees represented IAU membership.[5] Even today the IAU is the only one of the ICSU unions to allow individual members. Thus individual astronomers are able to have direct influence in their discipline's international affairs, and if they utilize the opportunities, they enjoy direct interaction with colleagues around the world. At IAU meetings one has the opportunity to speak with and to listen to the world's great astronomers. I recall Bart Bok, who, after sitting down at the Hamburg General Assembly, whispered to his neighbor wondering if Oort approved of his talk. There was also Fritz Zwicky, forging ahead in discussion in Prague, waving his arms, buttressing his argument by saying "... my Professor Einstein said... ." And then there was Sergei Gaposchkin, also at the Prague General Assembly, discussing the various light curves of variable stars in the Magellanic Clouds, in a presentation interspersed with slides of his family. Great memories!

AAS PRIZES

Constructive networking includes recognizing excellence among members of a group. Annie J. Cannon, of stellar spectral classification fame and an early and long-time Treasurer of the AAS, won a prize of $1,000 from the Association to Aid Scientific Research by Women. She in turn donated that sum, with its accumulated interest, to the AAS to establish an award to women for their work in astronomy.[6] Hence, the Cannon Prize was both the first AAS prize and the first to be endowed. The AAS

Council approved the rules for the Cannon Prize at its meeting in December 1933. The Cannon Prize continued to be given as an AAS Prize until 1971 when the designated recipient refused it because she felt that the Cannon Prize was discriminatory. To deal with the situation, President Bart Bok appointed a committee to determine the future of the Cannon Prize. The result was that the AAS gave the endowment and the Annie J. Cannon Prize name to the American Association for University Women (AAUW) Educational Foundation in 1973. The AAUW has continued to oversee the operation of the Prize with the AAS providing the astronomical expertise in the recommendation of the awardee.

TABLE 2. *Number of U.S. and IAU Members.*

Year	No. Adhering Countries	Total IAU Membership	No. IAU Members from USA	Percentage from USA
1922	17	207	52	25.1
1925	22	248	58	23.4
1928	23	288	72	25.0
1932	24	405	77	19.0
1935	24	510	89	17.5
1938	26	524	95	18.1
1948	31	611	159	26.0
1952	33	809	195	24.1
1955	36	888	208	23.4
1958	38	1,120	282	25.2
1961	38	1,081	276	25.5
1964	42	1,276	334	26.2
1967	43	2,009	396	19.7
1970	46	2,602	728	28.0
1973	47	3,185	920	28.9
1976	48	3,805	1,108	29.1
1979	49	4,538	1,363	30.0
1982	49	5,200	1,527	29.4
1985	50	5,687	1,615	28.4
1988	55	6,649	1,924	28.9
1991	63	7,260	2,069	28.5
1994	57	7,898	2,190	27.7

The second AAS prize to be established evolved from a plan created by Harlow Shapley to honor his old teacher, Henry Norris Russell. Bok presented the idea to the Council at its meeting June 8, 1945 in Cambridge, Massachusetts, and the Council agreed to endorse a broad fund raising campaign among AAS members and patrons. The prize was designated the Henry Norris Russell Lectureship, and has become the Society's most prestigious and senior award, given for a lifetime of eminence in astronomical research. The first Russell Lecturer was Henry Norris Russell himself in 1946.[7]

The Annual report of the AAS Treasurer dated May 31, 1952 showed that Helen B. Warner had donated $5,000 to the AAS to establish the Warner Fund. Within a matter of days, Council discussed the best use of the Warner Fund. During Council's December 1952 meeting, J. J. Nassau suggested that a new Prize be established to

Figure 2. Arlo Landolt was Secretary of the Society from 1980 to 1989 during the period when the Executive Office transferred to Washington, D.C. Irwin photograph, May 1971, AIP E. Segrè Visual Archives, Irwin Collection.

recognize research by young astronomers, young being defined as under 30–35 years of age. The Warner Prize rules were set at Council's meeting in August 1953, and the first winner, Aden B. Meinel, was announced in December 1953.[8]

The Minutes of the 138th Council meeting in August 1972 recorded a statement by Bok that the widow of Newton Lacy Pierce (Mrs. Beatrice Rieke Pierce Hess) wanted to donate a sum of money for the purpose of making an award in observational astronomy. Later Minutes discuss in great detail Mrs. Hess' wishes, a major point of which was "... to encourage young astronomers to develop and use new instrumentation or to undertake observational work in astronomy. The award should normally be made annually to an astronomer under 35 years of age who, by publication or otherwise over the preceding five years, has given proof of outstanding achievements." The first Pierce Prize winner was Edwin M. Kellogg in 1974.[9]

Several years went by before the AAS considered the possibility of another prize to honor scholarship among astronomers. At its 160th meeting in June 1982 Council voted to accept in principle a proposal by Sandra Faber to create the Beatrice M. Tinsley Prize, in honor of that most capable astronomer who died early in life. The final rules governing the Tinsley Prize were adopted by Council at its 165th meeting in Tucson in January 1985. In line with Tinsley's own scholarly activities, the Tinsley Prize recognizes research contributions of an exceptionally creative or innovative character that have played a seminal role in furthering the understanding of the universe. The first Tinsley Prize winner was S. Jocelyn Bell Burnell in 1986.[10]

The most recent Prize voted by Council to be sponsored by the AAS is the George Van Biesbroeck Prize. This Prize for service to the greater astronomical community, had its origin in 1988 when a group of astronomers led by Helmut A. Abt created it by forming a non-profit corporation. They turned the endowment and responsibility for overseeing the George Van Biesbroeck Prize over to the AAS at the Council's 189th meeting in Toronto in January 1997. The goal of the prize is to encourage and recognize exemplary and unselfish service to the greater astronomical community.[11]

The author wishes to acknowledge with thanks both the enhancement and confirmation of the data in Table 2 from Ms. Monique Orine of the IAU Secretariat's Office in Paris, the help of Ms. Sheri Thompson in searching old AAS files, and the editor's support in final preparation of this chapter.

My Years as AAS Secretary

Laurence W. Fredrick

BECOMING AAS SECRETARY

Little did I know that the holding of the 126th meeting of the American Astronomical Society in Charlottesville in April 1968 was going to be a test of my organizational skills and suitability for office. Shortly thereafter, a small Society delegation asked me if I would agree to serve as Acting Secretary with the almost lead pipe cinch of being elected Secretary in 1970. There was some agonizing and a long discussion with then University of Virginia President Edgar Shannon. My long term goal was the building of astronomy at the University of Virginia and I would have to be careful not to damage that goal or let it take precedence over the needs of the AAS. In any case, the position would bring some attention to the University and that was a plus. The cost to the University was in providing space and donating my time. The latter was not inconsequential by the time I finished my term as Secretary.

The position began with a bang. My first meeting as Secretary, the 129th, in Honolulu in March 1969, required a decision breaking the late paper rule without George McVittie (my predecessor) there to lean on. The paper reported the discovery of interstellar formaldehyde which I agreed was important enough to sidestep the rule. I violated the rule twice after that but enforced it vigorously otherwise.

The decision to take a look at me as a candidate for Society Secretary may have occurred two years earlier than I indicate above. In 1967, I was able to get the Society to lend its name to allow me to rent a Boeing 707 to carry 154 astronomers to Europe to attend the International Astronomical Union meeting in Prague. I made my pitch at Ithaca, and Bengt Strömgren was very enthusiastic. We pulled it off without using an advance from the Society. The airplane cost $40,000, so each person went round-trip for $260. Strömgren was not one of our passengers.

After becoming Secretary and getting a few meetings under my belt, something that impressed me about our meetings was that they take on a life of their own. Once the venue is agreed upon, the meeting will occur even if everything goes wrong. And once in motion, they run to the bitter end, whether you want them to or not.

The most difficult meeting during my tenure was the 153rd in Mexico City in January 1979. Our colleagues there had fully prepared me for what to expect. They went into great detail and I regarded most of their reports as horror stories. But I did take certain precautions just in case, such as carrying 700 abstract booklets as personal baggage. When I went to get my luggage to go through customs—no boxes of booklets. It continued from there. To top the meeting off, there was a mild earthquake during the banquet.

The Presidents who served the Society during my terms were a dedicated lot, to say the least. Martin Schwarzschild, filling in for Al Whitford at the 129th meeting in March 1969, saved the day with his typical quick thinking. At the banquet, a music

★ 101 ★

student from the University of Hawaii was having great difficulty tuning her instrument (an ungainly musical device with an unpronounceable name) and was in tears—her great moment shot by an uncooperative instrument. Martin came to the rescue by saying in a very fatherly manner that there wasn't an astronomer in the room who didn't know the frustration of trying to work with an uncooperative instrument. We burst into laughter, the musician's face turned to a smile, the instrument decided to cooperate after all, and her performance finished with a crescendo of applause.

I think the most interesting President was Bob Kraft. He had the knack of avoiding things that neither he nor the Society could do anything about. He concentrated only on issues where there would be a positive effect. Across the bay, Ivan King, on the other hand faced the toughest situation as President and smoothed most of the ruffled feathers with great diplomacy. The issue at hand was how the Society would honor the Equal Rights Amendment. The other two Presidents during my tenure were Bart Bok and Margaret Burbidge. All five of them put the Society ahead of their other work.

When I joined the AAS in 1953, there were about 800 members, and meetings were held in one smoke-filled room with perhaps forty or fifty attendees. When I became Secretary, the Society numbered about 2,300 and was running parallel sessions at every meeting. When I finished being Secretary in 1980, the Society numbered around 3,800 and six parallel sessions were the rule. We introduced poster sessions for the late papers and were about to use them as regular sessions.

ELECTION TO THE SOCIETY

I was elected to the Society in 1954 when I was at Swarthmore. In those days you had to present a scientific paper along with your dues check. For some reason, I could not attend the meeting in Ann Arbor so Adriaan Blaauw, who was then passing through, took my paper and check to the meeting and presented both. Thus began a long and fruitful friendship with Blaauw and the Society that has lasted a lifetime. By the way, I still have the canceled check.

I missed quite a few AAS meetings those days. It seems that Peter van de Kamp needed me to do observing just when the meetings occurred. I made up for missing AAS meetings by attending the Neighborhood Meetings. These would be held once a year and covered the territory from Boston to Washington, D.C., i.e. along the old Pennsylvania Railroad. The Virginia astronomers would always show up at meetings held in Washington. These meetings were fun and very informal. The total attendance may have been thirty and the local astronomers put up the out-of towners in their own homes. The moving forces behind those meetings in the 1950s were Dirk Brouwer and Gerald Clemence of Yale.

The first meeting of the AAS that I actually attended was the 107th in New York City in 1960. I have lasting memories from that meeting. In those days, if you wanted a breath of fresh air you had to leave the meeting and go outside! There were no parallel sessions and the big wheels chaired each session. That meeting was held in the Hotel Roosevelt with perhaps 50 or 60 astronomers in attendance. The first evening, I was sitting in the lobby wondering what I should do for supper when Allan Sandage, Guido Münch and Armin Deutsch strolled by. Allan, whom I had just met about two years earlier, called me by name and asked what I was doing for dinner. I allowed that

I had no plans, so he insisted that I join them. I don't recall where we went to eat but I do recall being overwhelmed with the astronomy discussed. It was very reassuring to learn that these people were human and cared about young astronomers.

I attended most of the AAS meetings after that and all of them when I became Secretary, except the ones while I was on sabbatical in Austria. This leads me back to the Society.

RECOLLECTIONS OF A TOUR OF DUTY

During my term as Secretary I argued that meetings in the winter should be in warmer climates and those in the summer in cooler locations. I kept to this line. At one point I tried to organize a meeting on a cruise ship. It fit most of the criteria (in one place, no one can escape, etc.) plus mine, as long as the cruise was in the Caribbean in the winter or near Alaska in the summer. There were the usual jokes about my effort—suppose some graduate student decides to open some job opportunities by renting an attack submarine. But the real show-stopper was an aside comment by the then Director of the astronomy program at the National Science Foundation (NSF). Clearly, astronomers should not appear to be enjoying themselves with government support.

Another point that I tried to stress was that the Society was the professional society for all of North America and as much of the rest of the Western Hemisphere as could make regular contributions to the meetings. I tried to avoid conflicts in scheduling with the Canadian organizations and with the ASP and succeeded. There was no e-mail then, so this was all done by telephone.

A major change in the Society during my time as Secretary was the formation of Divisions. I did not like to see it occur, but it was inevitable. Narrowly focussed meetings are more important in honing the science than general meetings. To keep the Divisions in the fold, we hit upon a plan to have the Divisions, each in turn, handle an invited session during a meeting and give their prize lectures, etc. There were some rough edges at first, while the organizers got used to how much detail was involved. Once over this hurdle, the meetings went smoothly again.

By 1974, the meetings were growing larger and larger and taking more and more of everyone's time and money, so we began to consider changes. One of the obvious problems was the cost of attending three meetings a year. We therefore accepted the need for multiple sessions and formally established the limit of two meetings per year in 1975. I believe we started to experiment with poster sessions the next year.

At the meeting banquets I would try to avoid the head table. My wife Frances and I would pick a table with some young astronomers whom we did not know. I could learn a lot about how the Society was doing by listening to their comments to each other about the speaker, about the entertainment, or whatever was going on.

Despite what my colleagues may have thought, the paper sessions were not put together by numbering the papers, putting corresponding numbers on a cork board and throwing darts to determine the order. Three or four of us from the University of Virginia and the National Radio Astronomy Observatory would go through the stack and carefully sort them by object and/or subject. Of course, there was always one session of papers which didn't fit with each other nor anywhere else.

One of the penalties for being an officer in the Society was being stuck with chairing the late paper sessions. If there was only one such session, I was it. This is why the poster sessions were a blessing. The authors felt less like outcasts in the poster format and I was free to catch the 6 p.m. plane back home.

The Madison, Wisconsin, meeting in June 1978 provided some excitement. The people in charge of the meeting space for the Council threatened to run me out of town for plugging in my tape recorder myself. That was a job for a union technician. Such a technician duly appeared, he looked like an electrician to me, unplugged my recorder and plugged it back in. That seemed to satisfy everyone, so we were allowed to continue.

Another memorable meeting was my last as Secretary. It was held at College Park, Maryland, in June 1980. I received the obligatory engraved plaque but more important was the case of Simi Cabernet Sauvignon. That is the way one wants to be recognized for service. Even more important, at that meeting our Mexican colleagues gave me ten kilograms, yes 10 Kg, of fully-roasted Mexican coffee beans. On its way back to Charlottesville, my Mazda RX-7 was worth its weight in gold and the aroma was magnificent.

I had another brush with the administration of the Society in 1988. I was asked to substitute for Boyce for eight or nine weeks, one day a week. My job seemed to be to answer questions from various sources when one of the staff didn't know the answer. On one occasion there was a fair amount of work, but I have forgotten what that was. I had to stay overnight, so it must have been important.

I believe I should comment upon the unsung heroes of the Society. Frank Edmondson was a pillar of strength and the encyclopedia of the history of the Society. He seemed to know every astronomer I ever heard of. One of his successors (after Bill Howard), Harold Weaver, complained that had he known how much work was involved he would have thought twice about accepting the position. In sum, Frank and Harold logged a total of 33 years as Treasurers of the Society.

Paul Routly, Hank Gurin, and Peter Boyce were the Executive Officers during my time. It was clear that the Society would have to change its mode of operating by the middle 1970s. There was equal pressure to relocate the office in a small school setting following the Princeton model but away from Princeton and in Washington, D.C. where most of the funding and policy-making organizations resided. Though we were much smaller, we adopted the model of the American Optical Society, and they had their building in D. C. Everyone recognized that this would be a major change and would require more salaried people. Peter Boyce certainly put an enormous amount of energy and enthusiasm into the job and carried the Society through difficult changing times.

All in all, I regard my almost twelve years serving the Society as a plus. Astronomers far and wide pitched in when asked to help and my memory of the cantankerous few is, that they were not too cantankerous.

PART 4

THE MODERN SOCIETY

THE POST-WAR SOCIETY: RESPONDING TO NEW PATTERNS OF PATRONAGE

David H. DeVorkin

INTRODUCTION

After World War II, the American Astronomical Society (AAS) became the platform for debate over how to respond to a new source of patronage, made possible largely through the lessons of war. In this chapter we outline the process by which a committee, chosen by the Council of the AAS and administered by the National Research Council, advised the Office of Naval Research on the needs of American astronomy. We will examine how the Committee deliberated over the use of this new source of funding and how it reflected the concerns held by many in the Society who feared that such a profound change in patronage might alter the very fabric of the discipline itself.

WARTIME ACTIVITIES

Throughout World War II, the Society struggled to hold its meetings and attract papers from those few astronomers still engaged in some form of research. The Society also did its part for mobilization. Following a tradition set during World War I, Society officers, including Secretary Dean B. McLaughlin, organized a manpower survey for the National Academy of Sciences, which helped to identify pools of talent for a wide range of research and development projects. As Bart Bok proudly recalled years later, astronomers acted as substitute physicists, and through the experience many came to better understand the world of physics as it was pursued in major laboratories, such as MIT's Radiation Laboratory or Harvard's Radio Research Laboratory.[1]

Most of the major observatories — such as Mount Wilson, Yerkes, and Lick — either lost their junior staff to wartime jobs elsewhere, or transformed their shops to become military contract laboratories. Staffs at universities like Princeton and Harvard either stayed on campus teaching navigation or worked at any one of dozens of military centers around the nation. A few meetings — like one in Cambridge in May 1943 — were well attended and lively, because many astronomers were detailed to wartime projects there and because Harlow Shapley, as Society President, drew them all together.

In the depths of war, during 1944 and 1945, the Society departed from its traditional two meetings per year and met only annually, in Philadelphia and again in Cambridge. Most meetings were rather sparse, since few astronomers were working full-time in astronomy, which also had a negative impact on both *The Astronomical*

Journal and *The Astrophysical Journal*, where both subscriptions (from Europeans) and submissions were seriously reduced. By this time, the Society had taken control of the former journal and was increasing its editorial oversight of the latter.[2] Thus the Society began to take on a greater role in the discipline at large, and this role would continue to expand.

POST WAR ASTRONOMY

In 1943, asked by the editors of *Popular Astronomy* to survey the past 50 years of astronomy as the first in a series of "Astronomical Summaries," Otto Struve chose to highlight the terrific growth of observatories in the U.S. The rise of the modern observatory in the past 50 years was an American phenomenon, he argued. Europe now lagged behind:

> The chief cause was undoubtedly the war and the fact that nearly all European observatories are operated by their governments. And governments rarely have enough money for pure research, especially when they are preparing for war.[3]

Struve was thinking, of course, of both world wars, and was thinking more of the future than the past. He knew that over the past centuries, monarchies and republics alike had established the most important observatories the world had ever known, ranging from Tycho's Uraniborg to the Greenwich and Paris Observatories to the U.S. Naval Observatory and even to his ancestral Pulkovo Observatory. With the exception of Potsdam and the Astrophysical Observatory of the Smithsonian Institution, however, no government had as yet invested heavily in modern astrophysical practice. The greatest observatories of that type had been built in the last half century by personal and corporate philanthropy. These were the observatories Struve knew would dominate the future of astronomy.

Despite his concerns, Struve knew that some form of government support was going to be necessary in the future to maintain America's lead, even though it had been so well supported up to that time by private munificence. "Such a course will have many disadvantages," Struve warned; government control, he argued, may provide protection and require better planning, but it also meant the possibility of external control. He predicted that in the previous half century astronomy had seen the last in major private support for new observatories, "and that the next half century will see the gradual assumption by the taxpayer of the responsibility for developing pure research in astronomy."[4]

Struve was a very complex man, and his vision for the future of astronomy was far from clear. Closer to the end of the war, he reveled in the many new technologies, from rocketry to electronics, that stood to reshape astronomy. But his concerns about costs and control were reflected by more than one astronomer. Harlow Shapley argued in November 1946 that the government's "...intercession in American science...has become ominous...Those who were worried about domination of freedom in American science by the great industries, can now worry about domination by the military."[5]

Whereas Struve was really concerned about obtaining greater support for astronomy and the need for central planning by astronomers, Shapley was more fearful that military needs would divert available scientific talent from the universities and observatories and that remaining scientists would be diverted to areas of potential utility to the military. Shapley also was among those, Leo Goldberg recalled, who believed that, "any money from the military was blood money."[6] They all worried about autonomy, loss of control, and a loss of traditional forms of support. Home institutions might lessen their support when they saw that sciences like astronomy could attract outside funding, and, as Struve and Shapley and other observatory directors knew, government patronage in any form, if not channeled through traditional lines of authority, also held out the possibility that hierarchical patterns would change. For astronomy, it could mean the loss of the autonomy, power, and authority of the observatory director.

Such concerns were not peculiar to astronomers, but astronomers tended to harbor more parochial fears than those who looked at the bigger picture. One was Manny Piore, director of the new Office of Naval Research (ONR) Physical Sciences Division, who in December 1947 told an AAAS audience meeting in Chicago that, "As the Federal Government enters itself more and more into the scientific activities of the country, the question arises as to who will do the planning and administration of any program."[7]

Figure 1. (l to r) Harlow Shapley, Otto Struve and Joel Stebbins, en-route to Copenhagen in March 1946 to attend a conference to revive the International Astronomical Union. Shapley, leading the American delegation, was then President of the AAS, Stebbins was immediate past-President and Struve would become the next President. The Executive Committee of the United States section of the IAU consisted of two representatives from the AAS who were members of the National Research Council as well as the President and Secretary of the AAS. Courtesy of AIP Emilio Segrè Visual Archives, Shapley Collection.

The government in all its forms was getting into the peacetime civilian research business to a degree never before known. Knowing full well that the success of the Navy program required that the Navy be satisfied that it was gaining the attention and the allegiance of the scientific establishment, Piore strongly advised his colleagues that if they wanted the job done right, "Scientists must now develop a tradition [where] they leave their laboratories for periods of one or two years and come to Washington to participate in the planning, direction, and administration of research."[8] Eventually some astronomers did this, acting as program managers for astronomy programs at ONR and later NSF. But these changes were still in the future and were only a small part of what Piore was really concerned about: how to preserve what he felt was the autonomy of pure science in America. The question immediately at hand, however, was, "What could be done now to restart the scientific infrastructure of the nation?"

Everyone knew that astronomy had always been one of the most expensive physical sciences; certainly the way it was practiced at major American observatories centered on huge telescopes and large staffs. And there was every expectation that astronomy would get even more expensive, as new technologies, many born of wartime programs, inevitably filtered into the discipline as those who helped to develop them or became familiar with them returned to their observatories. Kuiper sensed the change in his first few weeks at Harvard's Radio Research Laboratory in mid-1943, and at first he did not like what he was seeing. There was, as he wrote to Chandrasekhar:

> ... a danger: lots of people work in this field without a full or even a half-understanding of its principles. The growth is so rapid that some of it is wild, and needs trimming. But such half-understood science is probably common in all fields of engineering. The danger is if youngsters think that this is the way science should always be.[9]

Only a few weeks later, Kuiper had been converted to the new way to do science on a large scale. Beyond the interests of national security it would be good, he thought, for science to maintain this new heady pace, if only to keep "employed some of the best young men in each field."[10] Kuiper did not share Shapley's concern for just what this new generation of scientists would be doing, but then again, at the time he did not have an observatory to worry about.

Indeed, both Struve and Shapley had observatories to restart after the war that were among the largest and hungriest in the world. Thus, even though the Harvard staff was deeply divided on the issue, and both Struve and Shapley worried that government money would stimulate even greater independence among their staffs, they could not prevent many of their more aggressive subordinates from seeking military funding for their personal projects, using connections they had developed during the war. Jesse Greenstein, Gerard Kuiper, Donald Menzel, Fred Whipple, and soon Lyman Spitzer, Leo Goldberg, and others opened new and fresh conduits of funding from military and government patrons they had come to know during wartime. Those who were not observatory directors, and most of them were not at first, looked forward to an independence of action that was unknown prior to the war.

The war had opened many doors for those who had the contacts and expertise and took the initiative to use them. Greenstein's involvement in optical design and fabrication at Yerkes made him a prime candidate to build automatic spectrographs for V-2 rockets. Menzel's interests in the sun and its influence on the Earth's ionosphere blossomed into many new opportunities to expand his domain at Harvard and at its High Altitude Observatory in Colorado. Whipple, equally interested in the upper atmosphere and the interplanetary medium, soon found funding for hyperballistic studies in meteor research; whereas Kuiper and Goldberg exploited their wartime contacts to build new instruments to probe the infrared. These men worked as individual entrepreneurs. Some were limited only by their imaginations, whereas others, at Harvard and Yerkes particularly, remained subject to limits set by their observatory directors. Men like Struve and Shapley would not allow their autonomy as directors to be weakened to the point where they could not control the course of research.

It must be appreciated that Shapley and Struve dominated much of American astronomy in a manner that would be hard to appreciate today. In the years preceding World War II, the American astronomical community consisted of less than 250 active (publishing) members. There were less than two dozen major research centers, and most were at semi-autonomous observatories funded primarily by institutional endowments fueled by corporate philanthropy or local patriots. America by then dominated the world in observational astrophysics, and the course of American astronomy had been defined by relatively few people, all observatory directors.

RESPONDING TO THE CALL

As some form of civilian science foundation was being planned and interminably debated in Congress, an activity that drew Shapley's continued and often heated partisanship, the Office of Naval Research quietly approached the National Research Council to assess the needs of American science and determine how the Navy might help science meet its own postwar goals. Since George Ellery Hale had created the NRC during World War I, it had acted as a coordinator for various attempts to fund science on a national scale (none worked out). Unlike the numerous boards created during wartime to manage and restructure the interface between science and the military, the NRC remained wholly civilian and was, in fact, already a contractor to the ONR. The Navy decided that it was the best agency to develop mechanisms through which each scientific discipline could set its own priorities for research. ONR told the NRC that it wanted each discipline to create a panel of senior scientists who would "stimulate the submission" of proposals from good candidates and also evaluate them. Accordingly, the NRC asked professional societies to create committees to deliberate on how they might spend government money.[11]

ONR pushed hardest in areas most central to its mission, like oceanography, geophysics, and the areas of physics that had proven themselves most valuable to application. Astronomy was a well known commodity as far as navigation and time keeping were concerned, but as a discipline it was farther from Navy interests. Therefore it was one of the later disciplines to be approached by ONR, even though the pace was quite rapid. As news of the formation of the first disciplinary advisory panels spread in 1947, people like Menzel and Whipple, who were familiar with ONR, lobbied for astronomy's inclusion. As a result, Mina Rees, head of ONR's mathematics division, asked Shapley, who had just stepped down as President of the AAS, to describe the needs of his discipline and how those needs could best be represented to ONR, partly to see how well an astronomer's view matched the ONR's vision of patronage. The sole guideline set by Rees was that each discipline would disburse some $50 thousand yearly. This was almost an order of magnitude greater funding than had been managed by the National Academy for astronomy prior to the war, but it was small compared to the individual grants and contracts ONR was writing with the most aggressive individuals and institutions, like Spitzer, Menzel, and Goldberg.

Responding to his own staff's interests as well as to his own, Shapley limited the needs of astronomy to traditional problem areas, paying most attention to those specialties which were, in his opinion, in the greatest need of support, such as galactic and extra-galactic astronomy, "a field which lacks even the remotest connection with military or industrial activity." Ever mindful that the new ONR program was far smaller in scope than the individual grants and contracts the Navy already provided Harvard for solar research, meteor studies and upper air experiments, Shapley noted first that programmatic asteroid orbit studies needed special support — at least one fifth of the total — disbursed by a small committee of orbit specialists. The remaining $40 thousand would best be spent for short term research projects, and, if the NSF failed to materialize before the GI Bill ran out, for supporting graduate students. Shapley envisioned that a committee of astronomers, acting under the NRC and appointed by the AAS, could manage the dispensing of funds. This committee of peers, Shapley argued, had to be given the greatest range of freedom to respond to the needs of the community. Rees had little interest in the details Shapley presented, though his call for a peer-review process and for support for graduate training and post-doctoral support dovetailed nicely with ONR's own ideas. Thus her staff lightly redrafted his proposal and sent it to the AAS in late 1947, asking the Society to form a committee.[12]

Both Struve and Shapley found the Society an excellent platform through which they could determine how the astronomical community would respond to the prospect of government funding on a more general level. The ONR proposal was easily ratified by the Executive Council of the AAS at its 78th meeting in December 1947 at Columbus, Ohio. Struve, succeeding Shapley as president of the Society, became chair of a new "Committee on Astronomy, Advisory to ONR." Bart Bok became vice-chair, and members included Ira S. Bowen (Mount Wilson-Palomar), C. D. Shane (Lick), Lyman Spitzer, Jr. (Princeton), Dirk Brouwer (Yale), and Albert E. Whitford (Wisconsin). With the exception of Bok, who was in every respect standing in for Shapley, they were all observatory directors; only Struve and Shane were members of the Council. Thus, consistent with tradition, observatory directors were once again in control.

Both Rees, of ONR, and R. C. Gibbs, of the NRC, knew how important it was to maintain the hierarchical *status quo* in astronomy; if observatory directors did not play ball and see the program in their own best interests, it was unlikely that rank and file staff members would be able to propose to the ONR. Gibbs therefore supported the membership of the committee and put the program on a fast track, since ONR wanted to establish its program within all the major disciplines before Congress could create the NSF. Gibbs wasted no time calling meetings of the new AAS committee even before the general membership of the Society knew of its formal existence. By February 1948, the AAS announced the program to its members with a call for proposals, and in a matter of weeks, astronomers sent in 32 applications asking for at least $100 thousand in support, twice what was available. In March 1948, the committee divided up the pie, trying to make their funds travel as far as possible, shaving and paring even the best proposals.[13] In its haste to serve its patron, the NRC pushed through this first round of grants to the bewilderment of the new astronomy committee, which resolved in the next year to allow for at least three months' notice.

Notwithstanding his concern that their deliberations had been hasty, Struve regarded community response as "extremely gratifying" and reported later that, "The Committee was impressed by the complete freedom it was given by the ONR." Decisions were based only upon "scientific merit, ability, and experience", as well as upon the degree of encouragement the money would give to smaller institutions as well as for the training of new students. The Committee wanted to aid those smaller astronomical centers "least likely to benefit from large Government contracts and whose work was in serious danger of being slowly starved through lack of adequate support."[14]

The funding made available for this grant program was small compared to the individual grants and contracts ONR maintained with those few astronomers forceful enough to deal competitively with ONR, other military agencies, and soon with the new Atomic Energy Commission. Less than half a dozen were in this category, and therefore were somewhat out of step with those, like Struve, who accepted governmental support for large-scale programs, but remained uncomfortable with its consequences. When Jesse Greenstein's first rocket spectrograph failed, Struve resisted giving him a free hand to continue his Navy contract, which he thought would jeopardize his mainstream research at Yerkes Observatory, and, especially, his teaching. There were as yet very few in astronomy comfortable with spending in the tens to hundreds of thousands of dollars; most found the initial cap of $5 thousand per project set by ONR more than adequate.

Astronomy received and disbursed about the same amount of funding as did the other disciplines, and did so in about the same manner, trying to spread funding as far as possible.[15] The Astronomy committee, however, seemed to be more conservative than most; acting as elites serving a small community, it was the last to introduce a formula for member rotation and thought of itself as a standing committee.[16] It was also one of the most cautious of committees, taking few initiatives in its first year. But the NRC was pleased; as Gibbs advised Detlev Bronk in March 1948:

> I believe we are making very effective progress…these advisory committees are working out very satisfactorily to all concerned. Furthermore, these meetings have served to develop a better understanding among the astronomers on the committee of each other's work and to foster thinking on the over-all needs for astronomical research in the country as a whole.[17]

Gibbs now believed that the astronomers were ready to take the next step. As they had with the other disciplines, Gibbs and his ONR liaison officer asked the astronomers to take on a new but related task, "What were the overall needs of astronomy in the United States?"

THE NEEDS OF ASTRONOMY

Struve needed little encouragement to think globally. He had long worried about astronomy's infrastructure, especially its publications and institutions, and he had already taken strong steps to establish a cooperative observatory scheme between McDonald Observatory, Yerkes, and Indiana University. Thus when asked to estimate the needs of the entire profession, in anticipation of the still-debated NSF, Struve asked Lyman Spitzer to determine how much money astronomers had spent in the past, as a rough estimate of astronomy's present and future needs.

To arrive at an estimate for the cost of maintaining the astronomical research of the nation, Spitzer looked back 25 years to sum up costs of building new observatories since 1923, and added these to estimates of normal operating expenses (exclusive of salaries) of the top dozen astronomical institutions. He found that support for research had increased somewhat in recent years, but the cost of research, especially its instrumentation, had grown much more. Prior to 1940, the estimated peacetime annual expenditure was $1 million, and the annual cost of new observatories, including the 200-inch telescope, was about $400 thousand, averaged over the entire period. Without doubt, Spitzer concluded, "astronomical observatories have constituted about the most expensive item of research in the physical sciences." In each case, private funds built the major instruments that now dominated the astronomical landscape. "The cost of these instruments, together with the special equipment which they require, must be included in any over-all estimate of the expense of astronomical research."[18]

The Committee endorsed Spitzer's estimates, making only a few corrections. Struve left the sums intact and converted them into a proposal asking for $1 million for operations and $400 thousand for equipment per year. Even though the Committee knew that Spitzer's estimate was conservative, neither Bok nor anyone from Harvard commented on the fact that Shapley, less than two years prior, asked Harvard for an equipment budget that was equal to Spitzer's estimate for the entire community. Even Bowen remained quiet, though his own observatory operating budget was one quarter of Spitzer's estimate for the entire community. The Committee evidently was satisfied that it had made a responsible statement, useful for planning for a future not so different than what the past world looked like. Most important, the committee felt that this funding should not be more than supplemental to their traditional sources of support.

Spitzer's assessment lay fallow until late 1949 when the prospect of a National Science Foundation was again bright. In the interim, the Committee continued with its task of evaluating and prioritizing small research grant proposals to ONR. Throughout 1949, the Committee faced many questions and concerns as the NSF bill loomed—they were asked once again, in fact, to help plan astronomy's needs for the new funding agency. Should they request sizable sums for bricks and mortar, going the way of physicists like E. O. Lawrence, who had increased his dependency upon governmental support by a factor of 30 times prewar rates of expenditure? Or should they continue to question the safety of such unprecedented rates of expansion, and opt for a more prudent course?[19]

Doubtful of the permanency of federal support, and fearful that home institutions would be only too happy to give over their traditional responsibilities, the Committee always maintained a vigilance lest the program get out of hand. It always demanded that home universities of proposers carry their fair share of the research support burden, and not get comfortable with soft money support for staffing. In January 1949, it warned that, "The Committee does not normally wish to recommend the payment of the salary of an employee of an observatory, nor does it look favorably upon the payment of a salary of an individual who, in effect, becomes a full time employee." In that year, the Committee was proud to be able to hand back money to the Navy: It only approved $71 thousand out of the available $80 thousand that had been allotted.[20]

The leadership of the Committee viewed fiscal conservatism as a moral duty, especially since it wished to guard against becoming overly dependent upon ONR. But the Committee also began to face increased demands and pressures from its constituents and their institutions: there was talk of interdisciplinary funding for research in new fields, especially from the AEC for nuclear astrophysics. And there were new demands from home institutions for larger overhead limits. Overhead was still a very new idea, but it was a necessary evil given the state of the profession, since support for training and manpower had to carry with it considerations for resuscitating campus infrastructures. Shapley's outcry in 1946 about the hunger of the military and industry for scientific talent was all the louder now because, during the war, little or no graduate education took place at the major institutions. In 1950, Leo Goldberg told C. D. Shane that although they had some 15 graduate students in residence at Michigan at that time, they had not yet awarded a single Ph.D. in the postwar years.[21] Bowen reported that Caltech had not awarded any Ph.D.s since 1945 and that the first in astronomy were not expected until 1951.[22] Bowen, a physicist and student of Millikan, appreciated as well that astronomical training was terribly insular. He had helped to bring Jesse Greenstein from Yerkes to Caltech to begin a vigorous training program in astrophysics based firmly upon physics, but it was just barely underway and needed more support.[23] Even though it recognized that replenishing the manpower base was critical, the Committee continued to evaluate proposals primarily upon scientific merit and the seniority of the applicant, with lesser priority given to how it might aid graduate training, although this concern would appear again the next time astronomers came to ponder their needs for the NSF.

Planning for the NSF put all these issues into sharper focus: should ONR and NSF support only short term projects, or long term programs — it was all a question of dependency. The committee continually resisted increased dependency on any federal institution. At their March 1949, meeting Spitzer brought up the bricks and mortar question again:

> Are we convinced, for example, that supporting [small continuing projects] would be more beneficial to astronomy than the organization and continuing support of a spectroscopic observatory in the southern hemisphere?[24]

Spitzer asked the Committee to consider if it was ready to propose long-term commitments to ONR, or did it wish to remain merely reactive to short-term interests? Whitford, in response, feared the encroachment of vested interests:

> While no observatory or university can be guaranteed a promise of support from the Office of Naval Research beyond a single contract period, there is a tendency for moral obligations to play a role, and something approaching a vested interest could easily be established.[25]

For the present, Whitford preferred supporting new and fresh starts; short term projects, up to three years, deserved priority, because ONR would probably be willing to see them through. Leaving Spitzer's deeper question aside, Whitford felt it was more important to consider the community's real present needs. He called for a statement to ONR asking for consideration of some longer term grants to five years, in light of the long-term character of many astronomical projects.

Whitford's concerns were echoed by the Committee in following years, and more than once were brought up during meetings of the AAS Executive Council. In 1950, when Struve handed over the Committee to C. D. Shane, Shane resurrected Spitzer's 1948 memorandum and reformulated it into a draft proposal for the not-yet-created NSF. Shane's committee felt, above all, that the new NSF needed the same sort of guidance now being given to the ONR to avoid the "danger of unwise dictation of the astronomical program" by "officials no longer directly connected with astronomical research," referring to those who might once have been engaged in scientific research, but now were bureaucrats administering to science.[26]

Combining the types of support ONR had provided all of astronomy, Shane envisioned three categories of NSF grants: small ones similar to those now being granted by ONR; large projects that promote "new methods of approach to observational problems" and third, the procurement of "continually improved equipment" along with support for 20 graduate fellowships and $20 thousand for astronomical publications. All totalled, his funding request came to $520 thousand, similar to Spitzer's 1948 assessment for equipment alone. Shane argued, "It is evident that the budget proposed here for support of astronomy by the National Science Foundation would provide only a fractional increase in the funds spent annually on astronomy in this country."[27]

But this was his point. Shane and his new committee asked only for equipment grants and made a conscious decision to keep the government out of operations, fearing that universities would be only too happy to "use the available government money to escape the expenditures for astronomy that they would otherwise make." The proven, trusted sources could not be allowed to wander.

PRESERVING TRADITIONAL VALUES

Many of the original concerns American astronomers held continued to dog the Committee as it deliberated over its report to the NSF: the loss of autonomy and control, the fear that home institutions would lessen support when they saw that astronomy could attract outside funding, and concerns that the Committee was not paying enough attention to new technologies, such as electronics, upper air research with rockets and radio astronomy. Whipple and Goldberg argued that Shane's cost estimates were seriously below what was really needed, and worried as well that if the military ceased to fund some of the most innovative research techniques there would be no backup by the NSF. Many new programs would dry up overnight. Greenstein, especially concerned that there was a serious gap between traditional optical astronomers and the new radio astronomers, who came largely out of radio engineering and ionospheric research, expressed the concern shared by other committee members in February 1950 that radio astronomy was a field "in which astronomers have perhaps missed some major opportunities for effective cooperation with ionosphere and electronic[s] research." He hoped that the Committee would encourage ONR or NSF to hold symposia that would bring the two communities together.[28] But this did not happen for several years.

Overall, even though no one wished to replace the successful funding patterns that had brought America to prominence in astronomy in the first half of the 20th century, everyone knew that unless the infrastructure itself was supported, through continued university-based largess or at the worst through overhead on direct grants for long-term programs, the discipline itself would fracture. Small fissures grew into fault-lines between factions on the Committee and successive Presidents of the Society. Alfred Joy, who succeeded Struve in 1949 as President, was emphatic that support for publication costs should be doubled; he and other senior members of the Executive Committee felt that the support of *The Astronomical Journal* was a first priority. Younger members of the Committee were less concerned with their seniors' desire to spread the funding among as many small projects as possible and did not worry if the number of fellowships outstripped the number of professional positions available. They pushed for growth and remained uncomfortable with the frugality the leadership maintained.[29]

Debate over all these issues heated up in the spring of 1950 and prompted the Committee to use the June meeting of the AAS at Bloomington as an open forum to air differences over how astronomers wanted to express their needs to the new NSF. Whipple by now had broken ranks with the senior leadership, arguing that the astronomy report was too timid. Closer than most of his colleagues to Washington politics, he feared that once the NSF was operational, the far larger grants from ONR and elsewhere in the military would be cut off. Unless they impressed the NSF with their real needs at the outset, they were likely going to be left out in the cold. In every way Whipple agreed with Greenstein and Struve's insistence that their "budget must be an honest one" but for Whipple this meant far more than merely competent proposals. It meant taking chances, experimenting with new technologies and new institutional ways to pursue astronomy. Knowing that new technologies were not considered under the present draft proposal to NSF because the Committee decided to ignore them, Whipple called for a poll of astronomers to find out what they "would actually be able to use efficiently."[30]

Whipple's concerns were aired but then passed over by the Committee and by those who attended the forum who favored Shane's pruned budget. The single concern that held astronomers back from a bolder vision for NSF, one even Whipple shared, was fear of government dominance. In suggesting that they ask for more than they really needed, Whipple admitted to a lack of "mutual confidence between the [governmental] donors and the [astronomical] recipients" adding:

> Such a course is an obvious one in a University, where there is a longtime contact between the same individuals. My own reaction has been that in Washington it is generally assumed that all budget requests are padded thoroughly...[31]

Ultimately, conservatism won out once again. In their final report to the NSF, the Committee made it perfectly clear that they would not promote anything that would reduce traditional university support for astronomy. Some university administrators had already made demands for more overhead, which served as a warning to the Committee that they had as much to fear from within their own institutions as they did from the government:

There is a real danger that in the course of time observatories might become so dependent on federal funds that they would lose their freedom of action. If for any reason these funds were withdrawn they might suffer a great disorganization.[32]

In late July 1950, Shane submitted the Committee's report to Gibbs, who appreciated the astronomers' effort even though the new Foundation was still very far from being operational. Gibbs also issued what was a rather sullen report on the recently passed NSF bill, which only vindicated the conservatism Shane and the Committee harbored and astronomers' deep conviction that only university support was trustworthy. Shapley had been an ardent supporter of the original NSF. But now, with delays and downsizing, neither he nor his colleagues wished to depend upon it.[33] As historian Daniel Kevles has pointed out, in the four years of debate before its birth, the NSF concept went from being the "government's chief sponsor of fundamental research" to being "only a puny partner in an institutionally pluralist federal research establishment."[34] Thus the Committee felt it served the astronomical community well by its insistence upon the *status quo*. More telling, Gibbs reported back to Shane that the ONR panel itself still had a life of its own. It could plan to meet in January 1951, immediately after the Haverford meeting of the Society, to distribute another $75 thousand.

With the emergence of the NSF in the early 1950s, which was based largely on the ONR model, the scale of the enterprise did not change appreciably. In its first years, there were repeated calls for the transfer of the ONR small grant program to NSF. When ONR Chief Scientist Alan Waterman transferred to the NSF, he predicted that the ONR program might end. And in September 1952, as Gibbs introduced a newly reformed Astronomy Committee Advisory to ONR to other members of the NRC division, he noted that, "It is likely that the function of this Committee will be assumed by NSF after the current year."[35] Greenstein, making the transition from ONR committee member to NSF committee member in 1952, justified his move by the rumors that with the NSF a reality, ONR support for astronomy would dry up; he looked forward to strengthening the relationship of the NSF to the AAS.[36] Thus most scientists expected the ONR program to cease, but it did not, and it lasted for many years, continuing with its small grants program, as well as larger equipment grants for radio astronomy and other programs in instrument development. After limping through the late 1950s, the ONR program blossomed by a factor of ten in the post-Sputnik years and was only ended by the Mansfield Amendment at the end of the 1960s.[37]

FACING THE INEVITABLE

The longevity of the ONR small grants program and the Society's acceptance of its apparent *laissez-faire* attitude reveals overall the conservatism senior astronomers harbored, mainly observatory directors, who were comfortable with pre-war elite patronage that centered control in themselves and in the predominance of optical astronomy. The patrilineal nature of the community had over the years, partly by its observatory-based structure and partly by its small size (since the 1930s it had produced an average of only 10 Ph.D.'s per year and an annual growth rate of some

4%, which did not change significantly through the 1950s), maintained a strong sense of community among astronomers that was hard to break. Even a younger astronomer like William Baum at Mount Wilson, who had trained under Ira Bowen and had worked in Richard Tousey's rocket group at the Naval Research Laboratory at the end of the war, thought of the astronomical community in 1959 as a well-defined, more or less homogeneous "small family." And many astronomers throughout the 1950s still followed Shapley's narrowly focussed concept of astronomical research: work performed in optical observatories defined along traditional lines.[38]

However, by the mid 1950s, forces were also at play that were destined to break up the family tradition in favor of new patterns of behavior and greater levels of national planning. Partly due to the rapid growth of radio astronomy, made possible by a quickening influx of radio engineers and physicists and of large sums of money, competition for resources rapidly increased and new voices made appeals to NSF for astronomical research support. This raised the question of who was actually in control of those resources and who would speak for the astronomical community itself, if it indeed was to remain as a coherent body of workers. Although the ONR maintained its two-tiered program, continuing its small grants program and its larger individual and institutional interests, the NSF had already greatly expanded its role in planning for "large-scale facilities" by creating two new committees to begin detailed planning for national astronomical institutions for radio and optical astronomy.[39]

The NSF initiative, prompted both by its own internal mission and by the impassioned lobbying of both physicists and astronomers, was not happily received by the senior astronomers on the original NSF Committee for Astronomy (those who led the traditional optical community) who had already rejected a proposal to consider funding a cooperative photoelectric observatory. Now they regarded NSF's formation of these new committees as an attempt to gain control of what they perceived was their responsibility. In response to NSF's actions, Struve, still a leader of the traditional optical community, at last responded to what Goldberg and Whipple had been concerned about all along: if astronomers representing the traditional, dominant optical community did not unite to plan their own futures in the new realms opened up by radio, electronics, and computers, NSF would do it for them: "Our traditional caution has led us away from a bold stand for what astronomy needs," Struve warned in January 1955; now was the time to organize and to reverse what he feared would lead to a real fracture in the community.[40]

At last Struve sensed the true meaning behind Manny Piore's 1947 warning that science had to look out for its own interests. He now saw that what he feared about government gaining control with ONR funding might actually happen if the NSF were allowed to make decisions. As Piore warned, astronomers had to act forcefully to reestablish their common voice. Struve and Whipple thus called for a meeting of the 3 overlapping NSF astronomy-related committees, to come to terms and to make a unified statement about needs and goals. By the end of 1955, they decided upon a five-year plan that supported both radio and optical astronomy.

Summarizing the results of the conference committee's deliberations, Albert Whitford held his banquet audience at attention at the November 1955 meetings of the AAS in Troy, New York. Their plan included the establishment of a site for a national optical observatory and the building of a first generation of new telescopes, planning for building far larger telescopes, and most definitely the creation of some new type of "cooperative association of universities" that would represent "the eastern and midwestern sections of the country which would be the most frequent users of the telescope." Whitford did not have to say what everyone already knew, that a national facility for radio astronomy was already well started and would be administered by something other than a traditional astronomical institution. But he did want to reemphasize to the rank and file of the Society that, although the time had come to act on behalf of optical astronomers, the community's leaders were not going to let the NSF forget its now-traditional small grants program based upon the ONR model.[41]

> It does seem significant to me, however, that astronomers have been asked to sit down and think about what they need in order to make their science a strong and healthy one in this country. The recommendations that have been made by the panel for which I am reporting, are admittedly only a part of the answer. Certainly the support of short-term research projects by annual grants must continue undiminished, and the National Science Foundation has assured us that it has no other intention.[42]

No matter how hard it tried to maintain a sense of family among American astronomers, assuring everyone that they would share according to their needs in the support ONR and NSF had been providing, successive leaders of the AAS realized by the end of the 1950s that the structure and scale of pre-war astronomy in America held little relevance for the future. Even the Society could no longer exist as a unitary body as more and more specialities demanded larger investments in manpower and technical support and pushed for a greater portion of a rapidly expanding pie in the post-Sputnik era. The process initiated by the ONR and expanded by the NSF led astronomers into new realms of coordinated planning but they also provided the means through which factions within astronomy could grow to the point of establishing new specialties that could exist, in theory at least, quite independent of the Society. How the Society grew to accommodate these initiatives will be the subject of later chapters.

ACKNOWLEDGEMENTS

This chapter is a distillation of a much longer unpublished study of the influence of ONR and NSF on astronomy. An earlier version of this paper was read and commented on by David van Keuren, Frank Edmondson, Jesse L. Greenstein, Leo Goldberg, Lyman Spitzer, A. E. Whitford, Fred Whipple, Paul Forman, Karl Hufbauer, Woody Sullivan, Allan Needell, and Ron Doel. A longer version, in Historical Studies in the Physical and Biological Sciences **28** (1998), examines astronomers' concerns for autonomy. I am indebted to Frank Edmondson for providing archival material on the origins of the NSF program and national observatory, which is now embodied in his book *AURA and its US National Observatories* (Cambridge, 1997). Archival materials are from National Research Council Central Files, National Academy of Sciences Archives (NRC/CF); Fred Whipple Papers, Smithsonian Institution Archives (FLW/SIA); D. H. Menzel Papers, Harvard University Archives, HUG 4567.5.2 (DHM/HUA); Ira S. Bowen Papers, Mount Wilson Archives, Huntington Library (ISB/HL); Vannevar Bush Papers, Library of Congress (VB/LC); S. Chandrasekhar Papers, University of Chicago

Library (SC/UCL); Jesse Greenstein Papers, California Institute of Technology (JGP/ CITA); C. D. Shane Papers, Lick Archives (CDS/LA); Berkeley Astronomy Department Papers, Struve/NSF folder, Bancroft Library (BA/BUA); American Astronomical Society Records, AIP Niels Bohr Library (AAS/AIP); W. O. Roberts Papers, University of Colorado Archives (WOR/UC); and Historical Office, National Science Foundation (NSF). Oral histories from the American Institute of Physics collection (AIP) are also cited, with acknowledgement.

THE MODERN SOCIETY: CHANGES IN DEMOGRAPHICS

David H. DeVorkin and Paul Routly

CHANGES IN OFFICERS OF THE SOCIETY

By the early 1950s, vestiges of the old Society were still strongly felt; it was still centered on major observatories and their directors. But many pressures for reform brought about some significant changes in the way the Society conducted business. Nominations were now done by committee rather than at the meeting itself, but it was typical for the Nominating Committee to present a ballot with single names for each major office, rather than a slate. This procedure was generally followed until some members objected in the late 1950s and the rules were changed. Here we present an overview of the changing demographics of the Society: who was elected to lead, who could become a member, where meetings were held, and how the structure of the meetings changed over time.

The average age for Presidents over all time was 58 years at election, and their professional age (age since attainment of highest degree) was some 32 years. Vice-Presidents averaged a bit younger: 52 at election at a professional age of 25 years. The age ranges for both categories was quite broad: the youngest Presidents were elected in their late 40s and the oldest in their early 70s, with the mode near 58. The youngest Vice-President was George Ellery Hale who was only 31 at election, but most were elected in their early 40s through their 60s. The mode for Vice-Presidents was 45 years. These numbers were relatively constant over time, but after the 1950s average ages at election did drop a bit.

Six Presidents classified themselves (from Who's Who-type entries) as theorists, 22 as observers, and 7 as mixed. For Vice-Presidents, the numbers were 10, 69, and 5. The most popular specialty among both offices was stellar astronomy and spectroscopy. Institutions most frequently providing Presidents and Vice-Presidents were also among the largest in the field: Lick (5, 5), Harvard (4, 4), Mount Wilson (3, 7), Princeton (3, 4) and Wisconsin (3, 4). Six women held office as President or Vice-President, the first in each category being Margaret Burbidge (President, 1976) and Charlotte Moore Sitterly (Vice-President, 1958).

By far the greatest number of Presidents and Vice-Presidents were observatory directors at time of election (19 and 41 respectively); those who were full professors and not observatory directors numbered 10 and 23, respectively. Three officers classified themselves primarily as physicists (B. Burke, R. Tousey, and E. Salpeter) and about ten included physics as one of several specialty categories. Over time, those elected President and Vice-President migrated from a dominance by observatory directors to a more general mix of department chairs at major universities and senior professors. This was in fact a reflection of the changing nature of the discipline itself, as the power base moved more to university campuses, and as more and more departments of astronomy were created, mainly at the state university level.

Most Presidents and Vice-Presidents were American by birth (25, 58). Canada (2, 4), England (2, 6), and the Netherlands (2, 3) followed. Others were born in Australia (0, 2), Austria (0, 1), China (1, 1), France (0, 1), Germany (1, 1), India, Israel, Mexico and Puerto Rico (0, 1), Russia (1, 2), Scotland (0, 1), and Sweden (1, 0). Only one person traditionally classified as an amateur was elected to high office; R. R. McMath was President from 1952 to 1954. See Tables 5, 6 and 7.

CHANGES IN MEMBERSHIP

Although the question of the status of amateur astronomers and creating different forms of membership arose sporadically in the first half-decade of the Society's life (*see* Rothenberg and Williams this volume, page 40), the issue of "Classes of Membership" arose seriously in the early 1950s. Donald Menzel was asked to chair a committee to deliberate on how to broaden the membership profile, and reported at the 87th meeting in Victoria in June 1952 that the committee could not agree on much. But they were unanimous not to open any door to large-scale admission of amateurs: "The committee feels that any changes made with the aim of increasing funds should in no way alter the basic structure of the Society or the character of its meetings." Ironically, the Victoria meeting was held in conjunction with the ASP, which had always been open to amateurs. In distinction, Menzel's committee and the Council agreed that only those amateurs deemed "highly qualified" would be considered. The class of membership called 'Patron' however, was approved: Patrons were elected in recognition of the gifts and support they provided, and would not be judged by their scientific contributions. Election would "be based on financial rather than scientific contributions."[1] Patrons and corporate members were sought out by the Society; by the late 1950s corporations and commercial patrons had the right to exhibit at meetings of the Society. Especially

TABLE 1. *Past Presidents of the American Astronomical Society.*

Simon Newcomb	1899–1905	C. S. Beals	1962–1964
Edward C. Pickering	1905–1919	Leo Goldberg	1964–1966
Frank Schlesinger	1919–1922	Bengt Strömgren	1966–1968
W. W. Campbell	1922–1925	Albert E. Whitford	1968–1970
G. C. Comstock	1925–1928	Martin Schwarzschild	1970–1972
Ernest W. Brown	1928–1931	Bart J. Bok	1972–1974
Walter S. Adams	1931–1934	Robert P. Kraft	1974–1976
Henry Norris Russell	1934–1937	E. Margaret Burbidge	1976–1978
Robert G. Aitken	1937–1940	Ivan R. King	1978–1980
Joel Stebbins	1940–1943	David Heeschen	1980–1982
Harlow Shapley	1943–1946	Arthur D. Code	1982–1984
Otto Struve	1946–1949	Maarten Schmidt	1984–1986
Alfred H. Joy	1949–1952	Bernard F. Burke	1986–1988
Robert R. McMath	1952–1954	Donald E. Osterbrock	1988–1990
Donald H. Menzel	1954–1956	John N. Bahcall	1990–1992
Paul Merrill	1956–1958	Sidney Wolff	1992–1994
G. M. Clemence	1958–1960	Frank H. Shu	1994–1996
Lyman Spitzer, Jr.	1960–1962	Andrea K. Dupree	1996–1998

after 1957, many new corporate members were recruited from the optical, electronic and aerospace industries. In 1960, oil and commercial airlines were excluded but aircraft industries were included "because of their growing interest in astronautics."[2]

The standards maintained by the Society, and its general lack of attention to education, both professional and popular, bred insularity, which was noticed by the National Science Foundation in the mid-1950s. At a time when the Society was already feeling pressure to limit the lengths of papers and avoid simultaneous sessions (see below), the NSF created a panel for the study of the relation of astronomy to the general public. The panel found that the public was not well informed, and that the

TABLE 2. *Past Vice-Presidents of the American Astronomical Society.*

George Ellery Hale	1899–1901; 1901–1908	S. Chandrasekhar	1956–1958
W. W. Campbell	1902–1912; 1915–1916; 1916–1919	A. N. Vyssotsky	1957–1959
G. C. Comstock	1908–1911; 1912–1915; 1919–1920	Charlotte Sitterly	1958–1960
E. B. Frost	1911–1912	Leo Goldberg	1959–1961
Frank Schlesinger	1912–1916; 1916–1919	Guillermo Haro	1960–1962
Walter S. Adams	1919–1921	Fred T. Haddock	1961–1963
John A. Miller	1921–1923	Ira S. Bowen	1962–1964
Henry Norris Russell	1922–1924	John S. Hall	1963–1965
Ernest W. Brown	1923–1925	Richard Tousey	1964–1966
Heber D. Curtis	1924–1926	A. E. Whitford	1965–1967
S. A. Mitchell	1925–1927	S. W. McCuskey	1966–1968
A. O. Leuschner	1926–1928	Martin Schwarzschild	1967–1969
J. S. Plaskett	1927–1929	W. W. Morgan	1968–1970
V. M. Slipher	1928–1930	David S. Heeschen	1969–1971
Robert G. Aitken	1929–1931	Bart J. Bok	1970–1971
Joel Stebbins	1930–1932	Morton S. Roberts	1971–1972
C. G. Abbot	1931–1933	Edwin S. Salpeter	1971–1973
Benjamin Boss	1932–1934	E. Margaret Burbidge	1972–1974
Harlow Shapley	1933–1935	Victor M. Blanco	1973–1975
C. A. Chant	1934–1936	Arthur A. Hoag	1974–1976
Frederick Slocum	1935–1937	Donald E. Osterbrock	1975–1977
R. S. Dugan	1936–1938	Arthur D. Code	1976–1978
Frank E. Ross	1937–1939	Harlan J. Smith	1977–1979
Philip Fox	1938–1940	Leonard Searle	1978–1980
Edwin P. Hubble	1939–1941	George Wallerstein	1979–1981
H. R. Morgan	1940–1942	Frank Kerr	1980–1982
Otto Struve	1941–1943	Ray Weymann	1981–1983
J. H. Moore	1942–1944	Michael J. S. Belton	1982–1984
Robert R. McMath	1943–1945	Anne P. Cowley	1983–1985
J. A. Pearce	1944–1946	John A. Graham	1984–1986
Alfred H. Joy	1945–1947	Gart Westerhout	1985–1987
Donald H. Menzel	1946–1948	Andrea K. Dupree	1986–1988
Paul W. Merrill	1947–1949	Stephen E. Strom	1987–1989
Fred Whipple	1948–1950	J. Roger Angel	1987–1990
Dirk Brouwer	1949–1951	Frank H. Shu	1988–1991
C. S. Beals	1950–1952	Harvey D. Tananbaum	1989–1992
C. D. Shane	1951–1953	Paul W. Hodge	1990–1993
G. M. Clemence	1952–1954	James E. Hesser	1991–1994
Seth B. Nicholson	1953–1955	Donald B. Campbell	1992–1995
Robert M. Petrie	1954–1956	France A. Cordova	1993–1996
Jesse L. Greenstein	1955–1957	Jonathan E. Grindlay	1994–1997
		Neta A. Bahcall	1995–1998

TABLE 3. *Past Secretaries of the American Astronomical Society.*

George C. Comstock	1899–1909
W. J. Hussey	1909–1915
Philip Fox	1912–1918
Joel Stebbins	1918–1927
R. S. Dugan	1927–1937
John C. Duncan	1937–1940
Dean B. McLaughlin	1940–1946
C. M. Huffer	1946–1955
J. Allen Hynek	1955–1961
Harlan J. Smith (Act.)	1961–1962
George C. McVittie	1961–1970
Laurence W. Frederick (Act.)	1969–1970
Laurence W. Frederick	1970–1980
Charles Tolbert (Act.)	1972–1973
Arlo U. Landolt	1980–1989
Roger A. Bell	1989–1995
Arlo U. Landolt	1995–

AAS was doing little to help the situation. Presented with this fact, the Council, composed of members like Menzel, Edmondson, Spitzer, and J. Allen Hynek, expressed its concern, knowing full well that "the future of astronomy, its support, and the support of science in general, by government agencies, by industry, or by individuals, depends in large part upon how well astronomers themselves interpret their science to the general public." The Council added that it "deplore[d]" the stigma associated with popularization and wanted to erase any such feelings from its membership.[3] The Council, however, took no definite action at the time to reverse the situation.

At the time, the Society ranked educators far lower than researchers. The Society had yet to define its role in astronomy education in any meaningful fashion (*see* Fraknoi and Wentzel this volume, page 194). And as one can easily discern from the listings of Presidents and Vice-Presidents, each was distinguished primarily as a researcher;

TABLE 4. *Past Treasurers of the American Astronomical Society.*

Charles L. Doolittle	1899–1912
Annie Jump Cannon	1912–1919
Benjamin Boss	1919–1932
Frank C. Jordan	1932–1941
Keivin Burns	1941–1946
J. J. Nassau	1946–1954
Frank K. Edmondson	1954–1975
William E. Howard, III	1975–1977
Harold F. Weaver (Act.)	1977–1978
Harold F. Weaver	1978–1987
Leonard V. Kuhi	1987–1988
Harold F. Weaver (Act.)	1988
C. Robert O'Dell	1988–1996
Leonard V. Kuhi	1996–

TABLE 5. *Distribution of AAS Presidents and Vice-Presidents by Position at Election.*

Position	P	VP	Position	P	VP
Associate Professor	0	1	Head Astronomer	1	1
Astronomer	2	10	Observatory Director	19	41
Astrophysicist	0	1	Physicist	0	2
Director	0	2	Scientist	0	1
Dominion Astronomer	1	1	Senior Astrophysicist	1	1
Full Professor	10	23	Super. Naut. Al.	1	0

Number of AAS Presidents and Vice-Presidents by Country of Birth.

Country	P	VP	Country	P	VP
Australia	0	2	Israel	0	1
Austria	0	1	Mexico	0	1
Canada	2	4	Netherlands	1	2
China	1	1	Puerto Rico	0	1
England	2	6	Russia	1	2
France	0	1	Scotland	0	1
Germany	1	1	Sweden	1	0
Holland	1	1	United States	25	58
India	0	1			

although many were gifted and memorable mentors and teachers, their election to office was for their contribution to research.[4]

The first effort to expand the Society's venue beyond the strictly defined borders of astronomy came in 1957. At that time the Council approved a suggestion that the Society become an affiliate of the Institute of Radio Engineers so that Society members interested in radio technology could be affiliates of the IRE and receive their publications.[5] Radio astronomy was becoming more and more visible at Society meetings, as was southern hemisphere astronomy. The Council discussed the ramifications of a National Research Council proposal to develop southern hemisphere science in August 1959, and began to organize a protest to keep the radio bands important to astronomers open.[6] Clearly, special interests among the membership were making their voices heard through the Council by this time.

A milestone in opening up membership to a broader population came in the Spring of 1960 when Society President Gerald Clemence appointed a committee headed by Lyman Spitzer to deliberate again over classes of membership, especially to create a "junior" membership category. Members had been complaining that many new training programs were being created and more students were flowing into astronomy now, and there had been more nominations of serious young amateur astronomers and students, but most had been turned down: "The issues concern the balance between having untried young people in the Society, with the possibility of the emergence of a large floating population, and of discouraging good talent. The President spoke to this point and stated that he wished that 'there was something that we might do for undergraduates beside slapping them in the face — and we have been doing that for many years.'"[7] Margaret Burbidge volunteered to find out how the

TABLE 6. *Distribution of AAS Presidents and Vice-Presidents by Primary Field at Election.*

Primary Field	P	VP	Primary Field	P	VP
Astronomical Spectro.	4	11	Planetary Astronomy	0	2
Astrophysics	2	3	Positional Astronomy	3	2
Celestial Mechanics	2	3	Radio Astronomy	2	3
Dble, Eclip, & Var Stars	2	6	Solar Astronomy	2	7
Galactic Astronomy	2	7	Solar System Astronomy	0	3
Interstellar Astronomy	2	2	Spectroscopy	1	6
Lunar Astronomy	1	1	Stellar Astronomy	6	12
Photometry	5	7	Theoretical Astronomy	0	3
Physics	0	2	X-Ray Astronomy	0	2

Royal Astronomical Society handled the matter. Meanwhile, until Spitzer's committee did its work, the nomination of students such as Harry Crull, Jr., were tabled.

Spitzer reported favorably at the next meeting of the Society, in Mexico City in August 1960. He proposed two new classes of membership: Junior, for those under 26 years of age, and Associate, for those over 26, who were not professional astronomers, but who were "seriously interested in the advancement of astronomy" either as graduate students or advanced amateurs. His report led to a vigorous discussion since some on the Council feared that amateurs "and other hobbyists" would dilute the quality of the membership. Menzel noted that there were no amateur physicists: "Our problem is different because of the wide emotional appeal of astronomy to many classes of people." The majority remained with Spitzer and agreed to amend the

TABLE 7. *Distribution of AAS Presidents and Vice-Presidents by Institution at Election.*

Institution	P	VP	Institution	P	VP
Adler Planetarium	0	1	MIT	1	0
Allegheny	1	2	Mt. Wilson	3	7
Arizona	0	4	Nat. Opt. Astr. Obs.	0	1
Berkeley	2	2	NRAO	1	2
Bureau of Standards	0	1	NRL	0	1
Cal Tech	1	1	Ob. Astron. Nac.	0	1
Case	0	1	Pennsylvania State	0	1
Cerro Tololo	0	2	Princeton	3	4
Chicago	0	2	San Diego	1	1
Cornell	0	2	SAO	1	3
Dominion (Canada)	1	5	Stromlo	1	0
Dudley Obs.	0	1	Swarthmore	0	1
Harvard	4	4	Texas	0	1
Inst. for Adv. Study	2	0	Toronto	0	1
Kitt Peak	0	2	USNO	2	3
Lick	5	5	Virginia	0	2
Lowell	0	2	Washington	0	2
Maryland	0	1	Wesleyan	0	1
Massachusetts	0	1	Wisconsin	3	4
Michigan	1	3	Yale	1	2
			Yerkes	1	4

bylaws to create these new classes of membership. A leading concern of Council members favoring Spitzer's plan was that there was then a national deficit of qualified astronomers for positions opening in universities, government and industry. Clemence made this point and recommended further study of ways to reverse the "national shortage of astronomers." The issue was referred to the Committee on Education.[8]

At the next meeting, at the Hayden Planetarium in New York City in December 1960, where education was appropriately highlighted, the amended bylaws admitting Junior and Associate members was ratified, and the general annual dues were raised to $5.00. One result of this change can easily be seen in the subsequent growth in the membership of the Society, illustrated in Figure 1.

Even though the Council rejected outright a suggestion raised in 1960 that the Society establish a higher class of "fellow," in fact from its beginning distinguished foreign astronomers were made honorary AAS members. Sir David Gill was the first to be elected at the 14th meeting in August 1912, followed by Arthur Auwers and Oscar Backlund in the next year. J. C. Kapteyn was named in 1915 and Frank Dyson in 1920. Most of the earliest were observational astronomers, although Willem de Sitter was elected in 1931 and Einstein in 1933. The first non-European to be elected was Hisashi Kimura in 1936, followed by Megh Nad Saha in 1946. As of 1949, all honorary members were male.

WHERE THE AAS MEETS

One of the larger problems facing the Council in its first few years of existence was where to hold the next meeting. In the early years, freedom to travel was not readily

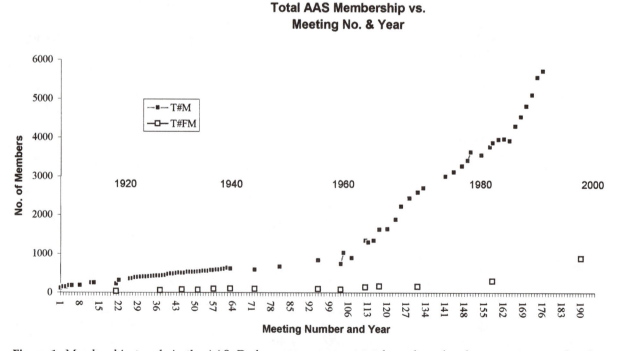

Figure 1. Membership trends in the AAS. Dark squares represent total number of males; open squares, females. Membership numbers derived from a variety of sources, including AAS records, AIP membership statistics, AAS Council records. The AIP and AAS statistics differed by up to 10% in the 1980s, possibly due to different polling techniques or to the inclusion or exclusion of corporate members and affiliates.

available to the rank and file; observatory directors represented their institutions. Lick's W. W. Campbell was able to travel to New York City, but rarely would a member of his staff appear farther afield than the Midwest. In its first two decades of life, therefore, the concentration of meetings reflected the geographical distribution of members. The majority of the meetings were held in the East (Mid-Atlantic states) and Northeast (the New England states and New York) (13 total); next came the northern Midwest (9), followed by the Southeast (Atlantic seaboard states), the West and Canada (1 each). None were held in the deep South, the Rocky Mountain, or Southwest regions.

This pattern remained relatively stable during the next three decades, from 1921 to 1950. Now the Northeast dominated as the region of choice, followed by the Midwest, and the East. Three meetings were held in the West and in Canada, reflecting a slight strengthening. Many of the more outlying meetings were held in conjunction with the AAAS.

The greatest change came in the second half of the century where the distribution was more equal among the identified regions. Air travel was becoming more common, and individuals gained freedom to travel provided by governmental funding (The Office of Naval Research starting in the late 1940s, the National Science Foundation in the 1950s, and NASA in the 1960s). See Figure 2.

CHANGES IN MEETING STRUCTURE

When the Society was small, at least small enough to meet either in Pickering's salon in 1898, or in the comfortable confines of the lounge in the Union Building on the Indiana University campus in December 1937, as Frank Edmondson recalls in this volume, the meetings were unparalleled. No one missed anything. Typically the Council would meet in private before the paper sessions, to be sure everything was in order to ratify the program, and to conduct its business. Sometimes, when there was much business to conduct, the Council met throughout the three-day meetings, between the paper sessions. Gradually, the Council confined itself to meeting the day before the paper sessions would start, and then would report to the membership.

The two classes of papers George Comstock created in the early 1920s, 'communications' of less than ten minutes, and 'papers' less than 30 minutes, were never rigidly enforced. Gradually, as more and more papers were submitted — according to the bylaws a member could not be denied the right to present a paper, even two or more — the pressure on time limits grew. The December 1937 Bloomington meeting may have been the first where a mechanical timer was used to enforce limits, but it probably was needed long before then.

By the 87th meeting in Victoria, in June 1952 in conjunction with the Astronomical Society of the Pacific, all papers were limited to ten minutes. Any member who wanted to give a second paper had to wait till everyone spoke, and absentee papers, read by proxy, were placed last.[9] The meetings were still running all unparalleled sessions, but the pressure was rising, and a number of members evidently felt that their presentations were given short shrift. There were calls for accommodations to allow everyone the time they wanted to speak.

A year later, at the Boulder meeting in August 1953, the Council was presented with a new paper session plan as its first order of business and was not happy to see that it contained parallel sessions to allow everyone the time they requested in the three-day format. Council vetoed the plan, trying to compress the sessions by limiting time on papers by absent authors and second papers by authors present — many would be read by title only.[10] They managed to squeak through, but again their decision was not a happy one. Not everyone could afford to travel to meetings at a time when there were little or no institutional travel funds or grants from NSF or ONR, and before NASA existed. So the absentee papers, mainly by junior members, were not given the exposure they deserved.[11]

At the 90th meeting in Nashville in December 1953, the Council knew well in advance that the pressure would not be great, because not many astronomers would show up. But wise to the problem, they knew they had to plan for the 91st meeting in

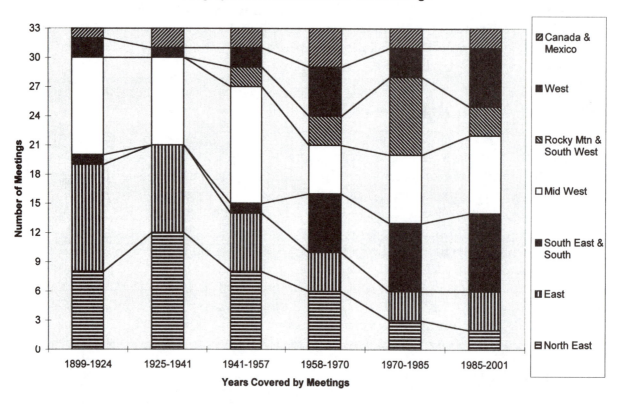

Figure 2. The geographical distribution of AAS meetings, taken in equal lots of 33 for the time periods illustrated, reveals that over the decades, the original dominance of meetings in the East and North East has eroded in favor of a greater proportion of meetings in the West, South East and South. The Mid West began strong and has maintained much of its share of meetings, whereas the South and South East have grown the most and the North East has diminished the most. The variable time periods are a reflection of the variation in the number of meetings per year. The regions were defined as follows: **Canada & Mexico:** Ottawa, Toronto, Victoria, Montreal, Calgary, Vancouver, Mexico City; **West:** San Francisco, Pasadena, College, Seattle, San Diego, Honolulu, Berkeley; **Rocky Mountain & South West:** Tucson, Boulder, Denver, Flagstaff, Las Cruces, Las Vegas, Albuquerque, Phoenix/Tempe; **Mid West:** Williams Bay, St. Louis, Put-In-Bay, Pittsburgh, Cleveland, Evanston, Ann Arbor, Chicago, Northfield, Madison, Delaware, East Lansing, Columbus, Lincoln, Minneapolis, Kansas City, Ames; **South East & South:** San Juan, Atlanta, Gainesville, White Sulphur Springs, Hampton, Charlottesville, Tampa, Winston-Salem, Lexington, Nashville, Austin, Baton Rouge, Houston, San Antonio; **East (Mid-Atlantic):** New York, Washington, Philadelphia, Swarthmore, Atlantic City, Princeton, Frederick, Haverford, College Park, Baltimore, **North East:** Cambridge, Boston, Albany, Northhampton, South Hadley, Middletown, Poughkeepsie, Hanover, Rochester, Nantucket, New Haven, Amherst, New London, Williamstown, Wellesley, Troy, Ithaca.

Ann Arbor in June. It was a popular location and would be a crowded meeting. The Council worried that the paper crush would be very heavy, so for the first time they allowed for simultaneous sessions "only if absolutely necessary, and as a last resort." They also restricted all late papers to five minutes, reinstituted the read-by-title-only injunction if required, and warned all speakers at Ann Arbor that they would be pushed into an earlier session if time was available. Clearly they made every effort to avoid parallel sessions at the end of the meeting.[12]

But the writing was on the wall for the 92nd meeting at Princeton in April 1955, as the membership of the Society neared 800 members. Again the Council was presented with a paper session schedule that included a simultaneous session on the last day, and now the demand was sufficiently great that they could not avoid it. Donald Menzel was then Society President and had approved the publication of the printed program, but he needed Council approval. A reluctant Council approved, but rededicated itself to making the load lighter: papers by absent authors would be placed at the end and would be limited to five minutes. Even so, the meeting required one set of simultaneous sessions, and the trend seemed inevitable, even though many fought it as hard as they could.

William Baum recalls that when he started going to meetings in the early 1950s, it was mainly to meet astronomers because, though he had been hired by Ira Bowen at Mount Wilson, his training was all in physics. Typically Baum found that 100 astronomers would show up to a meeting, and he "came to know most of them, or know who most of them were." In a short span of time Baum found that there were relatively few new faces at meetings; most of the people he met at his first meetings became familiar faces subsequently.[13] The membership was relatively stable and, as Baum also recalls, meetings in the early 1950s were more relaxed than those at present. There were fewer new faces trying to establish their niche in the profession. Baum felt no competition from the others he met.

But at mid-decade, he sensed the growing pressure to hold simultaneous sessions, and the pressure to adhere to strict time limits, which had been lax in the past. At his first meetings, he found it not unusual for the chair to allow the session to run up to a half-hour behind, and only then would the chair "politely suggest that perhaps we should get on with the meeting..."[14] This informality disappeared as meeting schedules tightened.

During the open business meeting at Princeton, many voiced fears that erupted into vigorous discussion, as William Baum recalls. Martin Schwarzschild in particular did not want parallel sessions, fearing that the "Society would fragment and we would all lose touch with parts of our field." Everything had to be done to avoid that.[15] Schwarzschild proposed a quota system on papers to relieve the pressure. This was not a popular idea, and stimulated counter-proposals from other members, including Cecilia Payne Gaposchkin. At the conclusion of the business meeting the Council invited all members to submit their ideas: the main options seemed to be: simultaneous sessions; quotas for the number of papers each institution could present; four-day sessions; and three meetings per year. The Council also suggested that henceforth, no paper would be accepted without an abstract, to be submitted well before the meeting, for publication in the meeting program and later in *The Astronomical Journal*.[16] But this too needed ratification by the membership.

The Council did receive numerous suggestions over the next several months, enough so that at the Troy meeting in November 1955 they believed they had the sense of the membership. First, everyone agreed that the abstracts would be a great improvement to professionalize the meetings. Abstracts would force members to think about what they were going to say, and would be a great aid if simultaneous sessions actually took place. A significant majority opposed "on principle" the restriction of the number of papers through a quota system. There was more sympathy for simultaneous sessions, longer meetings, or more meetings per year though the sense was that parallel sessions were inevitable and "a necessary price to pay for the growth of the Society." At the business meeting, the Council reported that henceforth, abstracts would be required, and that they were going to try to hold three meetings per year. One meeting would be with the AAAS and would be for papers only; no Council meetings or prize lectures would be held. This would allow for more papers to be read. "[S]imultaneous sessions for papers will be held when, and only when, deemed necessary." No quota system would be enforced.[17]

Adding a third meeting in the year did not relieve pressure because there were popular meetings and unpopular meetings. The 94th meeting at Columbus, Ohio in March 1956 was wide open, but the next meeting, at Berkeley, in August 1956 in conjunction with the ASP, was going to be huge. Everyone wanted to be in Berkeley and present a paper. Simultaneous sessions were held on the last day. The 97th meeting in Cambridge in May 1957 also required simultaneous sessions, but now the Council decided to double up morning sessions, leaving the afternoon sessions unparalleled, and thus relieve the pressure on the last day.

The policy of holding simultaneous sessions only when necessary became moot in a few years, especially in the 1960s when the membership began to grow at a much faster pace (*see* Figure 1). Doubling sessions became common practice; the first meeting where all paper sessions were doubled was in Tucson in April 1963. Doubling up soon proved to be inadequate to the increased demand for time, as did the ten-minute time limit. The first triple sessions were held at Yerkes in June 1967; the first quadrupling came in August 1968 at the Dominion Astrophysical Observatory and the first quintupling in June 1970 at Boulder, though the majority of sessions remained triple and quadruple.[18] The number of papers was not the only factor; at some meetings, rooms were not large enough to accommodate the growing audiences. The only suggestion that was never attempted was to initiate a quota system on institutions or individuals. Every member could still present a paper, even if it was only five minutes. In the late 1970s poster paper sessions were introduced sporadically to ease the pressure further, but they did not become common practice, or acceptable to many, until the 1980s.[19]

Without doubt, simultaneous paper sessions changed the flavor of AAS meetings. Choices had to be made. There was much conflict and tension; fears of balkanizing the Society were based on the feeling that in time, simultaneous sessions would be devoted to different topics. Indeed, by the 1970s, the "Program" announcements for meetings carried information on the distribution of papers in 11 categories defined at the December 1970 meeting in Tampa ("Instruments and Techniques;" "The Sun;" "Galactic Structure," etc.). The listings indicated the number of papers in each category and the sessions where they were to be found. At first they were spread around, but quite soon they were organized thematically.[20]

Dick Walker recalls his first meeting at Georgetown University in December 1963. There were three meetings that year: in Tucson; in College, Alaska; and finally in Washington, D.C. He sensed that three meetings were exhausting for the Council and the organizers, but most clearly he felt the anxiety caused by multiple sessions. "There were only two sessions, each across the hall from the other." Even so, many astronomers seemed "very upset with the arrangement, because there were papers across the hall they wanted to hear at the same time there were papers here." Sessions were already roughly thematic; stellar and galactic were in one room whereas planetary and solar were in another on the first day, but, as he recalled, "I wanted to hear it all." There was constant moving between the two rooms as astronomers would whisper to their colleagues "'Sorry I have to miss this,' or, 'You take notes.'"[21]

As dual sessions gave way to multiple sessions and poster sessions, each new step was taken with trepidation. Baum recalls that he first shunned the poster sessions, feeling he could communicate better orally and with slides and transparencies, which allowed him to field questions on the spot. Now he feels that posters, or display papers as they are called, turned out to be a fine change, "and perhaps the only solution to the very large meetings that occur today, but I had to be converted by seeing it."[22]

At the Tucson meetings in January 1995, Dick Walker found Baum standing at the end of a long aisle of posters during a break at the vast Convention Center. "Bill," Dick said, "you look as confused as I am." Bill scanned the hall, from the ranks of terminals at the far end to the corporate exhibits near the main entrance, across a sea of some 1,200 astronomers. "I don't know any of these people!" Bill lamented, "I don't know any

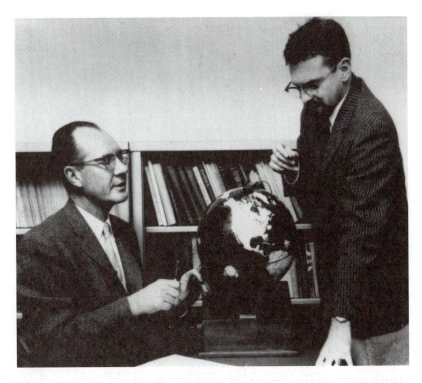

Figure 3. (l - r) Fred Whipple and J. Allen Hynek contemplate satellite orbits during the International Geophysical Year. Hynek was Secretary of the AAS from 1955 to 1961. Whipple was a Vice-President from 1948 to 1950. American Institute of Physics, Emilio Segrè Visual Archives, Irwin Collection.

of them! But they're all looking for jobs, they're all so bright, just brilliant, and I just hope they find jobs doing something they like."[23]

To handle what is now a large and extremely diverse meeting, with all its needs, its complexities and its problems, and to offset the growing sense of loss of community, the Society has initiated newsletters; issued both preliminary and formal programs; and has standardized meeting structure not only to keep its membership informed but to help the Society retain a sense of familiarity and commonality among its members. After all, for whatever purpose, to convey information, to get a job, or simply to get away from the office, the basic idea of the meeting is to meet people, just as Pickering always thought it had to be.

One other profound change has taken place at Society meetings. The first time Dick Walker gave a paper was in June 1978 at Madison. He recalls speaking about a double star whose components were of the same brightness, but what he remembers more than anything was the smoke-filled room. It was a stuffy classroom on the Wisconsin campus, extremely dark. "I'll never get over that — the projector in the back, with all this blue smoke just choking me. No one smokes anymore in the Astronomical Society."[24]

TABLE 8. *Record of AAS Meetings.*

No.	Location	Date	No.	Location	Date
1	Williams Bay, WI	Sept. 1899	56	Cambridge, MA	Sept. 1936
2	New York, NY	June 1900	57	Frederick, MD	Dec. 1936
3	Washington, DC	Dec. 1901	58	Williamstown, MA	Sept. 1937
4	Washington, DC	Dec. 1902	59	Bloomington, IN	Dec. 1937
5	St. Louis, MO	Dec. 1903	60	Ann Arbor, MI	Sept. 1938
6	Philadelphia, PA	Dec. 1904	61	New York, NY	Dec. 1938
7	New York, NY	Dec. 1905	62	Berkeley, CA	Aug. 1939
8	New York, NY	Dec. 1906	63	Delaware, OH	Dec. 1939
9	Put-in-Bay, OH	Aug. 1908	64	Wellesley, MA	Sept. 1940
10	Williams Bay, WI	Aug. 1909	65	Philadelphia, PA	Dec. 1940
11	Cambridge, MA	Aug. 1910	66	Williams Bay, WI	Sept. 1941
12	Ottawa, Ontario	Aug. 1911	67	Cleveland, OH	Dec. 1941
13	Washington, DC	Dec. 1911	68	New Haven, CT	June 1942
14	Pittsburg, PA	Aug. 1912	69	Evanston, IL	Dec. 1942
15	Cleveland, OH	Dec. 1912	70	Cambridge, MA	May 1943
16	Atlanta, GA	Dec. 1913	71	Cincinnati, OH	Nov. 1943
17	Evanston, IL	Aug. 1914	72	Philadelphia, PA	June 1944
18	Berkeley, CA	Aug. 1915	73	Cambridge, MA	June 1945
19	Swarthmore, PA	Aug. 1916	74	New York, NY	Feb. 1946
20	New York, NY	Dec. 1916	75	Madison, WI	Sept. 1946
21	Albany, NY	Aug. 1917	76	Cambridge, MA	Dec. 1946
22	Cambridge, MA	Aug. 1918	77	Evanston, IL	Sept. 1947
23	Ann Arbor, MI	Sept. 1919	78	Columbus, OH	Dec. 1947
24	S. Hadley, MA	Aug. 1920	79	Pasadena, CA	June 1948
25	Chicago, IL	Dec. 1920	80	New Haven, CT	Dec. 1948
26	Middletown, CT	Aug. 1921	81	Ottawa, Ontario	June 1949
27	Swarthmore, PA	Dec. 1921	82	Tucson, AZ	Dec. 1949
28	Williams Bay, WI	Sept. 1922	83	Bloomington, IN	June 1950
29	Boston, MA	Dec. 1922	84	Haverford, PA	Dec. 1950
30	Pasadena, CA	Sept. 1923	85	Washington, DC	June 1951
31	Poughkeepsie, NY	Dec. 1923	86	East Cleveland, OH	Dec. 1951
32	Hanover, NH	Aug. 1924	87	Victoria, B.C.	June 1952
33	Washington, DC	Dec. 1924	88	Amherst, MA	Dec. 1952
34	Northfield, MN	Sept. 1925	89	Boulder, CO	Aug. 1953
35	Rochester, NY	Dec. 1925	90	Nashville, TN	Dec. 1953
36	Nantucket, MA	Sept. 1926	91	Ann Arbor, MI	June 1954
37	Philadelphia, PA	Dec. 1926	92	Princeton, NJ	Apr. 1955
38	Madison, WI	Sept. 1927	93	Troy, NY	Nov. 1955
39	New Haven, CT	Dec. 1927	94	Columbus, OH	Mar. 1956
40	Amherst, MA	Sept. 1928	95	Berkeley, CA	Aug. 1956
41	New York, NY	Dec. 1928	96	New York, NY	Dec. 1956
42	Ottawa, Ontario	Aug. 1929	97	Cambridge, MA	May 1957
43	Cambridge, MA	Dec. 1929	98	Urbana, IL	Aug. 1957
44	Chicago, IL	Sept. 1930	99	Indianapolis, IN	Dec. 1957
45	New Haven, CT	Dec. 1930	100	Madison, WI	June 1958
46	Delaware, OH	Sept. 1931	101	Gainesville, FL	Dec. 1958
47	Washington, DC	Dec. 1931	102	Rochester, NY	Mar. 1959
48	Cambridge, MA	Sept. 1932	103	Toronto, Ontario	Aug. 1959
49	Atlantic City, NJ	Dec. 1932	104	Cleveland, OH	Dec. 1959
50	Chicago, IL	June 1933	105	Pittsburg, PA	Apr. 1960
51	Cambridge, MA	Dec. 1933	106	Mexico City, Mexico	Aug. 1960
52	New London, CT	Sept. 1934	107	New York, NY	Dec. 1960
53	Philadelphia, PA	Dec. 1934	108	Nantucket, MA	June 1961
54	Toronto, Ontario	Sept. 1935	109	Denver, CO	Dec. 1961
55	Princeton, NJ	Dec. 1935	110	Cambridge, MA	Apr. 1962

TABLE 8. *Continued.*

No.	Location	Date	No.	Location	Date
111	New Haven, CT	Aug. 1962	154	Wellesley, MA	June 1979
112	White Sulphur Sprgs, WV	Dec. 1962	155	San Francisco, CA	Jan. 1980
113	Tucson, AZ	Apr. 1963	156	College Park, MD	June 1980
114	College, AK	July 1963	157	Albuquerque, NM	Jan. 1981
115	Washington, DC	Dec. 1963	158	Calgary, Alberta	June 1981
116	Flagstaff, AZ	June 1964	159	Boulder, CO	Jan. 1982
117	Montreal, Quebec	Dec. 1964	160	Troy, NY	June 1982
118	Lexington, Ky	Mar. 1965	161	Boston, MA	Jan. 1983
119	Ann Arbor, MI	Aug. 1965	162	Minneapolis, MN	June 1983
120	Berkeley, CA	Dec. 1965	163	Las Vegas, NV	Jan. 1984
121	Hampton, VA	Mar. 1966	164	Baltimore, MD	June 1984
122	Ithaca, NY	July 1966	165	Tucson, AZ	Jan. 1985
123	Los Angeles, CA	Dec. 1966	166	Charlottesville, VA	June 1985
124	Williams Bay, WI	June 1967	167	Houston, TX	Jan. 1986
125	Philadelphia, PA	Dec. 1967	168	Ames, IA	June 1986
126	Charlottesville, VA	Apr. 1968	169	Pasadena, CA	Jan. 1987
127	Victoria, B.C.	Aug. 1968	170	Vancouver, B.C.	June 1987
128	Austin, TX	Dec. 1968	171	Austin, TX	Jan. 1988
129	Honolulu, HI	Mar. 1969	172	Kansas City, Mo	June 1988
130	Albany, NY	Aug. 1969	173	Boston, Ma	Jan. 1989
131	New York, NY	Dec. 1969	174	Ann Arbor, MI	June 1989
132	Boulder, CO	June 1970	175	Washington, DC	Jan. 1990
133	Tampa, FL	Dec. 1970	176	Albuquerque, NM	June 1990
134	Baton Rouge, LA	Mar. 1971	177	Philadelphia, PA	Jan. 1991
135	Amherst, MA	Aug. 1971	178	Seattle, WA	May 1991
136	San Juan, PR	Dec. 1971	179	Atlanta, GA	Jan. 1992
137	Seattle, WA	Apr. 1972	180	Columbus, OH	June 1992
138	East Lansing, MI	Aug 1972	181	Phoenix/Tempe, AZ	Jan. 1993
139	Las Cruces, NM	Jan. 1973	182	Berkeley, CA	June 1993
140	Columbus, OH	June 1973	183	Washington, DC	Jan. 1994
141	Tucson, AZ	Dec. 1973	184	Minneapolis, MN	June 1994
142	Lincoln, NE	Mar. 1974	185	Tucson, AZ	Jan. 1995
143	Rochester, NY	Aug. 1974	186	Pittsburg, PA	June 1995
144	Gainesville, FL	Dec. 1974	187	San Antonio, TX	Jan. 1996
145	Bloomington, IN	Mar. 1975	188	Madison, WI	June 1996
146	San Diego, CA	Aug. 1975	189	Toronto, Ontario	Jan. 1997
147	Chicago, IL	dec. 1975	190	Winston-Salem, NC	June 1997
148	Haverford, PA	June 1976	191	Washington, DC	Jan. 1998
149	Honolulu, HI	Jan. 1977	192	San Diego, CA	June 1998
150	Atlanta, GA	June 1977	193	Austin, TX	Jan. 1999
151	Austin, TX	Jan. 1978	194	Chicago, IL	June 1999
152	Madison, WI	June 1978	195	Atlanta, GA	Jan. 2000
153	Mexico City, Mexico	Jan. 1979			

THE ORIGINS OF THE EXECUTIVE OFFICE AT THE AMERICAN ASTRONOMICAL SOCIETY, 1959–1964

David A. Attis

INTRODUCTION

In the history of science, administrators are rarely the heroes, yet, particularly in the realm of twentieth-century "big science," they play a central role in shaping the organization of science and thus make it possible for scientists to continue their research. Most likely, Lyman Spitzer had these issues in mind when, acting as President of the American Astronomical Society (AAS), he wrote to Paul M. Routly in 1961 to offer him the newly created position of Executive Officer of the AAS. Spitzer declared, "When the history of astronomy in this century is written, some fifty years from now, I can well imagine that the role played by the Executive Office of the AAS will seem one of the most important items in the picture."[1]

Though Spitzer's statement was in part designed to inspire the young Routly to temporarily leave his professorship and accept an administrative position, Spitzer's comment also demonstrated his own feeling, and that of many others, that the AAS was at an important historical crossroads and that the Executive Officer would play an essential role in shaping the future of the AAS and thus the future of American astronomy. To face the challenges of the quickly changing world of post-war and post-Sputnik astronomy, Spitzer and others believed the AAS would need someone to dedicate himself full-time to the AAS's increasingly important role in education, as well as to its relationships with government and industry. In this chapter we look at some of the reasons why the Society felt the need for an Executive Office with a full-time staff, in addition to some of Routly's earliest duties as Executive Officer.

A CHANGING WORLD FOR AMERICAN ASTRONOMY

The purpose of the AAS since its foundation in 1899 has been "the advancement of astronomy and closely related branches of science." In the late 1950s, however, the Society found that the means for advancing astronomy had become increasingly varied. Astronomers shared in the science boom that followed World War II, though at first in a much smaller degree than the physicists. After Sputnik, however, astronomy took off; increase in Ph.D. production rates went from 4% in the 1950s to 20 percent in the 1960s.[2] American astronomy was expanding both in terms of the amount of funding it received, as well as in terms of the variety of sources for funding. Traditional sources like the home university, the Carnegie Institution, and the Rockefeller Foun-

Figure 1. Lyman Spitzer, Jr., President of the AAS from 1960 to 1962, promoted the formation of the Executive Office. AIP Emilio Segrè Visual Archives.

dation continued to support astronomy, but after the war, with the establishment of the Office of Naval Research and then the National Science Foundation, government support increased and eventually dominated.

With the expansion of astronomy came a greater need for young astronomers, and, in addition to funding particular research projects, the NSF helped the AAS set up programs to support astronomy education. In the mid-1950s, the AAS revived a committee on education, with support from the NSF, and began a program to allow leading American astronomers to visit colleges and universities that lacked strong programs in astronomy. The visitors would stay for about two days, give general addresses to the student body, lecture on astronomy to both beginning and more advanced students, and advise the faculty and administration on how to start an astronomy program or expand existing offerings. During the 1959–1960 academic year, twelve leading astronomers visited 62 colleges, and in 1960–1961, 32 astronomers visited about 100 colleges.[3] The AAS also administered a program funded by the NSF for foreign astronomers to visit American observatories.

Additionally, in 1957 the AAS put out a pamphlet entitled "A Career in Astronomy" containing suggestions for high school study programs, lists of colleges and universities offering degrees in astronomy, as well as a short description of employment opportunities for astronomers. The pamphlet was revised in 1960 and again in 1962 in order to keep it up-to-date. By 1963, over 8,000 requests per year for this pamphlet were being answered. Also in 1960, plans were made for the AAS Committee on Education to produce a series of short films on astronomy for high school students to generate interest in the profession (see Franknoi and Wentzel this volume, p. 194).

Clearly, the administrative duties of the committee members were beginning to exceed what could be accomplished by astronomers in their spare time. Education, however, was not the only area in which the AAS faced greater administrative needs. The growing role of industry and government in science meant that the AAS had increasing official contact with other large organizations. On the industry side, for example, there was the matter of corporate membership. In order to raise additional funds for its conferences and educational programs, the AAS like many other societies decided to create a special membership category for corporations in 1959. Regular corporate members would pay $100 per year, while sustaining corporate members would pay $500 per year, for which they would receive a journal subscription as well as the right to exhibit during meetings (with the approval of the Council). By December 1960, there were 21 corporate members, including Edmund Scientific, Perkin-Elmer, Eastman Kodak, IBM, and Douglas Aircraft.

On the government side, the rise in government funding and the need for science advising led to greater official contact between the Society and the government. In May 1960, the AAS was asked to testify before the Federal Communications Commission on the issue of the protection of frequencies for radio astronomy, and in 1961 they were asked by the Subcommittee on Reorganization and International Organizations of the Senate Committee on Government Operations for assistance in improving the flow of pre-publication information on current research. Some members of the AAS realized that in order to promote American astronomy properly, the Society had to represent the interests of American astronomers in Washington.

CREATING THE POSITION OF EXECUTIVE OFFICER

It is against this backdrop of increasing administrative demands that the Council of the AAS decided to create the full-time position of Executive Officer. According to Lyman Spitzer, the need for full-time staff had been discussed since 1959, but the first real action appears to have been taken at the Council Meeting on December 27, 1960 during the AAS meeting in New York. (The Council then consisted of the President, the President-elect, the two previous Ex-Presidents, Vice-President, and nine Councilors.) At the meeting, councilor Walt Roberts pointed to the experience of the American Meteorological Society (of which he was also a member), which had recently appointed an Executive Secretary, and Gerald Clemence, the past President, proposed hiring an Executive Secretary on a trial basis for three years with funds raised from outside. After Frank Edmondson framed the general discussion into a formal proposal and Clemence seconded it, the Council decided that the AAS Secretary would remain the secretary to the Council while the Executive Secretary would carry out educational programs and build up public relations. The Executive Secretary would be called the Executive Officer to avoid confusion.[4]

In August 1961, Spitzer wrote a detailed memo to the Executive Committee (which consisted of the President, Vice-Presidents, Secretary, Treasurer, Ex-President, and

President-elect) explaining the need for the new position as outlined in the December 1960 Council Meeting. (A copy of the memo was circulated to the members in May of 1962.) He explained,

> With the rapid and accelerating growth of science in general and of astronomy in particular, new responsibilities are falling upon the Society, since no other organization is so well situated for representing the interests of astronomy to the nation. These new responsibilities are outlined in the following tentative and partial list.
>
> (a) Public Education. In view of the great shortage of astronomers it is important to encourage young people to enter astronomy. The AAS is in a better position than any other organization to undertake this important work, which should include such items as popular and technical lectures on astronomy, astronomical films, assistance to high schools and colleges in arranging astronomical programs, answers to inquiries by high school students, etc.
>
> (b) Relations with Government. Government activities are becoming increasingly important to astronomy, both through support on the one hand and interference on the other. Intelligent contacts with both the executive and legislative branch of the government are vital for the future welfare of astronomy. Such contacts should refer not only to government support of astronomy and space research as a whole and of Society activities in particular, but also to such matters as contamination of space, allocation of radio frequencies, etc.
>
> (c) Relations with Other Societies. Collaboration of astronomers with physicists has always been very close. The increasing role of geophysics in planetary astronomy emphasizes the importance of collaboration with geophysicists also. The increasing organization of these other disciplines makes contacts directly between Societies important as, for example, in the organization of joint symposia.
>
> (d) Relations with Corporations. Financial support from this source may be of increasing importance to the Society. On the other hand, corporation exhibits at Society meetings may be mutually advantageous.[5]

The new Executive Officer would be responsible for these new duties while the Secretary of the Society would continue to perform the previous duties of arranging meetings for the AAS, keeping track of membership, elected offices and committee appointments, and preparing the minutes of the Council meetings. The new position, therefore, represented not simply an increase in the size of the Society, but a change in the ways in which astronomical research was to be promoted in the second half of the twentieth century.

These changes were due not only to the longer trends of post-war growth in science, but as well to the boom in astronomy due to the space race. In his May 1962 memo to the members of the Society, Spitzer explained, "The enormous effort going into space research is likely to generate a very great expansion of astronomical activity, and the society should be prepared to face the increasing responsibilities which such expansions should entail." The AAS had to prepare for the new responsibilities of American astronomers in the space age and that required a full-time staff. Spitzer had originally intended the Executive Office to be located in Washington, D.C., but it was decided that a university setting would be more appropriate due to fears that an office in Washington might lose touch with academic astronomy. The office was located at

Princeton University (which had agreed to provide office space rent-free). A decade later, when fears of losing touch with astronomy were overcome by increased political needs, the office was moved to Washington for more effective contacts with government.

FINDING THE MONEY

Clearly a new Executive Office would require money, and the Society took steps to raise it both internally and externally. At the New York meeting in December 1960, the Society opened up two new classes of membership in order to expand its member base. Associate Membership and Junior Membership were open to "any person who is seriously interested in the advancement of astronomy or related fields." Spitzer explained in a grant application that, "These new types of membership were set up in order to attract the many scientists and engineers in government and industry who have become interested in astronomy through their contacts with space research."[6] By tapping into the growing area of space research, the AAS could increase its membership while continuing to advance the interests of astronomy. At the Nantucket meeting in June 1961, membership dues and journal subscription prices were increased. The Council calculated that the increased dues could cover about one third of the cost of the Executive Office, while overhead on government contracts could cover another third.

In order to obtain the remaining one third of the budget, Spitzer applied for grants from the Research Corporation and the Ford Foundation. In a letter of February 14, 1962 to the Ford Foundation, Spitzer emphasized the importance of the AAS's role in astronomy education:

> Until recently the only function of our Society has been the communication of scientific results among professional astronomers, both through professional meetings and through technical journals. Within recent years a need has arisen for effort in other areas. In particular the expansion of scientific research has led to an acute shortage of astronomers. The enormous efforts going into space research in this country indicate that the need for astronomers will certainly increase during the next few years. The quality of the nation's growing research effort in astronomy and, in particular, the effectiveness of much of our huge space program will depend critically on the number and ability of young people trained in astronomy and astrophysics. While many agencies are involved in science education, and in encouraging young people to choose science as a career, relatively little effort along these lines is oriented specifically toward astronomy.[7]

Spitzer explained that the AAS was in a unique position to meet these needs as the only professional society that included most astronomers in America and because it already had a number of small but active educational programs. He explained, "An Executive Officer would devote more than half his time to the organization of expanded programs in the field of astronomical education." Additionally, he explained, it was only through the creation of a new full-time position that these programs could continue since they had reached the limit set by the present volunteer organization.

Spitzer predicted that the position would soon become self-supporting, pointing to the expansion of the Society's regular and corporate membership. It would be the responsibility of the Executive Officer to attract Associate Members from the space industry, as well as to expand the list of Corporate Members. The increase in income, he estimated, would cover the administrative costs in about two years. The Ford Foundation agreed to grant $22,000 over two years beginning in July 1962.

THE FIRST EXECUTIVE OFFICER

While Spitzer was looking for funds for the new position, he also searched for the right man for the job, and, at the end of November 1961, Paul M. Routly of Pomona College (a former student and collaborator of Spitzer's) was offered the position. Joseph Miles Chamberlain had declined Spitzer's initial offer earlier that year, as did other

Figure 2. Paul Routly, Executive Officer of the AAS from 1962 to 1969. Irwin photograph, December 1971. AIP Emilio Segrè Visual Archives, Irwin Collection.

astronomers, including J. J. Nassau, of the Case Institute of Technology, Otto Struve, of Berkeley and the National Radio Astronomy Observatory in West Virginia, and Thornton Page, of Wesleyan. Many found it difficult to leave research (even temporarily) for an administrative position, but Routly was up for the challenge. He took a one-year leave of absence from Pomona and began work officially on August 15, 1962.

Paul Routly recalls that he was first approached by Spitzer to become Executive Secretary when they met on the West Coast. Later, he attended a meeting of the AAS at the Greenbrier Hotel in White Sulpher Springs, West Virginia, in December 1962 to get the flavor of Council meetings, and although he had just been promoted to a full professorship at Pomona College, he was interested in making a change and accepted the offer. So he and his wife moved to Princeton.

Despite the arguments laid out by Society officers, it seemed at first that the duties of the Executive Officer could be completed part-time. After the first few months, Routly felt that 60% of the job was trivial and could be done by a secretary. He missed teaching and research and suggested that he take the position back to Pomona with him and split his time between teaching and administrating.[8] C. S. Beals, who succeeded Lyman Spitzer as President of the AAS from 1962–1964, liked the idea of a part-time Executive Officer, writing, "I have some doubts... whether anyone in your position could do as good a job without having a foot in either the teaching or research camps."[9] G. C. McVittie, however, Secretary of the AAS, worried that the office would be too distant from Washington. "It seems to me," he wrote, "that there will be more and more need for dealings with the government if astronomy, and especially radio astronomy, is to continue developing in this country."[10] Routly wrote in December 1962 that the Executive Committee felt that the position would probably have to become full-time in three or four years but was not yet at that point. Spitzer agreed that Routly might make the position part-time in the interim, but that in the long term, it would have to be full-time.[11]

However, Routly's duties soon increased and the position remained full-time. In June 1963, he organized a major symposium co-sponsored by the American Astronautical Society on "The Exploration of Mars." Then at the Alaska meeting in July 1963, the Society decided that the Domestic and Foreign Visiting Professor Program would be administered entirely from the Executive Office, and in January 1964, the AAS was given $188,000 by the NSF to produce three 30-minute astronomical films for secondary schools. The Executive Office not only negotiated the grant but also supervised all aspects of the project. Routly also stepped up efforts to interest new Corporate Members after being empowered to approach any firm he thought suitable. Regular Corporate Membership was now $500, Sustaining Corporate Membership $1,000, and Sponsoring Corporate Membership $2,500.

Routly warmed to the position, and, with the aid of a secretary, Carol Crandall, worked hard to administer to the Society's educational and outreach efforts, as well as to manage the business side of the office, using an accounting firm to keep the books in proper shape. He attended Society meetings and took minutes during Council deliberations, but the organization and planning of the AAS meeting was the responsibility of the Society Secretary. The Society Treasurer, Frank Edmondson, continued to

Figure 3. Hank M. Gurin, Executive Officer of the AAS from 1969 to 1979. Irwin photograph at the Seattle meeting, April 1972. AIP Emilio Segrè Visual Archives, Irwin Collection.

manage the Society's books. Routly was responsible only for the budget of the Executive Office, which included routine expenditures, salaries, and grant monies. Eventually, partly because he did not have a vote on the Council, after seven years and successive changes in AAS officers, he tired of his inability to influence change. He was also not interested in moving the office to Washington, even though he recalls growing pressure for such a move from leading Society members. He resigned the position in 1969 after Kaj Strand invited him to a position at the U.S. Naval Observatory. Routly was replaced by H. M. Gurin, who managed the Executive Office in Princeton for another decade, amidst growing pressures to become more attuned to Washington politics and funding sources.

CONCLUSION

Although the creation of a new administrative position might not seem at first like a milestone in the history of astronomy, it should be clear that the creation of the position of Executive Officer at the AAS represented the Society's response to the rapidly changing world of American astronomy. While previously the advancement of astronomy had required little more than the planning of conferences and the publication of journals, in the late 1950s the future of astronomy depended on improved efforts in education, as well as increasingly vital relationships with government, industry, and other scientific societies. Though professional astronomers may have been hesitant to give up teaching and research or to establish a headquarters in Washington, they realized that the AAS could no longer meet the needs of American astronomy without a full-time administrative staff with close ties to government and industry to handle these new responsibilities and opportunities.

Figure 4. The Princeton University Observatory (as it appears today on FitzRandolph Road) was the first headquarters of the Executive Office of the AAS. Routly's (and later Gurin's) office was to the immediate right of the garage doors, and the secretarial office was at the far right. Robert P. Matthews photograph, courtesy of Princeton University Observatory and Don Hortenbach.

Moving to Washington, the Cannon Prize, and Other Thoughts

Margaret Burbidge

The Burbidges' own personal library of *The Astrophysical Journal* gives dramatic proof of the strength and growth of the American Astronomical Society (AAS). We used to have our volumes bound, and Vol. 109 (1949) sits proudly at the top of new shelving which we hope will accommodate the three fat issues per month through the rest of our lives!

MY FIRST AAS MEETING

Geoffrey and I were at Harvard College Observatory in the early summer of 1952. Arne Wyller, a graduate student there, his wife Ingrid, and her mother were planning to drive from Cambridge across the U.S. to attend the AAS 1952 meeting in Victoria, B.C.; they had room for a passenger (only one) and asked us whether one of us would like to go with them. They planned a three-week drive, camping and picnicking on the way to make the trip as low-cost as possible (in those days, graduate students lived a frugal existence and funds for travel were minimal). Geoff and I tossed a coin to decide on the lucky one, and the toss fell my way.

It was a wonderful trip; we traveled by roads very different from today's super highways, and we did not stay in paved, guarded, monitored campgrounds, few of which existed then, but we parked by the roadside, unrolled ground-sheets and sleeping bags, got out the picnic food and went to sleep with the starry sky as roof and the chirping of night creatures as music. Our only stay in a formal campground was in Yellowstone Park, and the journey remains in my mind as a very happy memory. The meeting was a wonderful experience. Parallel sessions were years in the future, and a photographer had no problem in lining up all those attending for a group picture.

Our next memorable AAS experience was the joint award of the Warner Prize in 1959, and the invitation for one of us to present the Warner Prize Lecture at the Christmas meeting in Cleveland, Ohio. The prize was awarded for our work in stellar spectroscopy and the synthesis of the elements in stars, but in 1959 we had been working for two years on the spectroscopy of galaxies — measuring rotation curves, velocity dispersions, determination of masses, etc. with the McDonald Observatory 82-inch telescope. Therefore, Geoffrey presented the Warner Lecture on what we felt was an exciting new topic.

WOMEN IN ASTRONOMY

Following this, I was elected to the AAS Council (1959–1962), and gained insight into the AAS operations. Ten years later, Geoffrey was elected to the Council. In May

1971, I was told I had been selected for the award of the Annie Cannon Prize in Astronomy, a prize specifically for women astronomers who were not at that time eligible for the premier AAS award, the Russell Lectureship. On May 27, 1971, I wrote to Larry Fredrick, AAS Secretary, declining the award and giving my reasons for not accepting a prize which emphasized the subordinate role of women in astronomy. The Prize had been set up by Annie Cannon in her will to redress the discrimination against women which extended from access to major telescopes to their consideration as equals with men in our national organizations. Some members were not pleased by my decision, but encouraging letters were received from Beatrice Tinsley, Carl Sagan, Elizabeth Scott, Vera Rubin, Jesse Greenstein, among others. The AAS Treasurer wrote with his hope that I would reconsider my decision, which he felt would "damage the American Astronomical Society on a short-term basis." The result was, however, that both the Russell Lectureship and Presidency of the Society were opened up to women (Cecilia Payne Gaposchkin was the first to be awarded the Russell Lectureship, and it was my privilege as the first woman President to introduce her on the platform).

THE EXECUTIVE OFFICE AND THE MOVE TO WASHINGTON

A quarter of a century after the small 1952 AAS meeting described above, it was clear that Sputnik, the space program, the moon landings, the national observatories, the role of the Federal Agencies in supporting astronomy and astronomers, had changed irreversibly the nature and practice of our subject. The functions of the Executive Office of our National Society no longer belonged on a single university campus, no matter how prestigious that campus and how dedicated its Executive Officer, Hank Gurin. It was time to move the Executive Office to our nation's capital, where direct contact with the power structure and people on Capitol Hill could be a daily occurrence, and interaction with NSF and NASA could be as meetings between friends over coffee or lunch. Plans for moving the Executive Office to Washington began in 1976, and the serious search for a new Executive Officer began in 1978, and brought applications from many talented people from which a short list for interviews was drawn up, and the search committee (Ivan King, Larry Fredrick, Margaret Burbidge, Harold Weaver, John Bahcall, and Gart Westerhout) met in the conference room at the AUI headquarters in Washington with a carefully prepared list of questions and topics for discussion. Peter Boyce, at that time working at NSF, easily made the top of everyone's list.

His Washington experience while he had worked for Congressman Udall was seen as an excellent background, and his goals for improving the AAS Executive Office and setting it up in Washington were exactly what we were looking for. In the interview, Peter also said that he would plan to take part in the Astronomy Decade Review, would continue close contact with NSF, and would regularly attend its advisory group meetings.

The offer of the position was made, and following Peter's acceptance, a new era for the AAS began.

Moving the AAS Executive Office to Washington

Peter B. Boyce

It was the year 1975. The American Astronomical Society (AAS) had been functioning since the turn of the century serving the needs of the North American astronomical community by holding meetings and publishing research results. In a nutshell, the Society's job was to enable the communication of research results and other information of interest to the astronomical community. As the last quarter of the twentieth century approached, it was clear to the forward looking officers and councilors of the AAS that the traditional ways of funding science had changed and that the astronomical community could benefit from maintaining a closer contact with the government in Washington. The AAS was headquartered at that time in Princeton, New Jersey, in the form of an Executive Office which had a limited number of duties. There was virtually no organized contact between the Society and the government in Washington.

Yet, as John Bahcall's efforts with Congress on behalf of the Space Telescope showed, it seemed clear that the AAS and the astronomical community should develop a more organized Washington presence. After some discussion and delay, the decision was made to move the Executive Office to Washington and, since the Executive Officer, Hank Gurin, did not wish to move, this would mean choosing a new Executive Officer as well. Plans were laid and the job was advertised. It was at this point that I first contemplated working for the AAS. Little did I expect that 18 years later I would still be working for the AAS. Little could I foresee the subsequent evolution of technology, of our science, and of the organization. Little was my realization how joyful it has been to work with smart, often selfless, astronomers and wonderful, dedicated staff to develop what has become one of the most active and effective scientific societies for its size anywhere in the world.

SELECTION OF NEW EXECUTIVE OFFICER

From my standpoint the selection process for the job of AAS Executive Officer included being interviewed by a committee of six leading astronomers, which could have been rather intimidating. Having thought about what the AAS was not doing for me as a member, I had developed a proposed plan of action for the Society. The committee had apparently also decided that the AAS was going to need a strong plan to improve communication with the membership as well as with the outside world. Since my plan of action meshed with the selection committee's goals, I found myself the new Executive Officer of the AAS within a very short time.

FIRST DC OFFICE

The AAS was embarking upon a more expensive operation than had been the case with the Executive Office in Princeton. It was a great help during the transition that Associated Universities, Inc. (AUI), offered to house the AAS Executive Office rent free for its first year in Washington. The staff of two, myself and my secretary Bill Rampley, set up a small office in the rear of the AUI suite. We benefited more, perhaps, from the experience and guidance of the long-time Washington staff in the AUI office than we did from not paying rent. As the AAS Executive Office became established in Washington, the AUI staff provided valuable advice, help and discussion.

The first year was a very exiting time as we started several new programs and services for the AAS members and established a strong program in public policy, one of the first small societies to do so. In 1979 we published the first issue of the AAS *Newsletter* (*see* Figure 1), devoting a major portion to federal science policy issues, advice on how to prepare a good research proposal, and a description of how the federal budgets for NSF and NASA move through Congress.

At the same time we successfully applied to the NSF for funding a program of small international travel grants, a program which continued effectively until 1997 when NSF declined to fund a routine renewal proposal. The AAS itself has contributed Society funds to this program by supporting part of the administrative costs.

A proposal to NASA to fund a program of small research grants was, likewise, successful. This program continues to the present day, reportedly receiving very high marks from the peer reviewers. The only change in operation was an increase in the upper limit to the amount of the awards from $3,000 to the present $5,000. The AAS small research grant program is based on the philosophy that small amounts of money can enable otherwise unsupported astronomers to engage in high quality research. Our goal has been to make this happen with the least possible bureaucratic burden for the applicants.

From the beginning, the AAS has contributed Society funds sufficient to allow the support of one or two grants per year for foreign astronomers or for projects not sufficiently related to NASA programs to qualify for NASA funds. The small research grant program has also attracted some private support. Katherine Haramundanis established a fund in honor of her parents Cecilia and Serge Gaposchkin to support one award every other year for a particularly noteworthy project in areas of research which were of interest to the Gaposchkins. Edith Woodward provided funding for three awards for research on contact binary stars, and the Wray Foundation provided a substantial contribution to the program in the 1980s. Finally, the success of the AAS small research grant program was a major factor in the decision of the Dudley Observatory to establish a set of research awards modeled upon the AAS program.[1]

Outside of Sigma Xi, which has a long-established program of small research grants, the AAS is the only society to my knowledge which has a program to support the research activities of its members. It has always been a puzzle to me why other scientific societies have not established a program of research grants, especially since, as shown by the AAS results, these small awards can be very helpful for young scientists just starting their research careers. Astronomy as a science may be unique in that,

JULY 1979   * * * * * * * *   AAS NEWSLETTER #1
               *   AAS   REPORT   *
               * * * * * * * * *

Inaugural Message from the Executive Officer

I am delighted to be able to start this newsletter to members of the American Astronomical Society. Through this AAS Newsletter the officers, councilors and I expect to increase the information available to members. I hope to include full coverage of items of interest to astronomers. With your feedback I hope to produce an informative, helpful and (with luck) interesting Newsletter. Comments about the format, content and style of the newsletter will be very welcome.

I expect to report on Society busines, actions of the Council, summaries of the annual business meeting, announcements of interest to the members, results of ballots, etc. In addition I will include a section about activities in Washington which affect astronomy, e.g. NSF and NASA budget prospects, information about the granting process, tips on little known funding programs at various agencies, etc. A general news section will follow, and, eventually, a calendar of events will be included.

From my perspective I can see very clearly the importance of Federal funding actions to the whole science of astronomy. The Federal Government now supports more than three-quarters of all the astronomical research done in this country. For better or worse the time has passed when we could spend our time simply teaching and doing research. Our collective future is going to depend upon Government funding decisions. As astronomers we have the advantage of a strong popular appeal to the public and to Congressmen. If we can present our case well we will be able to continue to do our research. If we fail to speak out we may well see astronomy funding cut. Not everyone feels that astronomy funding should continue to grow. During hearings on Jan. 25, 1978, the House Subcommittee on Science, Research and Technology asked why NSF doesn't spend more money on astronomy. The director of NSF, Dr. Richard Atkinson, replied, "I have heard some of the astronomers' plans for new facilities, and the expenditures are astronomical. I hope you will not give the astronomical community too much encouragement."

I am concerned that if astronomy is to prosper we must all pitch in- and make our voices heard. I expect to be doing what I can here in Washington. I will be glad to help any of you who wish to make your own statements to your own Congressman and to the agencies. I hope the Washington News part of this newsletter will help to keep you sufficiently well informed that you can make a knowledgeable statement if you so desire.

I am sure that this newsletter, which we plan to produce four to six times a year, can develop into a forum for other areas of discussion if you, the members, desire it.

Dr. Peter B. Boyce
American Astronomical Society
Suite 603, 1717 Massachusetts Ave.
Washington, DC, 20036
Phone: 202-232-3077

Figure 1. The first AAS Newsletter, July 1979.

with a small amount of funding, an astronomer can use the national observatories, mine the archives of NASA space missions, or even use private facilities as a visitor and accomplish first class research. Perhaps this explains why the AAS remains alone in offering research support to its community. Of course, the other reason may be the work involved in setting up and carrying out the tasks associated with processing and ranking 150 proposals a year and generating the necessary proposals and reports to the funding agencies.

The job situation for young astronomers was not particularly bright in 1979, and it was clear that a more centralized registry of jobs within astronomy would be helpful. To this end, one of the first major tasks in the Washington Executive Office was to totally upgrade the Job Register to a monthly publication; actively soliciting job announcements, expanding the mailing list and improving the format for easier readability. For many years the AAS Job Register has served as the prime source for job listings in astronomy, expanding to a mailing list of 2,500 by 1990, making the Job Register an expensive ($100,000 per year) service to the community. Even the $100 charge per ad was insufficient to cover the costs. In 1993 we started posting the Job Register electronically, sending paper copies only to institutions and to individuals who requested it. The resultant cost savings have turned this once expensive service into a break-even operation. With the advent of electronic mail, the Job Register is attracting a growing number of European ads, serving a clientele far beyond the North American community.

```
American Astronomical Society - JOB REGISTER    SEPTEMBER 1979
Suite 603, 1717 Massachusetts Ave.
Washington, DC  20036  Phone: 202-232-3077
```

The AAS Job Register Policies

This register of jobs available in the field of astronomy is maintained and published by the American Astronomical Society as a service to members of the Society. The following policies prevail:

* There is no charge for listing jobs.

* The listed jobs are now certified to this office as being real openings not already promised to some candidate. If uncertainties in funding exist we ask that this be noted in the listing.

* Personal subscriptions to the Job Register are available free of charge to members of the AAS upon request. We ask that this request be based upon need to keep down the costs of printing and mailing.

* The complete listing is published quarterly. New job listings, if sufficient in number, are published monthly in a supplement.

* The AAS plays no part in the job seeking or negotiation process other than publishing the listing of available jobs.

* Other than requiring certification of the reality of the job, the AAS takes no responsibility for the accuracy of the job descriptions.

Figure 2. An early AAS Job Register.

By the end of the first year in Washington, we were ready to strike out on our own. The AAS Executive Office moved to space in a building owned by the Optical Society of America (OSA). As with the AUI, the staff of the OSA quickly became a valuable source of advice and information. Scientific societies are all generally organized to serve their members, help them communicate research results by holding meetings and publishing scholarly journals, and to promote their science. Sharing similar goals, scientific societies face similar problems, and new executive officers can benefit greatly from discussing problems with their colleagues in other societies. In particular I would like to identify three people who were very helpful: Lois Chew, the AUI office manager, provided invaluable advice in setting up and running a small office in Washington. Jarus Quinn, Executive Officer of the OSA, was particularly generous in sharing ideas and offering advice. As we both were members of the AIP Executive Committee and traveled together to their meetings several times a year, we had a lot of time to discuss what constitutes a good scientific society and how to put our ideas into practice in the real world. Calva Lottridge (now Leonard) of the OSA was reorganizing the OSA office to accommodate their growth and shared her insight on cost accounting, personnel matters, and other organizational matters which go into making a society office run smoothly.

RELATIONS WITH THE AIP

The AAS is one of ten member Societies which comprise the American Institute of Physics (AIP). Originally established to help member societies produce their scientific journals, AIP now has a number of programs which serve the overall physics and astronomy communities, such as maintaining the statistical attributes of the member societies by surveying and sampling the membership. The AIP also maintains the Center for History of Physics, which, among other things, serves as the archive for the official papers of the AAS. However, one of the most valuable aspects of belonging to the AIP is the chance for elected officers and paid staff of all the AIP societies to share information among themselves about society operations, about new government rules and regulations and about ideas for services and programs.

As one of the AIP member societies, the AAS is entitled to three positions on the AIP Governing Board, one of which has always been filled by the AAS Executive Officer. As one of the smaller societies, the AAS has not carried much weight in setting the policies of the AIP. The American Physical Society (APS), being ten times larger, has always been the dominant influence. Yet, during the discussions of whether the AIP should move to the Washington, DC, area, the example of the AAS in establishing contacts with Congress helped to support the decision to move.

Over the years, the AIP has provided a number of services to the AAS at cost, including the maintenance of the membership records of the AAS, carrying out the annual dues billing and publishing the *AJ* and the *BAAS*. As the AAS Executive Office matured, and as computer technology became less and less expensive, it was apparent by the late 1980s that it made sense for the Executive Office to take over the management of the membership system. Not only was it less expensive, but the responsibility would be vested in the AAS staff who were closer to the members and would certainly meet a good fraction of the AAS members in person at the semi-annual meetings.

DEVELOPMENTS

Along with assuming the duties of maintaining membership data, the AAS Executive Office added a large number of responsibilities during the 1980s. It may help to recall that when the Office first moved to Washington in 1979, the main functions of the AAS were still being performed mostly by volunteer officers. The Society meetings were then organized by the Secretary and the accounts were maintained by the Treasurer. There was, in fact, very little for the Executive Office to do. This was a holdover from the days when the AAS had 1,500 members and the meetings were attended by 200 people. But, the AAS had grown since 1960. The membership stood at 3,500 in 1979, the San Francisco meeting attracted a record 650 people, and the Society budget was approaching $2 million. Operating an organization of this size had grown into a serious endeavor. It's no wonder that the volunteer officers were feeling overworked!

Yet, in 1980, the Society was just entering a phase of even more rapid growth. Fueled by increasing support from NASA for the astronomical research community, astronomy in the United States grew more rapidly in the 1980s than ever before. Currently in 1997 the AAS has 6,200 members, a yearly budget of over $7 million and meetings which have exceeded 2,200 in attendance. Organizing large meetings can not be done on a part time basis. Responsibly handling millions of dollars and tens of thousands of individual financial transactions each year is a full-time professional job. Assuring compliance with increasingly complex government regulations takes special expertise. And developing effective relations with Congress and government agencies requires dedicated attention from someone experienced in the ways of Washington. It was inevitable that the Executive Office would have to assume the full job of operating the Society.

Various operational responsibilities were transferred to the Executive Office throughout the 1980s, and we in the Office expanded many of the things we did in order to make the outcome more useful to the members. One prime example of the latter was the *AAS Membership Directory*, which evolved over time to become a general source of information about the AAS. The evolution of the *Directory* mirrors the development of the AAS, starting with an emphasis on communication, adding features suggested by members and culminating in a pioneering effort to enhance electronic communication.

When the production of the *Directory* moved into the Executive Office, considerable effort was made to improve the readability of the entries, to add fax numbers, to update the list of institutions and to add descriptions of the various AAS programs, awards, divisions, and subscriptions. Shortly thereafter, in recognition of the growth of astronomy around the world, we added the list of international institutions to the *Directory*. Then, in 1989, as e-mail began to be used by the members, the AAS jumped into the electronic era by being one of the first societies in the world (maybe the first) to add e-mail addresses to their *Membership Directory*. In fact, that year the e-mail addresses were provided in a special supplement, prepared and published by the Executive Office, which included a dozen pages of instruction about how to use e-mail, how to send messages to people on another network, and how to connect to colleagues in Europe and elsewhere. At least a dozen other societies reprinted the AAS e-mail instructions as they followed the AAS into the world of electronic communication. As usual, many AAS members helped us with expertise, comments, and suggestions. In particular, Don Wells of the National Radio Astronomy Observatory (NRAO) gave us the extra push needed to get the Executive Office started with using e-mail and Bob Hanisch of the Space Telescope Science Institute (STScI) saw to it that the AAS got our first e-mail account on their computers. They were both willing and patient teachers as we in the Executive Office developed our expertise.

Despite all our concern in the Executive Office for effective communication, it took one of our members to suggest that it would be handy to have a list of future AAS meetings included in the *Directory*. We all felt incredibly sheepish about overlooking such an obvious step and quickly added the list of future meetings in the *Directory*. The Society has benefited greatly from the willingness of members to suggest changes and useful additions to all aspects of our operation.

NEW BYLAWS AND CONSTITUTION

The AAS had been incorporated in 1926 in the state of Illinois, where the Treasurer's Office had been located at the time. As the years passed, and all the officers of the Society were located elsewhere, it became a particularly onerous task to appoint someone as the AAS registered representative in Illinois, to file the necessary reports, and to pay the yearly fee. One year our representative was unavailable, away on sabbatical, and the notice was not dealt with, almost causing us to lose our incorporated status. In 1983, AAS Treasurer Harold Weaver and I recommended to the Council that we move the AAS incorporation to the District of Columbia.

The AAS operating practices had long since outstripped the old AAS Constitution and bylaws, and this would provide an opportunity to bring them up to date and to bring them into accord with the District of Columbia (DC) Corporation Statutes. So began a two-year project by the author, Harold Weaver, and Arlo Landolt to modernize the bylaws and Constitution of the AAS.

The AAS Constitution had to be replaced by new "Articles of Incorporation" whose contents were explicitly specified by DC law. The Council rebelled at the thought that the AAS would no longer have a "Constitution," a dilemma which was solved by including an article which states, "These Articles of Incorporation shall be known to the members of the Society as the Constitution." This was but one of many areas in which we had to walk a fine line between traditional wording and modern practices and requirements. Some peculiarities in the old bylaws were hard to fathom and others reflected outmoded procedures. But some of them (although probably unenforceable) were written to benefit one person and demonstrated a remarkable degree of irresponsibility toward the welfare of the Society on the part of the Council which adopted such wording. The first of these stated that the salary of the Executive Officer shall not be changed without the consent of the Executive Officer. The second stated that "the location of the Executive Office shall not be changed without the express consent of the Executive Officer." It is my understanding that the second of these articles delayed the move of the Executive Office to Washington for some time. One can only speculate about whether this did any permanent harm to the Society.

One anomaly concerned the AAS Vice-Presidents. Under the old bylaws, the senior Vice-President had no duties but to stand in if the President should be unable to serve. The VP did not pass on to become President. We wrote the new bylaws to give the VPs the responsibility to oversee the scientific content of the meetings and lengthened their term to three years to provide more continuity on the Executive Committee. After the new bylaws were adopted in 1986, feedback from the members indicated that the breadth and quality of the invited talks and the special sessions at AAS meetings improved. Selection of the speakers and topics is taken very seriously by the Vice-Presidents and the discussion of whom to choose is both substantive and enjoyable. It has been a pleasure to participate in this activity with the Vice-Presidents.

Perhaps the most substantive change in the bylaws involved the setting of the annual membership dues, which had been done at the annual Business Meeting of the Society by the vote of those in attendance. Since this normally amounted to 30–40 people who had not seen or discussed the Society budget until ten minutes earlier, it seemed to make much more sense to place this responsibility in the hands of the Council. So ended the town meeting aspect of AAS governance.

Perhaps in part because we had to discuss each and every aspect of the operation of the Society so thoroughly during the rewriting of the bylaws, a strong and mutual bond developed among the three long-term officers. There was Treasurer Harold Weaver who adroitly managed the finances of the AAS during a period of intense

Figure 3. Harold Weaver was Treasurer of the AAS from 1977 to 1987 and then was appointed again in 1988. Weaver guided the investment strategy for the Society during a period of steeply rising expenses. Irwin photograph, August 1973, American Institute of Physics Emilio Segrè Visual Archives, Irwin collection.

growth, yet was still able to quietly build up the reserves of the AAS so that we could face the transition to electronic publishing without worry. Secretary Arlo Landolt was the second member of the bylaw Committee. Dedicated to the AAS, Arlo is a genuine selfless public servant who worked long hours without reward, as did Harold. I was the third long-term officer and felt fortunate that the three of us managed to build such a good working relationship — one which served us so well during the era when the operations of the AAS were changing and expanding at a fearsome rate. The nine years the three of us spent together as colleagues and friends remain one of the highlights of my term as Executive Officer.

AAS MEETINGS

Beginning with the January 1981 meeting in Albuquerque, the responsibility for fully managing the meetings was transferred to the Executive Office. At that time we added an additional staff member to the Office, making a grand total of three. At this point we were leaning heavily upon the local organizing committees to handle a lot of the work involved, including the management of the registration process, arranging for audio/visual (AV) equipment, arranging for the rooms and their set-up, and handling the money. It was a lot of work, and we expected all this to be provided by the local institution for free. Small wonder that invitations to host an AAS meeting were becoming hard to obtain. Our only option, as meeting size was growing and institutions were less willing to foot the bill for the meetings, was to raise the registration fees to cover the actual meeting costs. The Executive Office gradually assumed nearly all of the burdensome responsibilities and costs of the meetings, which now operate on a break even basis. Of course we still have need for a local organizing committee to make suggestions for invited speakers, provide local information and directional signs, and to organize the crew of volunteers who operate the projectors, put up the numbers on the display boards, and do the other myriad things which make meetings run smoothly.

As the AAS staff gained experience with running meetings, we learned how to negotiate with hotels, sometimes gaining large concessions in the room rates. We learned where to find AV equipment and how to ensure that it worked. We learned tricks for keeping the cost of coffee breaks within reason, and we built up a store of knowledge about what commonly goes awry and how to prevent that from happening.

But, my first meeting was an eye-opening experience. I had no idea there would be so many last-minute problems to solve. Since we were meeting in New Mexico, I had followed the lead of our host, R. Marcus Price, and had purchased an inexpensive brown cowboy hat to add to the southwest flavor. This turned out to be a real boon. It became common practice to "find the man in the cowboy hat" to solve all problems. Eugene Milone, host of the next meeting in Calgary, felt it was inappropriate for me to appear in a brown cowboy hat in Calgary, whose symbol is a white cowboy hat. The entire local organizing committee generously presented me with a fine, albeit enormous, white cowboy hat which served as my identification at the meeting—and at subsequent AAS meetings for the next decade. At some point it dawned on me that my staff had become the problem solvers and there was no real reason for me to wear the hat. The hat was retired from service, and it has subsequently fallen victim to moths.

During the 1980s, attendance at meetings of other societies was falling off, and the percentage of AAS members attending was, likewise, falling. The Executive Office put a lot of work into sampling opinions about the good and bad points of AAS meetings. From time to time various Councilors also had good suggestions. The problem was how to structure a meeting to accommodate all the papers without expanding the number of parallel sessions beyond reason. I felt that poster papers, which I had seen used to very good effect by the Division of Planetary Sciences, offered the answer. But there were problems to be solved in a way that would be acceptable to the members. First, we named them Display Presentations, since many members had trouble obtaining travel funds from their academic deans to give just a "poster paper." Changing the name was remarkably successful. Second, we made the Display Presentation sessions the central events of the meeting, with exhibits around the edge, coffee breaks in the middle, plenty of free space, and 1.5 hours per day devoted only to the poster sessions. At first we had to switch a number of papers, but soon we were getting two-thirds of the papers submitted as displays and one-third oral, which made for a nice balance. The result was that our meetings included an expanded set of invited summary talks and prize lectures, plenty of time for informal discussion, and generally no more than four or five parallel sessions; all things which our feedback indicated were desirable attributes for a meeting. As a result, meeting attendance tripled between 1980 and 1995. In any given year, more members attend an AAS meeting than vote in the Society elections, perhaps regrettable, but a tribute to our success at one of our primary functions as a scientific society.

Figure 4. Pamela Hawkins, Peter Boyce and E. Margaret Burbidge at the Austin, January 1988 meeting. Photograph by Andrew Fraknoi.

THE ELECTRONIC ERA

From the beginning, the AAS Executive Office in Washington had put an emphasis on using technology as a tool. There was always at least one personal computer for each staff member. Limited though the first ones were, they greatly enhanced office productivity and prepared the way for us to use e-mail and the Internet when the time came. The Executive Office started with Xerox 820 computers running the program "Electric Pencil" for word processing and using 8-inch floppy disks which stored 90 Kbytes each. When the IBM PC came out we switched to standard PCs with 10 Mbyte hard disks. We have upgraded machines regularly, staying far enough behind the curve to remain cost effective.

One early experiment with technology is worth recalling. For the two 1983 meetings we had offered the ability to connect to the AAS computer by phone and modem to transmit abstracts. This proved to be too difficult for routine use and was discontinued.

E-mail connectivity came to the AAS in 1988, and the NASA Science Internet provided full Internet connectivity in 1991. By 1989 a significant proportion of the astronomical community had incorporated network connectivity into their daily routines. Jaylee Mead suggested that we ask NASA to set up Internet connectivity at our meetings so the exhibitors could have "live" demos and attendees could have e-mail during the January 1990 AAS meeting. We never envisioned the popularity of this service. The 10 e-mail terminals had waiting lines five to ten deep all day long and we had to physically shut down the connection to get astronomers to leave the room at the end of the day. So began one of our most popular services at the meetings.

The members' favorable response to the Internet triggered our process of planning how to make use of the Internet for scholarly communication. Again, Jaylee Mead was the broker, bringing the AAS together with people from the NSSDC and elsewhere in a workshop on the publishing of scholarly journals in an electronic format, which led to NASA's Project STELAR, a 2-year attempt to distribute page images of the AAS journals electronically. While not successful, as such, Project STELAR, by demonstrating the drawbacks to distributing page images (enormously large files and the inability to search the text), encouraged us at the AAS Executive Office to set our sights higher.

By the end of 1991, I had returned to the idea that we should be offering our members a way to submit meeting abstracts by e-mail. I made the decision, clearing it only with the Treasurer, to offer electronic abstract submission, and paid for the development of a system to accomplish this. It worked. Over half the abstracts were sent electronically, and within two years we were getting 99% electronic submissions. I suspect that if we had opened this decision to Council debate, we would have had a delay of at least six months, probably one year, while a committee investigated and reported back. We could not have afforded such a delay. Some things just need to be done when the time is right.

The time was also right to plan for further actions, and in the spring of 1992, a year before Mosaic and the World Wide Web were announced, we set out a plan for moving into electronic publishing within three years. I formed a team in the AAS Executive Office that moved the AAS journals into the electronic environment. By the fall of 1995, we were publishing the *Astrophysical Journal Letters* on line, and even today, it still remains one of the best scholarly electronic journals in the world.

INTERESTING MEMORIES

One of the most vivid pictures I carry with me to this day is the picture of President Dave Heeschen pounding the table and vowing never to go before Congress as part of his Presidential duties, and then in the next breath saying that was his personal attitude, and he recognized that the other Councilors and many of the younger members that he knew disagreed with his stance, and that he would support the formation of a Committee on Astronomy and Public Policy and would back any actions they took to work with Congress for the betterment of astronomy.

Such actions, in which individuals put their own parochial interests aside in favor of the broad considerations of astronomy as a whole, have been the hallmark of most officers and Councilors of the AAS. But not all Councilors have been paragons of rationality and responsibility. During the early 1980s the costs of producing *The Astrophysical Journal* started rising rapidly, causing the *ApJ* to operate at a large deficit for two years in a row. The Council and the Editor were unwilling to raise subscription rates and page charges enough to cover the costs. The Journal was on the verge of going broke. The only solution seemed to be to reduce costs, and the University of Chicago Press was not being particularly cooperative. At the same time, *The Astronomical Journal* was being produced at a much lower cost by AIP, so Treasurer Harold Weaver and I obtained an informal indication that we could bring the *ApJ* back to fiscal health if we had AIP publish the *ApJ* in addition to the *AJ*.

This issue came to a head during the January 1981 Council meeting in Albuquerque. For some Councilors, the suggestion that we consider moving the *ApJ* bordered on the heretical, or unthinkable. It led to the stormiest session I ever witnessed in some three dozen Council meetings. For some Councilors, emotion ran higher than reason. A motion was introduced forbidding the Executive Office to ask other publishers to quote on producing the *ApJ*. The motion was amended to preclude any informal inquiries as well, specifically "...that the Society not pursue an informal approach to the AIP..."[2]

Such a motion to abandon responsible business practices was counter to the Society's articles of incorporation and was probably unenforceable. Fortunately, we never had to put that to the test as the motion lost by a vote of 6 to 5. It was probably also fortunate that the Council did not realize that we had already obtained an informal quote from the AIP as that would have exacerbated the situation, perhaps beyond repair.

As it turned out, the Council discussion, and the fact that we had talked to the AIP, sent the desired message to the University of Chicago Press which began an aggressive campaign to cut costs. But the most important fallout of this episode has been the long period of increasing cooperation between the Press and the AAS, culminating in the exceptionally close working relationship which has been crucial to the successful development of the electronic versions of the AAS journals.

ERA AMENDMENT AND THE AAS

In my first year as Executive Officer, I found out just how deeply our members hold their convictions. This involved the reaction by some AAS members to the passage of the Council resolution which prohibited the AAS from meeting in states which had not yet ratified the Equal Rights Amendment (ERA) to the U.S. Constitution. The Council took the ERA boycott action at the Austin (January 1978) meeting. There was a significant reaction by some vocal members about this stand of the Council's, including a strong call to rescind the boycott. Throughout this affair, about a dozen members actually resigned from the AAS.

As a side note at least two of the resigned members continued to subscribe to the *ApJ* at the member rate. At that time the *ApJ* bill was separate from the dues bill, and the lists were not often effectively cross checked. When I called them, one rejoined quietly and the other dropped his subscription.

The Council held a special public session at the Mexico City (January, 1979) meeting, where people could make their views known. There was very little interest in this session. The Council also polled the full membership of the Society and commissioned Art Code to lead a committee to analyze the pros and cons of rescinding the action. The "Code Report" indicated that only 25% of the members responded to the ERA Poll which asked the members to choose one of three options:

1. Leave the ban in place.
2. Leave the ban but refer future sensitive issues to membership for decision.
3. Rescind the ban.

Of those who responded, 51% voted to rescind, so that was half of 25% of the membership—not a "mandate."

The Council gathered in record numbers at the Wellesley meeting to consider the issue; all Councilors were present for the first time in years. The issue was considered during an afternoon and evening session and the Council voted unanimously not to rescind the boycott, stating that "the Council believes that the repercussions of a rescission would constitute a far more conspicuous action than the original—open to interpretation by those in favor of the Council's ERA action, to be an unnecessary and damaging blow to their hopes for full equality for women."[3] As I reported at the time, "Two of the Councilors who voted against the original action were present at the meeting and voted against the rescission."[4]

A full report of the Council decision was made at the business meeting which attracted a record attendance of about 75 members. Following Council's explanation of its reasoning, and aside from a vocal few, there was little sentiment expressed at the Business Meeting for rescinding the ban. The Council's decision not to rescind generated more mail and concern, but the membership as a whole seemed glad to put the acrimony behind us. And so the Society weathered a very emotional issue.

Since then, the Council has considered the pros and cons of new political issues very carefully before taking action. I think the experience with the ERA issue has kept the Council out of some contentious areas into which they otherwise might have ventured.

SUMMARY

By borrowing ideas from everywhere, enlisting the aid of our members, and staying attuned to (and perhaps a bit in front of) changing circumstances, the AAS has completed the transition from a small, volunteer run organization to a professionally run organization better able to serve the members' needs in today's changing world. The challenge will be to continue to keep close to the members, to maintain a strong sense of community, and to serve the changing expectations of astronomers in North America and throughout the world.

Part 5

The Publications of the Society

A BRIEF HISTORY OF
THE ASTRONOMICAL JOURNAL

Paul W. Hodge

Of the two journals owned and run by the American Astronomical Society the older and, at least currently, the smaller is *The Astronomical Journal*. Predating the founding of the Society by fifty years, the inception of the Journal marked a significant early milestone in the history of American astronomy. Now, 150 years later, the *AJ* has shown a renewed vitality and is jumping into the electronic publishing era with enthusiasm. The future of the Journal as an arm of the Society looks full of exciting opportunities for service and innovation.

IN THE BEGINNING

American astronomy in the first half of the 19th century lay in the shadow of dominant European astronomical institutions. There was no formal organization to bring astronomers together; communication of astronomical results was largely done by letters and informal circulars, distributed by mail among the few practicing astronomers.

By the middle of the century, however, there was enough astronomical activity occurring throughout the country that a need was clear: better, more regular and more available dispersal of astronomical news and results. The person who recognized this need was a young astronomer in Boston named Benjamin Apthorp Gould.

BENJAMIN GOULD

A graduate of Harvard College and a Boston native, Benjamin Gould began his career as a teacher at the famous Boston Latin School. After a year of this, however, he decided that he would rather devote his life to the pursuit of science. To prepare himself, he designed and carried out what we would today call a graduate program in astronomy. In July 1845, he sailed to Europe. After spending three months learning about astronomical research at the Greenwich Observatory he crossed the Channel and partook of French science for four months at the Paris Observatory. This was followed by a full year's visit to the Berlin Observatory and four months at the Altona Observatory (near Hamburg, Germany). These longer study periods were interspersed with shorter visits to Göttingen, Zürich and Pulkova, as well as Hungary, Austria and Italy. [1, 10] They were topped off by a month at the Gotha Observatory in Türingen. Gould returned to Boston in 1848. Now thoroughly acquainted with the research traditions of European astronomy, exemplified by the great pioneers Gauss, Encke and Schumacher, Gould was ready to embark on his rather remarkable career.[2]

Just a year after his return from Europe, Benjamin Gould began what would soon become the standard organ of American astronomical results, *The Astronomical Journal.* His explanation, published in the first issue of the Journal in 1849, still reads so well that it is better to quote than to paraphrase it.[3]

> The enthusiasm of astronomers and the liberality of friends of science in America have enabled me to commence the **ASTRONOMICAL JOURNAL**, with the full conviction that it will be permanently supported. Of its importance, — its necessity, indeed, — for the proper development of astronomy in our country, there can be but one opinion. Astronomy has already reached a stage of development in America, which entitles it to claim a higher position than has yet been accorded it, and which requires a larger scope for its future growth. The influence which a purely scientific journal, devoted exclusively to astronomy and its kindred departments of inquiry, may exert upon the future progress of the science is very great; and it is, therefore, with diffidence, but without hesitation, that I begin the work.

> Such a work ought to support the dignity of a pure science, striving for the extension of the realm of human intellect; it should furnish the means of publication and prompt dissemination of discoveries and researches; and should promote harmony among astronomers, laboring for a common end, — while it furnishes an opportunity for the manly expression of differences of opinion.

> It will be distinctly understood that the publication of statements or opinions implies no indorsement of them by the Editor. No communication will be published without the name of the author; and I desire to be held answerable for the accuracy of such articles or researches only, as may be published with my name or initial.

> In the earnest hope that the establishment of *The Astronomical Journal* may be hereafter referred to, as an era for astronomy in America, I commend it to the sympathy and cooperation of the lovers and votaries of science.

WAR INTERVENES, AS DOES ARGENTINA

After an excellent start, with publication of issues thrice monthly, the Journal ceased temporarily in 1861 with the outbreak of the Civil War.[4] The Editor joined the war effort behind the lines, but did not stop his own astronomical research when time permitted. In this period he built an observatory in Cambridge and used its transit instrument to measure precise positions of a large number of stars near the north pole.

The war ended in 1865 but before Gould could re-start publication of his Journal he embarked upon another astronomical adventure. He was greatly concerned about the lack of astronomical data for the southern hemisphere and had managed to convince his Boston friends to finance an astronomical expedition to South America. The Argentine Minister to the U.S., Domingo Faustino Sarmiento, became enthusiastic about the idea and helped promote it. Later, as President of Argentina, he helped his friend Gould to establish a National Observatory for Argentina in Cordoba, and as its Director, Gould enthusiastically went about the task of establishing basic stellar data for the southern skies, marking ``an epoch in modern astronomy, the equalization of our knowledge of the two celestial hemispheres'' (2). Among the pioneering aspects of his work in Cordoba was the extensive use of the new technique of photography which was revolutionizing the field of astrometry.

Figure 1. Benjamin Apthorp Gould in 1888. Photograph courtesy Nancy Langford, Dudley Observatory Archives.

After returning to the U.S., Gould (Figure 1) realized his hope of resuming publication of *The Astronomical Journal* in 1886. From then on, the Journal was published regularly. Gould continued as Editor until his death in 1896 when that position was assumed by his long-time assistant, Seth Carlo Chandler.

CHANGING TRENDS IN ASTRONOMY

In their introduction to the first Index for *The Astronomical Journal*, which covered the first 50 volumes, Gerald Clemence and Louise Jenkins pointed out that "*The Astronomical Journal* is... a history of American astronomy. Founded in the days when our oldest astronomical institutions were still in their infancy, it contains contributions from virtually every eminent American astronomer... The growth and decline of interest in many subjects, as well as the rise and fall of some astronomers, can be traced in its pages."[5] With its long temporal base-line, the Journal does serve as a guide to the evolution of American astronomical research. A look at Volume 1, followed by a glance at a recent volume, demonstrates the extremes of this evolution. The former was devoted to the fields of celestial mechanics and precise positional astronomy, while the latter is dominated by papers on galaxies, objects which didn't even exist as subjects when Gould was Editor. Nevertheless, the proverbial thread can be followed across the 150 years; exciting new developments in gravitational physics are still being published in the Journal, as exemplified by highly-refined tests of General Relativity. Astrometry is still an important element of the Journal's pages, as exemplified by recent papers devoted to radio interferometric position determinations, as well as results from astrometric spacecraft such as *Hipparcos*.

Table 1 compares the distribution of topics of papers published in Volume 1 with that for the October and November 1997 issues of the Journal, which have four times as many pages as Volume 1 did, which covered two years, in itself a measure of change both in the Journal and in astronomical activity. The table dramatically demonstrates the shifts in emphasis over the years but also shows a very small but gratifying amount of common ground.

TABLE 1. *AJ* Papers by Subject: 1850 vs 1997.

	Volume 1 (1849–1850) (percent)	October & November 1997 (percent)
Celestial mechanics	36	1
Astrometry	28	3
Geodesy, general physics	8	0
Planets (other than orbits)	1	0
Comets (other than orbits)	18	0
Asteroids (other than orbits)	5	0
Stars	4	24
Star clusters	0	12
Instellar matter	0	12
The Galaxy	0	1
Galaxies and quasars	0	36
Clusters of galaxies	0	10
Cosmology	0	1

Clemence and Jenkins' claim that the Journal also traced the rise and fall of many astronomers is also notably true. Figure 2 is an example. Eagle-eyed astronomer E. E. Barnard published his first *AJ* papers in Volume 7 and he continued to publish there regularly until his death in 1923, publishing a total of 219 papers in the *AJ*. He probably holds the record for the most *AJ* papers published posthumously, as nine papers were published in volumes following his obituary notice. He may also hold the record for the number of Errata published in the *AJ* (a total of 16). It would be interesting to try to discover why no Errata were published after 1914, when he became an Associate Editor of the Journal.

THE RISE OF ASTROPHYSICS

The last few years of the nineteenth century saw a fairly dramatic change in the emphasis of astronomical research. As Osterbrock and others have thoroughly and eloquently recorded, a new branch of astronomy, called astrophysics, was then being defined.[6] With an emphasis on stellar spectra and the application of a newly-developing physical understanding of the microscopic nature of matter, astrophysics was a considerable departure from earlier astronomy, with respect to both the instrumentation used and the basic physical laws employed. It is generally accepted that American astronomers, especially at the new giant observatories in the Mid-west and, later, the West, were impatient with the staid, old-fashioned *Astronomical Journal* and so they decided to start a new journal for their new science. Osterbrock and others have suggested that Gould and Chandler as Editors did not welcome papers of an astrophysical nature and that *The Astrophysical Journal* and its brief predecessors were born out of desperation. An alternative interpretation is that the young spectroscopists considered the *AJ* to be too traditionalist and they wanted to establish a separate identity.[6] G. E. Hale, the prime advocate for a new journal, was a creative, ambitious, and wealthy young scientist, and these characteristics were important ingredients for the establishment of something as monumental as *The Astrophysical Journal*. It is notable that the young B. A. Gould, 50 years earlier, had these same characteristics.

The creation of *The Astrophysical Journal* provided a natural but unnecessarily-sharp division in American astronomy. The exciting results from the giant new telescopes in California, even results that were not spectroscopic, found their way into the new, more glamorous journal to the decided detriment of its older brother. Famous names from the early twentieth century are hard to find in the *AJ*. Edwin Hubble published only one paper there (on stellar proper motions) and Harlow Shapley only two in the pre-AAS *AJ*, one on the asteroid Mildred, which, curiously, has the same name as does Shapley's daughter, who was born years later.[7, 8, 9] Other famous names do occur, but most are now unfamiliar (e.g., W. W. Dinwiddie, Esther Doody and many others). Whether the result of editorial policy or of natural selection, *The Astronomical Journal* gradually settled into the role of an old-fashioned and unassuming

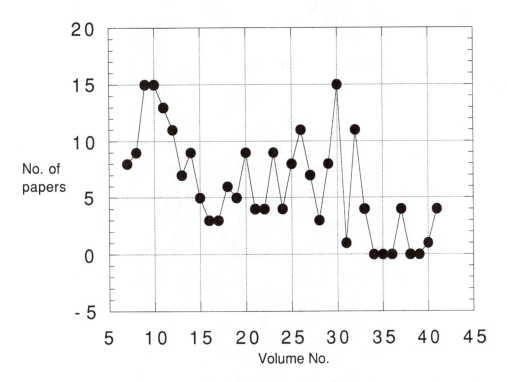

Figure 2. The number of papers per volume published by E. E. Barnard. He became Associate Editor with Volume 28 (in 1914) and died in 1923 (Volume 35).

depository of traditional, classical astronomy, securing a distant second place behind its young competitor.

THE ALBANY YEARS

For two intervals of time *The Astronomical Journal* was edited from the Dudley Observatory in Albany, New York. In 1855, Benjamin Gould was appointed Director of the young Observatory, which had been founded just three years before. He brought the journal with him to Albany, where, with financial help from some friends of astronomy, publication continued. Gould's tenure at Dudley was brief, however. He "equipped and organized the institution, and carried it on without remuneration and at his private expense."[2] After four years as Director he left, following, in Chandler's words, a "severe struggle to preserve the institution for purposes of scientific investigation."[2, 10] Both Gould and the Journal returned to Cambridge, Massachusetts.

Four years as director of an observatory might not seem to be a particularly brief time by today's standards, but it definitely was anomalous at that time. Benjamin Boss, (Figure 3) for example, directed the Dudley Observatory from 1912 to 1956, an amazing 44 years, during part of which he also edited *The Astronomical Journal* (from 1912 to 1941). The Journal had moved back to the Dudley Observatory in 1909, when Chandler

Figure 3. Benjamin Boss, editor of the *AJ* from 1912 to 1941. Photograph courtesy Nancy Langford, Dudley Observatory Archives.

offered it to the then Director, Lewis Boss (Benjamin's father), who was Editor until his death in 1912.

ACQUISITION BY THE AAS

In 1941 Benjamin Boss approached the American Astronomical Society with an offer to transfer *The Astronomical Journal* to the Society. His reason was that he found "the editorial duties consumed too much of his time."[11] The Society had used various journals for the publication of its proceedings and related material, including *Science, Popular Astronomy* and its own *Publications of the American Astronomical Society*. Furthermore, it had been considering how to formalize its relationship with *The Astrophysical Journal*. Just two years before Boss' offer, the Society had accepted a bequest from the preeminent student of the Moon's motion, E. W. Brown, who had been Associate Editor of the *AJ* from 1911 to 1938. The generous gift ($5,000) was intended to ensure that the Society "founds or acquires and has full control of a journal devoted to astronomical research."[12]

Probably bolstered by Brown's bequest, the AAS Council received Boss' offer warmly and voted at its September 1941 meeting to accept. The Council also voted to ask Dirk Brouwer, Director of the Yale University Observatory and a prominent practitioner of celestial mechanics, to be Editor. Louise Jenkins, also of Yale and a specialist in positional astronomy, was appointed Assistant Editor, and the Journal offices were moved to New Haven, Connecticut.[13]

WHAT GETS PUBLISHED?

The decision of what is published and what is not is a matter of concern for every editor, publisher, author and reader of a journal. Both the nature of the material and its quality are issues for discussion. With regard to the form of the contributions, a considerable evolution has occurred for the *AJ*. Early volumes included many more kinds of contributions than are published now, including brief announcements of discoveries (Figure 4), letters from abroad, reviews, translations, and obituaries. Many of the "papers" published in early volumes were actually portions of letters sent to Gould. The style of the Journal was informal, perhaps, but the words and the spirit of presentation were highly formal.

Reviews of books and other publications were included in the first 18 volumes (to 1898). It is amusing to note that although the practice was discontinued exactly 100 years ago, some publishers and authors still send notices of publication and review copies of books to the present Editor.

The variety of material and its style of presentation both changed with the acquisition of the Journal by the AAS. Brouwer complained about the existing format, which he found difficult to use. After deliberation by various committees, it was decided to adopt a format like that of the *Physical Review*, a policy which has continued to the present with only modest changes.[14] More importantly, the nature of the papers changed along with the format. The new Journal marked the culmination of the evolu-

ASTRONOMICAL JOURNAL.

EXTRA.

NEW PLANET.

Mr. DE GASPARIS discovered in Naples, November 2, a New Planet, resembling a star of the 9.10 magnitude.

Professor SCHUMACHER announces the discovery in a circular dated November 14, and states that Mr. DE GASPARIS made the discovery by means of the Zones in the vicinity of the ecliptic, which he had constructed to aid him in his search for planets.

The observations are,

At Naples, by Mr. DE GASPARIS.

1850.	M. T. Naples. h. m. s.	α	δ
November 2	7 3 6.5	$30^{\circ}\ 31'\ 49''.9$	$+7^{\circ}\ 58'\ 55''.0$
3	7 21 41.4	30 14 58.3	$+8\ \ 0\ 18.5$

At Altona, by Dr. PETERSEN.

1850.	M. T. Altona. h. m. s.	α	δ
November 13	13 25 45.2	$27^{\circ}\ 34'\ 25''.0$	$+8^{\circ}\ 19'\ 38''.6$

Dr. PETERSEN estimates it as of the 10 magnitude.

B. A. GOULD, JR.

Cambridge, 1850, December 5.

Figure 4. "Extra! Extra! Read All About it!" An unusual feature of Volume 1 was this "Extra", a circular to subscribers announcing the discovery of a new "planet" (asteroid). At the beginning of 1850, only 10 asteroids had been discovered.

tion of the scientific "paper" from a heterogeneous mix of notes (Figure 5), bare tables and letters, to a formalized, fully-developed scientific report.

But in the 1940s the *AJ* did not publish only original scientific papers. The Society decided to discontinue the *Publications of the American Astronomical Society* and elected to place the abstracts of papers presented at AAS meetings, as well as the "Reports of Observatories," in their newly-acquired journal. It was also decided that the *AJ* should publish one review article each year.[15]

With regard to the quality of material published in the *AJ*, there has always been a certain amount of discontent, as is true for most journals. Authors sometimes think that editors are too particular and editors sometimes think that authors are too careless. The introduction of Associate Editors helped to modulate this natural source of conflict and provided the Journal with a body of people to help make general decisions, as well

MELLISH'S COMET (1915 a),

On the Condensations or Secondary Comets of May 12.

By E. E. BARNARD.

On May 12 Mr. SULLIVAN and I examined MELLISH's comet with the 40-inch telescope. The sky was misting over, with a storm approaching from the west. The comet was already dim to the eye from the dense haze.

There were two round condensations or secondary comets in a line with the head and preceding it. Calling the main comet A, these would be B and C, in the order of distance. B was very faint and nearer C. C was quite bright and was perhaps 1½ or 2 times less bright than A. Except for brightness it resembled A very much and was a little smaller. They were all involved in the nebulosity of A, and were in a brighter region, perhaps the axis of the tail. The following measures were made. Central Standard Time (6^{h}0^m slow of G.M.T.)

POSITION ANGLE AC

1915 May 12^d	13^{h}30^{m}28^s	286°.11	(5)
	13 39 13	284 .32	(4)

DISTANCE AC

1915 May 12^d	13^{h}34^{m}39^s	26″.53	(4)
	13 36 30	27 .84	(4)
	13 41 29	28 .62	(3)

Hastening to the Bruce Observatory, I made an exposure of ten minutes on the comet with the 6-inch and 10-inch telescopes. The comet was disappearing in the haze when the exposure began and was completely blotted out at the end of the ten minutes. The sky remained cloudy. The plates show A and C, but with insufficient exposure to produce a good picture.

Yerkes Observatory, Williams Bay, Wisconsin, May 13, 1915.

Figure 5. Not all *AJ* papers had the formal trappings of today's journal articles. This example is from 1915.[19]

as more particular decisions about what to publish. The Associate Editor tradition continued into the era of AAS ownership. The list of past Associate Editors includes many famous names, including some from the sub-field of astrophysics.

In spite of such precautions, the early *AJ* was not entirely free of papers of dubious value. As Clemence and Jenkins explain in describing the first General Index, "all articles have been given equal treatment..., including a few that ought never to have been printed."[5] No such statement was made in the last General Index.[16]

As astronomy and the Journal both grew, the practice of having the Associate Editors serve both as reviewers and advisors gradually changed. I have not found records that pin-point the exact time when outside referees became the general rule, but the transfer of the advisory role of the Associate Editors to an AAS Publications Board is well-documented. The last issue of the *AJ* to list the advising Associate Editors was that of December 1978. In subsequent years, the title of Associate Editor of the *AJ* was reserved for one person, appointed by the AAS Council, whose duties were to act as Editor in the absence of the regular editor. Since 1984 that person has been Karl-Heinz Bohm.

THE *AJ* AT YALE

Starting in 1941 Brouwer and Jenkins guided the Journal through the remainder of the difficult war years and into the second half of the century. With the rapid development of high-speed computers, exciting new results became possible in the traditional *AJ* fields of research, including celestial mechanics and astrometry. During this period precise photometry using photoelectric photometers became another strong component of the *AJ* menu. Brouwer continued as Editor for 25 years, nearly matching Benjamin Boss' record. When he died in 1966, the Journal had had only five editors in the 117 years since its founding.

A new position, Co-Editor, was introduced in 1959, when Harlan Smith joined the staff, with the primary responsibility of looking after papers on stellar and extragalactic astronomy. When he left Yale in 1963 to become Director of the McDonald Observatory, G. M. Clemence became Co-Editor, a position he held until Brouwer's death. From January 1966, until December 1967, Clemence served as sole Editor.

THE COLUMBIA EDITORS

The January 1968 issue of the Journal was the first to be published under the new Co-Editors, Lodewijk Woltjer and Norman H. Baker at Columbia University. Both men represented a new set of research interests for the Journal, though the profile of the subjects published showed only a gradual concomitant change. By 1984, the last of the Columbia years, however, the *AJ* looked different. Celestial mechanics and astrometry no longer dominated the Journal; stars and galaxies had taken over.

Another change affecting the Journal at this time was the withdrawal of both the "Reports of Observatories" and "Abstracts of Papers Presented." The latter had been published after each AAS meeting since Brouwer had become Editor, but both of these features were removed to the *BAAS* in 1968. A more sporadic feature, reports on various special-topics meetings, also ceased at about that time, and the Journal became exclusively an organ for complete, formal scientific papers.

The editorship changed twice after the Journal's move to Columbia, with Leon Lucy replacing Woltjer when he left for Europe and, later, with Baker becoming sole Editor when Lucy left for Europe. Baker's tenure first as Co-Editor and later as Editor was notable for its quiet dignity and the smoothness of its operation. Also, not since Gould had an Editor written such felicitous editorials. They appeared seldom but were a pleasure to read.

"OLD WINE IN A NEW BOTTLE"

The January 1984 issue of the *AJ* began with an editorial titled as above, in which Editor Baker introduced the new *AJ* format.[17] Conceived as a new departure by George Abell, who had been selected as the new Editor for the Journal several months earlier, it instead became a "kind of memorial" to him, as he died of heart failure before he was to assume editorial duties. It was Abell who designed the new *AJ* cover and who laid out the rules for selecting the cover art. It was a wise move, as more than one astronomer has confessed to have sent his or her important paper to the *AJ*, hoping to have a chance for the cover.

In March of 1984, the transfer of the Editorial Offices from Columbia to the University of Washington was completed. What happened after that will not be described here, as it belongs to the category of current events, rather than history.

FINANCIAL MATTERS

This essay will end with a brief account of the financial history of the *AJ*. Although the Journal is financially secure at the time of this writing, it has had a few periods of budgetary crises in its long lifetime. At the beginning, Gould used his own funds and that of some of his friends to maintain publication. The subscription rate was $5 per volume, with a volume consisting of 24 issues published approximately monthly. Thus astronomers received this highly-professional journal for a mere $2.50 per year.

Gould's first years were rather difficult financially. At the beginning, the budget was comfortably balanced.[1] There were 75 subscribers ($375) and 8 "promoters" (5 put up $100 each and 3 put up $50 each), giving a total income of $1,025. Expenses for volume 1 were approximately $900. However, by 1855, Gould was seeing a deficit of some $600 per volume and was becoming discouraged. His move to the Dudley Observatory occurred in that year, at which time 12 citizens of Albany pitched in and donated enough funds to keep the Journal solvent for six more years.[10] After those six years, the question of budget became moot as the Civil War began and the *AJ* temporarily ceased publication.

The subscription rate for the *AJ* remained remarkably stable for a very long time. At the turn of the century it was still $5 per volume (though by then, volumes were published approximately annually) and even 100 years after its founding the rate had not changed substantially. The first copy of the *AJ* in this writer's collection is from volume 58 (1953), which cost $8 per year for a regular subscription. Inflation and a growing page count eventually changed things, however; an AAS member subscription was $85 per volume in 1997. Although this might seem to be quite an increase, one must realize that the $85 bought 6,000 pages of carefully and professionally-prepared science, a real bargain when compared to scientific books or many other journals. The AAS seems to have made a wise decision in 1941 to acquire the Journal and to maintain it as a non-profit enterprise.

When the AAS acquired the Journal, the financial situation was satisfactory; there was income amounting to nearly $1,000 per year from the Gould Fund, an endowment established by Gould's daughter in 1897 and administered by the National Academy of Sciences. There was also income available from the E. W. Brown Fund, amounting to about $130 per year.[18] In the financial statement for the year June 1942 to May 1943, the receipts were $2,637 and the expenses were $1,525, with an end-of-year balance of $2,294 (including carryovers from previous years.)[13] Such a healthy budget was largely the result of the war; there were fewer papers to print than before or after that troubled time. Comparing the 1942 budget to the 1997 budget ($1,111,150 income vs. $1,053,084 expenses) it is clear that the *AJ* has grown enormously but at the same time has managed to balance costs and expenses, improve production quality, and maximize accessibility to the astronomical community.

The ideals with which the young Benjamin Gould began the life of *The Astronomical Journal*, nearly 150 years ago, continue to guide it. For nearly 60 years its new parents, the members of the American Astronomical Society, have cared for it wisely. As a modern and vital vehicle for the world-wide dispersal of astronomical knowledge, it has greatly benefited from "the sympathy and cooperation of the lovers and votaries of science."

THE AMERICAN ASTRONOMICAL SOCIETY AND *THE ASTROPHYSICAL JOURNAL*

Helmut A. Abt

INTRODUCTION

One of the most important functions of the American Astronomical Society (AAS) is the publication of journals of interest to its members. This chapter is a description of how the AAS acquired *The Astrophysical Journal* (*ApJ*) and how the *ApJ* grew, developed a new structure, an electronic version, a more active Publications Board, and became a truly international journal. We also make some guesses about what may be in store following the first centennial of the Journal and Society.

OWNERSHIP OF THE JOURNAL

As early as 1941, Otto Struve recommended that the *ApJ* be published "With the Collaboration of the American Astronomical Society," although that wording was not added to the title page until 1945. That addition allowed the *ApJ* to give reduced subscription rates to members of the AAS. Further he recommended that three new Collaborating Editors be appointed each year by the AAS on a rotating basis. Those aided the Managing Editor and several Assistant Editors in setting Journal policies and aided in the review of papers. That board of Collaborators had been in existence since 1902 and was selected by the University of Chicago; it replaced the "Associate Editors" that, since the start of the Journal in 1895, served the same purpose. Finally, Struve recommended in 1941 that eventually the AAS take over the ownership of the *ApJ*, although that was postponed. It was during the same year that the AAS started discussions about taking over the ownership of *The Astronomical Journal*, a move that was completed in 1944.

The AAS finally assumed ownership of the *ApJ* in 1972. Both were started in the 1890s primarily by the same person, namely George Ellery Hale. Both organizations soon became the preeminent ones in the field in America. But it was in 1971 that S. Chandrasekhar made the move that Struve had recommended much earlier. Chandrasekhar made many changes and innovations to the Journal that have already been documented.[1] However he, like Struve, felt that the leading American astronomical journal should be owned by the leading American astronomical society, rather than by a single university press. An unstated additional factor that must have influenced the University of Chicago Press to relinquish ownership of the Journal was that in 1971 the first Managing Editor had been appointed (Helmut A. Abt) who was not a member of the University of Chicago faculty, and therefore the Press and University were losing some control over the Journal. Therefore in 1971 the Press, represented primarily by

Chandrasekhar, and the AAS, represented by President Martin Schwarzschild and Treasurer Frank K. Edmondson, negotiated the ownership transfer.

The conditions of the transfer involved many issues, most of which were specified by the revised AAS bylaws of 1971. The AAS selected the editors and an Editorial Board. It was specified that the AAS must maintain a reserve fund at a level of at least one-third of the annual expenditures (that was later changed to one-half). The existing reserve fund in 1971 was not transferred to the AAS until 1974; it was felt that by that time the fund had been accumulated primarily under AAS ownership. Moreover, there was a gentlemen's agreement, never written out, between the participants that *ApJ* and AAS funding should always be kept separate. The failure to include that provision led in 1985–1986 to the only disagreement between the AAS and *ApJ*. The AAS, being reluctant to raise dues further, decided to assess the journals 4% of their annual income to compensate for the extra expenses incurred to the Society. It argued that other societies also received funds from their journals. The *ApJ* Managing Editor argued that that was a violation of the gentlemen's agreement and that, unlike the cases of other societies that had to develop their own publications, the AAS received a successful journal free of charge plus a large reserve fund. However because the decision was up to the AAS Council, the action was taken without permitting any airing to the membership of the opposing point of view.

The University of Chicago Press has been retained as a contract publisher. While the AAS is free to select another publisher, it has been continuously pleased with the quality, promptness, cooperation, and innovation shown by the Press. The Press originally had an editorial division and a printing division. The latter was gradually phased out because it could not compete in the purchases of ever larger presses and printing equipment. The Journals Division has energetically sought bids every few years from various compositors and printers to minimize costs and to develop new methods. That has led to the format changes (larger sizes, frequency of publication, thinner paper, type changes, more words per page) that have occurred. However the complexities of preparing material for on-line publication preclude the possibility of shifting tasks to another compositor on short notice. The Press has also cooperated in allowing reasonable style changes, such as printing abstracts in full-sized type.

JOURNAL GROWTH

The *ApJ* underwent a remarkable expansion in the years following the transfer. Actually the expansion started in the early 1930s, probably due to the growth of atomic physics that allowed astronomical observations to be related to physical parameters. After an interruption caused by World War II, the growth continued at a constant exponential rate, showing very little sensitivity to the advent of the space age or ups and downs in funding.[1] However, the magnitude of that rise was not apparent until recent decades. Although the average paper length also more than tripled since early in the century, the numbers of papers and authors also increased by large factors so that the overall length of the *ApJ* grew by a factor of 100 since the beginning of the century.

This lack of sensitivity to funding changes seems difficult to understand. One cause is that research results are often slow in reaching publication, so an observation may not be analyzed, interpreted, and published for many years. Another cause is that when funding is decreased, applicants must try harder; and increasing publication rates is one way to compete. However, there is some evidence that the continued low funding in the 1990s and the reduced availability of positions are starting to cause a leveling of the publication rate. It is ironic that this is occurring just when the rate of recent discoveries in astronomy has reached a new high because of increased wavelength accessibility from space and new equipment on the ground.

The growth of the *ApJ* to its current content of 25,000 pages per year has been a cause for concern for many years. Librarians have complained about insufficient shelf space, and many astronomers have terminated their subscriptions for the same reason. The change to weekly publication has been postponed temporarily by the use of thinner paper; if we try to publish more than 600–700 pages per issue with the new thinner paper, the binding process will not work well.

A solution often proposed is to divide the Journal into sections by astronomical objects. Many knowledgeable people have advised that this should not be done because: (1) to divide the Journal would have the effect, as it did in physics, to divide the field with the result that astronomers will fail to keep aware of progress made outside their own specialties; (2) unlike physics, astronomy cannot be divided naturally into separate fields e.g., stellar astronomers should be aware of recent results in solar physics and extragalactic astronomers should remain aware of results regarding stars; (3) the libraries pay the bulk of the publication expenses, and they would subscribe to all parts in any case; and (4) separate publication and distribution would be more expensive. Instead we opted for the following solution: (1) to depend heavily in the future upon the on-line version, where the amount of material available in storage is irrelevant; and (2) to depend upon good indexing to recover needed material.

Since the 1960s, the Journal has led in the availability of good indexes. Every year there is an annual author and subject index in which the full reference (title, authors, and location) can be obtained for each author (up to a maximum of eight per paper) and for each of several subject headings without being referred to other listings. Every five years there is a cumulative index that is also distributed free to each subscriber. Also, in recent years there has been an author and subject index every two months. All these are programmed to be produced continuously so that, for example, the annual index is distributed before the end of each year.

In 1990 the editors of *Astronomy & Astrophysics* (*A&A*), *ApJ*, and the *Monthly Notices of the Royal Astronomical Society* (*MNRAS*) agreed upon an extensive set of about 250 subject headings that they use in common so readers would look under the same heading for similar papers in each journal. That many headings was necessary so that for 2000 papers published annually and about five headings per paper, there would be an average of 40 papers per heading; if there are far more than 40 papers for a given heading, searching becomes cumbersome. The subject headings are printed on each paper so that readers can guess where to search for similar papers.

ON-LINE EDITIONS

The development of the on-line editions of the Journal was due to the foresight and technical knowledge of Peter Boyce.[2] When he was Executive Officer of the AAS, Boyce obtained an NSF grant to produce an on-line edition of the Letters in late 1995 and of the Journal and Supplements in late 1996. This was done with the help of Heather Dalterio (AAS office), Chris Biemesderfer, and Evan Owens (Univ. Chicago Press). The on-line editions have the added feature of allowing readers to call up from the Astronomical Data Systems at Harvard (ADS) a past reference that had been optically scanned by the ADS. By late 1997, virtually all of the standard journals will have been scanned by the ADS and will be available for quick recall. This feature, plus the care with which the on-line editions have been planned, makes the field of astronomy the leader among the physical sciences in the availability of on-line journals.

We are aware of the availability of other huge data resources in the fields of law and medicine but only at a considerable expense to the readers. In designing the system for the *ApJ*, the AAS felt that the most practical system is one in which the library at each institution obtains a site license that would allow every scientist at that institution unlimited free access to the Journal. To collect a small reader's fee would have been too cumbersome and a large fee would inhibit usage. Actually, the added cost to libraries of the on-line editions is only about 20% (after subtracting the added cost due to the changing of editorial offices). For individuals, the on-line edition is much cheaper than the paper edition because most of the latter expense is in printing, paper, and postage.

PUBLICATIONS BOARD

In the 1970s, it had been the practice of the AAS to conduct a careful review of the *ApJ* every five years to help decide on policy matters. That function was gradually taken over by the Publications Board which studied individual problems, such as the cost structure of the journals (under William Kraushaar's chairship), the advisability of AAS-sponsored republication of important books (under Margaret Geller's chairship), and needs for on-line journals (under Catherine Pilachowski's chairship). The Publications Board continues to provide advice to the editors and advocates changes to the AAS Council. Since the Board's reorganization in 1979 as a more active committee, the chairpersons have been William L. Kraushaar (1979–1982), Margaret J. Geller (1983–1984), Patrick Palmer (1985–1986), John P. Huchra (1986–1988), Julie H. Lutz (1988–1989), Catherine Pilachowski (1989–1992), Hugh M. Van Horn (1992–1994), James W. Liebert (1994–1996), and Robert J. Hanisch (1997–).

INTERNATIONAL ASPECTS

The *ApJ* has steadily become more international in readership and authorship. Hale subtitled the Journal "An International Review of Spectroscopy and Astronomical Physics." Actually its partial role as a review journal gradually decreased during the first half of this century. We insist upon original research content in each paper, the exception being the catalogs and compilations occasionally published in the Supplements. Because the Journal is highly respected in the U.S. and the U.S. has been the leader in many branches of astronomy, the Journal has attracted more and more papers from abroad. At present about 35% of the authors are from outside the U.S. and the percentage has been growing by about 1% per year. A similar effect has been noted by many other scientific journals. About half of the subscribing libraries and individuals are abroad.

The heavy foreign readership and authorship has had several effects. One is the avoidance of all American slang and colloquialisms in the papers. Another is the availability of individual subscriptions to astronomers abroad at the same reduced rates offered members of the AAS. Another is the waiving of page charges for institutions in certain developing countries for which the charges, typically $1000–2000 per paper, are difficult to raise. That practice goes back at least to 1956 when the AAS Council voted for special funds to help some foreign authors with page charges. Also starting in 1987, the *ApJ* offered libraries in developing countries the option to subscribe at member rates, rather than at library rates. We also allow them the opportunity to subscribe by paying only for the cost of producing the Journal copies that they receive. These are major decisions because the reasons for assessing page charges are: (1) to allow relatively low library subscription rates; (2) to provide a stable financial base for the journals; and (3) to permit new ventures such as the indexes distributed free to subscribers, the video and CD-ROM series, and the on-line editions. Institutions and libraries, through the mechanism of page charges, provide about one-half of the publication expenses of the Journal while the individual subscribers pay only enough to cover the printing, paper, and mailing of their copies.

Another effect of the growing internationalization of astronomy, partly caused by the ease of e-mail communication, was to standardize some of the style requirements. Most astronomers as coauthors publish in a variety of journals and conference proceedings, caused in part by the growing cooperation between astronomers in different countries. Why should astronomers have to remember that some journals require roman numerals for section headings or tables while others use arabic numbers, or use one abbreviation for the *Monthly Notices* (*Mon. Not. Roy. Astron. Soc.*) while another uses a different form (*MNRAS*)? Therefore Abt organized two meetings between the editors of *A&A*, *ApJ*, and *MNRAS* (others were invited) to help reduce the diversity. The first meeting in 1988 concentrated on style requirements and led to changes in these three journals plus others.[3] Among those changes are a set of simple acronyms for the major astronomical journals, e.g., *MNRAS* and *PASP*. The second meeting in 1991 led to a common set of subject headings for *A&A*, *ApJ*, and *MNRAS*.

One additional aspect of the internationalization was the selection of a foreign astronomer (H. J. G. L. M. Lamers) on the Publications Board in 1992 on the grounds that if one-third of the papers come from abroad, it makes sense to have a representative from abroad on the Publications Board. I hope that this will become a regular practice.

REVISED EDITORIAL STRUCTURE

In 1971, Chandrasekhar ran the Journal with one Associate Editor (Dimitri Mihalas). He had one assistant (Donna Elbert), one production person at the Press (Jeannette Burnett), and one copyeditor (Jeanne Hopkins). Currently there are three editors (Abt, Dalgarno, and Avrett), 12 Scientific Editors, three Associate Letters Editors, nine assistants, seven production people, and 12 copyeditors at the Press. In addition there are three systems developers for the on-line editions and the Journal obtains additional help from the Press, especially from Journals Manager Robert Shirrell, and elsewhere (Jeannette Barnes, Chris Biemesderfer, Lee Brotzman).

Before 1990, the Managing Editor (Abt) and Letters Editor (Dalgarno) personally oversaw the reviewing of all the papers. While that was efficient, it became too much work. In that year two Associate Editors (Yervant Terzian and Virginia Trimble) were selected to help oversee the reviewing of manuscripts for Part 1 and the Supplements. By 1996 the number of Associate Editors (renamed Scientific Editors) increased to 12 and they were overseeing about 90% of the reviews of papers for Part 1 and the Supplements. The advantages were (1) the work of the Managing Editor (renamed Editor-in-Chief) was much reduced so that it could be transferred to another person; (2) the Scientific Editors were specialists in certain areas and were better able to understand and evaluate manuscripts and the assessments of those manuscripts in their specialties; and (3) the reviewing system and standards for the Journal became a matter of common consensus, rather than the wishes of a single individual. As the field grows, the number of Scientific Editors can also grow so that the burden upon those volunteers will not be excessive. Thus we have a structure that can grow and is not dependent upon the health and abilities of a single person.

JOURNAL CENTENNIAL

The *ApJ* celebrated its centennial in 1995 but only in a modest way. The proposal for a series of submitted essays on the likely future of astronomy in the next hundred

Figure 1. The current *Astrophysical Journal* staff in Tucson are shown in the Kitt Peak National Observatory library. The people are (left-to-right) Alice Prochnow, Janice Sexton, Helmut Abt, Cheyenne Ross, Candace Hauser, and Rachel Williams. The piles of volumes are those published in the first year of publication (left), 50th year (center) and 100th year (right).

years or less led to only one acceptable essay (by George Collins). Basically the Managing Editor was too busy with the flood of papers to plan a more elaborate celebration, such as is being done for the AAS in 1999. It remains remarkable that the Journal has been the preeminent one in world astrophysics for 100 years.

THE FUTURE

We look forward to many years of useful and exciting cooperation between the AAS and the *ApJ* with its concentration upon the publication of outstanding research results. It would be very difficult to predict the nature of that cooperation in the same way that we cannot predict most of the new astronomical results to be derived even ten years from now. But perhaps a few comments are appropriate.

The Paper Editions

Most astronomers do the bulk of their research and writing on a computer terminal, so we can expect that in the future they will do most of their reading there also. However I doubt that librarians will voluntarily give up receiving paper editions of the *ApJ* for many years to come because they have learned that new technologies in communication last only a decade or so. Can we now read IBM cards, paper tape, or 8-inch floppies? What will happen when CD-ROMs and videos are replaced by other storage media? Will part of the holdings of libraries have to be replaced at considerable cost?

On the other hand, if we were to give up the paper editions, there would be no need to hold papers until an issue is filled; papers would just be added to memory as they are accepted. And the formatting of journals would be more compatible with computer screens. The bulk of the *ApJ* plus other journals demands more compact storage space than is possible with paper editions, which is fine for individuals, but libraries will resist terminating the paper editions.

Faster Publication

The production of paper editions is a slow process that takes months. A paper *ApJ* manuscript goes through the mail 14 times before publication. It is produced carefully and authors see proofs twice (for correction) before publication. When they were given the option of shortening the publication delay by two weeks by seeing proofs only once, 85% of the authors declined. But now when most manuscripts are prepared electronically and transmitted by e-mail or ftp, and when they do not need to be keyboarded a second time, the copyediting and printing is much faster. In fact, during 1997 the University of Chicago Press expects to produce an on-line version of the Letters (without final pagination) in two weeks after receipt of the accepted papers.

We would all like to see faster publication because progress in astronomy some-times happens more quickly than the 3–6 month publication lag time. For one thing, publication in two weeks may diminish our dependence upon preprints (that are scientifically unreliable) and abstracting services. And it would make the dissemination of current information less dependent upon being on the right preprint mailing lists. New techniques and the use of electronically-prepared manuscripts have reduced *ApJ* publication times from six months to five; we can expect even greater reductions in the near future.

Less Expensive Publication

At $0.04 per page to libraries and less than $0.01 per page to individuals, the *ApJ* is already the least expensive major journal in the physical sciences.[4] Even if all the income came from subscriptions and no library subscriptions were lost, the cost would still be an order of magnitude less than many for-profit journals. Nevertheless, the large quantity of papers produced leads to high total costs. We constantly search for possible savings, so the cost increases during the past two decades have been less than the cost-of-living increases. Composition, paper, and mailing have traditionally amounted to more than half of the editorial and production costs. By using author-keyboarded manuscripts we save most of the first of these (except initially the copy-editing is more expensive) and for the on-line editions we save most of the last two. We can expect reduced expenses in the future.

Reader Use of Published Data

The increased flow of data from space telescopes and the ease of storing those data in computer-readable form makes it more likely that research projects can be done using published data only. This is similar to the continued widespread use of IUE and IRAS data even after the spacecrafts have been turned off. Many ground-based observatories have started to store CCD data, just as they formerly stored photographic plates. The CD-ROM set of Palomar Sky Survey plates is another example of making use of older data.

Increased Cooperation Among Journals

A common complaint among people asked to review manuscripts is that they just received manuscripts for review from several other journals. To my knowledge the record number of people who declined to review a single manuscript for that and other reasons is eight. When astronomers are asked to review observing request proposals, proposals for grants, recommendations for employment or promotions, advise students and colleagues about papers. etc., they have very limited time left to review manuscripts for journals.

We should develop a better system for selecting referees. The *ApJ* Editor-in-Chief and his 12 Scientific Editors have a common referee file and a policy that if any one of them has sent a new manuscript to a person, none may send another new manuscript to the same referee within two months. This can be done without letting editors know which papers have been sent to which referees. Would it not be helpful if such a common file were used by most of the major astronomical journals?

The North American astronomical journals have been collecting and publishing lists (the Yellow Pages; also on the WWW) of the titles, authors, and sources for preprints of papers submitted to (currently) eight different journals. Would it not be helpful to have that information for journals outside of North America too? Several journals have good indexes for their published volumes. Would it not be helpful to have a combined index for many of our astronomical journals?

Finally, undoubtedly improved search techniques will be devised in the future so that our requests for papers on a given topic will be better focused and will not produce too few titles or too many nonrelevant titles.

I am indebted to the Editor for supplying pertinent minutes of AAS Council meetings and a copy of the 1941 letter from Otto Struve to Henry Norris Russell in which Struve outlined his proposals for future cooperation between the AAS and *ApJ*.

PART 6

THE SOCIETY IN A CHANGING WORLD

COMMITTEE ON THE STATUS OF WOMEN IN ASTRONOMY

Susan Simkin

INTRODUCTION

It is difficult to satisfy everyone's perceptions and still write an "official" history of an event — such as the creation of the Committee on the Status of Women in Astronomy (CSWA) of the AAS, which was launched in response to political controversy. Much of the background for this activity is not in the AAS minutes and resides only in the (imperfect) memories of the active participants. Since my personal involvement in the events leading up to the creation of the CSWA was limited by geography (I was resident in the Netherlands and then Australia at the time), I have had to rely on firsthand accounts from those who were directly involved. My success in eliciting these accounts has been limited, at best. Thus, the summary reported here is sketchy but may (I hope) serve as a starting point for those who have greater access to historical documentation.

PROLOGUE

Although most elementary astronomy books emphasize the early history of such women as Annie Jump Cannon and Cecilia Payne-Gaposchkin, the number of women actually engaged in astronomy during the years leading up to WWII and after was very limited, in number of course, but mainly in their ability to achieve elite, independent roles in research. As with other scientific disciplines, the lack of male graduate students during WW II led to a *relative* increase in female astronomers but this was rapidly wiped out in the 1950s.[1]

Those of us who were graduate students in the 1960s and refused to believe that women were not suited for employment at major universities had a few examples such as Cecilia Payne-Gaposchkin at Harvard (who was well known nationally, but inaccessible to most of us), Helen Dodson Prince at the University of Michigan (whose students were referred to as "Helen's girls" by our male professors), Elizabeth Scott at Berkeley (who wrote papers about galaxies but was "really" a statistician), Helen Sawyer Hogg at Toronto, and Margaret Burbidge (who was, directly or indirectly, responsible for most of the women doing work on galaxies in the 1960s). Although all of these women (with the exception of Margaret Burbidge, who was a "lady" with a *very* outspoken husband) were trivialized in conversation (behind their backs) by many of our senior male colleagues, their very existence served as proof that it was possible to be female and still do good astronomy.

Figure 1. Cecelia Payne Gaposchkin — Recipient of the first Annie J. Cannon Prize of the AAS in 1934 and the first woman to be designated Russell Lecturer, in 1976. American Institute of Physics, Emilio Segrè Visual Archives.

Although the number of female Ph.D.s rose in the 1960s, the percentage of women in the AAS dropped to an all-time low of 8% by 1973.[2] The possibility of finding a job was particularly poor for those women who were married (we joked that we needed a certificate of infertility as part of the job application and were told to our faces that "the director didn't want to take a chance on a woman" or that we might be able to "work part-time (teaching two or three classes) until we started a family"). Amazingly, most of us accepted this attitude as "normal" even though we resented it and joked about its illogic.

This was all challenged in 1971 when Margaret Burbidge declined the Cannon Prize, giving as her reason that "the prize, available only to women, was in itself discriminatory."[3] At the time, the impression one gained from eavesdropping on the (male) elders of the AAS Council was that Margaret Burbidge's refusal was a disaster "because it would insult Cecilia Payne who was the first recipient of the Cannon Prize."

The Council's response was to set up a committee — The Special Committee on the Cannon Prize! As recalled by Anne Cowley, "...when Margaret Burbidge refused the old Cannon Prize, the AAS set up a committee on what to do about this. I was on the committee — I can't remember who else was, but I am pretty sure George Preston was either on it or chaired it. There were probably about 5 or 6 people on the committee ... so the committee was charged with recommending 'what to do' about what was then the Cannon Prize. Our committee recommended that it be given to the American

Figure 2. Charlotte Moore-Sitterly, the first woman to hold the Vice-Presidency of the Society, 1958–1960, and the second recipient of the Annie J. Cannon Prize, in 1937. American Institute of Physics, Emilio Segrè Visual Archives.

Association of University Women (AAUW). I think that there was some stipulation from the donor that it be used for women, which meant the AAS couldn't open it to men and women. We further recommended that it be a research award for which women in the early stages of their careers could apply for (I recall being careful not to stipulate an age limit as some prizes had/have). The Council bought this, and hence that is how the Cannon Award came into being. You will see that starting in 1974 the award went to much more junior women."[4] According to Sidney Wolff:

> I was a member of the committee that made a recommendation about what to do with the Cannon prize. We had to recommend something that was consistent with Cannon's bequest but took Margaret's feelings into account. We decided that women started with a number of disadvantages early in their careers and that it was appropriate to offer an award that would assist them when they were just beginning to do research. Hence the structure of the award as it is now and its management by the AAUW.
>
> I don't remember that I went to the council in person, although I may have... I also remember being struck by the fact that the situation of women had not improved at least in terms of numbers throughout much of the 20th century. At about the time we were meeting, a number of the very senior women were at or nearing retirement (Hogg, Prince, Gaposchkin), and they had not been replaced by the next generation.[5]

Although these recollections seem rather mild, in fact Margaret Burbidge's message acted as a clarion call. At the AAS meeting in Lansing, Michigan, in August 1972, the Special Committee on the Cannon Prize faced the primary issue directly and recommended that the Council set up a group to review the status of women in astronomy. According to Donald Osterbrock (who was an AAS Council member at the time):

> I was present at what I think must have been the first formal recognition of women as needing or deserving an organization of their own within the AAS... A delegation of women members of the AAS, about 4 or so as well as I can remember, but all the details are hazy in my mind, appeared, I believe at their own prior written request.

> Their message was that women weren't being considered for nomination to office, Council member, etc., nor for invited speakers, chairs of sessions, appointments to AAS committees, etc. Of course some women had been in all these slots, but not enough of them, these women who were there said. They wanted a formal statement that the AAS had done wrong in the past, and they wanted improvement in the future.[6]

This group of women was, in fact, the "special committee" appointed by the AAS Council in 1971.

ORIGINS

In response to this request, in 1972 the Council set up a second committee, the "Working Group on the Status of Women in Astronomy." The report of *this* working group (represented by A. Cowley, R. Humphreys, B. Lynds, and V. Rubin, with the help of 19 other AAS members) was accepted by the AAS Council on December 3 at the meeting in Tucson, Arizona and is published in the *Bulletin*.[7] The report contains a wealth of statistical information culled from questionnaires, AAS membership lists, journal indices, and NSF records. It concluded that:

> The percentage of women in the AAS is now (1973) the lowest that it has been in the history of the Society.

> Women have been generally under-represented as Society officers, committee members, prize recipients, invited speakers, session chairman, and journal editors.

and

> The US ranks seventh in the percentage of IAU members who are women... .[7]

Although the Working Group formed in 1972 was quite specific in its recommendations, matters moved slowly and the AAS Council again voted to establish an *ad hoc* Committee on the Status of Women at the 152nd AAS meeting in Madison, Wisconsin in June 1978. Ivan King made the motion which was seconded by Harlan Smith. This committee (consisting of Martha Liller, Chair, Anne Cowley, Paul Hodge, Frank Kerr, and Nancy Morrison) was charged with updating the 1973 report. Its principal conclusions were that: "the status of women (in the AAS) has changed very little since 1973" and that "the Council authorize the appointment of a standing Committee on the Status of Women."[8] The long-sought standing committee (the present CSWA) was established in June 1979 (with A. Cowley, Chair, Frank Kerr, Martha Liller, Bruce Margon,

Figure 3. E. Margaret Burbidge, the first woman to hold the Presidency of the Society, 1972–1974. She was the 1984 Russell Lecturer, and co-winner of the Helen B. Warner Prize (with her husband) in 1959. She turned down the Cannon Prize. Irwin photograph, August 1973. American Institute of Physics, Emilio Segrè Visual Archives, Irwin Collection.

and Catherine Pilachowski) and was asked to draw up its own charge, which was adopted by the Council in June 1980.

PROGRESS?

For several years after its inception, the CSWA members were appointed on a haphazard basis with the chair serving for only one year, often learning of the appointment in September with very little time to organize events for the annual meeting of the AAS in January.

The author served as chair of the CSWA in 1985/86 and decided to take a fresh look at the latest statistics on the post-Ph.D. employment of women in astronomy. Lacking a venue for this *ad hoc* analysis, I started a hard copy newsletter, *STATUS*, styled after the advice columns of the national dailies. The meager statistical analysis in the first edition of that letter suggests that there had not been much improvement in the percentage of female astronomers in academic, non civil service jobs.[9] Unfortunately, the newsletter's attempts at humor were deemed offensive by many of the younger women in the Society, and it faded into limbo sometime after 1988 (but was renewed again in more serious form in 1995 with Kathy Mead as editor).

In recent years the committee has achieved more long-term stability, with Debbie Elmegreen serving as chair from 1990 to 1997. A more successful effort at communication became possible with the widespread introduction of e-mail in the late 1980s, and Elmegreen started the *CSWA NEWSLETTER* (electronic) in 1992. This has proved to be an excellent vehicle for both the dissemination of information and interactive discussion.

A major advance in international recognition for women in astronomy was achieved in 1992 with the meeting "On the Status of Women in Astronomy" held at the Space Telescope Science Institute (September 8–9, proceedings edited by C. M. Urry, L. Danly, L. E. Sherbert, and S. Gonzaga). Out of this meeting came the "Baltimore Charter" whose goal is to promote a culture in which both women and men can realize their full potential in scientific careers. The AAS Council formally adopted a resolution of support for the Charter at the January 1994 meeting in Washington D.C., which read in part:

> Recognizing the principle that the inclusion of women and other under-represented groups in the ranks of professional astronomers is important and highly desirable, the American Astronomical Society is committed to addressing issues of attitude and procedure that negatively impact any groups. The American Astronomical Society supports the goal of the Baltimore Charter, which is to promote a culture in which both men and women can realize their full potential in scientific careers. We recognize that there are many differences in the institutional structure of astronomical organizations, and that no single strategy is likely to be suitable to all of them. We do, however, urge all astronomical programs to formulate strategies that will enable them to realize the goal of the Baltimore Charter.[10]

The Council also modified the AAS bylaws to reflect its "commitment to this goal." [10] The Baltimore Charter was distributed by Goetz Oertel to the presidents of all the AURA institutions. In the spirit of the Charter, the CSWA began to hold open meetings to explore issues such as job interview and hiring practices in astronomy and "what questions are illegal or legal." In this manner the Committee acts as both a network and a forum to air concerns that touch every life in the Society.[11]

WHAT NEXT?

When the CSWA met during the January 1997 AAS Meeting in Toronto, two discussion topics emerged which suggest different paths to progress. The first was a call for a new survey to help determine the current status of women in astronomy. This has been a recurring topic at CSWA meetings since the origin of the committee and the results of the surveys have shown only marginal progress. One hopes that an updated survey will be more encouraging.

A different theme at the 1997 January meeting, however, was a detailed discussion of educational outreach (particularly at the K–12 levels). This is a topic which has received increasing emphasis at recent CSWA meetings and may eventually lead to a new generation of students and scholars who will finally redress the imbalances which so far appear to have resisted major change.

ACKNOWLEDGMENTS

I am particularly grateful to E. M. Burbidge, A. Cowley, D. Elmegreen, I. King, D. Osterbrock, and S. Wolff for sharing their memories with me (and in the case of I. King, supplying valuable documentation). Naturally, the author alone bears all responsibility for any errors or misinterpretations which may occur in this article.

Astronomy Education and the American Astronomical Society

Andrew Fraknoi and Donat Wentzel

I t seems fair to say that the American Astronomical Society (AAS) — considering itself primarily as an organization of *research* astronomers — has had an ambivalent relationship with the world of astronomy education. While some members have felt that it was important for the Society to play an active role in this arena, many others looked upon educational work with disinterest and even disdain. Some officers of the Society occasionally advocated significantly greater AAS involvement in education, but the Council rarely followed up with the sustained political will or the resources needed to bring about effective change.

Our examination of Society records and publications shows that enthusiasm for astronomy education seems to have come in cycles — with periods of more concentrated activity alternating with stretches of unmourned inactivity. As summarized in Table 1, some education committee or task force would generally begin with great enthusiasm to reform or revive some aspects of education, only to fade away after a few years as its leaders became tired or felt that they did not have the support of the community. Then, often after a dormant period, a new generation of "reformers" would tackle the same issues (occasionally even using the same language and the same suggested solutions as their rallying cry), only to fall prey to the same problems or lack of support. And when Society leaders did take a more active interest in educational matters, it was often motivated (as it appears to be at the time we are writing this history) by concerns over jobs for astronomy graduates, and whether there were too few or too many astronomers to fill the positions then available to them.

Such ambivalence may be natural for a Society whose primary aim is encouraging research, but it also means that the kind of national coordination that has helped many of the research branches of astronomy become more effective has frequently been absent in the field of astronomy education. Despite many good educational initiatives from the AAS over the years, such lack of coordination continues to hamper efforts to improve astronomy education even today. We note that there has never been a journal or magazine devoted to astronomy education, and that some of the most important symposia in the field have been organized outside the aegis of the AAS (although they frequently obtained AAS co-sponsorship later for the prestige it afforded).

DEFINING ASTRONOMY EDUCATION

One crucial question, which was to emerge again and again in the relationship of the AAS and astronomy education, concerned what the term was to mean. To many astronomers, especially in the early years, astronomy education meant the training of new astronomers. If any aspect of education was to place a consistent hold on their attention, it was the issue of how to produce world-class scientists at a time when sources of support for the training of scientists were still meager and intermittent.

Yet from time to time, the question would come up whether a broader scope for the Society's educational purview was not necessary. Should not the AAS also concern itself with what we today call "general education courses" in college, with K-12 education, and with public education (through the media, through planetaria and museums, and other ways of reaching a much broader segment of the American public)? We shall see that there has been a gradual expansion of the scope of the Society's educational efforts with time. There were several periods, especially in the 1950s and 1970s, where groups within the Society clearly advocated taking a broader view of the appropriate purview for the AAS and undertook projects to help those working in these larger domains. Nevertheless, this question still remains a vexing one for a Society with limited resources, and recent AAS committees and Councils continue to grapple with it.

Still, our history will end on a hopeful note, since as the AAS Centennial draws near, the Council has voted a specific dues increase dedicated to expanding the Society's programs in education and has hired (for the first time) a paid education coordinator to spearhead these efforts.

TABLE 1. *AAS Educational Committees and Groups.*

Name	Dates of Existence	What Happened To It?
Committee on Cooperation in the Teaching of Astronomy [changed to the Committee on the Teaching of Astronomy]	1911–1921	Abolished by Council (was inactive at end)
Teachers' Committee	1941–1956	Dissolved; Chair had resigned saying there was a stigma attached to the committee
Committee on Education in Astronomy	1957–1972	Dissolved after the TGEA was appointed
Task Group on Education in Astronomy (TGEA)	1972–1985	Education Officer took over many of its tasks
TGEA Advisory Board (soon becomes Education Advisory Board)	1975–1997	Replaced by Education Board
Working Group on Astronomy Education	1991–	
Ad Hoc Committee on Education	1993–1994	Evolved into the Education Policy Board
Education Policy Board	1994–1997	Replaced by Education Board
Education Board (combines the Education Policy Bd. & the Education Advisory Bd)	1997–	

THE EARLY DAYS

The birth of the AAS corresponded to a generally discouraging time in astronomy education in the U.S. A series of academic conferences arranged by a group of ten college presidents and high school principals, known as "the Committee of Ten," in the last decade of the nineteenth century — reflecting broad trends in educational reform — had recommended (among other things) that astronomy be eliminated as a required course for college admission, and that physics, chemistry, and biology be emphasized. As an elective course not required for college, what little astronomy was still offered soon suffered from lack of enrollments, and the subject eventually disappeared from the curricula of most high schools and thus from the preparation of most elementary school teachers as well.

As a result, between the years 1900 and 1915 astronomy suffered a "precipitous decline in high school and college."[1] The inertia from these early school reform efforts left both pre-college and college astronomy education for non-scientists in a state of disarray and impoverishment from which it did not really recover until the Sputnik era ushered in its wave of funding for expanded science training.

The first record we have of an education paper at an AAS meeting was of one given by Sarah F. Whiting of Wellesley College at the Society's fourth meeting, in December 1902. The paper is listed by title only: "Astronomical Laboratory Work for Large Classes."[2] She gave another education-related paper at the seventh meeting, but there is little record of other members following suit.

During the course of the twelfth meeting in August 1911, the Council appointed a Committee on Cooperation in the Teaching of Astronomy, chaired by C. L. Doolittle of the University of Pennsylvania. One of the committee's first tasks, in 1912, was to undertake a survey of the availability of astronomy courses at a range of colleges and universities.

The report of the survey began with an eloquent statement that seems as appropriate today as it was almost a century ago: "At its late meeting in Ottawa, [the Society] was mindful of the fact that the advancement of science depends not only on the discovery of new truth, but on the diffusion of knowledge, and the scientific spirit which creates a friendly atmosphere for its reception. The Society considered the deplorable ignorance of persons, otherwise intelligent, in regard to the everyday phenomena of the sky, and the fact that astronomy lags behind the other sciences in adopting the modern method of laboratory work by the student." The 80 replies received, the committee reported, were disheartening. "Only a very small proportion of college men and women know much about anything off this little planet."[3]

The committee asked for the assistance of the Society in devising constructive plans for improving the situation, but no further reports on this subject appear in the Society's publications and the committee was abolished (with a list of other inactive groups) at the 26th meeting in 1921.

In 1915, the AAS held its 18th meeting in San Francisco and Berkeley, in what was to be the first of several joint meetings with the Astronomical Society of the Pacific (ASP). The ASP had been founded ten years before the AAS as an outgrowth of the cooperation between professional and amateur astronomers during the eclipse of January 1, 1889. Despite its regional name and origins, it would grow to be a national and international group, but it differed from the AAS in that it invited and accepted membership from everyone interested in astronomy and made public outreach a main concern from the outset.[4] In later years, a number of the AAS education projects would be undertaken in cooperation with the ASP.

A WARTIME REVIVAL

After the demise of the Committee on the Teaching of Astronomy (as it was known by 1921), astronomy education was absent from the published records of the AAS for almost two decades. However, this changed during World War II, when the need for trained "aerial navigators" made astronomy education a defense-related issue.

During the 66th AAS meeting in September 1941 at Yerkes, more than 70 teachers of college-level astronomy attended a Sunday afternoon conference and discussed a wide range of problems and techniques. On the agenda were the spelling and pronunciation of star and constellation names, finding appropriate laboratory materials and textbooks, the problems of switching from the old lantern slides to Kodak's new compact 2×2 design, and combating astrology (with a skeptical talk by Allen Hynek). Both the well-established *Popular Astronomy* and the new *The Sky* (which would later merge with *The Telescope*) expressed interest in publishing articles on the teaching of astronomy. An unofficial committee, chaired by J. H. Pitman of the Sproul Observatory, was appointed to continue the work of the group and plan future meetings.[5]

At the 67th meeting in December 1941, this Committee held three meetings and agreed that its "ultimate aim is to devise means for the encouragement of the teaching of astronomy in American Colleges and Universities, having in mind that its value lies, not only in its broad aspects of understanding the workings of the universe, but also in its cultural aspects."[6] This AAS meeting, by the way, was — it appears — the first to feature a public lecture. Harlow Shapley gave a talk at Cleveland's Severance Hall on "Galactic Explorations with Newer Telescopes."

At the 68th meeting, the Council formally accepted the group that had been operating for about a year and designated it as the AAS Teachers' Committee. The group organized sessions on astronomy education and the war effort at several meetings and sponsored talks and discussions on teaching navigation effectively. At the 69th meeting in December 1942, for example, they offered a symposium on "Science Courses in the War Effort" with several military instructors in attendance. Even after the war ended, "Teachers' Conferences" (where teacher meant college or university professors) were regular parts of AAS meetings. (And in the era before simultaneous sessions, this meant that the full meeting was "turned over" to the Teachers' Committee.)

The 72nd meeting in June 1944 featured a discussion on what sort of astronomy should be taught in the post-war liberal arts colleges. "Those actively engaged in teaching are evidently far from being perfectly agreed on just what should be emphasized and how it should be taught, but this is a healthy sign..."[7] Not much has changed in this respect in the intervening half century, we note! At the 80th meeting in 1948 there was again a broad discussion on the astronomy curriculum in American colleges and universities.

THE 1950s: THE ERA OF THE CEA

By the mid-1950s, however, much of the intensity of the war years was forgotten and the country settled into a more routine existence. The AAS resumed its strong focus on astronomical research and instrumentation. Freeman Miller, an active member of the Teachers' Committee between 1948 and 1954, recalls that he and Allan Hynek were often "fed up with lack of support by the Council [for the Teachers' Committee]." He remembers that they did "pry enough money from the Council to circulate a questionnaire to all astronomy departments, asking about their interests in education; possibly the response contributed to our feeling of lack of interest."[8] Between 1953 and 1956, committee members did write an occasional column called "Sky & Teacher" in *Sky & Telescope* magazine, however, to keep the astronomical community aware of educational projects and issues.

At the 92nd meeting, in April 1955, the Council was asked to pass a resolution in response to a National Science Foundation panel considering "the relation of astronomy to the general public." The resolution read in part:

> It is the opinion of the panel that astronomy does not fare as well in [this area] as many of its sister sciences, and that more attention should be given by professional astronomers to matters of inspiring future public and government understanding, interest in, and support of astronomy.... The Council of the Society, therefore, recognizes that a definite need exists for the dissemination to the public at large of accurate astronomical information, consistent with the dignity of the science; deplores that, in the past, some stigma appeared to be attached to such activities; and recommends that astronomers devote reasonable time and effort to the preparation of popular, non-technical articles and lectures on astronomy and closely allied topics.[9]

The problem the resolution referred to was dramatically illustrated just two meetings later, when the Chair of the Teachers' Committee, Carl Bauer of Penn State, resigned, saying that he had had trouble getting cooperation from members in setting up an educational session for the meeting. Bauer's words, as reported in the Council minutes, were that "it appeared as though these members felt that a certain stigma attaches to being asked to do something for the Teachers' Committee."[10] The Council expressed surprise and appointed a panel of former Teachers' Committee Chairs, headed by Helen Dodson of the University of Michigan, as an advisory committee on educational policy.

After hearing the report of the Dodson committee at their next session (the 95th meeting of the AAS in late 1956), the Council dissolved the Teachers' Committee and established a new Committee on Education in Astronomy (CEA), whose members would be appointed at the following meeting. It was during the same Council discussion, by the way, that the suggestion of what would eventually become the Shapley lectures was raised. The concept was borrowed from an NSF-sponsored program at the American Mathematical Society, and would involve visits from astronomers to smaller or less research-oriented colleges, often ones without active astronomy programs, to encourage the appreciation of astronomy by faculty, students, and the public. The AAS's project began in 1957 with the help of the NSF, and was first called the "Visiting Professors Program." Renamed in honor of Harlow Shapley after his death, it continues today as one of the Society's most visible contributions to the public understanding of science.

The new CEA was appointed at the 97th AAS meeting in 1957, with Joseph M. Chamberlain (then of the Hayden Planetarium in New York City) as its chair. The original members included such well-known names as Otto Struve, Carl Seyfert, Stanley Wyatt, and William Liller. The first years of the CEA coincided with the time of Sputnik, the concern in the U.S. that the country was falling behind in science and technology, and the infusion of significant federal funds into both science and education. It was not surprising, therefore, that many of the Committee's first activities dealt with what by 1960 was being called "the national shortage of astronomers" and with projects most likely to encourage more young people to enter the field. As the times changed in the 1960s, the CEA would broaden its mission to focus more on astronomy teaching and outreach for non-scientists.

The CEA began a number of the education and outreach programs that AAS members today associate with the Society. Among these were the "Careers in Astronomy" Brochure, first written by Struve and Gibson Reaves, which remains to this day the Society's most widely circulated publication. (In the first year and a half after publication, some 12,000 copies were distributed.) Two college level films on astronomy were produced with NSF support. A Foreign Visiting Professor Program broadened the outlook of many American graduate students by bringing astronomers from other countries to work at universities in the U.S.

The CEA debated the need for a newsletter on astronomy education, but decided that it was not worth the time and expense that would be involved.[11] Instead, members from larger institutions were encouraged to invite members in smaller schools to colloquia and other activities and to foster better communications among Society members engaged in educational work in whatever way they could. The lack of effective communication among astronomy educators at all levels remains a problem to this day.

Thornton Page represented the AAS and the CEA on a Cooperative Committee at the American Association for the Advancement of Science (AAAS), the umbrella group of U.S. scientific societies, which was then making recommendations for the reform of high school science education. The Council minutes report that: "...through Dr. Page's efforts, astronomy is now listed separately in AAAS curriculum guides, rather than as a happenstance item under general science."[12] Where to fit in seems to be a perennial problem for astronomy; in the new National Science Standards promulgated in the 1990s, astronomy wound up mostly under the Earth Sciences instead of the Physical Science headings.

In 1960, the Council discussed at length a report by Captain Carl Christie of the U.S. Navy on the need for more people with astronomical training (not necessarily Ph.D.s) and referred its recommendations to the CEA. At the December 1960 Council meeting Chamberlain reviewed what could be done to implement the Christie report, but many of the suggestions proved to be controversial and expensive. For example, the Council declined CEA proposals to keep track of statistics on graduate and undergraduate enrollments in astronomy programs, to appoint education representatives in each department or observatory, and to set up national programs of scholarships and fellowships through the AAS.[13] One has to see the reluctance of the Council in the right context however; this was a time when the work of the Society was done entirely by volunteers and any new tasks would fall on the shoulders of such volunteers or would require grants to be written by volunteers to NSF. Indeed, it was discussions like the one generated by the Christie report that led the Council around this time to explore the idea of a paid executive officer for the first time.

CONFERENCES AND WORKSHOPS

As part of the implementation of the Christie report, the CEA sought NSF funding for a conference on graduate education in astronomy, which was held in October 1962 at Indiana University. Organized by Chamberlain and a committee that included Donald Osterbrock, Lyman Spitzer, Jesse Greenstein, and Harold Weaver (all of them future officers of the Society), the conference brought together representative faculty and administrators from many institutions.[14] Participants discussed the goals of graduate education, the curricula needed to achieve these goals, and the problems of recruiting outstanding students for the field. As George Abell summarized the conference a few years later, "there was considerable disagreement about what the curriculum should be, and there wasn't even great agreement on what the goals should be."[15] However, departments learned a great deal about how other institutions operated, and some curricular changes were made at both the graduate and undergraduate level, especially as they related to the importance of a good background in physics to modern astronomical research. A similar set of conferences would be held by the AAS in 1996, but responding to an employment crisis of opposite direction—not too few astronomers but too few jobs.

In August 1969, at the 130th meeting, the CEA sponsored a conference on educational issues, the first such conference held as a regular part of an AAS meeting for well over a decade. After a keynote address by then CEA Chair Abell, six other speakers considered various aspects of astronomy education from the graduate to the K–12 level.[16]

In his eloquent review, Abell brought out a number of the issues facing those concerned about astronomy education in the late 1960s, including lack of training in modern astronomy among many community college, high school, and elementary school teachers, planetarium staff, reporters, and college graduates in general. He discussed the increasing growth of unskeptical belief in such pseudo-sciences as astrology, problems with the difficulty of some of the science reform curricula which had been devised in the 1960s, and student dissatisfaction with some of the features of the college education system (large lecture classes, memorization of facts as a prime standard for good grades, and the lack of relevance in the curriculum). He admonished his colleagues that, "if we do not turn our attention somehow to finding solutions [to these problems], we may find that science in general, and astronomy in particular, will suffer from a grave lack of support." These were prescient words, perhaps even more relevant in our own era of shrinking budgets and growing public expectations than they were in the turbulent 1960s.

Independently, Elske v. P. Smith and Don Wentzel (both of the University of Maryland) organized a workshop, one day after the same AAS meeting, on laboratory exercises in astronomy aimed at college non-science students.[17] To everyone's surprise, the 90 attendees included not only the astronomers who had been teaching non-science students but also much of the leadership of the AAS.

In 1971, with the sponsorship of the AAS and the N.Y. Academy of Sciences, Richard Berendzen, then of Boston University, organized a major conference on "Education in and History of Modern Astronomy" at the American Museum of Natural History. There were sessions on many aspects of education, from graduate training to planetarium shows, in the U.S. and abroad. The published proceedings of this conference stand as perhaps the best summary we have of the state of astronomy education in the 1960s.[18]

Figure 1. George Abell in 1982. Photograph by A. Fraknoi.

Abell was again the lead speaker, and expressed his vision of the most urgent need in astronomy education: "Far more serious today is the problem of selling astronomy to the public at large. Ultimately, the support of our science rests on the public's willingness to pay our salaries... . In the past, we have tended to leave it to others to carry the message of astronomy to the outside world, but now, as the public becomes increasingly disillusioned with science and concerned over increasing taxes...astronomy in the U.S. is losing support. Consequently, we have a responsibility to concern ourselves deeply with the problem of representing astronomy honestly and accurately to the public, and, hopefully, to gain appreciation and support for it."[19]

By the early 1970s, there was an additional impetus for astronomers to become involved with education: the employment picture in astronomy had swung to the opposite pole from the early 1960s. Now graduates of astronomy programs were having trouble finding research-oriented jobs, although positions in education were somewhat more numerous. During a discussion of the status of the AAS Placement Service by Executive Officer Hank Gurin at the 135th AAS meeting in Amherst, in

Figure 2. Bart J. Bok, circa 1978, was president of the AAS from 1972 to 1974, and at that time chaired the AAS "Aims Committee" on manpower to assess the needs of the profession. Photograph courtesy Bart Bok, DeVorkin collection.

August 1971, Bart Bok, one of the Society Vice-Presidents, rose to discuss at length the problem of unemployment among Ph.D. astronomers. He suggested that President Martin Schwarzschild appoint a committee to look into the matter, and found himself duly designated chair of an *ad hoc* "Committee on Manpower and Employment in Astronomy" along with Abell, D. van Blerkom, Don Goldsmith and John Trasco. Schwarzschild asked them to provide an interim report at the next AAS meeting. Included among the Committee's recommendations as reported at the San Juan meeting in December 1971, were the following suggestions:

> "Astronomy granting degree institutions should be encouraged to prepare their prospective graduates for careers in teaching, in which many of them will find themselves.
>
> We must help our Ph.D.'s and MA's...to develop ways in which they can apply for astronomically-oriented positions outside traditional colleges, universities, government laboratories and observatories... . [They especially emphasized educational positions in

smaller and junior colleges, planetaria, computer science, the Peace Corps, and even high school.]

Students beginning graduate work in astronomy should be given as honest an evaluation of the job market as possible before they begin their graduate studies.

The community should not enlarge and may even want to cut back on the production of Ph.D. astronomers. The Heads of Astronomy Departments should be urged to begin thinking in terms of limiting the sizes of their graduate schools.

This seems like a time in which we should urge the lower one third of each graduate group to terminate their graduate training with the Master's degree."[20]

It was a strong set of recommendations and represented a challenge to the larger departments of astronomy that boasted large graduate student populations. The Bok "Aims Committee" recommendations reverberated through the Society, but ultimately they were not widely put into effect, although a number of departments at the time did try to expand the placement of their graduates to non-traditional jobs, and a few tried to limit enrollment. Eventually, new instruments and increases in federal funding improved the employment situation, although the issues would return in the 1990s, as we shall see.

THE TASK GROUP ON EDUCATION IN ASTRONOMY

The late 1960s and early 1970s were an era of expanding popular interest in astronomy and the space program. The number of non-majors' college astronomy courses (and the number of students taking such courses) had begun to grow. New textbooks were being written and many popular-level books on astronomy attracted superb reviews in the mainstream media. Sensing the opportunities and challenges of this new era, the Board of the Astronomical Society of the Pacific began its new popular-level magazine *Mercury* in 1972 and hired its first executive officer, whose responsibilities included increased emphasis on public outreach. The kind of leadership that would be needed to turn the attention of the members of the CEA toward this larger arena, however, was not forthcoming; a new, more effective and pluralistic structure was needed for the AAS.

Martin Schwarzschild, Don Wentzel, and Gerrit Verschuur (NRAO) worked out the principles of a new organization within the AAS, the "Task Group on Education in Astronomy" (TGEA), and obtained approval by the Council at the summer meeting in 1972. Unlike the CEA, which was a small group appointed by the Council, the TGEA was open to anyone who wanted to become active in the realm of astronomy education and outreach. Wentzel and Verschuur were named the first coordinators of the TGEA for a three-year term. They obtained a three-year grant from the Program on the Public Understanding of Science at NSF's Educational Programs Division and enjoyed the active support of the key officers of the AAS in their endeavors.

It was clear that if the TGEA's work were to have a significant national effect, it would depend not only on the small number of astronomers who did not see themselves as primarily research astronomers, but also on cooperation with other scientific societies and groups. After all, many departments of astronomy at research institutions did not consider educational work beyond the regular college courses as an activity that would further an astronomer's career; at least two of the original members of the TGEA were told this quite explicitly by senior colleagues. This was a time when Carl Sagan's public activities (years before the *Cosmos* television series) were regarded skeptically by many astronomers and sometimes condemned as oversimplifying astronomy. Among those who became active in the TGEA were astronomers at museums and planetaria, as well as those teaching at institutions where research was not required.

Table 2 lists some of the projects undertaken by the TGEA, both under the initial leadership of Wentzel and Verschuur, and when Paul Knappenberger, of the Science Museum of Virginia, took over their position three years later. Note that many of these projects were initiated or undertaken by other organizations or institutions, but

TABLE 2. *Some TGEA Projects 1972–1979.*

Project	Leaders
Astronomy in the National Parks (sky interpretation workshops and materials for park rangers)	Von Del Chamberlain
Traveling Exhibit on Cosmology for Planetaria	Frank Jettner, Charles Smith
Four Brochures for High School Students on Topics at the Forefront of Astronomical Research	Gerrit Verschuur Paul Knappenberger
A Pilot Program of Radio Spots on Astronomical Developments (begun in Virginia)	Charles Smith, Paul Knappenberger,
Listings of Astronomy Education Resources (began before TGEA)	Richard Berendzen, David DeVorkin
Annotated List of Astronomy Lab Activities	Haym Kruglak
A Collection of Introductory Astronomy Course Syllabi	James Wertz
Workshops on Effective Astronomy Teaching and Student Reasoning Ability (which resulted in a published workbook)	Dennis Schatz, Andrew Fraknoi, R. Robert Robbins, Charles Smith, Paul Knappenberger
TGEA Newsletter (with eventual circulation of 560)	Don Wentzel, Gerrit Vershuur
Collections of Astronomy Activities for the Classroom	Dennis Sunal
Syndicated Newspaper Column on Astronomy (ASP & AAS)	Andrew Fraknoi
The Bok Prize for Outstanding High School Projects in Astronomy (begun by Boston U. and later taken over by the TGEA and ASP)	Michael Papagiannis
AAS Booth at Meetings of the National Science Teachers' Association	William Straka
Coordination with Other Organizations, including the American Association of Physics Teachers, American Chemical Society, AAAS, ASP, etc.	TGEA Members

received encouragement, funding, support, or prestige through the involvement of the AAS. TGEA reports appeared each year from 1972 through 1983 in the *BAAS*, and can be consulted by those who want more information on these projects.

One of the most innovative of the TGEA-sponsored programs was organized by Von Del Chamberlain (then from the Abrams Planetarium, later with the National Air and Space Museum), to help rangers in the National Parks give evening "sky interpretation" programs. With NSF support, regional workshops were held in Tucson and at the Goddard Space Flight Center, and four issues of a handbook full of activities and resources were published and distributed. Numerous astronomers visited parks as part of the program and provided sky interpretation and astronomy talks for both the park staff and the public. Even years later, astronomers volunteering to give a talk at one of the parks found the park management and rangers eager to use the opportunity. Upon Chamberlain's move to Hansen Planetarium, the program continued there at a reduced level.

PROGRAMS FOR TEACHERS AT MANY LEVELS

The TGEA's activities regarding college teaching were largely aimed at AAS members. A special TGEA session was held at the AAS meeting in August 1974 and included a panel discussion on how to train graduate students so that they would be ready to teach in small colleges. More and more Ph.D. astronomers were now taking positions in small colleges and committing themselves to heavier teaching loads than faculty at research universities. In recognition of the value of their contribution, these teaching astronomers have been awarded a significant fraction of the AAS Small Research Grants, which give priority to smaller, less well-endowed institutions. Thus the Society has aided such faculty in keeping their research going despite the heavy teaching demands on them.

By this time, papers at AAS meetings were divided into subject categories, with education relegated to "Other Topics." Starting in 1974, education was made a separate abstract category. The first contributed papers session devoted to education attracted 11 papers in August 1974 and anywhere from 5 to 12 papers during the next five summer meetings of the AAS. Summer meetings were emphasized since members whose primary interest was in teaching could more easily attend these meetings. Several specialized programs of invited talks were organized in 1977 and 1978, and such invited and contributed sessions have continued at AAS meetings ever since, with the number of sessions and papers rising and falling with the interest level of the local organizing committees, the priorities of the Society vice presidents, and the persuasiveness of the succeeding education committees and groups.

One of the most far-reaching initiatives of the TGEA was to begin programs to assist astronomy teachers at community colleges and high schools to improve their curricula. This was the time when science educators were discovering the work of psychologist Jean Piaget and others concerning the stages through which the reasoning level of students progress (and the importance of using hands-on activities when planning instruction at all levels.) A TGEA session at the June 1976 AAS meeting led to a plan of conducting and publishing a workshop on effective teaching strategies for introductory astronomy. Dennis Schatz, then of the Lawrence Hall of Science at the

University of California, Berkeley, obtained NSF support for this project. Two workshops were offered (in 1977 and 1978) and the materials from them were judged to be sufficiently useful to warrant wider dissemination.

The publication that resulted, *Effective Astronomy Teaching and Student Reasoning Ability* by Dennis Schatz, Andrew Fraknoi, Robert Robbins, and Charles Smith (1978, Lawrence Hall of Science), was distributed to instructors around the country and became quite influential in the small world of astronomy education. Much of the later work in developing effective astronomy activities in such programs as Project STAR at the Harvard-Smithsonian Center for Astrophysics and Project ASTRO at the ASP drew inspiration from this pioneering work.

Two of the leaders of this first workshop, Schatz and Fraknoi (then of Cañada College and later of the ASP) went on to lead a series of workshops specifically for teachers in grades 3–12 around the country, mostly through the ASP but for other organizations as well (including the IAU and National Science Teachers Association). These workshops, now called "*The Universe in the Classroom*," are still continuing at ASP meetings today. When the AAS later introduced its own workshops for high school teachers, called "Astronomer for a Day," the synergy continued with many of the materials and quite a few of the speakers coming from the ASP's workshops and publications.

Later, in 1984, the ASP and the AAS began a joint project to publish a newsletter on astronomy for teachers in grades 3–12, also called *The Universe in the Classroom* and edited by Fraknoi, but written with the help of many members of both Societies. Word about the free newsletter spread quickly and within a little more than a year, more than 10,000 requests for subscriptions had come in from around the U.S. and Canada.

Figure 3. Joseph M. Chamberlain receiving the Klumpke-Roberts Award of the ASP, 1988. Photograph by A. Fraknoi.

Scrambling to obtain the resources needed to meet the unexpectedly large demand, the ASP and AAS received support from the Canadian Astronomical Society, the International Planetarium Society, the Slipher Fund of the National Academy of Science, and several other groups. This newsletter is still being published, and is now translated into more than a dozen languages around the world (and then distributed locally).

THE AAS PRESS AND EDUCATION OFFICERS

During the first six years of the TGEA, astronomy education became a more "respectable" activity for professional astronomers. The TGEA certainly benefited from the change in astronomers' outlook, especially as the employment picture required a sober look at alternative job possibilities. At the same time, the TGEA contributed to this change, primarily by giving a new venue and visibility to those astronomers who, instead of or in addition to their research work, preferred to expand into educational spheres.

In 1975, when the TGEA's first charter needed to be renewed, the Council appointed a TGEA Advisory Committee, made up of more senior members of the Society and chaired by Owen Gingerich of Harvard. This advisory group eventually took on a life of its own, quite separate from the TGEA, and became known in the 1980s as the Education Advisory Board.

Encouraged by the work of the TGEA and feeling the need to relieve the Executive Officer of some of the work involved with educational activities as the office moved to Washington, the Council — at the recommendation of the TGEA Advisory Committee — in 1979 created the position of Education Officer, designed to be an

Figure 4. (left-to-right) Charlie Tolbert and Donat Wentzel at the 1988 IAU Symposium on the Teaching of Astronomy. Larry Marschall is standing directly behind Wentzel. Photograph by A. Fraknoi.

ex officio member of the Council. This new AAS Officer would serve as press liaison, coordinate the work of the TGEA, and oversee the other ongoing educational programs of the Society, such as the Shapley lectures and responding to public inquiries. Secretarial support would be provided, but there would be no salary for the person in the position.

Subsumed in the new position was the work of AAS Public Information Representative (PIR), which had been created in 1973 in response to one of the recommendations of the Bok Committee Report of 1971. At the urging of the TGEA, the Council instituted the office, (later changed to Press Officer) whose duties were to reach out to the news media. Of all the innovations during the TGEA era, this was probably the most effective one in the long run. The first PIR, appointed in 1973, was Kenneth L. Franklin of the Hayden Planetarium, briefly joined by William J. Kaufmann of the Griffith Observatory. They began to invite reporters to AAS meetings, to issue press releases for them about newsworthy work being discussed, and to arrange interviews with scientists during the course of the meeting.

The job was eventually combined with the work of the new Education Officer in 1979 and taken on by Harry Shipman, of the University of Delaware, but by 1984 it was clear that the two volunteer jobs really needed separate individuals. Steve Maran of NASA's Goddard Space Flight Center has held the post ever since, becoming over the years one of the most effective disseminators of science information to the media in the country. Largely as a result of his efforts, the AAS is now widely held up by reporters as a model for how scientific societies should conduct their meetings to be of maximum utility to the media. (See chapter on the Press Office, page 213.)

Figure 5. Left: Andrew Fraknoi in the mid-1980s. ASP Archives. Right: Harry Shipman in the early-1990s. University of Delaware photo by Jack Buxbaum.

During Shipman's six year tour of duty as both education and public information coordinator for the Society, the TGEA was still active, although in the 1980s its separate identity began to slip away as more and more of the AAS education program became consolidated in the Education Office. Regular reports of the Education Officer appear in the *Bulletin of the AAS* and, later, in the *AAS Newsletter*.

In 1985, Charles Tolbert of the University of Virginia replaced Shipman. It was under Tolbert's administration, in January 1988, that the AAS offered its first "Astronomer for a Day" workshop for high school science teachers. During the first workshop (in Austin), 60 Texas teachers participated in what was billed as "a research science meeting, but at a level that the teachers could understand. Some of what they heard was interesting, some esoteric, some exciting, and some dull (just like a real AAS session)."[21] In later years, the talks by research astronomers would be supplemented with talks and sessions by astronomy educators, and the teachers would be encouraged to attend some of the AAS sessions themselves.

Inspired by the success of the Education Officer concept for the AAS, the Division for Planetary Science appointed its own Education Officer, Martha Hanner of JPL, in 1990. Since then, Linda French of Wheelock College, and Larry Lebofsky of the University of Arizona have held the post. In 1991, the Education Advisory Board formed a Working Group on Astronomy Education. The existence of such a group would allow AAS members to present an education paper as well as a research paper at the same Society meeting and would provide those members interested in education with a group identity within the AAS. So far, the Working Group, headed by Stephen Shawl of the University of Kansas, has sponsored a number of sessions at AAS meetings and an electronic newsmail service on education issues (which is currently distributed to about 300 people, and can be consulted on the World Wide Web as well.)

THE "BENEFITS TO THE NATION" ERA

As the national budget deficits built up during the 1980s, the feeling of expansion and optimism that (rightly or wrongly) characterized much of that decade began to change into a concern for what would happen when the bills for all that spending would become due. As the 1990s began, astronomy, like many other fields, began to sense Congressional reluctance to fund many domestic programs and the increasing demand that programs that were funded demonstrate their relevance to immediate national concerns. As the 1990s wore on, permanent positions for astronomers again became more difficult to obtain.

For several decades, the astronomical community had organized a "decadal survey" of the needs of the profession, presenting its research priorities in a united front to the federal funding agencies. The most recent such survey, looking forward to the 1990s, chaired by John Bahcall of the Institute for Advanced Study, included a special panel on astronomy's "benefits to the nation," with education assuming a significant role in its report.[22] Astronomers may not be able to cure diseases, solve the energy crisis, or make the country more competitive with Asian economies, but, the report pointed out, the excitement of our exploration of the cosmos was a powerful tool in helping the nation's youngsters appreciate the value and effectiveness of the scientific method (and thus in helping to train a more technologically literate work force).

Many astronomers began to see that a modestly increased emphasis on astronomy education could be a politically and socially valuable step for the community to take. And, as in the 1970s, the education sector continued to be a source of employment for graduates of astronomy programs who could not obtain research positions. Several candidates for AAS offices ran and won on platforms of increased attention to education.

Among the suggestions of the Bahcall survey report was that the AAS might consider instituting a prize for education (in addition to the various prizes it gave for research). As it happened, Bahcall was elected President of the AAS from 1990 to 1992 and after sharing a taxi with the President of the Annenberg Foundation, took steps to create the Annenberg Foundation Award, funded by the Foundation on a five-year trial basis, to recognize achievement by an astronomer in the field of education and public outreach. The rules for the prize were recommended to the Council by the Education Advisory Board, and the first winner, in 1992, was, appropriately, Carl Sagan. Unlike the other AAS awards, this prize did not require its recipient to give an invited talk at an AAS meeting. Still a way was found for each of the winners to speak at the meeting where the Prize was awarded.

During the five years that the award was funded, however, the Annenberg Foundation changed presidents and priorities, and after the fifth award, there was no funding to continue the program and no active plan at the AAS to seek funding elsewhere. As we write this history, the award has been suspended indefinitely. One has to wonder whether the AAS Council would have accepted a new *research* prize without a permanent endowment or allowed it to disappear without involving more of the membership in efforts to find alternate funding?

In 1991, Mary Kay Hemenway of the University of Texas became the third AAS Education Officer and began to expand the activities of the Education Office significantly. She became active in a number of science education organizations, including the newly formed umbrella group called the Coalition for Earth Science Education. In 1992, the Society received funding from NSF for the supervision of the national program of "Astronomy Research Experiences for Undergraduates." Plans were also made to apply for a substantial NSF grant to fund a national program of secondary-school "Teacher Resource Agents" in astronomy, modeled on a successful program in physics run by the American Association of Physics Teachers. This grant was received by the AAS and an extensive program of teacher training was undertaken between 1994 and 1996.

At the meeting of the Council in June 1993, Hemenway set off a fire-storm of discussion by requesting one-quarter time salary support for her work as Education Officer. She was existing on soft money at her own institution, but there was also a sense that the level of activity in the Education Office was significantly greater than a volunteer should be asked to supervise. In response, President Sidney Wolff (NOAO) formed an *ad hoc* committee, chaired by Council member Suzan Edwards of Smith College, to review education policy and operations within the AAS and recommend how the Council should deal with Hemenway's precedent-setting request.

THE EDUCATION POLICY BOARD

After vigorous discussion about the issues and the role the AAS should take in astronomy education, the Edwards Committee made its final report to the Council in June 1994. Their recommendations went much further than Hemenway's simple request. They advocated that the Society should have a full-time paid Education Officer, together with an Education Policy Board that would function as the equivalent of the Society's Publications Board in the arena of education and public outreach. The Society had to take a "leadership role" in developing an education strategy for American astronomers "in order to maximize their contributions to enhancing the nation's literacy...and productivity in science." Furthermore,

> The AAS must also provide a framework and resource network to encourage and enable its members to become active and effective participants in furthering science education. Moreover, we need to ensure that these efforts ... engage the energies of the research community of astronomers. Not only can researchers expect to be increasingly called upon to justify how their efforts benefit society, but without the involvement of those who are at the forefront of acquiring new knowledge about the universe, the unhealthy separation of researchers from educators will remain a possible outcome.[23]

The new AAS President Frank Shu responded by appointing an "*Ad Hoc* Committee on Educational Policy," chaired by Edwards and Stephen Strom of the University of Massachusetts, to consider the broad policy implications of the Edwards Committee recommendations, what was happening in science education at the national level, and what ways might be found to expand the AAS education effort in the context of these national changes. The new Committee, which soon became known as the Education Policy Board, began by considering the state of astronomy education and opportunities for AAS leadership at all levels (graduate, undergraduate, K–12, and public outreach.) It drafted, with some encouragement from the NSF, a broad proposal for an "Education Initiative in Astronomy."

At its January 1995 meeting, the Council (after much debate) approved a $10 increase in Society dues specifically earmarked to support education and public outreach activities. There were several arguments in favor of such a move: In an earlier survey of the AAS membership, increased work in education had been the only area for which a majority of members was willing to pay greater dues. And to fund an expensive education initiative, NSF would surely ask the AAS to shoulder a reasonable share of the costs. (With about 5,000 members, a $10 dues increase would still only generate about $50,000, not a lot of money considering the work that needed to be done; certainly not enough to fund a full-time, senior level Education Officer with appropriate travel funds and support staff.)

In the summer of 1995, however, the AAS was told that the Policy Board's ambitious NSF grant would not be funded and everyone had to go back to the drawing board. By late 1995, the Education Policy Board scaled down its proposal to focus solely on graduate education in astronomy, and soon received NSF funding for a series of meetings, discussions, and a report on this subject. These occurred throughout 1996 and many of the ideas suggested in earlier AAS reports (such as the Bok report of 1971) resurfaced independently. A final report is being submitted to the Council in summer of 1997, as we write.

In the meantime, in 1996, the Council approved a new structure for the AAS education effort. The older Education Advisory Board and the more recent Education Policy Board would be merged into a single Education Board, headed by an elected volunteer Education Officer. Bruce Partridge of Haverford College assumed this role in 1997 and his group is charged with continuing some of the policy initiatives and community-wide discussions of the Policy Board. In addition, the Society has hired a half-time paid Education Coordinator (Douglas Duncan of the University of Chicago) who will begin an active campaign to expand the educational activities of the Society in many areas. With a budget from the AAS limited essentially to the funds generated by the $10 dues increase, Duncan will search for funds elsewhere and leverage the efforts of other institutions and organizations, much as the TGEA did in the 1970s.

Is the current effort for more educational involvement by the AAS simply another crest in a wave of interest in education, which will subside as time goes on? Or will the reality of a paid education staff member make a permanent institutional difference for education at the Society? We leave this question for future historians to ponder, noting only that the challenges facing our Society (and our society) at all levels of education remain formidable and worthy of our best efforts.

THE AMERICAN ASTRONOMICAL SOCIETY AND THE NEWS MEDIA

Stephen P. Maran

ASTRONOMY IN THE NEWS

The national meetings of the American Astronomical Society (AAS) are widely reported in the print and broadcast media today, and it is not unusual in recent years for 100 members of the media, or more, to attend a meeting. Thus, the press attendance at some recent meetings exceeds the total attendance at some early meetings of the AAS. But while the intensity of media coverage and attendance have increased markedly, the Society's meetings have always attracted significant interest. A front page "Special to The New York Times" on September 3, 1921 reported from the Society's 26th meeting, held in Middletown, Connecticut in late August, that, "... it is estimated that it takes light, traveling at the rate of 186,000 miles a second, a period of 1,000,000 years to travel from one edge of the universe to the other." The same brief article announced what might be "dark dust clouds of some sort of matter suspended in space," whose nature was disputed by the scientists.[1]

As often happens at current AAS meetings, the 26th meeting was the subject of continuing coverage. On September 4, another *Times* report of information from the Middletown meeting stated that the AAS Eclipse Committee was making plans to test the theory of "Professor Einstein who contends that rays of light which pass the sun are deflected...".[2] Thus, Relativity was then a newsworthy topic at AAS meetings, just as it is today (albeit in the guise of new findings on black holes and gravitational lensing).

THE CREATION OF THE PRESS OFFICER

From its early years the Society recognized the need to have a media representative, whether to accommodate press interest or to foster it. Typically, in the 1920s at least, the Council appointed a "press secretary" for each meeting. The Council minutes associated with the 31st Meeting of the Society, in December 1923, for example, state that "Mr. [Frederick] Slocum was requested to act as press secretary for the Vassar meeting."[3] This informal process did not change significantly for decades.

As pointed out by Wentzel and Fraknoi elsewhere in this volume, in 1973 the AAS created a "Public Information Representative" and asked Kenneth Franklin to perform the duty. In 1979, the duties of this position were incorporated in those of the newly created Education Officer when Harry Shipman assumed the post. Shipman administered both the Shapley Lectures program and press matters, a joint responsibility that gradually became onerous. The positions of Education and Press Officer were officially separated by the Council at the 165th meeting, in Tucson in January 1985, when I was asked to take on the duties of the latter.

ATTRACTING THE PRESS

My task was to intensify efforts to attract reporters to the meetings by offering greater numbers of news briefings and press releases. The strategy adopted was to select topics and individual meeting papers that are "newsworthy," a term that characterizes subject matter that reporters are likely to write about and which their editors are likely to allow space for in newspapers and magazines. In contrast, new results to be presented at the meetings could not be readily judged for scientific significance: generally, only abstracts are available in advance of the meeting, and if the work is familiar or has gained acceptance because it has been presented or published in some form previously it is unlikely to be "news." Where results publicized at one meeting were later withdrawn, journalists understood that they were witnessing and reporting the scientific process in action. (Independent experts are sometimes asked to participate in our press conferences and comment on the results announced there; they have not hesitated to question them, usually diplomatically.)

For each meeting, dozens of press releases and photo releases were solicited from authors who had submitted abstracts for the meeting. Reporters could get these releases, as well as those pertaining to the meeting press conferences, by attending the meetings. To advise the media that these materials would be available, we created a new AAS letterhead with "Press Release" printed in large red letters. The AAS Press Release or Press Kit was a summary of the individual stories that would be documented by press releases brought to the meeting by their individual authors. Once the AAS notices of the meeting were mailed to reporters, we began calling them to make sure they appreciated the numbers and magnitudes of the newsworthy stories that they would get if they attended. This was the then-essential "jawboning" process. But by the late 1980s and early 1990s, little or no jawboning was required. AAS meetings were making so much news that reporters routinely put them in their travel plans, called to verify the dates and preferred hotels, and awaited notice of the prime stories so that they could, where appropriate, negotiate with gatekeeping editors in advance of the meeting for major space in their newspapers on specified dates during the meeting.

Although we were distributing many meeting-unrelated press releases by e-mail year-round by the 1990s, we adopted a policy of refusing to distribute the major stories from our meetings in this manner. The underlying theory is that if reporters have to come to the meeting to cover a major story, they will also cover other stories at the meeting. But if they cover the story from their home office, they will only write one astronomy story. Press attendance at the meetings rose during the 1985–1995 decade from a dozen or so at the January meeting and a handful at the June meeting to a few dozen to 80 or more at the June meetings and 75 to 110 at the January meetings. The launch of the Hubble Space Telescope in April 1990 and the enormous public interest concerning its findings was an important factor as astronomers began announcing many of their HST discoveries at our meetings.

Discovery, further study, and sometimes, withdrawal, as noted above, are unavoidable themes in media coverage of science, which emphasizes what appear initially as quantum leaps although most good science is incremental. Nowhere was the scientific self-correction process seen so dramatically than at the 179th meeting, January 1992 in Atlanta, where in his invited talk before the Society, Andrew Lyne bravely and unexpectedly withdrew his recently published discovery of the supposed planet of pulsar PSR1829-10 and then strode to the briefing room to face the press. At the same meeting, Aleksander Wolszczan briefed the media on his just-published detection of planets in the PSR 1257+12 system, a finding that, thus far, has held up. The seeming detection of extrasolar planets and brown dwarfs, announced at our meetings but subsequently withdrawn or strongly disputed, all heavily covered by the media, became a sufficiently common experience during 1985–1995 that I developed an after-dinner speech on the topic, "The Best Evidence Yet," illustrated with slides of retrospectively amusing newspaper articles. Yet this was not a new phenomenon at the meetings, nor of the media: On April 19, 1963, the *New York Times* had run a story from the 113th meeting, at Tucson, headlined "Another Solar System Is Found 36 Trillion Miles From the Sun." It was an account of the work on Barnard's Star by the late Peter van de Kamp, and it cited two earlier reports of purported substellar companions of proper motion stars.[4]

PURPOSE OF MEDIA OUTREACH

It's important to understand the purpose of the media outreach effort at AAS meetings. Colleagues sometimes wonder why certain work was featured in the media, when other work seemed just as good, or maybe better. The intent, however, is not to publicize particular astronomers or their projects, but to keep before the public—using subject matter that seems most effective for that purpose—the story of current astrophysical research as an exciting, engrossing ongoing endeavor. The scientists who are featured may or may not benefit from the exposure that results from assisting the Society in these briefings (a few report that they feel they have suffered); but the profession collectively benefits from increased public interest and awareness. The participants are not "hams" but rather "guinea pigs," colleagues who have been good enough sports to expose themselves to potential notoriety in order to aid the Society's outreach effort. Often, the resulting reports include substantial illustrated "spreads" in daily newspapers, such as those regularly published in the weekly science section of the *Dallas Morning News* in the wake of an AAS meeting (Figure 1). The spreads have an obvious tutorial value; we suspect they are clipped and posted for classroom use.

PREPARING FOR PRESS CONFERENCES

Press Conferences just do not happen. They are planned. One of the most important planning steps is to read through the abstracts submitted to the AAS Executive Office in advance of a meeting and then to select topics for a slate of six to nine briefings to be held at that meeting. Because we are in search of topics that will be new to the veteran science writers who regularly attend our meetings, who receive large numbers of press releases and tips every week, and who even have been known to scan *The Astrophysical Journal* as new issues appear, the topics selected for briefings are more

Figure 1. First page of a typical astronomy spread, based on reports at a recent AAS meeting, in the *Dallas Morning News*. (Courtesy of T. Siegfried, *Dallas Morning News*.)

often chosen from unheralded contributed papers than from invited talks or prize lectures, because the invited presentations often focus on established work with which the writers are already familiar. The criteria we use were described (in part) by an observant journalist who wrote an essay on the press coverage at the 189th meeting, in Toronto: "... when something is first or biggest or smallest or worst or any other superlative, it catches the attention of both reporters and editors..." and "[the Press Officer] must mix things up... there could have been four black-hole press conferences, but what [news]paper was going to declare what would amount to 'Black Hole Week' in their news pages?"[5]

Besides trying to attain some balance between the different fields of astrophysics, we want to feature scientists from host organizations of the meeting, whenever possible, to encourage local media to take a greater interest in local and regional astronomy programs. Occasionally we offer "Seminars for Science Writers" in which the content is not necessarily new material nor intended for immediate reporting, but is a tutorial on a current "hot field" in astrophysics. Where feasible, there is a Press Tour during the national meeting, to visit a new research facility or one of historic interest. And occasionally, there is a "Photo Op" or Photo Opportunity, meaning an arranged time and place where a particular display of astronomical information or experimental apparatus is presented for still and video photographers (Figure 2).

Figure 2. Papparazzi crowded into a small room to record a Photo Opportunity at the 189th meeting. After filming a large display of a Milky Way CO survey on the opposite wall (not shown), they appear to be taping the display on astronomer Thomas Dame's video monitor. Photograph courtesy of James Cornell.

THE HARVEST

By the early 1990s, the broadcast media were taking a greater interest in our meetings, so that television and radio coverage was increasing. We found, however, that it was not productive to plan news briefings aimed at broadcasters, because (unlike science writers) broadcasters, recordists, and camera crews are typically assigned to cover an event at almost the last minute. Because few of them have astronomy as their regular beat, it is often difficult for them to judge the news value of an astrophysics press conference. Accordingly, our strategy has been to feature briefings aimed at the print reporters who specialize in astronomy and related sciences. We found that whether television cameras and radio microphones were present at a morning news conference or not, the heavy reporting of that briefing by print reporters during the day, carried by wire services hours or sometimes even minutes after the briefing (some reporters draft a story in advance of a news conference, touch it up with a quote or two from the briefing, and send it off by e-mail immediately thereafter), validated the importance of our stories to the radio and television assignment editors. Then the broadcast news correspondents played "catch up," running short stories on the evening news or more fully developed ones the next day.

By the mid-1990s, if not before, AAS meetings were recognized as major news sources by both cable and broadcast networks. Already, radio network services and syndicated programming services (such as the BBC World Service and the U.S.'s Monitor Radio) were assigning freelance correspondents to attend the meetings. Now, it was not unusual for organizations such as Cable Network News and Discovery Channel Canada to send correspondents or crews to attend the meeting for a day or two, or for the duration. Producers of television documentaries began setting up mini-studio operations at some of the meetings, taking advantage of the presence of large numbers of articulate, expert astronomers to record many interviews inexpensively in a short time for later editing. The enterprising producers of one series sent dual interviewers and backdrops to a meeting, so that it would not be especially obvious to viewers that multiple interviews were conducted at nearly the same time and place.

On occasion, as when the late Carl Sagan attended the 181st meeting in Phoenix in 1993, to deliver his AAS-Annenberg Prize lecture, interviews or news reports were televised "live" from the meeting. Events like the unveiling of the Hubble Deep Field and the announcement of the detection of putative planets orbiting 70 Virginis and 47 Ursae Majoris (all at the 187th meeting, in San Antonio, Texas) were covered by multiple camera crews from networks and documentary producers. Especially heavy media attendance at the 187th and other meetings led to briefings where all seats were individually reserved (so that, for example, publications or broadcast media that sent multiple representatives to the same briefing were restricted to one seat per organization) and the aisles sometimes were jammed by photographers (Figure 3). On at least two occasions, briefings were so well attended that they had to be shifted from the scheduled press conference room to a "breakout room" (a small auditorium normally used for sessions of oral papers or invited talks). The coverage of the 187th meeting included front-page stories in the *New York Times* on three consecutive days, and itself inspired further articles and editorials on the subject of the excitement of astronomical discovery and the resultant media frenzy, and on the process of media coverage of the meeting.[6]

EXPANDING THE NETWORK

Reporters followed astronomers as regular users of the internet, with a phase lag of a few years. Accordingly, we began to distribute our press notices of the meetings by e-mail and, by 1996, discontinued postal mailings of these materials. Soon, institutional press representatives at observatories and educational institutions began to ask us to pass on their astronomy-related press releases as well. This effort grew until, by August 7, 1997, there were 639 writers, editors, and producers and 120 institutional press officers on our distribution list. The releases are sent regularly to journalists in the Americas, western Europe, and Australia; thus far only a few science writers in Asia have subscribed, but Japanese news bureaus in the United States are well represented. Through a program initiated by the American Association for the Advancement of Science (AAAS), which accredits the participating reporters, we began to offer complimentary press subscriptions to the electronic editions of *The Astrophysical Journal* in June 1996; several hundred applications have since been granted.

MEDIA QUERIES AND BENEFITS

As science writers and broadcasters became increasingly familiar with the AAS, they began to direct inquiries about astronomy and space exploration to the Society at an increasing rate. Until recently, almost all were from North America and the United Kingdom and almost all came by telephone. Now many inquiries arrive by e-mail from reporters overseas. The great majority of queries are referred to individual astronomers

Figure 3. The crowded scene at a typical AAS meeting press conference on black holes, in this case at the January 1997 meeting in Toronto. Photograph by the author.

who are experts in the respective subject matter fields, or who teach large undergraduate classes, lecture at planetaria, or have otherwise distinguished themselves as good communicators.

Press coverage of Society meetings provides several benefits. First, it adds to the public understanding of science and keeps knowledge of astronomy as a significant ongoing enterprise alive in the minds of students, teachers, and our fellow citizens in general. Second, press coverage is noticed, read, and appreciated by staffers and principals in Congress and the Executive Branch, where policy makers are concerned that public outreach is necessary to maintain support for scientific research. Third, the media presence arguably increases interest in our meetings even for our own members. It helps to establish and enhance the reputation of the national meetings of the AAS as venues where much of the most interesting and novel new research in astrophysics is first presented and debated.

ACKNOWLEDGMENTS

Harry Shipman initiated me into the mysteries of AAS press relations and has been a constant source of encouragement. James Cornell generously gave of his time, skills, and knowledge as an advisor and occasional participant to help us establish the AAS as a principal point of contact between the news media and astronomers. Many institutional science writers and press officers from national observatories, universities, NASA and other agencies have been tireless volunteers in staffing the press room operations at AAS meetings since 1985. A few who have done so repeatedly at our national meetings include Daniel Brocious, Richard Dreiser, James Elliott, David Finley, Shireen Gonzaga, Caroline Lupfer Kurtz, and Ray Villard. To the named volunteers and the many others, I am deeply grateful.

It is a pleasure to thank Ruth Freitag (Library of Congress) and the editor for historical research in support of this article and Tom Siegfried (Science Editor, *Dallas Morning News*) for kindly furnishing the photographic reproduction shown here as Figure 1.

PART 7

THE DIVISIONS OF THE SOCIETY

The Origin of the Divisions of the American Astronomical Society and the History of the High Energy Astrophysics Division

Virginia Trimble

HOW IT ALL STARTED

Ew structures — political, architectural, or scientific — are assembled either by people with some new vision of what the world should be like or by people who are simply dissatisfied with the existing structures. The League of Nations, the Statue of Liberty, and George Ellery Hale's proposal for what eventually became the National Research Council (whose initial purpose was to enable scientists to contribute quickly and efficiently to the U.S. effort in World War I) are examples of the first category. Most small political parties, our new central library building, and the scientific research honor society, Sigma Xi (founded by people whose "non-liberal" interests made them ineligible for Phi Beta Kappa), are examples of the second category.

The first four (at least) divisions of the American Astronomical Society arose almost entirely out of dissatisfaction at a time (the late 1960s) when mainstream astronomy was generally thought to be the study of stars and galaxies, and people working in other areas began to feel that their interests were not being well served. Albert Whitford, AAS President at the time, was committed to a sabbatical in Australia, leaving the problem in the hands of his Vice President and successor Martin Schwarzschild (*see* page 233 for a table of AAS officers). Schwarzschild recalls the events as follows:

> Leo Goldberg, speaking for the solar astronomers, declared that the AAS poorly served solar astronomy and that, if the AAS did not develop a better setup for that group, they might leave to form a separate society. Similarly, the planetary astronomers, many of them more at home in the geophysical society [American Geophysical Union] than in the AAS, wondered about leaving. Finally, in a decisive move, the physical society [American Physical Society] asked Chandra[sekhar] to lead the formation of an Astrophysics Division for it, aimed to include high energy astrophysics.

> All of this I felt added up to the threat that the AAS might lose those branches which at that time were the most scientifically exciting and popularly attractive ones — a rather disastrous possibility. The foundation of divisions seemed to be the most effective possible countermove — though the thought of losing some of the unity of astronomy lingered in our minds. I think I felt this threat strongly and so went ahead, with much support of most of the Council, to plan the divisions.

The three divisions I mentioned above had, from the outset, strong leadership. The situation was less simple for the dynamics division because it intended to include two fairly separate groups, the celestial mechanicians for the solar system and the stellar dynamicists for galaxies. But after some negotiations, also that division got composed.

The division leaders naturally tended to want as much independence for the divisions as possible, but no legal and minimal financial responsibility. On the other side the Council — particularly, the more conservative Secretary [G. C. McVittie] and Treasurer [Frank Edmondson] — was much concerned to keep enough control necessary for its responsibilities. It was quite a balancing act.

Hank Gurin, then the Executive Officer — an extremely capable and modest person — and I drafted the bylaws of the divisions with much reference to the setups in the physical society [APS divisions date back to 1943] — just as we also drafted the bylaws for the *ApJ* (transferred from the University of Chicago to the Society in the same time frame) and for the new election proceedings. In due course, the Council adopted these drafts, if I remember right, with not much competition in this detailed work.[1]

Eugene Parker, who had primary responsibility for drafting of the HEAD-specific bylaws, also recalls a deliberate effort to break as little new ground as possible and to model them closely after working examples from other societies. That the origin of the High Energy Astrophysics Division lay largely in feelings of disaffection within the space astronomy community is confirmed by William Kraushaar, Maarten Schmidt, and Lodewijk Woltjer, who were among the initial officers and committee members (Table 4). Riccardo Giacconi phrases it somewhat more gently as, "to see that X-ray astronomy was properly represented at meetings."[2]

This feeling of insufficient representation was not entirely unprecedented. The relationship between radio and optical astronomy a decade earlier had been similarly uncomfortable, and the merging of the former into the mainstream, though rather gradual, was eventually accomplished without fragmentation.

How realistic were the perceptions of exclusion? A complete answer would require careful examinations of early membership lists and meeting programs that are not readily available. But one can set some limits. Between 1946 and 1969 (when the divisions were established), 143 names appear on lists of the Russell Lecturers, the Warner Prize Winners and the Society presidents, vice-presidents, and councilors. At least a few come from each of the disaffected subfields. Using "R" for radio astronomy, "P" for planetary science, "S" for solar physics, "A" for high energy astrophysics, "D" for dynamics, and "H" for history, these are (in chronological order in each category):

Russell Lecturers: Gerard Kuiper (P), Grote Reber (R), Richard Tousey (A), Otto Neugebauer (H), John Bolton (R).

Warner Prize: Joseph Chamberlain (P), Bernard Burke (R), Riccardo Giacconi (A).

Presidents: G. M. Clemence (D), Leo Goldberg (S).

Vice Presidents: Fred Whipple (P), Dirk Brouwer (D), Clemence (D), Goldberg (S), Fred Haddock (R), Tousey (A).

Councilors: Alan Maxwell (S), Peter Millman (P), Goldberg (S), Clemence (D), Kuiper (P), Robert Trumpler (D), Walter Orr Roberts (S), Ronald Bracewell (R), Chamberlain (P), Herbert Friedman (A), John Evans (S), Elizabeth Roemer (P).

Figure 1. Martin Schwarzschild, AAS President from 1970 to 1972. Irwin photograph, American Insitute of Physics, Emilio Segrè Visual Archives, Irwin Collection.

Notice that some names appear more than once. The remainder in each category were, indeed, theorists and optical astronomers working primarily on stars and galaxies (as were all the winners of the Cannon Prize during that period), though a few are a bit difficult to classify. How do you limit Jan Oort to a single subdiscipline?

The divisions clearly accomplished their purpose, in the sense that the four initial ones remain large, active parts of the AAS, organizing meetings of their own and sessions at general AAS meetings. The shakedown cruises in 1970–1972 revealed some minor structural problems connected with the handling of registration, abstract publications, and meeting publicity for various kinds of separate and joint sessions when a division met either with the main AAS meeting or with a section of some other society, like HEAD with the astrophysics section of the American Physical Society.

What became of the separatist movements? There is still no American Association of Solar Physicists (which is probably a good thing). Planetary science remains an active presence in the AGU as well as in the AAS. The APS went ahead in 1970 with its Division of Cosmic Physics (renamed Astrophysics in 1983), though S. Chandrasekhar was not the founding chair. In fact, 14 of the 15 chairs and secretaries who led DCP during its first decade were cosmic-ray physicists rather than from the X-ray and gamma-ray communities, though in recent years more of the leadership has come from theoretical astrophysics and from X- and gamma-ray astronomers. Its roughly 1,400 current members overlap less than 50% with the AAS membership (and by simple arithmetic, less than 50% with the 650 current members of HEAD). A 1972 proposal from Hale Bradt that HEAD and DCP might merge into a single unit with a single set of officers, meetings, etc. not unexpectedly mired swiftly down in bureaucratic mud.

At one point, the High Energy Astrophysics Division seemed to be working almost too well, in the sense of separating its community from the rest of the AAS, and Riccardo Giacconi and George Field were among its leaders who suggested that it should disband. The suspension of separate meetings between 1983 and 1993 (see "Meetings") appears to have been the main result of this suggestion.

Nevertheless, in comparison with substructures in other scientific societies (Table 1), the divisions of the AAS remain nearly pathological. In none of the other 10 societies shown are there divisions by subject matter that exclude the largest, core parts of the science(s) involved. This should not be taken as encouragement for energetic AAS members to propose organizing divisions of cosmology, high-resolution spectroscopy, stellar structure, infrared astronomy, or whatever!

The four commonest activities of scientific societies are: (1) recruitment of new members, (2) election of officers (some do nothing else: Richard Feynman included the National Academy of Sciences in that class), (3) organization of meetings, and (4) awarding of prizes. All five AAS divisions now do all of these. The following sections pertain primarily to HEAD and, after a discussion of how the meaning of the name has evolved, focus on these four activities.

THE SCOPE OF "HIGH ENERGY ASTROPHYSICS"

The phrase "high energy astrophysics" does not seem to be enormously older than the Division. The first printed definition I have found, in the proceedings of a 1965 Varenna summer school with that title, says, "The words...are thus meant to indicate not merely processes in which large amounts of energy are involved, but, mainly, those in which the rate of energy release per second and per gram is very high as compared with the more usual processes going on in normal stars and galaxies."[3] Gravitational collapse, supernovae, and quasi-stellar radio sources are among the examples given. Correspondingly, although the school included lectures on observational and theoretical X-ray and gamma-ray astronomy, comparable amounts of time were devoted to radio galaxies and quasi-stellars at optical and radio wavelengths; the strong interaction, equation of state of dense matter and relativistic star structure; and neutrino astrophysics and cosmology. That is, "high energy astrophysics" at this point meant "high energy per event," not "high energy per photon."

The Division bylaws initially provided a somewhat similar (though less grammatical) definition, describing the object of the Division as "to assist and promote the advancement of research and dissemination of knowledge of high energy events, particles, quanta, of relativistic gravitational fields and of related phenomena in the astrophysical universe, and to promote the coordination of this research and knowledge with other branches of science."[4]

Early Division committees and business meetings struggled with the issue a number of times. Kenneth Greisen in spring, 1970, asked his committee to think about, "why do we exist and what we should do to justify our existence," and their initial response was couched in terms of increasing contact between astronomers and physicists working on the same objects, events and systems from different points of view.[5] In December of that year, George Field raised the point again at the San Juan business meeting and asked for expressions of opinion on whether the scope should be limited

TABLE 1. *Substructures of Various American and Astronomical Societies in Comparison with AAS.*

Society	Approximate 1996 Membership	Substructure(s)
American Astronomical Society[1]	6,566	Five divisions representing nontraditional sub-fields; about 1/3 of members belong to one or more
American Physical Society[1]	41,000	14 divisions representing major subfields; topical groups (smaller subfields); forums (interdisciplinary); geographic regions; most members belong to one or more
American Chemical Society[4]	151,000	About 35 sections (etc.) representing major subfields; most members belong to one or more
American Mathematical Society[4]	29,000	Geographic regions
American Geophysical Union[4]	33,000	About 18 sections representing major subfields; most members belong to one or more
American Meteorological Society[3]	11,000	City and University chapters
American Assoc. for the Advancement of Science[1]	144,500	24 sections representing major sciences; 54% of members belong to at least one; geographic regions
Sigma Xi[1]	88,000	Local chapters joined in geographic regions (historically, an honorary)
Royal Astronomical Society[1]	3,000	None
European Astronomical Society[2]	1,586	None (society only about five years old)
European Physical Society[1]	70,000*	Seven divisions representing main subfields; subdivisions and interdivisional groups; most affiliated members do not belong to any
International Astronomical Union[1]	7,800	39 Commissions representing major subfields, recently grouped into 11 divisions; most members belong to one or more (historically, this was compulsory)

*Most are affiliate members by virtue of belonging to one of 36 national societies of physicists
[1] Information from society membership directories, newsletters, officers' handbooks, etc.
[2] Information from society officers
[3] Information from an active member
[4] Information from Washington offices

to X-, gamma- and cosmic-rays, or be more inclusive, after the fashion of the ''Texas'' Symposia on Relativistic Astrophysics. Similar remarks appear in Newsletter No. 5 in December, 1971.[6] The majority favored a broad construction of the Division's charge, but this was by no means unanimous. The second Chair, Kraushaar, indicated to Hale Bradt (as member of the program committee with Field and Stirling Colgate in 1972)

Figure 2. Leo Goldberg was AAS President from 1964 to 1966, a time when solar astronomers, himself among them, began thinking about the need for better representation in the Society. Irwin photograph, American Institute of Physics, Emilio Segrè Visual Archives, Irwin Collection.

that the scope should be "astrophysics that uses relativity," or a "travelling Texas symposium," and not just X- and gamma-ray astronomy. Bradt concurred, but soon after, a tabulation of all invited talks that had been sponsored by the Division showed that close to two-thirds had been in the cosmic-ray, X, and gamma regimes.[7]

This focus on the three core disciplines gradually came to be perceived as the norm (as is clear from the topics emphasized at the meetings listed in Table 5). Twenty years later, when I raised the question of "high energy per event" versus "high energy per photon" with the 1992 and 1993 committees (Table 4), opinion was overwhelmingly in favor of "high energy per photon."

The Commission on High Energy Astrophysics of the International Astronomical Union, founded almost simultaneously with HEAD, at the 1970 General Assembly in Brighton, illustrates the same phenomenon in even more extreme form. The founding officers and members (Table 2) display (a) a considerable overlap with the founders of HEAD, at least among the Americans, and (b) a range of scientific interests encompassing radio and optical observations and a wide variety of theoretical astrophysics topics, as well as X-rays, gamma-rays, and (marginally) cosmic rays.[8]

The Commission was always erratic (outstandingly so, by IAU standards) about producing its triennial reports (before successive General Assemblies) and its meeting reports (afterwards), but the early ones that exist indicate a scope of interest that includes assorted outbursts at radio, optical and gravitational wavelengths, pulsars,

TABLE 2. *Founding Members of IAU Commission 48, High Energy Astrophysics.*

President: Herbert Friedman*
Vice President: Martin Rees*
Organizing Committee: Alastair Cameron*, Vitaly Ginzburg, Thomas Gold*, Kenneth Greisen*, Philip Morrison, Franco Pacini, Dennis Sciama, Maurice Shapiro*, Iosef Shklovskij, Francis Graham Smith
Members: Luis Alvarez, Geoffrey Burbidge*, Talbot Chubb*, George Clark*, G. Dautcourt, Giovanni Fazio*, James Felten*, Carl Fichtel*, George Field*, Philip Fisher*, William Fowler*, Gordon Garmire*, Riccardo Giacconi*, Livio Gratton, Howard Greyber, Herbert Gursky*, Satio Hayakawa, Fred Hoyle, J. V. Jelley, Ben-Zion Kozlovsky, V. G. Kurt, Malcolm Longair, Masaru Matsuoka, Yuval Ne'eman, Minoru Oda, Eugene Parker*, Vahe Petrosian*, Kenneth Pounds, Hubert Reeves, Bruno Rossi*, Edwin Salpeter*, William Saslaw, Evry Schatzman, Peter Scheuer, Giancarlo Setti, Giora Shaviv, Sabatino Sofia, Peter Sturrock*, Rashid Sunyaev, S. J. Syrovatskij, Kip Thorne*, James Truran*, John Wheeler, Lodewijk Woltjer*, Yakov Zeldovich

*Commission members who also belonged to HEAD within its first decade. The IAU Commission requires that one cannot be considered for election within three years of obtaining the Ph.D. and that a new member is restricted to membership in a single commission for the first triennium. Therefore Trimble was elected to the IAU in 1973, into Commission 48 in 1976, and on to the organizing committee for the 1985-1994 terms.

supernovae, quantum gravity, nucleosynthesis and the early universe. The last report of any kind (of activities at the 1988 General Assembly in Baltimore) has only two talks out of 17 from outside the X- and gamma-ray regime. One can no longer ask about the interests of Commission members or about the fraction of founders who are still members because, in 1994, Commission 48 declared itself to be indistinguishable from Commission 44 ("Astrophysics from Space") and voted itself out of existence as a separate entity, at the urging of its President, Jeremiah Ostriker.

The history of the subject called "relativistic astrophysics" is remarkably different. The phrase was coined and provisionally defined in connection with the Dallas meeting in December 1963 that we retrospectively call the First Texas Symposium (the 18th of which met in Chicago in December, 1996). Initially focused on quasi-stellar sources, radio galaxies, and gravitational collapse, Texas programs rapidly expanded to include X- and gamma-ray sources, but also the early universe, large scale structure, gravitational radiation and lensing, and, at times, complex interstellar molecules and very large telescopes. Much territory has also been abandoned over the years,[9] but it seems most improbable that the standing committee responsible for the long-term organization of the symposia will declare its subject matter to be indistinguishable from cosmology, nuclear astrophysics or astronomy from space!

MEMBERSHIP, DUES, AND SUCH

The first activity absolutely essential to the existence of a scientific society is recruitment of members. The 85 AAS members who sent a check and a ballot to founding Secretary-Treasurer A. G. W. Cameron before the end of May, 1969, were declared to be the founding members of the Division (along with six late contributors, including the Secretary himself). They are listed in Table 3, categorized by whether they are still members of the Division (according to the 1997 AAS Membership Directory), members of the Society but not the Division, Members of the scientific community (in the sense of being members of APS, IAU, academic departments, etc.) but not of AAS, deceased, or lost to follow-up. Of the 81 living founders, 46 (or 57%) are still Division members. Phyllis Freier, the discoverer of heavy elements in cosmic rays, was the only female founder. Membership rose gradually to about 135 in late 1971 and 237 in 1978. The 1978 roster was published in the *BAAS*. Of the 237 members (18 women), 132 (56%) are listed in the 1996 AAS Directory as Division members; 55 (23%) are still AAS members but not in the Division; of these, about 16 are retired and a comparable number worked, and work, on topics like quasars, pulsars, and theoretical relativity that are no longer part of high energy astrophysics; 27 (11%) remain in the community and can be located as members of APS, IAU, RAS or academic institutions; 13 (5.5%) are deceased; and 10 (4%) could not be traced. Of the last, some may have died, but nine of them (according to their last AAS Directory entry between from 1979 and 1988) had addresses at industrial organizations, government labs, or private residences, and I suspect that most of the people are alive and well, but no longer think of themselves as astronomers, let alone high energy astrophysicists.

The most obvious reward of membership (besides voting privileges) was the *Newsletter*, issued four times a year beginning in November, 1970. Early ones were mimeographed and sent directly by the Secretary-Treasurer; later ones were reproduced by some more elegant technique and mailed out more centrally; and the current crop comes electronically (but the Secretary-Treasurer has to do the work again).

TABLE 3. *Founding Members of HEAD and Their Status in 1996.*

Still Division Members: Kinsey Anderson; James Bardeen; Hale Bradt; Geoffrey Burbidge; Edward Chupp; George Clark; Donald Clayton; T. L. Cline; Stirling Colgate; Brian Dennis; David DeYoung; Giovanni Fazio; Carl Fichtel; George Field; M. W. Friedlander; Gordon Garmire; Riccardo Giacconi; Paul Gorenstein; Donald Groom; R. C. Hartman; Robert Haymes; Richard Henry; Herbert Gursky; R. Hjellming; D. A. Kniffen; William Kraushaar; James Kurfess; Stephen Maran; Lloyd Motz; J. F. Ormes; E. N. Parker; P. J. E. Peebles; Jim Peters; Vahe Petrosian; Reuven Ramaty; Malcolm Savedoff; J. D. Scargle; Maarten Schmidt; Herbert Schnopper; Maurice Shapiro; J. A. Simpson; Leon Van Speybroeck; Kip Thorne; C. J. Waddington; Robert Wagoner; George Wallerstein

Still AAS Members: W. David Arnett; Stuart Bowyer; A. G. W. Cameron; Hong-Yee Chiu; Robert Christy; Talbot Chubb; Marshall Cohen; James Earl; Philip Fisher; Thomas Gold; J. L. Greenstein; Robert Kraft; Robert O'Connell; J. B. Oke; R. B. Partridge; Martin Pomerantz; Victor Regener; W. L. W. Sargent; Frank Scherb; M. Simon; Philip Solomon; James Truran; William Webber; Donat Wentzel; Gart Westerhout; Kenneth Widing; D. Wilkinson

Members of other societies or academic departments: Kenneth Frost; Kenneth Greisen; Morton Kaplon; J. H. Kinsey; Ian Lerche; Kandiah Shivanandan

Lost to follow up: Oscar P. Manley; Edmond C. Roelof

Deceased: S. Chandrasekhar; Leverett Davis; Robert Dicke; William A. Fowler; Phyllis Freier; Serge Korff; Howard Laster; Alan Moffet; Bruno Rossi; G. S. Vaiana

1978 Division members lost to follow-up: Doron Bardas; Richard Belian; Richard Borken; Betty Jean Bragg; Gabrielle Cohen; H. Grady Hughes III; Hugo Rugge; James Underhill; Matthew Vanderhill

1978 Division members since deceased (not founders): Jeno Barnothy; Satio Hayakawa; Jerome Kristian; Leona Marshall Libby; David Schramm

Membership oscillated between 200 and 300 through the decade after 1974, with peaks following particularly good meetings (at some of which immediate sign-up was possible). Numbers given in the annual division reports in the *BAAS* are clearly not perfectly accurate. For instance, 430 seems to have been copied from year to year from 1990 to 1994. Resumption of separate divisional meetings at which participants have been encouraged to join has produced another growth period, with (at some particular instant in each year) 576, 631, and 656 members in 1994, 1995 and, 1996, respectively.

Roughly 11 percent of AAS members who belong to one division actually belong to more than one (this comes from a count of every fifth page in the 1996 directory). There are 10 (5 x 4 ÷ 2) possible combinations of two divisions. Logical combinations are the most common, like people who work on orbits in the solar system and belong to both Planetary Science and Dynamical Astronomy, or people who work on solar flares and belong to both Solar Physics and HEAD, but all possible combinations occur. There are also ten possible triple memberships (think of leaving out two), most of which also happen. A few people belong to four divisions, but apparently, none to all five. To do so would add $40 to one's annual dues.

Initial dues were $3 per year, sent directly to the Secretary-Treasurer of HEAD. Billing was handed over to the American Institute of Physics in the fall of 1970. They recharged the AAS 50¢ per person, with the cost passed on to the Division. This used up an excessive share of the income, and the system reverted to direct collection by the Secretary-Treasurer. Members were expected to send $6 at a time for three years at a time (with resulting large fluctuations in membership!). Collection of all divisional dues in tandem with regular annual AAS payments began in the late 1980s and the fee for HEAD membership gradually crept up to $4 per year in 1988, $5 in 1994 and $6 at the present time. The initial $3 fee was set at a time when the AAS dues rate was $27 per year and a private subscription to *ApJ* was $10. The 1997 numbers are $105 for AAS and $180 for *The Astrophysical Journal*. The raw numbers make the Division today sound like a bargain and the Journal quite the opposite, but the number of printed pages you get in a year has expanded in a way that the benefits offered by Society and Division membership arguably have not.

ELECTIONS AND OFFICERS

The second essential characteristic of a viable, formal substructure is that it elects officers. In the case of HEAD, the Council of the American Astronomical Society appointed an organizing committee at its meeting on August 20, 1968. The members were: G. R. Burbidge, A. G. W. Cameron, T. A. Chubb, G. W. Clark, C. E. Fichtel, K. I. Greisen, E. N. Parker (temporary chairman), M. Schmidt, K. S. Thorne, and L. Woltjer. They, in addition to being responsible for the drafting of Division bylaws, served as the first nominating committee and, in accordance with those bylaws, assembled a slate for the 1969 election that included "at least one" candidate each for Chairman, Vice-Chairman and Secretary-Treasurer, and eleven candidates for Committeemen, the three receiving the largest number of votes to serve for two years and the next highest four to serve for one year. There was a good deal of overlap between this slate and the initial organizing committee, and three of the four defeated committee candidates were subsequently elected to office.[10]

The system has been self-perpetuating. Each year, the Chair, with advice from the committee, appoints a three-member nominating committee, with, at most, one member who is already on the committee; they choose the candidates for the next election; the Vice-Chair becomes Chair; and so around again the next year. The 1971 nominating committee included Herbert Gursky and Marshall Cohen, chaired by Robert Kraft; in 1972 Gursky chaired, with Cohen and Robert Wagoner. Terms were initially one year for Chairman and Vice-Chairman, two for Committeemen and three for the Secretary-Treasurer. Bylaw changes in 1994-96 expanded the one-year terms to two years (including the service of the past Chairman on the committee) and formalized two other changes that had gradually come about through usage. The first was language changes from Chairman to Chair (etc.), and the second was that there be "at least two" candidates put forward for Vice-Chair at each election, so that the winner would have somebody to triumph over (the bylaws don't quite say it this way).[11]

Table 4 is a complete list of those who have served in division offices and committees. Notice that the earlier cohorts are more likely to include radio, optical and relativistic astronomers than the later cohorts. Alan Moffet is the only past officer not still alive as this is being written. Of the other 101 people (16 women, beginning with Claire Max), 79 are still (or again) Division members, 19 are members of AAS but not of the Division (including one promotion to honorary membership and one switch to the history division); and three are no longer to be found in the 1997 directory. Two have retired and moved away from their professional institutions, and a third could not be traced. Of those who have left the Division but remain in the AAS, a few have significantly changed their research interests away from high energy astrophysics (narrowly or broadly construed). For most of the rest, the subject matter has moved away from them, as noted in a previous section. There is considerable "division loyalty" since 79 percent of the former officers are still Division members. This is totally unsurprising, since the officers have a stronger than average commitment to any organization (after, if not before).

HEAD elections are always settled by fewer than half of the members. Sporadic records in *BAAS* annual reports and records kept by some of the Secretary-Treasurers indicate that turnout has generally ranged between 25 and 35%. This is typical of the discipline. In the most recent (1996) election of the Astrophysics Division (formerly, Cosmic Physics) of the APS, 356 of 1,392 members, or 26%, cast ballots. Participation in society-wide elections is somewhat (not enormously) larger, and one wonders whether the Division elections might be combined with the general one to the benefit of both. The AAAS and some other societies already do this.

MEETINGS

The third most important activity for any scientific entity is the organization of meetings. Thus, the first trace of HEAD in the *BAAS* is the program of its first meeting in Washington, D.C., in April and May of 1970, held jointly with the Division of Cosmic Physics of the American Physical Society. Abstracts of the papers presented were divided between *BAAS* and the *Bulletin* of APS (April 1970). A quite wide range of subjects appeared on the program, including pulsar radiation mechanisms, infrared astronomy, relativity, and models and optical data for quasars, in addition to what

TABLE 4. *Past and Present Officers of HEAD.*

Year	Chair(man)	Vice-Chair(man)	Secretary-Treasurer	Committee(men)/members
1968–69	EN Parker			GR Burbidge, AGW Cameron, TA Chubb, GW Clark, CE Fichtel, KI Greisen, M Schmidt, KS Thorne, L Woltjer
1970	KI Greisen	WL Kraushaar	Cameron	TA Chubb, R Giacconi, RB Partridge, M Schmidt, GW Clark, KS Thorne, L Woltjer
1971	Greisen	Kraushaar	Cameron	TA Chubb, R Giacconi, RB Partridge, M Schmidt, GW Clark, KS Thorne, L Woltjer
1972	Kraushaar	GB Field	Cameron	Clark, Thorne, Woltjer, AT Moffet, WLW Sargent, JI Silk
1973	Field	P Morrison	HV Bradt	Moffet, Sargent, Silk, JN Bahcall, JE Felten, PA Sturrock
1974	Morrison	L Woltjer	Bradt	Bahcall, Felten, Sturrock, WD Arnett, GP Garmire, K Kellermann
1975	Woltjer	R Giacconi	Bradt	Arnett, Garmire, Kellermann, JM Bardeen, CE Max, PA Strittmatter
1976	Giacconi	LE Peterson	R Novick	Bardeen, Max, Strittmatter, AP Cowley, GG Fazio, JH Taylor
1977	Peterson	H Friedman	Novick	Cowley, Fazio, Taylor, JRP Angel, K Brecher, DN Schramm
1978	Friedman	GG Fazio	Novick	Angel, Brecher, Schramm, JE Grindlay, SS Holt, MM Shapiro
1979	Fazio	CE Fichtel	Schramm	Grindlay, Holt, Shapiro, DQ Lamb, R Ramaty, V Trimble
1980	Fichtel	Bradt	Schramm	Lamb, Ramaty, Trimble, C Canizares, PJE Peebles, JW Swank
1981	Bradt	Shapiro	Schramm	Canizares, Peebles, Swank, C Crannell, JC Wheeler, S Woosley
1982	Shapiro	SS Holt	Grindlay	Crannell, Wheeler, Woosley, R Blandford, M Israel, S Rappaport
1983	Holt	R Ramaty	Grindlay	Blandford, Israel, Rappaport, P Joss, FK Lamb, H Tananbaum
1984	Ramaty	Garmire	Grindlay	Joss, Lamb, Tananbaum, A Cowley, WD Evans, F Seward
1985	Garmire	R McCray	J Ormes	Cowley, Evans, Seward, R Chevalier, M Leventhal, J McClintock
1986	McCray	DS Helfand	Ormes	Chevalier, Leventhal, McClintock, W Cash, R Rosner, TC Weekes
1987	Helfand	FK Lamb	Ormes	Cash, Rosner, Weekes, E Boldt, C Jones, P Meszaros
1988	Lamb	Wheeler	R Haymes	Boldt, Jones, Meszaros, D Cox, A Harding, JP Henry
1989	Wheeler	F Cordova	Haymes	Cox, Harding, Henry, G Fabbiano, L Ozernoy, TA Prince
1990	Cordova	Lightman	Haymes	Fabbiano, Ozernoy, Prince, H Hudson, JA Tyson, S Kahn
1991	Lightman	DQ Lamb	N Gehrels	Hudson, Tyson, Kahn, DD Clayton, D Schwartz, CM Urry
1992	Lamb	V Trimble	Gehrels	Clayton, Schwartz, Urry, S Lea, B Margon, J Patterson
1993	Trimble	M Elvis	Gehrels	Lea, Margon, Patterson, H Ogelman, R Petre, B Wilkes
1994	Elvis	Gehrels	K Hurley	Ogelman, Petre, Wilkes, R Rothschild, M Ulmer, D Worrall

TABLE 4. *Continued.*

Year	Chair(man)	Vice-Chair(man)	Secretary-Treasurer	Committee(men)/members
1995	Elvis	Gehrels	Hurley	Rothschild, Ulmer, Worrall, C Kouveliotou, C Dermer, L Cominsky
1996	Gehrels	Garmire	Hurley	Kouveliotou, Dermer, Cominsky, P Szkody, C Meegan, D Burrows
1997	Gehrels	Garmire	A Marscher	Szkody, Meegan, Burrows, J Bechtold, D McCammon, N White
1998	Garmire	T.B.D.	Marscher	Bechtold, McCammon, White, three T.B.D.

eventually became the core topics of X-rays, gamma-rays, and cosmic rays (including solar ones from time to time). The first program committee included J. B. Oke and P. J. E. Peebles, chaired by G. R. Burbidge. The program committee is statutorily appointed by the Division Chair but, in practice, has generally consisted of the Division Vice-Chair and the three more senior members of the committee in recent years.

Table 5 is a reasonably complete list of subsequent divisional gatherings, including dates, locations, whether in association with DCP or regular AAS meetings, and major topics on the program (where the core topics are always to be assumed in addition). Records from the 1972 meeting in Pasadena leave one feeling a bit nostalgic. The local Chairman, W. L. W. Sargent, expressed concern that the Pasadena weather would not be tolerable until very late in October (we have been to much worse places!) and ended by providing an accounting to Division Chairman Kraushaar (who checked the arithmetic), reporting a profit of $9.24 on a total cost of $218.26 (mostly printing the programs, which were sold for $1 each, and lunches at the Athenaeum at $2.50 each), and refunded the profit to the Division. The Division was not yet exactly a plutocrat; the October 1971 bank balance was $1,289.85.

From 1983 to 1993, the Division met only in connection with semi-annual AAS meetings, with its business session and invited speaker sessions generally at the January meeting, though with occasional June sessions as well, and, from 1985 onward, the Rossi Prize Lectures. Among important non-core topics were Supernova 1987A at the January 1988 meeting; millisecond pulsars and the broad emission line regions of active galactic nuclei at the January 1989 meeting; multiwavelength astrophysics a year later; and solar neutrinos and supernova theory in January 1993.

Starting in 1994, the Division resumed separate meetings at roughly 1.5 year intervals. These were intended to replace, at least partly, the mission-oriented (ROSAT, CGRO, etc.) meetings that had meanwhile proliferated and, therefore, to reduce the total number of meetings. It is not clear that this has actually happened. Simultaneously, the Division has continued to present the Rossi Prize Lectures and to sponsor special sessions at the January AAS meeting, in recent years featuring briefings by representatives of sponsoring agencies.

THE ROSSI PRIZE

By 1983, the Division treasury had accumulated a sufficient reserve for the membership to start thinking of how to spend it. Engaging in the fourth common

TABLE 5. *Divisional Meetings.*

Date	Place	Participants	Important Program Topics
January 1970	Washington DC	DCP of APS	pulsar radiation mechanisms, core (including solar), infrared astronomy, quasar models and optical data, relativity
December 1971	Puerto Rico	DCP of APS after AAS	rocket astronomy, core (especially Uhuru, CR nucleosynthesis), radio observations of X-ray binaries, Li-Be-B, quasars and clusters, supernovae, hadronic matter, annihilation
October 1972	Pasadena CA	——	cosmological nucleosynthesis, clustering, core, early universe, galaxy formation and evolution, quasars, radio sources, submm background radiation
December 1973	Tucson AZ	DCP of APS after AAS	active galaxies in IR and optical, core (including solar, SAS II, X- and gamma-ray bursters), supernovae and massive stars, including nucleosynthesis, UV observations of ISM, clusters of galaxies, GR and gravitational radiation
December 1974	Gainesville FL	after AAS	(program and abstracts apparently never printed in BAAS)
January 1976	Cambridge MA	——	core focused on Uhuru, OAO, ANS, Ariel-5, OS0-8, SAS-3, Apollo-Soyuz results; X-ray bursters
April 1976	Washington DC	DCP of AAS	core, neutron stars, globular clusters, SETI and extraterrestrial life, neutrino astrophysics, observational cosmology
June 1976	Haverford PA	AAS special session	X-rays
January 1977	Honolulu HI	after AAS	"superrelativistic expansion" (radio), core, NASA high energy program
June 1977	Atlanta GA	AAS special session	COS-B
January 1978	Austin TX	AAS special session	HEAO-1
September 1978	San Diego CA	——	HEAO-1 results, X-ray source identifications, clusters of galaxies, diffuse backgrounds, types of X-ray sources, gamma bursts and transients
January 1979	Mexico City DF	AAS invited talk	significance of meteorite isotopic anomalies
April 1979	Washington DC	DCP of APS	core, early HEAO-2 results
June 1979	Wellesley MA	AAS special session	highlights from Einstein (HEAO-2)
January 1980	Cambridge MA	——	Einstein results and related topics-stellar coronae, SNRs, globular clusters, active galaxies, clusters, cosmological significance
January 1980	San Francisco CA	AAS special session	Einstein results, AGN theory, gamma ray line astronomy, cosmic ray transport
April 1980	Washington, DC	DCP of APS	core, including solar

TABLE 5. *Continued.*

Date	Place	Participants	Important Program Topics
June 1980	College Park MD	AAS special sessions	HEAO-3, optical observations of X-ray sources particle physics and cosmology
September 1980	Minneapolis MN	DPC of APS	gamma ray line astronomy (HEAO-3); cosmic rays (especially heavies)
January 1981	Albuquerque NM	AAS special session	X-rays, hot dark matter, cataclysmic variables
April 1981	Baltimore MD	DCP of APS	core topics
June 1981	Calgary AL	AAS special session	gamma bursts, active galactic nuclei, SS433, star burst galaxies
January 1982	Boulder CO	AAS special session + 1 day with DCP	core (especially Hakucho results), cataclysmic variables, supernovae, jets in AGNs, neutrinos
June 1982	Troy NY	AAS special session	core, coronae and rotation of late type stars
November 1994	Napa Valley CA	——	multi-mission perspective (CGRO, ASCA, ROSAT, etc)
May 1996	San Diego CA	——	ASCA, ROSAT, bursting pulsar, hard X- and gamma-rays, X-ray spectra first results from RXTE
November 1997	Estes Park CA	——	

activity of a scientific entity, the award of prizes, naturally suggested itself. The proposal for an annual award "for a significant contribution to high energy astrophysics, with particular emphasis on recent, original work" was put to a vote of the membership. Roughly half of the members responded, a higher yield than on elections for officers, presumably because money was involved. There were 109 yeses, 14 nos, and 13 more complex responses (including the present author's suggestion that the surplus be used to sponsor an annual reception at an AAS meeting).[12]

The Executive Committee recommended that the prize be named for Bruno Rossi (1905-1993), one of the founders of American X-ray astronomy, and drafted suitable amendments to the bylaws. These were approved, and the first prize was awarded in 1985 to Christine Jones and William Forman for work on X-ray coronae around early-type galaxies. Table 6 lists the subsequent winners with a brief description of the contributions honored. Of the 17 winners, six were resident outside the U.S. and Canada at the time (van der Klis, Sunyaev, the Kamioka Team, Bignami, Mirabel, and Rodriguez), and one was a woman (Jones). These patterns are fairly similar to the average of other division prizes and of the AAS-wide prizes for which there are no restrictions by location or gender (except that the location-unrestricted Russell and Heinemann prizes do not often find their way outside North America).

TABLE 6. *The Rossi Prize Lecture.*

Year	Winner(s)	Wavelength, Contribution	Date of Lecture at AAS Meeting
1985	Christine Jones and William Forman	X-rays; hot coronae around early type galaxies	June 85
1986	Allan Jacobson	gamma-rays; spectroscopy	June 86
1987	Michiel van der Klis	X-rays; quasi-periodic oscillations in XRBs	June 87
1988	Rashid Sunyaev	theoretical astrophysics; Soviet Space Program	Jan. 89
1989	IMB and Kamioka teams	Neutrinos; detection of SN 1987A	June 89
1990	Stirling Colgate	Theoretical astrophysics; models of supernovae	June 90
1991	John A. Simpson	cosmic rays	Jan. 92
1992	Gerald Share	gamma-rays; nuclear gamma rays incl. SN 1987A	Jan. 93
1993	Giovanni Bignami and Jules Halpern	X- and gamma-rays; identification of Geminga	June 94
1994	Gerald Fishman	gamma rays; BATSE	June 95
1995	Carl Fichtel	gamma rays; CGRO and EGRET	Jan. 96
1996	Felix Mirabel and Luis Rodriguez	radio; galactic superluminal sources	Jan. 97
1997	Trevor C. Weekes	gamma-rays; Whipple observatory	T.B.D.

ACKNOWLEDGMENTS

I am enormously grateful to the late Martin Schwarzschild for his (hand-written!) account of the beginnings of Divisions in the AAS and to William Kraushaar for the loan of an inch-thick, forgotten file of papers dated from February 1969 to December 1972, covering his period as Vice-Chairman and Chairman of the Division. Additional information also very much appreciated came from Rachel Pinker, A. G. W. Cameron, Riccardo Giacconi, Maarten Schmidt, Lodewijk Woltjer, Kevin Hurley, Neil Gehrels, Eugene Parker, Kenneth Greisen, Bruce Partridge, Ed Fenimore and Hale Bradt. My thanks to them and to all the section secretary-treasurers and chairs who prepared annual reports and abstract programs for the *Bulletin of the American Astronomical Society*.

THE SOLAR PHYSICS DIVISION

John H. Thomas

INTRODUCTION

The centennial year for the AAS, 1999, marks the 30th anniversary of the founding of the AAS Solar Physics Division (SPD). The purpose of the SPD is the advancement of the study of the Sun and the coordination of solar research between astronomy and other branches of science. In this chapter we examine the motivation and the events leading to the formation of this organization, which serves the professional needs of solar astronomers and solar physicists in North America. We also outline the more important activities of the SPD over the years and how they reflect changes in the field of solar physics, including changes in the relative emphasis on the astrophysical and geophysical sides of the subject.

FOUNDING OF THE DIVISION

The origins of the SPD can be traced to an initiative in the mid-1960s to organize a series of special AAS meetings devoted to solar physics. The idea for these meetings originated in early 1965 with suggestions made by Henry J. Smith, the chief solar physicist at NASA headquarters and formerly on the staff of Sacramento Peak Observatory, and by Leo Goldberg of Harvard College Observatory, then President of the AAS and a distinguished solar astronomer himself. Smith had been disappointed in the small turnout of solar astronomers at AAS meetings.[1] He had found that several solar astronomers were abandoning the AAS for other organizations because of the crowded schedules of AAS meetings, the tendency of the AAS to meet in the eastern U.S. while the majority of solar astronomers lived in the western states, and a general lack of appreciation of solar astronomy among other astronomers. In April 1965, at a meeting of NASA's Solar Physics Subcommittee, Smith proposed that NASA-funded solar physicists meet periodically to discuss their research. In the discussion that followed, Goldberg suggested as an alternative that the AAS sponsor an annual meeting on solar physics,* "perhaps as a first step in establishing a section for solar physics."[2]

Goldberg, as AAS President, was reluctant to raise this possibility directly with the AAS Council himself because several of the Council members were already concerned that increasing specialization was threatening the unity of astronomy. He felt the suggestion would be better received if it came from solar astronomers outside the Council. Similarly, Smith believed that such a suggestion would be better received from an observatory director rather than from a Washington bureaucrat like himself.[1]

---

*From the earliest stages of planning which led to the formation of the SPD, the term "solar physics" was used to describe the field, with the intent of being more broadly inclusive than the term "solar astronomy."

Smith and Goldberg settled on John Firor, then director of the High Altitude Observatory, as the best person to put forward such a proposal to the AAS Council.

Smith[2] and Goldberg[3] then both approached Firor and asked him to take the lead in proposing a series of solar meetings to the AAS Council. Goldberg was "rather partial to the idea of holding this meeting somewhere in the western or southwestern portion of the country, both because of the concentrations of solar astronomers in these regions, and because it would be highly appropriate for the AAS to hold one meeting a year somewhere in the West more or less as an established practice." Goldberg also said that "we may want to think of formally establishing a section on solar physics, with elected officials taking full responsibility for the organization of the meetings." Firor thought that such meetings would be quite appropriate and certainly worthy of a trial. He discussed the possibility with several colleagues in the solar physics community, most of whom liked the idea and urged that it be an annual event.

Not all solar astronomers were enthusiastic at first about the suggestion that the AAS establish a section for solar physics, however. For example, Robert Noyes of Harvard was concerned about any change that would tend to further separate solar astronomers from the rest of astronomy.[4] Noyes agreed that there was a need for separate meetings on solar physics but thought that these meetings should be organized outside the AAS.

Further impetus for an annual meeting devoted to solar physics was the success of the annual informal "Santa Fe meeting" of the scientific staffs of the High Altitude Observatory and Sacramento Peak Observatory, the two largest groups of solar physicists in the country. These lively, three-day meetings, which began in 1961, were held

Figure 1. John Firor, chair of the Organizing Committee of the Solar Physics Division. (1968 photo, courtesy of the High Altitude Observatory.)

in scenic Santa Fe, New Mexico, about midway between the two institutions. Although these meetings were primarily for the staffs of the two observatories, a few fortunate scientists from other institutions were invited each year. The word got around about these stimulating meetings, and a number of solar physicists at other institutions began to wish that they too could participate regularly in a meeting devoted entirely to their subject.

In July 1965, Firor presented a formal proposal for an annual AAS-sponsored meeting devoted to solar astronomy and closely related subjects, to be held in the western U.S., with a format designed to encourage discussion.[5] The proposal pointed out that the rapid growth in solar studies had not been accompanied by a similar growth in the time devoted to the Sun at AAS meetings, and that a number of the newer people in the field were physicists who had had little motivation for joining and attending meetings of the AAS. Although other organizations, such as the American Geophysical Union (AGU), could potentially fill the need for meetings devoted to solar physics, Firor urged the AAS to take this initiative so that "the traditional and valuable connection between solar physics and the rest of astronomy will be symbolized and encouraged." The proposal specified that the first such meeting would be held in Boulder, Colorado in 1966.

The AAS Council reluctantly and cautiously approved only one such meeting, on a trial basis, and AAS President Leo Goldberg appointed Firor, Donald Billings, Frank McDonald, and Oran R. White to organize this meeting.[6] This first AAS "solar meeting" was held in Boulder October 3–5, 1966, with scientific sessions in the auditorium of the Boulder laboratories of the National Bureau of Standards. The program featured special topical sessions on the solar corona and on energetic solar particles.

The Boulder meeting was judged to be a great success by those attending, and there was general enthusiasm for further meetings. The AAS Council approved a second solar meeting, which was held in Tucson, February 1–3, 1968. The Tucson meeting was hosted by Kitt Peak National Observatory and the University of Arizona and was organized by A. Keith Pierce (chair), Jacques Beckers, Firor, Goldberg, Robert Howard, and G. C. McVittie. The Tucson meeting had over 200 attendees, a full schedule of papers, and lively discussions. Shortly after the Tucson meeting, AAS Secretary McVittie proposed to the Council that the Society appoint a "solar secretary" to oversee the planning of future AAS solar meetings.[7] Shortly thereafter, Firor wrote to McVittie urging the Council to reconsider the original proposal to establish the AAS solar meeting as a continuing, annual event.[8] Firor argued against the idea of a "solar secretary" on the basis that other subdisciplines within the AAS would also want special meetings in their field and this might lead to a proliferation of such secretaries (e.g., a "quasar secretary" or a "gaseous nebula secretary"). Firor favored instead some sort of general mechanism for the organization of all such meetings within the framework of the AAS.

Indeed, at that time two other groups within the AAS were also asking for special attention to the needs of their subdisciplines. A group of planetary scientists was planning to establish scientific meetings in their specialty, under the auspices of the AAS or the AGU or perhaps even as a separate society. A group of high-energy astrophysicists, the majority of whom had been trained as physicists rather than conventional astronomers, was also trying to establish an organization and had in fact already applied to the APS for the formation of a division for high-energy astrophysics. These activities of the solar, planetary, and high-energy groups persuaded the AAS Council that, however much they might regret the increasing specialization of astronomy, it had become necessary to recognize the special needs of certain subfields within astronomy not only by providing for regular meetings in these fields but also by creating appropriate Divisions of the Society that would organize these meetings and otherwise attend to the needs of special fields.[9] The Council proposed an amendment to the AAS constitution providing for the establishment of Divisions, but with considerable reluctance.

> The step of forming these special divisions was taken only after thorough deliberations and after it became clear that any further postponement of this step would increase the danger to the AAS of losing these recently energized fields of astronomy to other related societies, such as the Physical Society or the Geophysical Union. All efforts are being made to insure that the formation of the special divisions will not increase the always present hazard of overspecialization in American astronomy.[10]

A ballot on the proposed amendment establishing Divisions was mailed to the membership in July 1968. The amendment was approved by the membership and was formally adopted, with minor changes, at the annual AAS business meeting in Victoria on August 22, 1968.

While the balloting was under way, in anticipation of approval, Martin Schwarzschild (then acting President of the AAS during A. E. Whitford's stay at Mt. Stromlo in Australia) asked Firor for suggestions for members of an Organizing Committee for the Division of Solar Physics. Firor responded by suggesting a list of names of scientists who were at the forefront of solar physics but who, for the most part, had not been deeply involved in matters having to do with the structure of the AAS or other organizations and hence might be more open to new meeting formats. The people suggested by Firor were duly appointed by the AAS Council at its meeting on August 20, 1968. The Organizing Committee for the Division for Solar Physics consisted of Grant Athay (HAO/NCAR), Jacques Beckers (Sacramento Peak Obs.), Robert E. Danielson (Princeton), William C. Erickson (Clark Lake Radio Obs.), John Firor (HAO/NCAR), Peter Meyer (Univ. of Chicago), Norman F. Ness (NASA Goddard SFC), and William H. Parkinson (Harvard). The committee elected Firor as their chair and went about the business of drafting a set of bylaws. A number of helpful comments on early drafts of the bylaws were made by Martin Schwarzschild, himself a pioneer in solar research.[11]

Meanwhile, in February 1969 a third AAS solar meeting was held in Pasadena, hosted by the Mt. Wilson and Palomar Observatories and organized by Robert Howard, Robert Leighton, and Harold Zirin. The proposed bylaws of the Division were discussed at that meeting and the Organizing Committee prepared a list of 61 "original members" of the Division. In July 1969 the proposed bylaws were approved by these founding members by mail ballot. [The original AAS documents and the original bylaws refer to the "Division on Solar Physics," but by the time of the first annual meeting in 1970 the Division was being called the "Solar Physics Division" (SPD) and generally has been ever since then.]

Firor asked Grant Athay to prepare a slate of candidates for the first officers of the Division, in consultation with other members of the organizing committee. Athay responded by preparing a slate which consisted of just one candidate for each position but which purposely excluded members of the organizing committee itself. In Athay's words, "the last criterion may raise a few eyebrows, but it was the only way to avoid some potential embarrassment."[12] The final slate of candidates prepared by the Organizing Committee was duly elected by the original SPD members in a mail ballot in summer 1970. Those elected were: John Jefferies, Chair; Gordon Newkirk, Vice-Chair; Robert Howard, Secretary; Elske Smith, Treasurer; and Mukul Kundu, Robert Noyes, Carl Fichtel and David Rust, members of the Committee.

SPD MEETINGS

The first official meeting of the newly formed Division was held in Huntsville, Alabama, November 17–19, 1970. (The newly formed Division of Planetary Sciences and Division of Dynamical Astronomy had already held their first meetings in January 1970.) It is interesting to note that, in spite of the initial thrust to establish an annual solar meeting in the west, the first official Division meeting was in the south. The program committee for the Huntsville meeting consisted of Firor, Pat McIntosh, and Zirin. The meeting overlapped with the meeting of the American Institute of Aeronautics and Astronautics (AIAA), held November 16–18, in Huntsville, and the two groups had a joint session on "Solar Physics and the Apollo Telescope Mount Project" on the morning of the 18th. The SPD meeting itself had 96 registered attendees and included sessions in parallel with AIAA sessions on November 17 and two parallel sessions of its own on the 19th, with a total of 50 contributed papers arranged into six sessions.

The first SPD business meeting was held on the evening of November 18, 1970, and was led by Firor who was chair of the Organizing Committee. Most of the discussion at that first business meeting concerned the format of future scientific meetings, leading to a decision that the next annual meeting would be conducted without parallel sessions. This was to be accomplished by giving the session chairs the power to limit subject matter, invite speakers, and select from among contributed papers. Thus began an intense debate among SPD members over the issue of single sessions (with only invited and selected papers) versus parallel sessions (accommodating essentially all submitted papers). Opinions were equally divided on this issue. A questionnaire sent to SPD members in early 1972 asking "should basically all submitted papers be accepted" received 28 yes votes and 29 no votes. The debate reached its peak at the second SPD meeting, in Maryland in 1972, when in protest Zirin organized an impromptu evening "rump session" for papers rejected from the official sessions. Although the SPD Committee officially disapproved of this rump session, it also found that improvements in the process of selecting papers for presentation were needed. Within a few years the SPD membership had grown to the point where single sessions were no longer a practical alternative and the debate subsided somewhat. The introduction of poster papers in the late 1980s seemed to provide some relief, but it soon became clear that posters deserve dedicated time too and cannot just be superimposed on a full day of oral sessions. The debate continues today, but in recent years the annual meeting has generally accommodated all submitted papers while not guaranteeing oral presentation.

Following the Huntsville meeting, of the next ten SPD meetings all but the Boulder meeting in 1975 were held jointly with a full AAS meeting. (A complete list of SPD meetings is given in Table 1.) These close ties with the AAS were largely due to a resurgence of interest in the astronomical side of solar physics in the mid-1970s, under the banner of "the Sun as a Star." The reasons for this renewed interest in solar-stellar connections included the following: the rapid development of the new field of helioseismology and its implications for solar and stellar structure; the prospects for asteroseismology; the emerging results of long-term programs of observations of solar-type stars (including the discovery of stellar activity cycles similar to the Sun's); advances in non-LTE, multidimensional models of the solar and stellar atmospheres; and the solar neutrino problem and its implications for stellar astrophysics.

TABLE 1. *Chronology of SPD Meetings, Chairs, and Hale Prize Winners.*

Year	SPD Annual Meeting	SPD Chair[1]	Hale Prize Winner
1969		John Firor[2]	
1970	Huntsville, AL	John Jefferies	
1971	none		
1972	College Park, MD[a]	Gordon Newkirk	
1973	Las Cruces, NM[a]	Jack Zirker	
1974	Honolulu, HI[a]	Peter Sturrock	
1975	Boulder, CO and San Diego, CA[a,c]	Robert Noyes	
1976	Haverford, PA[a]	Robert MacQueen[3]	
1977	Atlanta, GA[a]		
1978	Madison, WI[a]	Loren Acton	Eugene Parker*
1979	Wellesley, MA[a]		
1980	College Park, MD[a]	John W. Harvey	Paul Wild
1981	Taos, NM		
1982	Boulder, CO[a]	Alan Krieger	John W. Evans
1983	Pasadena, CA		
1984	Baltimore, MD[a]	Grant Athay	Leo Goldberg
1985	Tucson, AZ		
1986	Ames, IA[a]	George Doschek	Peter A. Sturrock
1987	Honolulu, HI		
1988	Kansas City, MO[a]	Hugh Hudson	Cornelis de Jager
1989	Laurel, MD		
1990	Albuquerque, NM[a]	George Withbroe	Richard Tousey
1991	Huntsville, AL	Spiro Antiochos	
1992	Columbus, OH[a]		H. W. Babcock
1993	Stanford, CA	Thomas Holzer	
1994	Baltimore, MD[b]		Douglas Gough
1995	Memphis, TN	John H. Thomas	
1996	Madison, WI[a]		Raymond Davis, Jr.
1997	Bozeman, MT	Stephen Kahler	
1998	Boston, MA[b]		Richard B. Dunn
1999	Chicago, IL[a]		

[1] Chairs take office at the annual meeting in June of the year indicated.
[2] Chair of the SPD Organizing Committee
[3] The term of office of the Chair was changed to two years in 1976.
[a] Joint meeting with the AAS.
[b] Joint meeting with the AGU.
[c] Two meetings held that year.
* Hale Prize lecture given at the Wellesley meeting in 1979.

For its first two years, the SPD survived on registration funds collected at the annual meeting. In 1972, the Division instituted annual dues of $4, which remained the same until 1982. Membership in the SPD grew to about 180 in 1975 and to about 250 in 1980. In 1980 the bylaws were amended to provide for affiliate membership in the SPD. Affiliate membership is open to members of other related scientific societies (such as the AGU and the APS) who are involved in solar research but are not members of the AAS. Affiliate members have all the privileges of membership except that they may not vote or hold office in the Division.

By 1981 there was again strong sentiment in favor of smaller, separate meetings, and the Division met alone in Taos that year. Through the 1980s the SPD followed a plan of holding every other annual meeting separately from the AAS. One of the motivations for forming the SPD was the fact that solar physics is in many ways an interdisciplinary subject with strong ties to fields outside of astronomy, especially geophysics. Many SPD members have closer ties with the AGU than with the AAS. At the urging of some of these members, the SPD held its 1994 annual meeting in conjunction with the AGU spring meeting in Baltimore, with the planning of the SPD sessions coordinated with the Space Physics and Aeronomy Section of the AGU. This meeting was well attended and was generally considered a success by the membership. This experiment will be repeated in 1998, when the SPD again meets jointly with the AGU at its spring meeting in Boston.

Of course, a majority of SPD members do consider themselves to be primarily astronomers and have their strongest professional ties with the AAS. A point of continual discussion among SPD members over the years has been the relative advantages of holding our annual meeting separately or together with an AAS meeting. Although meeting separately gives us more freedom and control over the meeting schedule and format, most members recognize the importance of maintaining close ties with the rest of astronomy.

There have been a number of experiments and innovations in the format of SPD meetings over the years. The Boulder meeting in January 1975 included a joint symposium with the American Meteorological Society on problems of mutual interest, including Sun-weather connections, atmospheric circulation, and turbulence. Poster papers were presented for the first time at the Atlanta meeting in June 1977. The Taos meeting in January 1981 had morning and evening sessions, with afternoons free for scientific discussions (or skiing!). The Memphis meeting in 1995 featured a series of four special invited lectures honoring Eugene Parker on the occasion of his retirement (the lecturers were Tom Holzer, Bob Rosner, Nigel Weiss, and Eugene Parker himself). For a number of years now, the annual Business Meeting has included presentations by the directors of solar-related programs at NSF and NASA on the status of current projects and funding opportunities, and by the directors of the national solar centers, NSO and HAO.

In addition to its annual meeting, the SPD has organized many special symposia and topical sessions at regular AAS meetings over the years, such as the symposium on "Observations of the Solar Corona from Skylab" at the AAS Tucson meeting in 1973. Also, the SPD has occasionally co-sponsored meetings or special sessions with other scientific societies and organizations, such as the meeting on "Solar and Interplanetary Physics" with the AGU and the APS in 1977 and the workshop on "Flare Research and the Solar Maximum Mission" with the University of Michigan in 1978. One of the most important of these co-sponsored meetings was the workshop on "Cool Stars, Stellar Systems, and the Sun" held at the Harvard-Smithsonian Center for Astrophysics (CfA) in January, 1980, and organized by Andrea Dupree. The SPD co-sponsored this meeting with CfA and contributed substantial funds to support it. This meeting launched the well-known series of Cool Star workshops which have been held nearly every year since 1980 (although without further SPD sponsorship).

THE HALE PRIZE

One of the most important early activities of the SPD was the establishment of the George Ellery Hale Prize for outstanding contributions to solar astronomy. Informal discussions about the need for an AAS lectureship and prize in solar astronomy began almost immediately after the establishment of the Division, if not before. Many were involved in these discussions, but it was Gordon Newkirk who took hold of the idea in 1971 and pushed it forward. Newkirk took over the directorship of the High Altitude Observatory in 1968, when Firor became director of NCAR. Also, Newkirk succeeded John Jefferies as chair of the SPD in 1972. In late 1972 and early 1973 Newkirk and Robert Howard, then at the Hale Observatories and also SPD secretary, drafted the first version of a proposal to establish the Hale Prize. This proposal was discussed at the Division's business meeting in Las Cruces in 1973. Early versions of the proposal called for a Hale Lecture at the annual SPD meeting, but this was later changed to a lecture at a full AAS meeting, the argument being that outstanding work in solar astronomy should be presented to the entire AAS membership. Some felt that the prize should be an AAS prize, not an SPD prize, because of the greater prestige and greater opportunities for fund raising it would provide. A feature of the very first draft proposal which did see its way through to the end was the provision that the selection committee should place heavy emphasis on a candidate's sustained contributions over an extended period of time rather than on a single discovery. Also, from the beginning the intent was that the Hale Prize would not be restricted to SPD or AAS members, nor to North Americans. Others who contributed significantly to the early planning for the Hale Prize include Jack Zirker, Walter Roberts, Frank Orrall, and Grant Athay.

The proposal was approved by the AAS Council in mid 1973, but the Council specified that the Hale Prize would be a Division, not a Society prize, and that fund raising to support the Prize was the responsibility of the SPD alone. Fund raising began in earnest in 1975, with a goal of $20,000, and the Division itself contributed $1000 out of its operating funds to get the ball rolling. The fund raising effort was led by Newkirk (chair), Roberts, and Zirker. A total of $5650 was raised by the annual meeting in June 1976, and $11,000 by the annual meeting in June 1977, when it was decided that $15,000 should be sufficient to fund the prize. Corporate donations were received from IBM, Lockheed, Corning Glass Works, Ball Brothers, Arthur D. Little, American Science & Engineering, Owens Illinois, and also from the Carnegie Institution of Washington, the Smithsonian Institution, the National Academy of Sciences, and the Sibyl and William T. Golden Foundation. A number of individual donors also contributed, including several members of George Ellery Hale's family.

The first Hale Prize was awarded to Eugene Parker at the Madison meeting in June 1978, for his "imaginative and stimulating contributions in which plasma and magnetohydrodynamical physics have been applied to astronomy." Parker delivered the first Hale Prize lecture at the joint AAS/SPD meeting in Wellesley in 1979. At the SPD business meeting in Madison, following the announcement of the Prize, a formal resolution was passed expressing special appreciation to Gordon Newkirk for his tremendous efforts in establishing the Hale Prize.

There have been eleven Hale Prize winners as of this writing; their names are given in Table 1. Of the eleven winners, three are foreign: Paul Wild (Australia), Cornelis de Jager (The Netherlands), and Douglas Gough (United Kingdom). The Hale Prize has been awarded for both observational and theoretical work, and for research spanning a wide range of subjects, including optical, radio, and neutrino astronomy; solar astronomy from the ground, from rockets, and from orbiting space vehicles; spectroscopy and the solar atmosphere; solar magnetohydrodynamics and plasma physics; and helioseismology.

The Hale Prize is nominally awarded every other year, in even-numbered years. However, the Division has decided to also award a Hale Prize at the AAS Centennial meeting in Chicago in June 1999, which will also celebrate the centennial of Yerkes Observatory. Because of George Ellery Hale's key role in the founding of both Yerkes

Figure 2. Gordon Newkirk, chair of the committee to establish the George Ellery Hale Prize and the principal fund-raiser for the Prize. (1978 photo, courtesy of the High Altitude Observatory.)

and the AAS (*see* D. Osterbrock, this volume, page 3), it is especially appropriate that a Hale Prize be awarded in Chicago in 1999.

OTHER SPD AWARDS

In 1980, the SPD began a program of financial awards to promising undergraduate and graduate students to enable them to attend the Division's annual meeting. These "studentship" awards are meant to encourage students who show interest in pursuing a career in solar physics. Graduate student winners are required to present a paper at the meeting. Typically, four to eight students have received studentship awards each year. Through the generosity of Kluwer Academic Publishers, the award has been supplemented by a one-year subscription to *Solar Physics* or, more recently, by a solar physics monograph of the winner's choice. The studentship program was organized by James Ionson in 1980 and then taken over in 1981 by A. Gordon Emslie, who has run it ever since then. The awards are supported by SPD dues and by donations. In 1982, the SPD increased its annual dues from $4 to $8 primarily to support the studentship program. A good many of the winners of the studentship awards have indeed gone on to productive careers in solar physics; examples include Mitchell Berger, Douglas Braun, Timothy Brown, Patricia Bornmann, Luc Damé, Deborah Haber, and Jim Klimchuk.

In 1997, the SPD began giving "Popular Writing Awards" for articles on solar physics in the popular press or in semi-popular journals. There are two such awards — one for journalists or science writers, and the other for professional solar physicists. The awards are intended to encourage articles informing the general public about important advances in solar physics and solar-terrestrial relations. These new awards reflect the Division's growing awareness of the importance of public outreach in justifying continued federal support for solar physics. The 1997 awards went to Kenneth R. Lang (Tufts University) and J. Madeleine Nash (*Time* magazine).

The SPD has been attempting to establish a prize for a young solar physicist, so far without success. Because the Hale Prize is meant to honor scientific contributions made over an extended period of time, young solar physicists are generally excluded from consideration, and yet many SPD members see a need to recognize our best young researchers. Efforts to establish a prize for a solar physicist in the early stages of his or her career began in 1990 with the appointment of a committee which developed a proposal. So far this proposal has been rejected by the AAS Council, for a number of reasons but primarily because the Council wishes to avoid a proliferation of prizes and already has difficulty in fitting all of the current prize lectures into the two AAS meetings each year. Discussions with the AAS about such a prize are still under way.

OTHER ACTIVITIES

In 1974, SPD Chair Peter Sturrock was considering the formation of an SPD committee to study the state of solar physics. This idea was abandoned when it became known that the National Academy of Sciences was organizing such a study, to be carried out under the auspices of the NAS Space Sciences Board by a committee chaired by Eugene Parker. This study had an important influence on solar physics. The SPD had considerable input, including recommendations for the makeup of the Parker committee and discussions at the annual meeting.

The SPD has from time to time taken official positions on particular issues involving the discipline. In 1975, the SPD adopted a resolution urging continuing support of three solar observatories that were then threatened with closure: Sacramento Peak Observatory, then run by the Air Force; the Aerospace Corporation's San Fernando Observatory; and the Lockheed Solar Observatory. Sacramento Peak, with its relatively large staff and important facilities (including its vacuum tower telescope and coronagraph), was crucially important to the U.S. solar community (and indeed to the world-wide solar community). In response to strong community support and the recommendations of an *ad hoc* committee (chaired by Martin Schwarzschild), the National Science Foundation took over support of Sacramento Peak from the Air Force in July 1976 and contracted with the Association of Universities for Research in Astronomy (AURA) to operate the observatory. In October 1983, Sacramento Peak was merged with the solar facilities on Kitt Peak to form the National Solar Observatory (NSO) under the auspices of AURA, and shortly thereafter the National Optical Astronomy Observatories was established, comprising Kitt Peak National Observatory, Cerro Tololo Inter-American Observatory, and the NSO. The Aerospace Corporation gave its San Fernando Observatory to California State University at Northridge in January 1976; this observatory is still in operation.

In 1975, only five years after its founding, the SPD sought to reestablish close ties to the rest of astronomy and astrophysics. Robert Noyes, then SPD chair, had been among those who were concerned that the establishment of the Division meant an unfortunate separation from the rest of astrophysics. Noyes appointed an *ad hoc* committee on the "Interaction between Solar Physics and Astrophysics" chaired by Andrea Dupree. Other members of the committee were Jacques Beckers, Lawrence Fredrick, Jack Harvey, Jeffrey Linsky, L. E. Peterson, and Arthur Walker. The committee underscored the strong interdisciplinary relations between solar physics and the fields of stellar astrophysics, atomic and molecular physics, plasma physics, magnetohydrodynamics, and high energy physics. It recommended that the SPD continue to hold its annual meeting jointly with the AAS and urged the Division to be more active in organizing topical sessions and providing invited speakers for AAS meetings. It also urged SPD members to be more active on scientific advisory committees and in public outreach and to encourage the appointment of solar physicists to faculty positions.

In response to one of the recommendations of the Dupree committee, in 1976 the SPD began appointing liaison officers to help maintain ties with other disciplines and other professional societies. The individual areas of responsibility of these liaison officers have varied somewhat over the years, but have generally included the following: stellar astronomy; solar-terrestrial relations (with ties to the AGU); interplanetary astronomy; high-energy physics (with ties to the APS Astrophysics Division); plasma physics (with ties to the APS Division of Plasma Physics); and media relations. Responsibilities of the liaison officers include keeping SPD members informed of activities in the related fields and societies, and organizing joint sessions and joint meetings between the SPD and the related societies.

The relatively poor representation of solar physicists on university faculties is a long-standing problem of the discipline. In 1983, Karen Harvey (SPD Treasurer) carried out a demographic study of the institutional affiliations of SPD members that documented this problem. Her study showed that only 35% of SPD members held positions in universities, compared to 55% for AAS members overall. (Among those SPD members in universities, many were not in regular teaching positions or otherwise able to supervise graduate students.) On the other hand 27% of SPD members were employed by agencies of the federal government, compared to 15% of AAS members overall. This under-representation of solar physicists on university faculties is even worse today and poses a serious threat to the future of the discipline.

Figure 3. Karen Harvey, treasurer of the Solar Physics Division for eighteen years (1977–1995) and a significant contributor to the SPD in many other ways. (Photo courtesy of J. Harvey.)

In 1982, the SPD passed a resolution urging the National Oceanic and Atmospheric Administration to maintain its small grant program for continuing synoptic solar observations under the aegis of its "World Data Center A" for Solar-Terrestrial Physics. In 1983, the SPD passed a resolution urging NASA to restore funding for the Solar Optical Telescope. This ill-fated mission, reborn twice under different guises, was ultimately canceled by NASA.

In 1976, the SPD began publishing a regular newsletter, with a logo designed by Jack Eddy. In 1988, SPD secretary David Hathaway began publishing *SolarNews*, a monthly electronic newsletter that serves not only SPD members but also solar physicists around the world. By 1996, *SolarNews* had established itself so firmly among the SPD membership that the Division could stop publishing its printed newsletter and instead devote effort to producing special issues for urgent news. The distribution of *SolarNews* is an extension of the "SolarMail" system, maintained as a service to the international solar community by the solar group at Stanford. This system, started in 1986 by Philip Scherrer and Richard Bogart in response to the needs of the GONG helioseismology project, now maintains a file of e-mail addresses of nearly every solar physicist in the world, all aliased in a uniform format (e.g., JThomas@solar.stanford.edu). Messages sent to a SolarMail alias are automatically forwarded from Stanford to the addressee. SolarMail is perhaps the only service of its kind that is based on discipline affiliation rather than institutional affiliation.

In 1995, the SPD established its WWW home page, kindly maintained by Joe Gurman at NASA Goddard Space Flight Center and accessible from the AAS home page. Browsers will find complete information on SPD membership, officers, bylaws, prizes, etc., and they can also access back issues of *SolarNews*.

THE PRESENT AND FUTURE

The SPD has been an organizing force for solar physics over the past 30 years and has served to keep solar physics under the umbrella of the AAS while reaching out to other disciplines and other organizations involved in solar research. The Division's membership has grown to over 400 regular members and some 75 affiliate members. It seems fair to say that the Division has fulfilled its main purposes, "the advancement of the study of the Sun and promotion of coordination of such research with other branches of science." It has been particularly effective in organizing a series of well attended, stimulating scientific meetings and in keeping its members informed of developments and opportunities in the field. To a lesser extent, it has served effectively in an advocacy role on issues for which there has been broad community agreement and support.

The SPD will no doubt continue to play an important supportive role for the field of solar physics in the future. In spite of tight federal funding, solar physics remains a very active, healthy, and innovative science. The quality of the research in solar physics has never been higher, and a number of outstanding young scientists have joined the field in recent years. On the observational side, there have recently been some highly successful space missions (e.g., SOHO and Yokoh), collaborative ground-based networks of telescopes (e.g., GONG) devoted to the exciting new field of helioseismology, and impressive advances in high-resolution optical observations from the ground, including the measurement of vector magnetic fields on the Sun through Stokes polarimetry. On the theoretical side, there have been remarkable advances in our ability to model complex plasma and magnetohydrodynamic processes on the Sun and in the solar wind, leading to a much better understanding of the solar activity cycle and its influence on the Earth.

Recently there has been a renewed emphasis on the geophysical side of solar physics, with the National Space Weather Program and NASA's Sun–Earth Connections program. At the same time, interest in the solar-stellar connection has grown because of the puzzling results of solar neutrino detectors and the discovery of more and more solar-like activity cycles in other late-type stars. There is no doubt that even in the mature discipline of solar physics there are many unimagined technical advances and surprising scientific discoveries ahead of us in the new century.

ACKNOWLEDGMENTS

I am very grateful to Karl Hufbauer for helpful comments and for sharing with me some of his notes on the founding of the SPD and his copies of the related Leo Goldberg correspondence. Caroline Moseley at the Niels Bohr Library helped me find my way through the SPD archives. Veda Emmett at HAO provided me with the photographs of Firor and Newkirk.

THE BEGINNINGS OF THE DIVISION FOR PLANETARY SCIENCES OF THE AMERICAN ASTRONOMICAL SOCIETY

Dale P. Cruikshank and Joseph W. Chamberlain

INTRODUCTION

We trace the origins of the Division for Planetary Sciences as the premier scientific society in North America for the promotion of planetary science. There was a time when the work of every major observatory in the United States included the astrometric or physical study of the myriad bodies of the Solar System. To appreciate fully the reasons for the creation of the Division, we must recall the highlights of the history of the subject matter area itself. Whether it was the positions of comets and asteroids, visual observations of the seasonally shifting tones of Mars' surface, the motions of planetary satellites, or the spectroscopy of Saturn's rings, planetary observations figured significantly in the regular programs of Lick, Yerkes, Harvard, Yale, the U.S. Naval Observatory, and others.

In the early 1900s, with the emergence of modern astrophysics, and perhaps partly as a consequence of the huckster-like promotion of Mars as the habitat of a technically advanced civilization, based on questionable visual observations, planetary astronomy was somewhat de-emphasized among professionals. While planetary astronomy continued at various institutions, the research of most American astronomers with an interest in the planets assumed a low profile and was conducted in parallel with work on stars, galaxies, or other topics. The story is much more complex than can be summarized in a few sentences, but the net effect was that a rebirth of planetary astronomy occurred in post-war American science, largely through the special efforts of a very few astronomers, aided by the patronage of the U.S. Government through the military and the agency that became the National Aeronautics and Space Administration.[1,2]

In the late 1940s, planetary astronomy began to evolve into a more broadly based planetary science, as the result of several specific events. German V2 rockets captured at the end of World War II were used at White Sands Proving Ground to take pictures from more than 100 km altitude, showing large-scale views of the geology and geography of the southwestern U.S. This helped give us some of our first perceptions of the Earth as a planet. This new material was incorporated into the program of a conference organized by the Dutch-born American astronomer Gerard P. Kuiper at the Yerkes Observatory, September 8–10, 1947, in conjunction with the fiftieth anniversary of the Observatory. The conference volume, *The Atmospheres of the Earth and Planets*, included contributions by astronomers, meteorologists, and "high-altitude specialists."[3] A second, revised edition was published in 1952, and included an updated version of one of Kuiper's most significant papers on the atmospheres of the Earth and other planets from an observational and cosmochemical point of view. The development of Kuiper's interest in the bodies of the Solar System has been described by Cruikshank and by Kuiper himself.[4,5,6]

At the same time, the origin and chemistry of the planets had caught the interest of Nobel Laureate Harold C. Urey, who published his landmark book, *The Planets, Their Origin and Development*, in 1952, which brought the study of the Solar System clearly within the view of chemists and geochemists, and offered a perspective on the Moon and planets of interest to traditional geologists.[7] In 1953, Kuiper edited the first of his four-volume compendium on the Solar System, *The Sun*, and the next year *The Earth as a Planet*, the cover of which shows a picture of a piece of the desert southwest from a V2 rocket.[8,9] This book clearly established the study of the planets as an interdisciplinary enterprise. Not only were the interior, mantle, and crust of the planet explored, but the dynamics of Earth and its interaction with the Moon were covered, as were its oceans, all levels of the atmosphere, and the aurora. Significantly, the biochemistry of the atmosphere was a part of this truly global view of Earth. Those aspects of Earth (albedo, color, polarization) that can be directly compared with telescopic observations of other planets, were reviewed by astronomer André Danjon. Inklings of what has more recently become a systems view of Earth's oceans, crust, and atmosphere, are seen in this extraordinary book.[10]

Although by the early 1950s planetary science had taken on the status of a multidisciplinary endeavor in principle, interested scientists continued for many years to approach their research from the vantage points of their foundations in the traditionally defined fields of astronomy, geology, meteorology, chemistry, and to a lesser degree, biology. Not until the 1970s did there emerge explicit university curricula in planetary science.

It is facile to abbreviate the story of the development of planetary astronomy in these few paragraphs, using conferences and books as guideposts; the details are compelling and interesting, particularly when they are derived from primary sources. Those details, with commentary, are given by Doel in a book that is an essential resource for understanding the development of studies of the Solar System in America.[1]

A key turning point in American planetary science was the formation, in 1969, of the Division for Planetary Sciences (DPS) of the American Astronomical Society. It is the story of the origins of the DPS that we tell here.

The view of the emergence of planetary science from its birthplace in astronomy, and in particular the establishment of the DPS, has been described by one of the present authors,[11] who helped define the multidisciplinary character of the field by organizing the first national society devoted to it. The present paper draws upon Chamberlain's reflections and perceptions, and it is augmented by key documents and accounts of pivotal events, mainly covering the period 1967–1971.

SPECIALISTS AND GENERALISTS

Young astronomers entering the field are commonly overwhelmed when attending their first full meeting of the AAS. Throngs of astronomers surge into multiple meeting rooms as the overlapping sessions begin early each morning. At coffee breaks the corridors are awash with astronomers lined up to fill their styrofoam cups with "the fuel of science." The din slowly rises as conversations accelerate, and then the sessions resume as the participants file back into the meeting rooms for more 5-minute presentations by them and their colleagues. This goes on for several days, and even the evenings are occupied with special presentations, the banquet, the business meeting, committee meetings, and more.

Years ago, AAS meetings were attended by fewer than 100 astronomers, sessions were serial rather than parallel, and presentations were far less hurried. Furthermore, each American astronomer was acquainted with the person and the work of every other American astronomer. The same situation prevailed elsewhere in the world; the late Boris A. Vorontsov-Velyaminov of Moscow, told one of us (DPC) in 1969 that he once knew every astronomer in Russia, but by 1965 he didn't even know all of the astronomers working in his own institute (Sternberg State Astronomical Institute).

This depersonalization, brought about by the population explosion within science, has afflicted most of the major scientific societies. As the attendance at meetings swell, the organization is overpowered and can no longer accommodate in three or four days of leisurely sessions all of the contributed papers, along with various special sessions and activities that must accompany a major meeting. The members must then choose from a variety of unpleasant alternatives, including a longer meeting, shorter papers, "poster" sessions, relegation of some papers to the status of "read by title only," or holding two or more simultaneous sessions for contributed papers. (*see* DeVorkin and Routly page 122.)

Simultaneous sessions were the dreaded Final Solution, 'devoutly to be fear'd,' especially by generalists. A generalist is an individual who understands quite a bit about every aspect of the entire subject of astronomy. In 1950, such a person attended most of the meetings of the AAS and read *The Astrophysical Journal* from cover to cover — all 130 papers per year, 1200 pages per year. In 1996, the *ApJ* published about 1800 articles in 18,450 pages, not counting the Letters and the Supplements; did any one person read all that? Even the Editor? Today the vestigial generalist attends both AAS meetings and one or two special meetings per year, and knows that if two sessions are run simultaneously, he will certainly miss something important.

Specialists, on the other hand, confine their interest to one major area of astronomy. They organize and attend their own conferences, sometimes publish in a specialty journal, and they agitate for a professional society that caters to their specific interests. As specialty groups spin off from a larger scientific society, two opposite effects occur. First, the specialty is strengthened, but its practitioners grow further from the broader, overarching subject. The compensating effect is that other specialists from other fields soon join with the splinter group and the new amalgam develops a character all its own. In the present case, when the planetary astronomers were no longer regarded merely as astronomers, scientists from other planetary disciplines (e.g., geophysics, atmospheric physics) joined with them in their new society.

As the population continues to grow, the inevitable and undesirable happens: the specialist society becomes too large to accommodate all activities, and its annual meetings suffer the same compressional fate as the original parent society did. Multiple sessions, large crowds, and unwieldy business meetings ensue. Furthermore, the "generalist" emerges anew, but redefined as a planetary generalist rather than an astronomy generalist.

FILLING THE NEED

Interest in the moon and planets got a big boost with Sputnik in 1957, as did every other scientific and technological endeavor in the United States. Tatarewicz has traced the post-Sputnik development of planetary science as the U. S. military sought specific information on the suitability of the moon and other bodies in space in the context of national security. At the Pentagon's behest, NASA looked for people "who knew what they were doing" when it came to understanding the Solar System.[2] The priority given by NASA to such specific things as determining the thickness of the lunar regolith, the surface pressure on Mars, and the water content of Venus' atmosphere, fostered the agency's sponsorship of the construction of three (later four) major telescopes and various other facilities. At the same time, NASA funding managers supported the activities of Kuiper and others to establish multidisciplinary university curricula in the new and broadly defined field of planetary science.

The growth in interest in the Solar System, plus the increasing facilities with which to conduct observations at the telescope and in the laboratory, and especially the exploration of the planets with spacecraft, created pressure within the community of planetary scientists to conduct their own meetings and eventually to establish their own society. The journal *Planetary and Space Science* began publication in 1959, and in May, 1962, Academic Press published the first issue of *Icarus*, an international journal devoted entirely to Solar System research.

To accommodate the increased need to maintain open lines of communication, various small conferences were created by planetary scientists. In the 1950s, Lowell Observatory hosted workshops on planetary atmospheres, and beginning in early 1967, a series of five annual symposia was organized by staff members of the Planetary Sciences Division of Kitt Peak National Observatory (KPNO). The Planetary Science Division at KPNO consisted of about a dozen professionals, including J. W. Chamberlain, M. J. S. Belton, J. C. Brandt, D. M. Hunten, Michael McElroy, Darrell Strobel, Lloyd Wallace, and frequent visitor Richard Goody. It was at that time one of the larger specialty groups in planetary science in the country. Together with the staff and students in Kuiper's Lunar and Planetary Laboratory, just across the street at the University of Arizona, there was a large concentration of planetary science talent in Tucson.

The Arizona Conferences on Planetary Atmospheres, as they were called, focused on different specific themes at the annual gatherings. In 1967 it was "The Atmospheres of Venus and Mars," in 1968 it was "The Atmosphere of Venus," in 1969 "The Atmospheres of the Jovian Planets," in 1970 "Motions in Planetary Atmospheres," and then "Aeronomy of CO_2 Atmospheres" in 1971.[12,13,14,15,16] Thus, planetary scientists had a forum for publication, and various means for organizing relatively small meetings, but a professional society was needed to bring planetary scientists of all persuasions together.

BIRTH OF THE DPS

The Space Science Board of the National Academy of Sciences convened a Panel on Planetary Astronomy, which held its organizational meeting in Tucson in late February 1967. This meeting, chaired by John Hall, was held in conjunction with the first of the Arizona Conferences. At its Summer Study at Woods Hole later that year, the Panel wrote its report, "Planetary Astronomy: An Appraisal of Ground-Based Astronomy."[17] The report stated that "The establishment of a national society for planetary sciences or of an affiliate of an existing society would be highly desirable to serve as a forum for discussion and a cohesive force to facilitate recruitment of personnel, to assist in obtaining financial support or facilities for projects of unusual merit, and to encourage publication of results."

Tobias C. Owen noted that it was Juan Oro who initially argued at the summer study for a separate society.[18] He also recalled that "Juan's suggestion became one of the study's recommendations. I went to Gerard [Kuiper] with this idea, but he declined to get involved, suggesting I talk to Carl [Sagan] instead. Carl in turn consulted with Frank [Drake]." Building on a draft composed by Drake, Sagan and Owen composed the second draft of a letter to Albert Whitford, then President of the AAS. On February 1, 1968, Sagan and Owen sent this draft to a number of colleagues with a cover letter.[19] Noting that there was favorable reaction in the community to a specialized society, but that the actual structure of such a society was the subject of debate, Owen and Sagan noted that:

> Possible conflicts with existing groups and the undesirability of additional journals and meetings have been cited as arguments against the formation of a new, completely independent organization. It is our opinion that the best hope for the realization of our common goals lies in the proposal outlined in the accompanying letter [to Whitford].

> It is suggested that we begin by forming as [a] branch of the American Astronomical Society that would be concerned primarily with Solar System problems. We have chosen the AAS for this purpose because most of the scientists interested in these problems are already members and because it appears that fractionation of the Society into sub-specialties is already occurring to accommodate the needs of solar physicists. By maintaining an affiliation in this way, we can avoid the difficulties inherent in the formation of a new organization, although such a step may become desirable at a later date. A necessary prerequisite for the proposed arrangement would be permission from the AAS to hold relatively autonomous meetings that would include an interdisciplinary flavor, a concentration on problems of special interest, and opportunities for extensive discussion which are currently lacking in meetings sponsored by the existing organizations.

The letter concluded with a solicitation for approval of the letter to Whitford, to be indicated by the recipient's signature on that letter, to be taken also as agreement to participate in the organizing committee for the first meeting, "...which might be held in the fall or winter of 1968–1969." At the same time Sagan and Owen canvassed their colleagues, they drafted a letter to Whitford outlining what they had in mind and laying out the substance of the issues that were at stake.

In brief, Sagan and Owen suggested that the AAS "sponsor annual or semi-annual scientific meetings devoted entirely to solar system studies, excluding solar physics."

They envisioned meetings that would be similar to AAS meetings, but focussed on one specialty allowing for more time for the presentation and discussion of papers. "Our concern for such meetings is motivated by the rapidly increasing interest and activity in the entire range of solar system studies, and by the lack of regular scientific meetings in which there is adequate time to present new results and related discussion. In fact, as a result of the diverse backgrounds of the scientists working in these areas, no suitable forum is currently available for the regular exchange of ideas and results on problems of mutual interest."[20]

Lunar and planetary atmospheres, surfaces, and interiors, and relevant investigations of asteroids, meteorites and comets were the topics Sagan and Owen identified, but they also wanted to encourage broadly based interdisciplinary participation: "We would encourage participation by specialists in celestial mechanics who are interested in problems associated with the evolution of the solar system, such as spin-orbit coupling. In addition, we would like to invite scientists who are not members of the AAS to give papers, particularly in such areas as chemistry, geology, and biology, where significant contributions to the field can be expected."

Sagan and Owen recognized that there were alternatives, such as transferring attention to other professional organizations, "as has been attempted diffusely and without vigor by the American Geophysical Union," which they thought was a "poor solution." They also argued that the formation of a new society was:

> ... unnecessary and undesirable in view of the existence of the AAS, which we feel provides a basic organizational structure and atmosphere — in particular an appropriate balance between formality and informality — which engenders productive interaction among scientists. The leading figures in solar system science seem closest, in the majority of cases, to the AAS. It also appears to us that there is no need for an additional journal, removing what might be a minor argument for a new society. We conclude that retaining solar system studies in the AAS is the most desirable means, at least for the present, to nurture growth in this field.

Among the recipients of the February 1 draft, apparently only Anders and Chamberlain made substantive suggestions for changes. Anders thought that clarification of the issue of the formation of a "branch" of the AAS devoted to solar system problems was needed, since such a suggestion did not appear explicitly in the letter to Whitford. Anders also favored holding the planetary meetings in conjunction with AAS meetings. He suggested that such meetings might be organized as symposia, thereby "enhancing the attractiveness of the AAS meetings for people with interdisciplinary interests." He did not want the planetary meetings to appear to be a "wholly separate activity run as a service by the AAS."[21]

Anders' suggestions were followed, so the letter finally sent to Whitford on March 18, 1968 argued that by creating symposia, "it would be possible to hold joint sessions in conjunction with regular AAS meetings when this appeared to be desirable." This would encourage scientists with interdisciplinary interests to attend AAS meetings, "while astronomers with an interest in planetary research would have an opportunity to confer with specialists from other disciplines. If the AAS should ultimately find that it is necessary to develop subgroups devoted to various branches of astronomy, participants in the proposed symposia would form a nucleus for the organization of a group devoted to planetary research."[22]

When Owen discussed their proposal with Whitford prior to crafting the final version of the letter, he learned that, as he later told those who had shown interest, "we have chosen a favorable time for our appeal." The Council was then also hearing from other solar and high energy specialists who were calling for similar recognition, and was planning to take the matter up at their next meeting in April 1968. John Firor was already taking the initiative among solar astronomers, while Eugene Parker was doing the same for the high energy astronomers.

Owen and Sagan reported that Whitford wanted to "retain solar-system studies within the framework of the AAS and would support their effort 'If no complications arise ...'."[23] Within the month, Owen learned from Whitford that the Council was "favorably disposed" to their petition, "In fact the Society plans to cooperate with sections of the membership interested in holding meetings devoted to the discussion of one restricted topic. This has already been done by the solar physicists and there will be others."[24]

The Secretary of the AAS, G. C. McVittie, had already been in touch with Harlan Smith about holding a planetary meeting on the day before the Austin meeting of the full AAS in December 1968. He offered the help of the Secretary's office in mailing announcements and in giving advice on procedure, but noted that the organizing committee of the planetary group would have to do the organizational work for the meeting itself, and suggested that the solar physics people, who had done it twice before, might offer useful suggestions.

The AAS meeting was scheduled in Austin in part to celebrate the opening of the NASA-funded Texas planetary telescope, and Whitford noted that a special meeting on planetary astronomy held in conjunction with the regular meeting would be particularly relevant. Pointing out that "The Council views the format as an experiment," Whitford reported that the Council wished that "the purpose of these restricted one-topic meetings will in general be best realized by a two-day meeting at a separate time and place." The Council was very interested to have the planetary astronomers' reaction to this suggestion, because it opened the door for future meetings held at times and places completely independent of the AAS general meetings, while the option remained for contiguous meetings as well.

Smith wrote to Owen to begin preparations for the Austin meeting, proposing to call the planetary session the "Special Meeting of the AAS on [Planetary Astronomy] [or whatever]." He told Owen that "Our fliers should be mimeographed or multilithed on a special conspicuous color of paper, and sent to McVittie, 2500 copies, unfolded."[25] On May 8, 1968, Owen and Sagan distributed the Whitford letter (of April 12) to their original list, with the cover memo soliciting input on possible topics for the Austin meeting. They proposed four possibilities:

1. Interpretations of cratering statistics for the moon and Mars.
2. Spin-orbit coupling and tidal effects in the solar system.
3. Organic molecules in the early history of the solar system.
4. Problems in planetary atmospheric circulation.[26]

These topics reflected the interests of the day. The Apollo 11 lunar landing just over a year away, and a session on crater studies would appeal to geologists working on planetary problems. Sagan's own interest in organic matter in the Solar System was clearly represented, although few astronomers were interested in the topic at the time.

With new data, old classical problems of planetary spins and resonances involving orbital periods were being reopened by a number of young scientists, rekindling the field of gravitational astronomy. Finally, planetary atmospheres appealed to much of the core group of Solar System researchers, certainly those who had attended the Tucson conference series sponsored by KPNO. Not everyone had the same priorities, of course; Smith replied to Owen that his own interest in the proposed topics was exactly in the reverse order to that which had been given in the memo.[27]

On July 17, Whitford in Santa Cruz phoned Chamberlain, who was spending part of the summer in La Jolla, to say that the AAS was about to send out a mailing on the organization of divisions. It was to contain guidelines for setting up the official machinery, and of course everything had to be consistent with the Constitution and bylaws of the Society. Chamberlain was asked to nominate about eight people for the Organizing Committee for a Division for Planetary Sciences. The first meeting would probably be in Austin at the time of the AAS meeting in December, and would afford an opportunity to set down the Divisional bylaws. Rather than have an earlier meeting to get started, Chamberlain preferred to communicate with his small organizing committee by phone and letter. Secretary McVittie wrote to Chamberlain and the other committee members officially announcing the Council's action:

> At the Annual Business Meeting of the Society on 22 August 1968, the membership approved the institution of Divisions of the American Astronomical Society devoted to Special Subjects. One such Division is that on Planetary Astronomy. The Council at its meeting of August 20, 1968, had agreed that you should be the members of the Organizing Committee for the Division on Planetary Astronomy.[28]

McVittie added that their first task will be to draw up bylaws for the Division, perhaps following the method used by the AAS. He asked for the proposed divisional bylaws in time for presentation to the Council at its meeting of December 10, 1968.

INFLUENCING FACTORS

Chamberlain was thus put in charge of organizing the planetary scientists, although Sagan and Owen had taken the initiative and gotten the attention of the Society. Chamberlain later wrote that on the basis of the Sagan and Owen letter alone the AAS would not likely have responded by setting up divisional structures.[11] Had it not been for the pressure brought by the high-energy astronomers, the planetary astronomers might have gone down one of the alternate routes that were emerging.

In particular, Chamberlain notes that because of the regard in which planetary astronomers were held in the American astronomical community in the 1960s, pressure for a special section of the AAS to accommodate Solar System interests would probably have resulted in an "invitation" to set up a completely separate society, had it not been for pressure from other astronomers in the AAS in pursuit of their special interests. The high-energy astrophysicists (including John Simpson, William Kraushaar, George Clark, Herbert Friedman, Eugene Parker, and others) had been agitating for a reorganization of the AAS that would accommodate the particular needs of their subdiscipline. Chamberlain asserts that the threat to secede by this influential community, "followed by the successful diplomatic intervention by Martin Schwarzschild, convinced the Council that divisions were definitely in the Society's future, like it or not."[11]

Schwarzschild's positive role in the reorganization, which was surely dreaded by the Council, proved to be critical to the successful birth of the DPS and to other divisions of the Society. Chamberlain recounts the events, noting that in 1966 Bengt Strömgren began a two-year term as President of the Society, but resigned after one year to return to Copenhagen. Albert Whitford, as the senior Vice-President, became Acting President for 1967–1968. Although Whitford began his own two-year term as President on July 1, 1968, he had previously committed to take a sabbatical leave at Mount Stromolo Observatory in Canberra, Australia, beginning in the late summer of 1968. In his absence from the U.S., Martin Schwarzschild, at that time the senior Vice-President, carried out the duties of President until Whitford returned in mid-1969. At that time Schwarzschild assumed the newly created office of President-Elect for 1969–1970 and became President for 1970–1972. This series of events put Schwarzschild at the center of action during the time of the reorganization to accommodate the new divisional structure of the Society.[11] As Whitford recalled, "I felt that I could go away with a good conscience, since the problem of dealing with the mounting pressure for specialized divisions in the AAS would fortunately be in the capable hands of Martin Schwarzschild."[29]

As Chamberlain drafted the bylaws of the planetary division, he was in frequent communication with Schwarzschild, exchanging ideas by letter and telephone. Schwarzschild worked to ensure that there were no conflicts with the Society's governing rules and that the emerging "Division did not go charging off in all directions without parental restraint." Chamberlain was intent on "ensuring a high degree of independence in the Division's operations: e.g., by allowing the affiliation of non-astronomers, in order to make the Division the preeminent society of its kind in the world." Indeed, the individuals on the Organizing Committee covered nearly all areas of planetary science as it was seen at the time, although Sagan in particular had suggested others with an interest in exobiology to Chamberlain. Overshadowing Chamberlain's efforts to draft the bylaws was the knowledge that the approval of the AAS Council was mandatory to guarantee the success of the venture.[11]

On September 17, 1968, well in advance of the organizational meeting to be held in Austin, Chamberlain, acting as Temporary Chairman, wrote to his Organizing Committee noting that one day of meetings of the Committee (December 9) would be adequate to get the bylaws in final shape for presentation to the AAS Council on December 10, which would be their own day "devoted exclusively to the scientific sessions on planetary astronomy."[30] Chamberlain then set out the functions of the Committee as follows:

> If the Organizing Committee can accomplish its functions at the Austin meeting, it could presumably pass out of existence at that time. However, until procedures are established for other members of the AAS to affiliate with the Section, membership of the Section consists solely of the Organizing Committee, who will presumably select the initial slate of Section officers at the Austin meeting, in accordance with procedures outlined in the Section bylaws adopted there.

Chamberlain added that to proceed "as expeditiously as possible" he appointed Carl Sagan as Temporary Secretary of the Section. Sagan would work with the AAS

Secretary to make arrangements for Austin and to publicize the meeting. "I have just learned from Martin Schwarzschild," Chamberlain reported, "that the Amendment to the Society bylaws for the 'Introduction of Divisions of AAS,' as adopted in Victoria, authorizes the Temporary Section Chairman to conduct the election of the Permanent Chairman of the Organizing Committee without necessarily awaiting the formality of a meeting. I favor this provision as it will allow the Permanent Chairman to organize the Austin meeting well in advance, and hopefully this should accelerate the formal organization of the Division."[30] Chamberlain enclosed a ballot card with instructions to return it to Toby Owen, the Teller for the first election. He also invited input to the Section bylaws. The result of the voting was that Chamberlain was elected Permanent Chairman of the Organizing Committee, to serve until the election at the Austin meeting.

On October 1, 1968, Chamberlain wrote to a wider list of scientists interested in the organization of the planetary sciences division, noting the Council's approval to proceed. He issued a call for papers for Austin. The morning program was to consist of an interdisciplinary symposium on "Organic Matter in Meteorites and on the Moon" (chaired by F. L. Whipple) and one on the "results of the most recent optical and radar investigations of the asteroid Icarus, chaired by Dr. A. Kliore." The afternoon session was to consist of contributed papers on lunar and planetary topics. Titles and abstracts were to be sent to Sagan.[31]

Figure 1. In the 1970s, Carl Sagan expressed how planetary sciences were changed by the space age: "In all the history of mankind, there will be only one generation that will be first to explore the Solar System, one generation for which, in childhood, the planets are distant and indistinct discs moving through the night sky, and for which, in old age, the planets are places, diverse new worlds in the course of exploration." Carl Sagan, *Cosmic Connection* (New York: Anchor/Doubleday, 1973), p. 69. Photograph from the Cosmos series, courtesy ASP Archives and Andy Fraknoi.

THE ORGANIZATIONAL MEETING, AUSTIN, DECEMBER 1968

In mid-October, Chamberlain distributed draft bylaws to the Organizing Committee, but Anders was the only one who "did his homework" and provided substantive input to a revised draft that was put on the table on December 9 in Austin. [32] Chamberlain recalls that "the Committee worked hard all afternoon, then recessed for a Mexican dinner and a stop at a wine shop, where Anders and Goody tried to 'out-winesmanship' one another. The result was that we had a peculiar combination of Chilean and Portuguese wines to speed up the decision making process in our evening session."[11]

At Austin an initial slate of officers was selected by the Organizing Committee from its own membership, with Anders nominated for Vice-Chairman and Chamberlain for Chairman. Nine people were nominated to fill six staggered terms as Committee members over the next three years.[33] The Division membership was established by a list drawn up by the Organizing Committee including everyone thought to be interested in becoming a member. Owen was appointed (over his objections) to Secretary-Treasurer *pro tem*, and arrangements were established for a Nominating Committee to be selected by the full membership at the first annual business meeting.[11]

The official program agenda of the 128th meeting of the AAS, distributed in advance of the Austin meeting, did not show that the special planetary meeting was scheduled for Tuesday, December 10, only that the Council would meet that day, followed by registration and an informal reception. Deeper in the brochure, however, under "Notices," was the following:

> **Symposia.** An interdisciplinary Symposium on Organic Matter in Meteorites and on the Moon, followed by papers on the asteroid Icarus will be held on December 10, 1968, at the University of Texas, Austin, Texas. Details may be obtained from Dr. Carl Sagan...

The AAS program made no specific mention that this symposium might be related to the formation of a new Division of the Society, or was even associated, except by proximity, with the 128th meeting of the AAS. The regular program of the AAS meeting included nine contributed papers about the Moon, Venus, Jupiter, comets, Pluto, and the origin of the Solar System, all presented on Wednesday, December 11. Nevertheless, the special planetary science session on December 10 was a success. In Session I chaired by Arvidas Kliore, five papers about asteroid 1566 Icarus were presented, followed by discussion. Session II on organic matter was chaired by Whipple. In that session Sagan provided an introduction, followed by a review on organic matter in meteorites by M. H. Studier, R. Hayatsu, and Anders. John Oro followed with "Carbonaceous Matter in Meteorite & Lunar Samples," Stanton Peal on "Water on the Moon," and P. R. Bell on "Lunar Sample Analysis in the Lunar Receiving Laboratory." A 30-minute panel discussion including the presenters, plus Harold Urey, Harold Masursky, and A. G. W. Cameron, finished up the symposium. The afternoon session consisted of 24 papers, including a special invited presentation by Urey on the history and implications of lunar mass concentrations.

TIDYING UP THE DETAILS

On December 30, 1968, following the Austin meeting, Chamberlain sent a memorandum to the "Organizing Committee of the Division for Planetary Sciences."[34] Note that the name now clearly identified planetary sciences rather than planetary astronomy. With this memo he solicited lists of individuals who may wish to be affiliated with the DPS. In January, Chamberlain wrote to Schwarzschild to expand upon a few items in the draft bylaws submitted to the Council by the DPS Organizing Committee. In particular, a provision was included to encourage involvement of outstanding foreign scientists in the DPS meetings, somewhat above and beyond the degree to which the AAS had at that time become accustomed. In particular, the DPS wanted its Committee to be able to designate especially worthy planetary scientists outside North America as Foreign Affiliates of the Division, giving them full rights to attend and present papers at the Division meetings. Other items were organizational details concerning co-opted Committee members and the term of the Secretary-Treasurer.[35]

Schwarzschild was concerned about the introduction of Foreign Affiliates desired by the DPS. He asked Chamberlain to clarify a few points about the election of Affiliates, but his main concern was that "...we could not defend it to the AAS membership at large if we spend funds or appreciable energies of our AAS officers for the benefit of people who are not members of [the main body of] the AAS."[36] Neither Chamberlain nor Anders were happy about Schwarzschild's allusion that the AAS Council might limit the Division's autonomy on the admission and treatment of Foreign Affiliates,[37,38,39] but in a memo to the Organizing Committee, Chamberlain noted that the AAS Council had considered the Division's bylaws at their meeting in Honolulu, and the results of the deliberations were communicated to Chamberlain by the Executive Officer H. M. (Hank) Gurin, who would also be acting as the liaison officer for the newly established Divisions.[40]

Among other changes requested by the AAS Council, the issue of Foreign Affiliates surfaced. The version advocated by the Council (denoted Version B by Chamberlain),[40] changed the qualification from one of "recognized accomplishment" to "outstanding accomplishment," and imposed a limit of five percent of the Division membership for the Foreign Affiliate category. Chamberlain expressed his personal view that the Council was making a mistake to restrict the Division's autonomy in this matter, but he recommended to the Organizing Committee that the language requested by the Council be adopted, concluding that, "If at some later date the fears of the Council subside, the bylaws could be revised." With that, he put the new draft of the bylaws to a vote by the Committee, requesting that ballots be returned by May 15, 1969.

With the Division bylaws approved by the Organizing Committee, on May 16, 1969 Chamberlain distributed an invitation to join the Division to a list of "Initial Members, Division for Planetary Sciences, AAS." Dues of $4.00 were to be sent to Owen. Just over 100 AAS members had expressed the desire to join the Division, plus "an additional dozen or so non-members" had indicated their intent to join the AAS and the Division. He urged all colleagues with an interest in the planetary sciences to affiliate with the DPS.[41]

ON TO SAN FRANCISCO

The success of the inaugural meeting of the DPS in Austin, especially its scientific symposium, led most of the active planetary scientists in the country to express interest in joining the Division. The approval by the AAS Council propelled Chamberlain and his Committee toward preparations for the First Annual Meeting, to be held in San Francisco in January, 1970.

Chamberlain had invited Richard Goody to chair the scientific program in San Francisco. Goody accepted and enlisted the help of M. B. McElroy and Owen. Local arrangements for the San Francisco meeting were handled by George Pimentel and Hyron Spinrad. The meeting was held at the Jack Tar Hotel (since renamed) on January 19–21; the registration fee was $10.

The program for Monday, January 19, consisted of a Symposium on Lunar Science, convened by W. Hess and W. Rubey, and a Symposium on Mars Imaging, convened by R. Leighton and T. B. McCord, followed by a Panel Discussion convened by H. Masursky. The next day began with a Symposium on the Atmosphere of Mars, convened by C. Leovy and M. McElroy, followed by the Annual Business Meeting (for DPS members only), and then a Symposium on Planetary Spectroscopy, convened by Owen and G. Münch. Wednesday, January 21, was occupied by 10-minute contributed papers, led off by Kuiper's paper on "Further High Altitude Spectra of Venus."

Figure 2. (l to r) Gerard P. Kuiper and Tobias Owen at the Texas radio telescope, near Marfa, circa 1970. Dale Cruikshank Photograph.

The minutes of the Business Meeting were kept by Owen. [42] Present were Chamberlain, Anders, Pettengill, Kliore, Smith, Owen, Goody, McElroy, Sagan, Gurin, and guest L. LeMoine (KPNO). The minutes show that the main items of business concerned classes of membership and arrangements for the following annual meetings. Münch, B. Murray, and S. Gulkis were appointed to take charge of the 1971 meeting, with Owen's assistance. The results of the election of officers for 1970 were announced: Chamberlain was elected Chairman and Anders Vice-Chairman. "Committeemen" serving until 1971 were Sagan and I. Shapiro; until 1972, Kuiper and McElroy, and until 1973, Smith and Pettengill, thus establishing the cycle of staggered terms on the Committee. Dues were kept at $4 per year, and a change in the bylaws was proposed to clarify an ambiguity in electing the Secretary-Treasurer. Owen's Treasurer's report showed that dues had been received from 135 members, and with various mailing costs deducted, the Division's financial balance as of January 15, 1970 was $471.17.

With the successful scientific meeting in San Francisco, and a Business Meeting that dealt primarily with mundane matters, the Division for Planetary Sciences was decisively launched. Looking ahead to the 1971 meeting, Chamberlain had already asked Anders to take on the program chairmanship to ensure avoidance of "any show of indecisiveness in San Francisco," in part because "Sagan is starting to make noises again about being left out of things... ."[43] Anders replied quickly, declining because of the "mess" that the lunar program had made of his life. "NASA is running it [the lunar program] like a military operation."[44] But Anders soon relented. Chamberlain's term as Chairman ended at the 1971 meeting in Tallahassee, when he turned the podium over to Anders as the incoming Chairman. Anders paid tribute to Chamberlain's years of effort on behalf of the DPS with a nautical metaphor: "Joe has helped launch the Good Ship DPS and, over the past two years, has steered its course through uncharted waters — some say in the wrong direction, but at least we're still afloat."[11]

TOPICS FOR FUTURE EXPLORATION

The early years of the DPS were not without interesting incidents that could reasonably be attributed to the "growing pains" expected of any new organization. Some of these may merit a deeper historical study, using the materials in the archives of the DPS and the papers of some of the principals involved. Here we note just a few points of interest.

A. Strife Over the Division Structure in the AAS

Not long after the adoption of the Division structure in the AAS, discord arose between the divisions and the Council of the parent organization. On January 20, 1972, A. G. W. Cameron sent a four-page memorandum to all members of the Council of the AAS and all officers of the divisions. The memorandum began, "The American Astronomical Society, in its great wisdom, is promoting the fragmentation of astronomy into many non-communicating pieces." The principal issues included the apparent indifference to the divisions on the part of the Council, and a lack of communication among the governing entities. The divisions were not usually represented at the meetings of the Council, the distribution of minutes of those meetings was not always reliable, and there were disputes over the costs incurred by the AAS in mailings that included divisional materials to the full membership. The strong tone of Cameron's memorandum sparked interest in the divisions and in the AAS Council to adopt policies for distribution of meeting minutes, payment for mailings, and inclusions of division materials in the *Bulletin of the American Astronomical Society* to help remedy the situation. Discussions on the issue of communication among the divisions and with the parent society continue to the present day.

B. The Journal Icarus is Adopted by the DPS

Carl Sagan became the Editor of *Icarus* beginning with Volume 10 in January 1969. At that time, *Icarus* was transformed from a journal in which papers were recommended for publication by one of two or three editors, to one in which submitted papers were fully refereed in what has become the standard method of operation for peer-reviewed scientific journals. A Publications Subcommittee, organized in 1971 and chaired by C. R. Chapman, began to discuss with Academic Press the establishment of a Divisional affiliation with *Icarus* in 1972 or 1973. With Sagan's encouragement, the DPS moved to adopt *Icarus* as the official journal of the Division, and starting with Volume 24, No. 1 (January 1975), the cover of the journal bears the imprint, "Published in affiliation with the Division for Planetary Sciences, American Astronomical Society."

C. A Secessionist Movement in the DPS

As the DPS membership grew in number and attracted scientists from non-astronomical disciplines (notably geology and meteorology), the relationship of the Division to the parent AAS was frequently questioned in the Committee and at the open Business Meetings. Non-astronomers reported treatment as second-class members, among other things. But of deeper concern, the DPS began to seek greater autonomy from the AAS in order to exert some political influence on the annual NASA budget that so strongly affected funding for planetary science. The discontent was relayed to AAS President E. M. Burbidge in January, 1977 in a letter from AAS Treasurer William E. Howard III, and in subsequent correspondence preserved in the DPS archives. Donald M. Hunten, the DPS Chairman for most of 1977, attended the Atlanta AAS meeting of the Council on June 11 of that year. He found that the Council clearly wanted to retain the affiliation of the planetary scientists with the AAS, and an agreement was reached by which the AAS would provide more support in the preparation of the program of the DPS annual meeting through the use of the *BAAS*. In order to give the Division more political flexibility, it was agreed that the DPS Chairman "may write letters as long as the AAS President is notified (or the Secretary in her absence)."[45] As a consequence of this action by the Council and President Burbidge, the secessionist movement evaporated.

D. Establishing the DPS Prizes

In 1973, DPS Secretary-Treasurer David Morrison, who served from 1971 to 1977, began to promote the idea of DPS Prizes to be awarded to meritorious planetary

Figure 3. Fred L. Whipple of the Smithsonian Astrophysical Observatory was the second winner of the G. P. Kuiper Prize of the DPS in 1985. Irwin photograph, August 1973. AIP Emilio Segrè Visual Archives, Irwin Collection.

scientists, primarily to call attention to achievements in planetary science and to the professional activities of the Division. The concept met with mixed reactions. In a poll of the membership that Morrison conducted in 1973, he found that of 95 responding members, a small majority favored the prize. Of those who felt strongly about the issue, twice as many approved as disapproved. The matter was delayed, but Morrison later arranged for corporate funding of two prizes, which were finally instituted; in 1984, E. M. Shoemaker was the first recipient of the G. P. Kuiper prize, recognizing a lifetime of exceptional contributions to planetary science, and D. J. Stevenson received the first Harold C. Urey prize for outstanding contributions by a planetary scientist under the age of 36. The Harold Mazursky award for meritorious service to planetary science was first presented in 1991, to Carl Sagan.

E. The DPS and the Press

Most of the leadership of the DPS in the early years, and certainly the bulk of the membership at large, was inexperienced, uninformed, and somewhat naive about the promotion of planetary science in the press. Outreach to the public, who through their taxes pay for planetary science, was recognized as highly desirable, in part for the pure motive of education and in part for the delicate but practical reality of influencing public policy-making at the highest governmental levels. The DPS at its annual meet-

Figure 4. Joseph Wyan Chamberlain, circa 1960, taken at Kitt Peak. Photograph courtesy J. Chamberlain.

ings sought to interest the press by issuing rather bland invitations to recognized science writers from a few national newspapers. This fundamentally passive approach had little effect.

Jonathan Eberhart, the Space Sciences Editor of the weekly *Science News*, attended his first DPS meeting in 1974, in Palo Alto, California. At the next meeting, in 1975 in Columbia, Maryland, Eberhard was the only reporter present. He took an immediate liking to the DPS scientists and the meeting style, not to mention the windfall in new results to report in his weekly science magazine. In a long letter to Carl Sagan, Eberhard gave detailed and specific suggestions for improving and expanding the public awareness of planetary science.[46] His suggestions were discussed among the DPS leadership, and most of them implemented, thus affecting the way in which the organization of the annual meetings interfaces with the press and local educators in the meeting city each year. At the Palo Alto meeting in 1991, the DPS honored Eberhart by arranging to have asteroid 4764 named Joneberhart, to recognize his contributions and loyalty to the Division.

A NOTE ON SOURCES

The letters and other documents referenced here are held in the Archives of the Division for Planetary Science housed at the Niels Bohr Library of the American Institute of Physics in College Park, Maryland. Copies of some of these materials will also be found in the professional papers of some of the principals mentioned in this chapter. Historical notes on the DPS, consisting of minutes of business meetings, lists of former officers, meetings, and prize recipients, are published with the abstracts from the Division's annual scientific meeting in the *BAAS*.[47]

THE FOUNDING OF THE DIVISION ON DYNAMICAL ASTRONOMY— A FEW RECOLLECTIONS

R. L. Duncombe

DIRK BROUWER'S LEGACY

The story of our Division must begin with Dirk Brouwer, Figure 1. He more than most others recognized the importance to Celestial Mechanics of the development of high-speed computers and the demands of the burgeoning Space Age for trained personnel. Although he was not present to actually take part in the founding of the DDA, it was his legacy through the Summer Institutes in Dynamical Astronomy, which he started in 1959 at Yale, and his Annual Seminars in Celestial Mechanics, which began in 1962, that provided the impetus for our Division.

Brouwer's meetings were carried on by others and provided the opportunity to discuss current problems and solutions at length, which proved to be far more stimulating than the occasional session with 10-minute presentations allowed by the Astronomical Society. Thus through Brouwer's example, a number of specialists felt it was imperative to create a special interest group in Dynamical Astronomy. This feeling was, moreover, part of a growing trend in the Society since three other groups had already petitioned Albert E. Whitford, Society President, to secure the Council's approval to amend the bylaws to allow the organization of special interest groups within the framework of the Society. Martin Schwarzschild, as acting President, was delegated the task of dealing with the petitions.

By the late summer of 1968, petitions for three divisions (high-energy astrophysics, solar physics, and planetary science) had been submitted and on September 20, Samuel Herrick submitted a very short proposal for a Division on Celestial Mechanics. It had been prepared by Derral Mulholland and had only 15 signatures. This petition prompted a most thorough response (five and one-half single-spaced typewritten pages) from Schwarzschild on October 18, 1968. At first glance, we thought Schwarzschild was creating procedural and perfunctory roadblocks to stall our petition, but on closer reading of his carefully crafted letter, we realized that he was asking for just the type of information he required to convince the AAS Council of the need for this division.

SCHWARZSCHILD'S QUESTIONS

Schwarzschild emphasized that his letter was advisory only, since he was standing in for Whitford. He wanted to be helpful. First and foremost, he was surprised at the

Figure 1. Dirk Brouwer. Photograph appeared originally as the Frontispiece to the Celestial Mechanics Journal, volume 1 (June 1979). Reprinted with kind permission from Kluwer Academic Publishers.

brevity of the petition, which "consists of one sentence asking for the formation of the division, signed by 15 names" together with a supporting statement from Herrick. This was hardly enough to convince the Council. Schwarzschild predicted that the Council would want "substantive information regarding the need for the formation of this division..." Schwarzschild clearly did not want to present the petition in its present form only to see it rejected, or delayed. He suggested to Herrick ways to strengthen the argument, relieved, in his special humorous way, that this would delay proceedings just enough so that when a proper petition was received, Whitford would be back in power and would have to deal with the matter.[1]

Despite his self-effacing friendly manner, Schwarzschild knew just what the Council would ask, and advised us well. His first question dealt with need, "why are the general AAS meetings either insufficient or unsatisfactory as they stand[?]" As if to let us know we were not alone, he added to Herrick:

> Your personal comment that you have felt out of place in the world of astrophysicists and have ceased attending AAS meetings for that reason I rather suspect is a reaction that is not at all limited to celestial mechanicians but is entirely general for all of us who, whether we like it or not, belong to the older generation.

Schwarzschild recalled the "glorious days" when any well-trained astronomer could grasp the entirety of the papers at a AAS meeting. But now, astronomy had "blossomed out to a degree that even the brightest of the present youngsters have a tougher time with regard to general understanding than we had at their age."[2] It was a very different world.

Having said this, Schwarzschild then advised that the bylaws, as they had recently been amended for the first specialist divisions, did not explicitly allow for a division on celestial mechanics, but this did not preclude the creation of another division as long as good arguments could be made for it; arguments were required that were distinct from those that had been made by the planetary, solar, and high-energy people. "I feel however that the formulation of these reasons should be the task of the proposers...," Schwarzschild wanted the initiative to reside with the specialists, who knew best their own needs. He did warn that the Council would want to see good reasons for "as radical a move as the formation of a new division" instead of allowing for moderate changes in the structure of the general meetings of the Society to accommodate specialist themes.[3]

The Society was already taking steps to make the latter option a distinct possibility. Even though only a few years earlier Schwarzschild himself resisted the creation of parallel sessions at general Society meetings, he now saw them as an opportunity to allow specialists to hold sessions in their field. The Society was rapidly moving to four and five parallel sessions, more than enough to give every specialty a chance to talk to itself. The celestial mechanicians had to show how this new feature of general meetings, "already a bit of the character of a divisional meeting," did not meet their needs. More parallel sessions also relaxed time restrictions so longer papers could be entertained.[4]

Schwarzschild then advised Herrick to define the research area that the proposed division would cover. Would it be orbit theory, or would it include galactic dynamics and astrometry? Where were the boundaries? Would it include "applied celestial mechanics" for artificial satellite needs, or would the field be purely astronomical? Schwarzschild carefully advised Herrick, who was well known as a prominent leader in the new field of astrodynamics, that the Council would look very closely at the applied question, and suggested that the creation of a purely applied or a purely theoretical division might not be looked upon with favor. He knew that Brouwer had set a "magnificent example" of combining observation and theory, and, after talking with Gerald Clemence and Fred Whipple, both of whom favored the new division, Schwarzschild admitted that the needs of the specialty were unique, and might well be justified as a theoretical entity alone, excluding astrometric interests. "Nevertheless this point I would feel needs substantive elaboration in a serious petition."[5]

Schwarzschild also believed that the petition would be strengthened greatly if it included examples of how previous specialist meetings — those at the Jet Propulsion Laboratory and those at Yale — had helped the field coalesce. Even a listing of names would be helpful, but he hinted that more would be expected. He also suggested that the petition should identify the institutions most likely to host specialist meetings of the division, and how costs of such activities, separate from the Society, would be supported. Here he felt NASA was an obvious source of support, certainly several of its centers were most interested in astrodynamics. But the Naval Observatory and the Smithsonian would also be likely supporters. He had no problem with such institutions, as long as "no division becomes entirely dependent on governmental hosts." A few universities had to be interested as well.[6]

Schwarzschild's last point was the most direct. Did the scant list of 15 names represent the breadth and interests of the specialty? He sensed a "strong geographical and institutional unbalance" which would give the Council serious pause. More names, from a broader range of institutions, would help the petition immeasurably. He also advised that people who signed the petition had to include more than elite patrons, but those willing to work, and the latter had to be identified explicitly. After all, running a division was not a trivial task. It was time consuming and needed dedicated manpower. He was particularly concerned to see younger (under 45 years of age) workers on the list.

THE REVISED PETITION

In fact what Schwarzschild provided was a clearly defined road map to guide the petitioners. Accordingly, Mulholland, with input from others, then revised the petition, meeting Schwarzschild's requirements. One major modification was a change of title from Celestial Mechanics to Dynamical Astronomy since it was more representative of the interests involved. Mulholland also found more people willing to sign, and though many still came from those institutions most active in the field, the second list of some 45 names did cover a wider portion of the community of workers (see Table 1).

The revised petition was sent to Schwarzschild in time to be presented to the AAS Council at its December 1968 meeting at Austin. Supporting information regarding the types of programs initiated by Brouwer was provided by Victor Szebehely, who outlined in great detail the recent Summer Institutes in Dynamical Astronomy and the Annual Seminars in Celestial Mechanics. He pointed out how Brouwer had created the former at Yale and how they travelled around the country, meeting at Stanford, Purdue, and MIT, with more planned for various NASA Centers. The 4 to 6-week Summer Institutes had been created for the "continued education of college teachers" but now included both government and industry scientists who desired basic training in celestial mechanics, the lunar theory, planetary theory, etc. Szebehely was not convinced that the Institute model translated into a Society activity, but pointed out that the endorsement of the Society would provide "moral support to such undertakings."[7]

Szebehely then described the Annual Seminars in Celestial Mechanics, which Brouwer had also created in 1962 but gave over to Szebehely in 1964. These were normally two to three days in length, devoted to single topics in celestial mechanics, and due to their great success had been growing steadily each year as the only forum available to celestial mechanics specialists. "One of the services the Celestial Mechanics Division of the American Astronomical Society could perform would be to call such an annual meeting." He did not think, however, that the standard Society pattern of short talks would translate well — "In our seminars emphasis is on the free discussion of important details."[8]

In sum, Szebehely strongly endorsed the need for a division, using the popularity and growth of the annual seminar as an example. He agreed with Duncombe's suggestion that, if the Council approved of the plan in general, it would appoint a small committee of specialists to work out the details.

At the Austin meeting, the AAS Council looked favorably on the new petition, agreed that a new division was called for, and told the petitioners to organize it. In late December 1968, Schwarzschild asked Mulholland, John Danby, Irwin Shapiro, and

TABLE 1. *A Proposal for a Division of Dynamical Astronomy.*

I. Petition

We, whose names follow below, do hereby make formal request of the Council of the American Astronomical Society that it approve the establishment of a division of Dynamical Astronomy, pursuant to the bylaws of the Society. We do further petition Council to appoint an Organizing Committee and designate one of that number to be Temporary Chairman thereof, so that the rules of organization can be drawn at the earliest opportunity.

Robert d'E. Atkinson, Goethe Link Observatory, Indiana University
Robert M. L. Baker, Jr., System Sciences Corp.
Richard Barrar, University of Oregon
Roger Broucke, Jet Propulsion Laboratory, CIT
Dan L. Cain, Jet Propulsion Laboratory, CIT
Gerald M. Clemence, Yale University Observatory
Leland I. Cunningham, University of California at Berkeley
J. M. A. Danby, North Carolina State University
Andre Deprit, Boeing Scientific Research Laboratories
Raynor L. Duncombe, U. S. Naval Observatory
David W. Dunham, Yale University Observatory
J. S. Griffith, Lakehead University
Paul Herget, Cincinnati Observatory
Jaques Henrard, Boeing Scientific Research Laboratories
Samuel Herrick, University of California at Los Angeles
Paul Janiczek, U. S. Naval Observatory
I. Jurkevich, Flower and Cook Observatory, University of Pennsylvania
W. J. Klepczynski, U. S. Naval Observatory
E. Leimanis, University of British Columbia
Jay Lieske, Jet Propulsion Laboratory, CIT
Charles A. Lundquist, Smithsonian Astrophysical Observatory
Brian G. Marsden, Smithsonian Astrophysical Observatory
S. W. McCuskey, Warner and Swasey Observatory, Case Western Reserve University
William G. Melbourne, Jet Propulsion Laboratory, CIT
Irving Michelson, Illinois Institute of Technology
J. Derral Mulholland, Jet Propulsion Laboratory, CIT
Paul M. Muller, Jet Propulsion Laboratory, CIT
Peter Musen, Goddard Space Flight Center, NASA
Douglas A. O'Handley, Jet Propulsion Laboratory, CIT
Mary H. Payne, Electronics Research Center, NASA
Gerald E. Pease, Jet Propulsion Laboratory, CIT
Harry Pollard, Purdue University
Eugene Rabe, Cincinnati Observatory
Allan F. Schanzle, Wolf Research and Development Corp.
P. Kenneth Seidelmann, U. S. Naval Observatory
William L. Sjogren, Jet Propulsion Laboratory, CIT
E. Myles Standish, Jr., Yale University Observatory
Victor G. Szebehely, University of Texas
Byron D. Tapley, University of Texas
John P. Vinti, Massachusetts Institute of Technology
Michael R. Warner, Jet Propulsion Laboratory, CIT
Edgar W. Woolard, U. S. Naval Observatory
J. William Zielenbach, Jet Propulsion Laboratory, CIT

Duncombe to name candidates for an organizing committee that would prepare the division's bylaws. Schwarzschild again outlined in great detail just how this should be done, asking the four to act as advisors to the new committee. "I always hate to put administrative work on people who are effective researchers," Schwarzschild added, but he hoped the burden would be kept to a minimum, especially if the committee followed the course taken by the other divisions and the Society in framing their own bylaws.[9]

After much telephone consultation, the four advisors produced a slate of names which Schwarzschild relayed to the AAS Council at its Hawaii meeting, where final approval for the Division on Dynamical Astronomy was granted. Official notification came from G. C. McVittie, AAS Secretary, who empowered the organizing committee to prepare the bylaws. The committee was chaired by Duncombe, and included Danby, W. M. Kaula, Ivan King, Brian Marsden, Mulholland, Shapiro, Szebehely, and Alar Toomre. Hank Gurin, recently appointed Executive Officer of the AAS, supplied the bylaws of the other three divisions as examples to follow. Most of our work was carried on by mail and telephone, but the Summer Institute in Dynamical Astronomy held at MIT in July 1969 afforded us the first opportunity to meet together. Gurin attended as a consultant and all the details were worked out to everyone's satisfaction. With the bylaws completed, the committee drafted an announcement inviting colleagues to join the new Division on Dynamical Astronomy. The reaction from AAS members was very heartening and the $2 entrance fee was a bargain; in a scant four months the membership swelled to 98 people.

THE FIRST MEETING

But the work had just begun. The organizing committee had to produce a slate of candidates for officers of the Division and conduct an election. More difficult, they had to find a place to hold the first meeting. The list of candidates was chosen according to the bylaws, with counsel from Martin Schwarzschild and Hank Gurin. They tried to create a slate that represented the various areas of interest represented by the Division. The choice of a place to hold the first Division meeting was a tougher problem. Our treasury was practically empty (the January 1970 Treasurer's report indicated a balance of $166.19). Could we find an already established and funded meeting in our area of interest that might allow us to be a co-sponsor? This would allow us to take part in the scientific agenda and permit us to hold a business meeting where the organizing committee could relinquish the reins to the first elected officers.

Szebehely came to the rescue with an invitation to hold the first Division meeting jointly with the Eighth Annual Seminar on Current Problems in Celestial Mechanics at Austin, Texas, in late January 1970. Although other suggestions competed, a consensus was finally reached to accept Szebehely's offer. Tony Danby later wrote, somewhat wistfully, that although he agreed with the decision he had somewhat favored a spring meeting in Florida because he understood that Brian Marsden was willing to arrange for an eclipse of the sun at about that time.

The January 1970 meeting was a resounding success. The final meeting of the organizing committee turned into the first business meeting of the Division, which 40 people attended. Duncombe recounted the process through which the Division was

Figure 2. Some Division meetings are every bit as large as full AAS meetings were a half century earlier. The DDA met at the Lowell Observatory for its 28th annual meeting in April 1997. Photograph courtesy Alan Fiala.

organized, and Mulholland, acting as Secretary *pro tem*, reported that membership had reached 125, with 115 eligible to vote. The voting (81 ballots were cast) brought Duncombe in as the first Chairman, Shapiro as Vice-Chairman, Mulholland as Secretary, and Marsden as Treasurer. The duly elected officers now took responsibility for planning and operations. We had asked three of our elder statesmen, Gerald Clemence, Wallace Eckert, and Paul Herget to be candidates to lend an aura of respectability to our new Division, and they kindly agreed to serve 1-year terms on the Division

Figure 3. Gene Shoemaker (on right) was the banquet speaker at the April 1997 DDA meeting. Relaxing with him are (l to r) Don Osterbrock and Bob Millis. Photograph courtesy Alan Fiala.

committee. Danby, Deprit, and S. McCuskey were elected to 2-year terms, to begin the rotation cycle.

The new committee wasted no time planning for a new nominating committee and for the election of new officers prior to the next meeting. Both Ivan King and Tony Danby pointed out, rightly so, that the composition of our Division Committee was not representative of the many interests of our Division and that this should be kept in mind in nominating the next slate of candidates. Danby was duly appointed chairman of the Nominating Committee.

Since the January 1970 joint meeting had been such a success, we asked Schwarzschild if we could meet jointly with the AAS at its winter meeting in Tampa. At first he cited bylaw restrictions which precluded simultaneous meetings of divisions with the parent organization. Later action by the AAS Council, however, removed this obstruction and Schwarzschild then invited us to hold the next DDA meeting concurrently with the AAS in December 1970 with no charge for meeting rooms and other facilities. At this meeting Shapiro and the other new officers assumed control of the Division.

THE BROUWER LECTURE

It was during 1970 that the suggestion for a Brouwer Lecture Award was first proposed but action was not taken until 1971 when a Brouwer Fund Committee was established. Duncombe was asked to chair the committee. We immediately brought the wrath of the AAS Council down on our heads by approaching AAS corporate members for money at the same time the AAS was asking them to support the Society's own awards. Morris Davis later assumed charge of this effort and was successful in getting an award from the Perkin Foundation to reach the first goal of $2500, which emboldened us to set a new goal of $5000. Since that time contributions have brought the fund to its present level of about $25,000. The first Brouwer Lecture was scheduled for the AAS meeting in Austin in January 1978. The selection committee included Boris Garfinkel, Ivan King, and Paul Herget as chair. The first lecture was given by Victor Szebehely and the entire series of Brouwer Lectures has been of exceptional quality. Thus the story of the founding of the Division on Dynamical Astronomy begins and ends with Dirk Brouwer, but its existence was due in large part to the convictions of a few dedicated specialists and to the patience and thoughtful guidance of Martin Schwarzschild.

THE HISTORICAL ASTRONOMY DIVISION

Katherine Bracher

Dear Colleague," the letter read, "We have reason to believe that you may be interested in becoming a 'charter member' of the new Historical Astronomy Division (HAD) of the American Astronomical Society (AAS)..." Dated April 24, 1980, it went on to describe the goals of the new Division, how to join, and was signed by Kenneth Brecher for the Organizing Committee. A year and a half later the HAD boasted 267 members and held the first of its (so far) 23 successful meetings. But this newest Division of the AAS had been in the planning stages for more than a year before the Council approved it and it began to solicit members.

The original impetus for the founding of a Historical Astronomy Division came from conversations between John S. Eddy, Owen Gingerich, and Kenneth Brecher during the fall of 1978, when Eddy was on leave from the University of Colorado and spending some time at the Center for Astrophysics in Cambridge, Mass.[1] Each of the three had interests in the history of astronomy, and they began to realize that these interests were shared by other members of the AAS. Gingerich had already published extensively in traditional history of astronomy, especially on Copernicus. Eddy had investigated historical records of sunspot activity (rediscovering what is now known as the Maunder Minimum) and was also interested in the Native American medicine wheels as possible astronomical constructions. Brecher's interests lay in the areas of supernovae and stellar evolution (such topics as the reported red color of Sirius in antiquity). But main-stream astronomers, by and large, regarded such topics as marginal to their concerns.

At the Mexico City AAS meeting in January 1979, Brecher organized a session on archaeoastronomy, which was attended by approximately 200 people. At this session, he circulated a petition to find members who might be interested in the formation of a Division concerned with the history of astronomy and with archaeoastronomy; over 80 people signed this document. Brecher, Eddy, Gingerich, and others discussed this project further, and felt that this indicated a strong interest within the AAS; they also felt that if (as was the case with other divisions) people could be affiliate members without belonging to the AAS, substantially more members might come from the ranks of historians of science and archaeologists.[2]

As a result of these discussions, Eddy, Gingerich, and Brecher became a self-appointed steering committee to begin the process of forming a division. The name Historical Astronomy Division was chosen, rather than History of Astronomy Division, because, as Owen Gingerich recalls, they "wanted to include uses of historical evidence for modern astronomy as well as archaeoastronomy," in addition to the more traditional history of astronomy.[3] The Division has continued to maintain this broad range of interests, although archaeoastronomy has been less prominent in recent years.

The steering committee prepared a draft set of bylaws for the new division, which they sent to the AAS in May 1979.[4] These bylaws were modeled closely on those of other divisions, with an opening statement of purpose:

> "The Division shall exist for the purpose of advancing interest in topics relating to the historical nature of astronomy. By historical astronomy we include the history of astronomy; what has come to be known as archaeoastronomy; and the application of historical records to modern astrophysical problems. Meetings shall be organized to promote adequate discussion among participants and shall attempt to provide a forum for discussion of recent developments in these areas. The Division will assist the Society in the commemoration of important historical anniversaries and in the archival preservation of current materials of importance to future historians of astronomy."

These bylaws went to the AAS Council at their meeting in the summer of 1979, along with a request for the formation of a new division.

The Council determined that it was necessary first to appoint an organizing committee; they selected Eddy, Brecher, Gingerich (as chair), P. Morrison, R. Berendzen, and W. Sullivan. This group reworked the bylaws, adopted them on October 31, 1979, and submitted them to the AAS in November.[5] With a few minor changes in wording to avoid gender bias, the bylaws were adopted by the AAS Council at the San Francisco meeting in January 1980, and the new Division was formally approved. The bylaws specified the election of a Chair, Vice-Chair, and two Council members, each to serve 2-year terms, and a Secretary-Treasurer to serve a 4-year term. Gingerich continued as Chairman *pro tem* of the Division until an election could be held, and Brecher was Secretary-Treasurer. Brecher's first official duty was the letter soliciting members, quoted above.

In early November 1980, Gingerich sent a letter to all those who had joined by that time, inviting them to contribute papers for the first meeting of the HAD, scheduled for Monday, January 12, 1981 as part of the Albuquerque AAS meeting. The response was excellent; in addition to nine invited speakers, 11 contributed papers provided for two full sessions. The morning session was devoted to more traditional historical topics, such as Gingerich on Copernicus, W. A. Donahue on Kepler, J. Lankford on photography in America with long-focus refractors, and A. M. Heiser on E. E. Barnard's unpublished treatise on Mars. The afternoon session dealt predominantly with native American archaeoastronomy, and included papers on Fajada Butte (K. Frazier), Skidi Pawnee cosmology (V. Del Chamberlain), and Pueblo Indian sun watching (R. A. Williamson).

Another feature of this first meeting, the first of several such ventures, was a field trip on the Sunday preceding the meeting. Organized by Michael Zeilik, this all-day trip took interested astronomers on a 4-hour drive to Chaco Canyon, where they visited Casa Rinconada and Pueblo Bonito. Many also took the two-mile hike to see the Penasco Blanco pictograph of the 1054 supernova. All who participated agreed that this was a very successful outing, and boded well for the future of the HAD.

In December 1980, a mail ballot had been sent to the membership, and the first elected officers took over at the January 1981 meeting: Eddy as Chair, Gingerich as Vice-Chair, and J. B. Carlson and D. H. DeVorkin as members of the HAD Council. Brecher continued as Secretary-Treasurer. These officers planned the second HAD meeting in conjunction with the AAS at Boulder, Colorado, in January 1982. Since that time, the Division has met at least once a year, for a total of 23 times, as of early 1998.

From its inception the HAD has considered itself somewhat different from the other divisions of the AAS, since its interests are not directly scientific. Its membership includes not only astronomers who belong to the parent society, but also affiliate members from areas including the history of science, anthropology, and archaeology. At present these members are listed in the AAS directory, may present papers, and may vote in Division elections, but may not hold office. The HAD also negotiated with the AAS, in the Division's early years, so that members presenting a scientific paper might also present a paper in a HAD session. The usual AAS time limit of five minutes for oral papers was also increased to ten minutes for contributed HAD papers. HAD sessions at AAS meetings have been popular with other members of the AAS, who frequently come to hear the oral papers and sometimes to contribute their own recollections on more recent topics.

The Colorado meeting in 1982 included a special workshop on "The Use of Archaeoastronomy in Astronomy Teaching," chaired by John Carlson and Von Del Chamberlain. This was the first of a number of topical sessions held at HAD meetings. In addition to this workshop there were three sessions of invited and contributed papers: one on archaeoastronomy, one on general historical topics, and one on modern history. Owen Gingerich presented an invited AAS lecture on "The Galileo Affair in Contemporary Perspective." Every few years since then, an invited talk by a Division member to the full Society has taken place, and these have been well-attended by AAS members.

Archaeoastronomy continued to be a focus of the Division, and most meetings through 1990 had one session whose principal focus was on this area. But the topic was controversial, and in 1993 at the Phoenix meeting there was a special afternoon session on critical problems in archaeoastronomy. A panel discussion included archaeoastronomers and a professional archaeologist, and the exchanges among panelists and members of the audience were lively and provocative. A consensus grew that those interested in this area need to communicate better with the archaeological community, which by and large does not think archaeoastronomy deals with questions that they care about. Archaeologists are interested in what they can learn about cultures and societies from the available evidence; they are less interested in whether ancient people observed the sky but in how this activity influenced their society. Some archaeoastronomical research, particularly concerning the possible alignments of buildings or tombs towards astronomically significant directions, is seen by archaeologists (and many others) as on the fringe of legitimate interpretation of the evidence. If archaeoastronomers are to be taken seriously, they need to persuade archaeologists that they have something important to contribute, and they need to present their work in the language of archaeology in order to do this.[6]

The energetic discussions led Steven Dick, HAD Chair in 1993, to appoint an Archaeoastronomy Committee to facilitate communication with other disciplines. This committee has been largely inactive, although its new chair, David Diadevaia, hopes to revitalize it.[7] Since 1993, archaeoastronomy has been conspicuous by its absence in HAD paper sessions. Efforts to find an archaeoastronomer willing to run for a position on the HAD Council have also proven unsuccessful. It is not clear what the future of this subject and its role in the Division may be.

The HAD officers considered, almost from the beginning, the possibility of holding occasional meetings at places and times that were not connected with an AAS meeting, although there was concern that not enough members would be able to come, given the exigencies of funding for travel. By 1992, however, they decided to try it, and the HAD held a special joint meeting with the Division for Dynamical Astronomy (DDA), at Chicago's Adler Planetarium. (This was an effort at furthering relations with other divisions.) The meeting was a resounding success. The DDA held a day of papers of its own, followed by two days of primarily HAD papers; the latter covered topics ranging from archaeoastronomy to early twentieth century computer technology. A total of about 60 people attended, with about 25 from the HAD. Chairman John Lankford noted that attendees could "listen to a series of invited and contributed papers and engage in informal discussions, unconstrained by the pressures of the larger AAS meeting."[8] In addition, participants had the chance to visit the fine collection of astrolabes at the Adler Planetarium, as well as other exhibits on early navigation. A banquet at the planetarium topped off the events.

The following year another meeting was held separately from the AAS, at the Huntington Library in San Marino, California. This took place a few days after the AAS meeting in Berkeley in June 1993. On June 13 some 25 people participated in a tour of the Mount Wilson Observatory, including the historic 100-inch Hooker telescope and

TABLE 1. *HAD Officers.*

	Chair	Vice-Chair	Secretary-Treasurer	Council
1980	Owen Gingerich			Kenneth Brecher Richard Berendzen John Eddy Woody Sullivan Philip Morrison
1981–83	John Eddy	Owen Gingerich	Kenneth Brecher	John Carlson David DeVorkin
1983–85	Owen Gingerich	Edwin Krupp	Kenneth Brecher	Brian Marsden Spencer Weart
1985–87	Edwin Krupp	Donald Osterbrock	David DeVorkin	Katherine Bracher Von Del Chamberlain
1987–89	Donald Osterbrock	Katherine Bracher	David DeVorkin	Arthur Hoag Barbara Welther
1989–91	Katherine Bracher	John Lankford	David DeVorkin	Ruth Freitag Woody Sullivan
1991–93	John Lankford	Steven Dick	David DeVorkin	Dorrit Hoffleit Peggy Kidwell
1993–95	Steven Dick	Woody Sullivan	LeRoy Doggett	Ronald Brashear Sarah Schechner Genuth
1995–97	Woody Sullivan	David DeVorkin	LeRoy Doggett[1] Thomas Hockey	Richard Walker Barbara Welther
1997–99	David DeVorkin	Virginia Trimble	Thomas Hockey	Barbara Becker Kevin Krisciunas

[1] Died April 1996.

the solar telescopes. On June 14 and 15, three sessions were held at the Huntington. Owen Gingerich gave an invited paper on Copernicus' *De Revolutionibus* in retrospect; Gale Christianson gave an invited talk on Edwin Hubble at Oxford; and the contributed talks dealt with some of the early work at Mount Wilson, as well as other topics. An exhibit at the Library entitled "Constructing the Heavens: 450 Years of Astronomy" drew the rapt attention of the 50 participants. This marked only the second time the Division had met in a location distinctly separate from the full AAS meeting; but attendance was good and interest was high, due to the appeals of both the Huntington Library and the proximity of Mount Wilson.

In addition to these events, it has become quite common for the HAD to schedule a special session on a day immediately prior to the regular AAS session. This practice began with an invitation to hold a special session at the National Air and Space Museum in Washington, D.C., on Saturday, June 9, 1984, two days before the AAS meeting in Baltimore. Members were able to visit the Museum early in the morning, before it was open to the public and before the paper sessions began. Talks in the morning focused primarily on American astronomy, while those in the afternoon ranged more widely. A reception in the late afternoon at the Smithsonian's Museum of American History allowed members to see some of the historical astronomical instruments on display there. On Sunday morning, a number of visitors participated in a tour of the old Naval Observatory; then members made their own way to Baltimore, where sessions resumed on Monday. Since that auspicious beginning, special sessions have usually taken place whenever a local host or a member of the local organizing committee has invited us.

Among these special sessions, one which stands out was entitled "Astronomy and the State: US and CIS Perspectives," and was held in Washington on January 11, 1994. This session grew out of a concern expressed to the AAS as early as 1992: that astronomers in the former Soviet Union needed help. Severe funding cuts due to major economic problems in the former Soviet republics had led to the cancellation of astronomical journal subscriptions in all Russian libraries, and the Soviet Astronomical Society asked for assistance from the AAS. The result was a committee which solicited money from AAS members to support a small grant program in the former Soviet Union; this plea resulted in some $47,000 being collected in just a few months.

Robert McCutcheon of the HAD brought the plight of Russian historians of science to the Division's attention, and an International Relations Committee was appointed to determine what the Division could do. The special paper session grew out of this as the organizing committee sought funds to support the participation of four historians from the former Soviet Union. Thanks to grants from the Smithsonian and from the International Research and Exchanges Board, three were able to do so (the fourth had a visa problem). Alina Eremeeva outlined the repression of Russian astronomers in the 1930s, the arrests of many, and the 1937 execution of B. P. Gerasimovich, director of the Pulkovo Observatory. Alexander Gurshtein described the postwar rebuilding of Pulkovo as a symbol of the importance of science to Communism, and he lamented that no one was doing oral history interviews in Russia, due in part to a lack of the necessary equipment. Victor Abalakin gave an invited talk to the full AAS; he described KGB documents which indicated the fates of astronomers "purged" under the Stalin regime, and discussed the difficulties Russian scientists had in obtaining visas for international meetings. In addition to the Russian historians, several Americans gave talks on the politics of U.S./Soviet astronomy in the 1950s (Ron Doel) and on other aspects of political repression and state support for astronomy.[9]

In another special session in June 1990, the HAD met at the University of Michigan's 1854 Detroit Observatory, which was being restored. On the afternoon before the regular AAS meeting, five invited talks were presented in the Observatory, related to the Observatory and to astronomy at the University of Michigan; these drew about 25 members of the Division. The Observatory's 12-inch Fitz refractor and a beautiful meridian circle by Pistor and Martins were featured attractions. Special sessions have also been held in Seattle (1991) on "The Opening of the Electromagnetic Spectrum," in Tucson (1995) on "History in Astronomy Education," and in Washington, D.C. (1990) on "National Observatories," among others.[10]

The Historical Astronomy Division has had several important issues to which it has devoted time and energy. An early concern, raised in 1981, was the preservation of historical astronomical materials for the use of future historians. In particular, many observatory publications from the late nineteenth and early twentieth centuries are deteriorating due to the acid in the paper on which they were printed. The Division expressed an interest in seeing this material preserved, perhaps on microfilm; but this would cost money. A subcommittee of the HAD, consisting of David DeVorkin and Brenda Corbin, was appointed to look into this matter. This Committee on Preservation produced a report which was sent to members in November 1982, and the issue was discussed at the business meeting of the HAD in January 1983 in Boston and also in June 1984 in Baltimore. The Committee identified sources of about $25,000 for microfilming; but noted that this was not enough to begin such a large project. Several HAD members also pointed out that new electronic technologies for copying materials seemed to be imminent, and that it might be wise to wait and see what developments occurred on this front. The Division concurred with this at its 1984 meeting.

Since that report, progress has been slow. It seems now that the most effective way to deal with much of this material will be to preserve it electronically; but there is little consensus yet on the proper electronic format. Most historians and archivists still prefer microfilm whereas astronomers believe in electronic storage. An informal consortium of members from such organizations as NASA and the Smithsonian Astrophysical Observatory is pursuing the project of scanning observatory reports, but the work has not yet begun. The HAD has continued to write endorsements for this cause, and Brenda Corbin is particularly active in working with those who are interested.

Perhaps the most visible of HAD projects, to the AAS membership at large, has been the publication of obituaries of astronomers in the *Bulletin* of the AAS (BAAS). This program, first suggested by John Lankford in 1984,[11] was proposed again in 1989 by Steve Dick and others, who pointed out that there was no longer any mechanism for noting the passing of members of the astronomical community. Well-known figures would of course have obituaries in such places as *Physics Today*; but astronomers of lesser renown might pass from the scene unnoticed. This presents a problem for future historians who may be interested not just in the seminal figures but in what the rest of the astronomical community was doing. At the January 1989 meeting in Boston, an *ad hoc* committee chaired by Dick was appointed to look into this matter and make recommendations.

A year later, at the January 1990 meeting in Washington, Dick's committee recommended that obituary notices should be published in the *BAAS*. They also encouraged members to support the program when they responded to the AAS Survey which had been distributed to all the program members. The *Bulletin* seemed the appropriate place for such accounts to appear, since it is the official journal of record for the AAS; it was anticipated that no more than 25 pages or so annually would be devoted to obituaries. The committee further recommended that page charges should be waived for this purpose, and they suggested that the HAD could provide assistance, perhaps in the form of an editorial board for obituaries. The HAD membership endorsed these recommendations to the AAS Council.

The AAS Council accepted the idea and voted that the HAD should establish a committee to oversee the task of producing these obituaries for the BAAS, with page charges to be covered by the AAS. When this was announced at the Philadelphia meeting in January 1991, the Division voted to set up an Obituary Editorial Board chaired by the HAD Vice-Chair, including two HAD members, plus a member appointed by the editor of the BAAS and another by the president of the AAS. Obituaries would be published for all deceased AAS members, and they might range from a brief notice to as much as two pages, the length to be determined by the Board.

The first set of obituaries appeared in 1992 for 14 astronomers, including William A. Hiltner, John S. Hall, and Harlan J. Smith. In 1996 the obituaries recorded the passing of 22 astronomers, including S. Chandrasekhar and Gerard de Vaucouleurs, but also outstanding teachers, such as Sarah J. Hill and Robert Chambers, and long-time AAVSO Director Margaret W. Mayall. This service to the astronomical community has been welcomed by many astronomers both outside and inside the HAD.

In 1994, Woodruff Sullivan proposed establishing a HAD Prize for work in the history of astronomy, broadly interpreted. After a few years of talking about it, such a Prize was approved by the members at the HAD business meeting in San Antonio in 1996. This Prize is to be granted biennially, to an individual who has significantly influenced the field of the history of astronomy, either by a recent publication or by a career-long effort. Soon after the Prize was approved, the HAD suffered a grievous loss in the death of its Secretary-Treasurer and long-time active member, LeRoy Doggett, of the U.S. Naval Observatory. A generous donation in Doggett's memory became the initial endowment for the HAD Prize, which was then renamed the LeRoy E. Doggett Prize for Historical Astronomy. A Prize Committee was appointed to make the selection, and the first Doggett Prize was awarded in 1998 to Curtis Wilson.

Another of the Division's interests has been the commemoration of significant anniversaries in astronomical history. The first such occasion was the sesquicentennial of the Harvard College Observatory and the centennial of the Smithsonian Astrophysical Observatory, which were celebrated by a joint symposium in Cambridge on January 7, 1989. A full day of invited papers on the topic "Astronomy at Cambridge" was held at the Harvard College Observatory, attended by approximately 150 people. Three sessions dealt with Harvard's many contributions to astronomy, including the Pickering and Shapley eras, the women who worked for them, and Harvard-encouraged projects such as the American Association of Variable Star Observers and *Sky & Telescope* magazine. An afternoon session covered the founding and early years of the Smithsonian Astrophysical Observatory in Washington and its subsequent move to

Figure 1. (l to r) Ruth Freitag of the Library of Congress, whose exhaustive bibliographies in the HAD Newsletter have been so valuable; Katherine Bracher, HAD chair from 1989 to 1991, and Cynthia W. Shelmerdine. All photographs on this page were taken at the Phoenix/Tempe meeting, January 1993 at a surprise party to celebrate David DeVorkin's retirement from eight years as HAD Secretary/Treasurer. Much of the celebration (on DeVorkin's part) was due to the fact that LeRoy Doggett was the incoming Secretary/Treasurer! Photograph by Tom Williams.

Figure 2. (l to r) David DeVorkin; John Lankford, (HAD Chair, 1991 to 1993); Steve McCluskey, guru for the history of astronomy listserv HASTRO-L; and LeRoy Doggett, Secretary Treasurer from 1993 to 1995. Photograph by Tom Williams.

Figure 3. (l to r) Steve Dick, HAD Chair from 1993 to 1995; Virginia Trimble, HAD Chair, 1999–2001; Dorrit Hoffleit of Yale; and Robert McCutcheon, Chair of the International Relations Committee of the HAD. Photograph by Tom Williams.

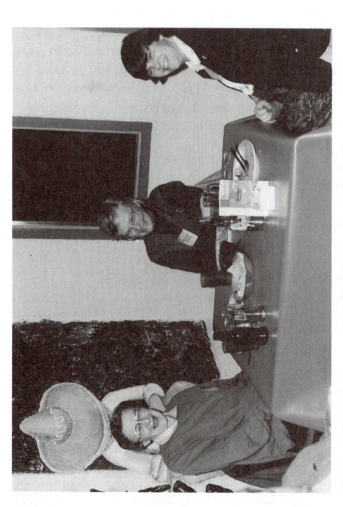

Cambridge.[12] In connection with the meeting, receptions on the afternoon of January 8 opened two special exhibits celebrating astronomy on the Harvard campus. A display at the Pusey Library showed letters and early astronomical photographs from the Archives related to astronomy at Harvard since colonial days. At the Science Center the curator of Historical Scientific Instruments presented an array of astronomical clocks and instruments for time-keeping.

Most recently, the HAD has been involved in planning for the centennial of the AAS, to occur in 1999. On the HAD's recommendation, the AAS appointed a Centennial Committee chaired by Donald Osterbrock (a former HAD Chair); this Committee came up with several ideas, including the present volume on the history of the AAS' first century. HAD member Sara Schechner Genuth led another effort, to arrange a historical exhibit for the 1999 Chicago AAS meeting, which might then travel around the country to other astronomical centers. Historical talks at the meeting, and a probable field trip to the Yerkes Observatory, are also being planned. The HAD is actively involved in all these efforts.

The HAD Newsletter, which has appeared three or four times a year since 1985, has been the Division's principal means of communicating with its members concerning meetings, dues, elections, etc. However, it has included other material as well. By far the most valuable part, in the view of many historians of astronomy, is the series of bibliographies prepared by Ruth Freitag of the Library of Congress. The first of these appeared in April 1988 and listed recent books and articles related to the

TABLE 2. *HAD Meetings.*

1.	Jan 12, 1981	Albuquerque, NM
2.	Jan. 11–12, 1982	Boulder, CO
3.	Jan. 10–11, 1983	Boston, MA
4.	June 9–11, 1984	Washington, DC/Baltimore, MD
5.	Jan. 14–15, 1985	Tucson, AZ
6.	Jan. 5–6, 1986	Houston, TX
7.	Jan. 8–9, 1987	Pasadena, CA
8.	Jan. 10–11, 1988	Austin, TX
9.	Jan 7–9, 1989	Cambridge/Boston, MA; joint symposium Jan. 7 and 8 to celebrate HCO sesquicentennial and SAO centennial
10.	June 11–12, 1989	Ann Arbor, MI
11.	Jan. 13–14, 1990	Washington, DC
12.	Jan. 14, 1991	Philadelphia, PA
13.	May 26–27, 1991	Seattle, WA
14.	Jan. 13, 1992	Atlanta, GA
15.	June 4–6, 1992	Chicago, IL (with DDA)
16.	Jan. 3–4, 1993	Phoenix, AZ
17.	June 10, 1993	Berkeley, CA
	June 14–15, 1993	San Marino, CA
18.	Jan. 11–12, 1994	Washington, DC
19.	Jan. 8–9, 1995	Tucson, AZ
20.	June 1995	Pittsburgh, PA
21.	Jan. 14–15, 1996	San Antonio, TX
22.	Jan. 12–13, 1997	Toronto, ON
23.	Jan. 1998	Washington, DC
24.	June 1998	San Diego, CA (Palomar)
25.	June 1999	Chicago, IL (Yerkes)

Figure 4. Owen Gingerich at the August 1988 International Astronomical Union Symposium on the Teaching of Astronomy at Williams College. Photograph by A. Fraknoi.

history of astronomy. Since that time the bibliography has been a regular feature of most Newsletters, and has grown from three pages in 1988 to 22 pages in 1996. Articles in languages ranging from English and French to Polish, Russian, and Chinese are included, sometimes with a one-sentence summary; topics span millennia from ancient Egypt to modern times. For anyone planning a historical project, Ruth's bibliography is now an indispensable resource.

Another recent feature of the Newsletter is a column entitled "Class Notes," in which various authors have set forth brief anecdotes suitable for use in teaching classes which include historical material. In the first of these, in November 1993, David DeVorkin discussed the Indian astrophysicist Meghnad Saha. Others have dealt with Hertzsprung and Russell, with the naming of the satellites of Jupiter and Saturn, and with Kepler's laws. The Division actively recruits members to contribute such columns from time to time.

The Historical Astronomy Division has had a strong and dedicated membership of between 200 and 300 for its 18 years of existence. It seems that many astronomers (particularly as they get older) develop an interest in the history of their science, and some pursue it actively as a secondary research area. The opportunity to interact with professional historians of science is a very valuable one, for both astronomers and historians, and the diverse membership of the Division makes this possible. We look forward to even more cross-disciplinary work, with an increased interest in the uses of historical astronomy in education as well as in archaeology, ethnographic and international studies, and other areas limited only by one's imagination.

PART 8

COMMENTARY BY RECENT AAS PRESIDENTS

Prioritizing Science: A Story of the Decade Survey for the 1990s[1]

John N. Bahcall

What are the most important aspects of the universe to explore? What are the best ways to make discoveries in astronomy and astrophysics? These are tough questions because researchers have many different approaches, and it is usually not clear, until the most interesting problems are solved, which method will yield the most important results. Individual astronomers present strong arguments for many potential approaches that require federal funding.

We are well into an era of limited research budgets, however, and choices have to be made. We astronomers have recognized that if we do not set our own priorities, then funding agencies and congressional officials will do it for us, and will do it less well. Moreover, we have learned over the years that the process of trying to convince colleagues in different specialties both improves our projects and provides a broader and more reliable basis for support.

The Decade Survey of Astronomy and Astrophysics for the 1990s gave specific answers to the hard questions of what to fund and, by implication, what to cut. Working under the auspices of the National Research Council, we astronomers — acting as a community — recommended funding for a limited number of initiatives, ranked in order of priority. Only one out of every ten highly promising initiatives survived this rigorous selection.

We have been spectacularly successful in getting a very large fraction of our recommendations implemented, as can be seen from the tables that are collected near the end of this article. The tables summarize the fate of the projects we ranked highly.

In this article, I will describe, from my perspective as chairman of the survey committee for the 1990s, how we came to a consensus on what to recommend. I hope that an understanding of our experience may be useful in future surveys.

THE SURVEY COMMITTEE

The group charged with setting priorities, the Astronomy and Astrophysics Survey Committee, was established by the National Research Council (NRC) in May 1989, following my appointment as chair in February 1989. The membership of the committee is shown in Table 1. The report of the committee, *The Decade of Discovery in Astronomy and Astrophysics*, was published in March 1991 by the National Academy Press.

The first step was to find an outstanding group of scientists who were willing to sacrifice a significant part of their research time in order to serve on the committee. I spent most of the months between February and May 1989 talking to hundreds of

TABLE 1. *Astronomy and Astrophysics Survey Committee.*

John N. Bahcall	Institute for Advanced Study, Chair
Charles A. Beichman	Institute for Advanced Study, Executive Secretary
Claude Canizares	Massachusetts Institute of Technology
James Cronin	University of Chicago
David Heeschen	National Radio Astronomy Observatory
James Houck	Cornell University
Donald Hunten	University of Arizona
Christopher F. McKee	University of California, Berkeley
Robert Noyes	Harvard-Smithsonian Center for Astrophysics
Jeremiah P. Ostriker	Princeton University Observatory
William Press	Harvard-Smithsonian Center for Astrophysics
Wallace L. W. Sargent	California Institute of Technology
Blair Savage	University of Wisconsin
Robert W. Wilson	AT&T Bell Laboratories
Sidney Wolff	National Optical Astronomy Observatories

astronomers about potential members who might serve on the advisory panels of the survey and on the executive committee (hereafter, the survey committee). I also wrote to the chair of every astronomy department in the U.S., as well as to many other prominent astronomers, requesting nominations. I invited each person to suggest themes and questions for the study. In addition, I wrote to a number of distinguished astronomers abroad asking about astronomical programs in their countries and requesting advice about possible international collaborations.

I filled nearly all of a looseleaf notebook with comments made by astronomers about the judgment and vision of their colleagues. (I later put this notebook into a secure trash can out of respect for the confidential nature of these conversations.) After many conversations, consistent pictures emerged. Some astronomers and astrophysicists were always mentioned with the highest respect by the people with whom they worked. These were the scientists we wanted to serve and, with only two exceptions out of our first 15 choices, nearly everyone I asked agreed to make the required personal sacrifice.

I am convinced that the unanimity which was achieved among astronomers in support of our recommendations was due in large part to the scientific distinction and judgment of my colleagues on the committee. In retrospect, I believe I could have assembled a different committee of 15 people with approximately equal scientific qualifications. But, I am certain that I could not have improved significantly upon the high level of respect of the astronomical community for the achievements and insights of the committee members. This respect was our most important asset.

The 15 members of the survey committee were nominated by the appropriate committees of the NRC and were appointed by Frank Press, the chairman of the NRC and the president of the National Academy of Sciences. The survey committee contained six members of the NAS, two Nobel Prize winners, and two directors of national observatories. In addition to the committee itself, Frank Press took an active role in supporting and representing the work of the decade committee within Washington. (For astronomers not familiar with Frank's past, I note that he is a distinguished geophysicist and a former national science adviser to President Carter. Throughout the survey, Frank provided immediate access, strong support, and valuable guidance and insights.)

I believe that the most important decision we made as a survey committee was to base our recommendations on scientific merit, independent of political considerations. We had credibility as scientists judging science. We did not have special expertise in guessing which way the political winds would blow. Early in the survey process, some individuals who worked for a federal agency tried to tutor us in the best political strategies, but I do not remember a single case in which these tutorials were repeated after we made clear that we were limiting the criteria for our prioritization to scientific merit. I believe that our insistence in judging only science greatly simplified our task and contributed to the lasting value of the survey report.

If I could made just one recommendation to future participants in decade surveys, it would be: "Stick to the science." Other committees and studies are charged with the responsibility for devising the best possible strategy for implementing science priorities in a timely way. Only the decade committee is charged with setting science goals.

WASHINGTON VISITS

Prior to the formation of the survey committee, Frank Press and I visited major agency heads and congressional and administration leaders in order to obtain their advice on what issues the report should address and in what form the results should be presented. I did not ask for support of any projects on these "get-acquainted" visits, but I did hope to create a favorable climate for future consideration of astronomy initiatives. I also did not ask what answers would be politically most desirable. Participants in the survey were encouraged to solicit facts from agency and administration authorities, but we evaluated ideas and initiatives independently and in confidence. Agency leaders, congressional staffers, senior people at the Office of Management and Budget, and the President's science adviser (who had gone through a similar experience as chair of a previous NRC decade survey for physics) all provided valuable advice.

The consultations in Washington ultimately resulted in several important sections of the final report: a chapter on the lunar initiative (requested by the Administrator of NASA); a chapter on high speed computing (suggested by the Director of NSF); an emphasis on priorities for technology in this decade that will lead to science in the next decade (proposed by the Deputy Administrator for Space Science of NASA); recommendations of what astronomers should do *pro bono* to help with the crisis in education (requested by Dick Mallow, then a senior Congressional staffer and now a senior AURA officer); an examination of the technical heritage of proposed initiatives (requested by people at OMB); realistic estimates of the costs for each of the new projects; a chapter on astronomy as a national asset; an examination of the role of American astronomy in the international context with some guidelines for assessing when international collaborations would be fruitful; and thumb-nail sketches of major projects that could be used conveniently by staffers helping to draft legislation. Where I have not made specific attributions, similar suggestions were made by several different people we visited.

THE PANELS

The first task of the survey committee was to select the chairs of 15 advisory panels for different subdisciplines, based on discussions with astronomers of different specialties at institutions throughout the country. The survey committee decided that the subject matter covered by the different panels should reflect the subdivisions that astronomers generally use in identifying their specialties, especially the wavelength or technique used to make astronomical observations. It would have been more logical to have organized the panels along scientific goals, independent of wavelength or technique, but I am convinced that the more logical organization would have been less effective. The similar viewpoints and experiences that were shared by people within a given technical subdivision of astronomy made it easier to reach a scientific consensus. The survey committee was responsible for integrating the advice by the different discipline panels and formulating the highest priority science program.

Future decade surveys may well choose to organize themselves differently. The revolutionary opportunities provided by, for example, the VLA, the HST, COBE, x-ray satellites, and the Keck telescopes have all forced astronomers to realize that in order to solve scientific problems they have to use different techniques. Many of the younger astronomers now identify themselves in terms of the scientific problems they work on rather than the techniques they use to solve problems. I think this is a healthy development.

Table 2 lists the chairs of our panels. In choosing the panel chairs, the survey committee again used scientific distinction and widely respected judgment as the primary selection criteria, but we also took account of the necessity of obtaining expert advice about the major research fields and techniques.

TABLE 2. *Astronomy and Astrophysics Survey Panels.*

Panel	Chair
Astronomy as a National Asset	Virginia Trimble
Computing and Data Processing	Larry Smarr
High Energy from Space	Bruce Margon
Infrared Astronomy	Frederick Gillett
Interferometry	Stephen Ridgway
Optical/IR from Ground	Stephen Strom
Particle Astrophysics	Bernard Sadoulet
Planetary Astronomy	David Morrison
Policy Opportunities	Richard McCray
Radio Astronomy	Kenneth I. Kellermann
Science Opportunities	Alan Lightman
Solar Astronomy	Robert Rosner
Status of the Profession	Peter B. Boyce
Theory and Laboratory Astrophysics	David N. Schramm
UV-Optical from Space	Garth Illingworth
Working Group on Astronomy from the Moon	Charles A. Beichman and John N. Bahcall

The panel chairs and the survey committee jointly selected 300 people for the advisory groups. The members of these groups had a high level of scientific achievement and also represented different research approaches, different kinds of institutions, and different geographical areas. The survey committee itself considered projects that spanned more than one subfield or which fell between the assigned responsibilities of the panels.

The panels met at different sites in the U.S. in order to help stimulate wide participation by the astronomical community. I also wrote to each of the panel members and asked them to solicit the views of colleagues at their home institutions. Local discussions of issues in individual astronomy and physics departments generated valuable ideas and helped consolidate support for the final recommendations of the Decade Survey.

Much of the difficult work of the survey was done within the panels. The panel chairs (*see* Table 2) were forced to exercise tact, scientific insight, and organizational skills. Scientists from groups that had traditionally worked in competition with each other had to develop unified recommendations. Perhaps the most difficult task, brilliantly achieved, was to form a consensus set of recommendations within the optical and infrared community (Chair, Steve Strom). The lack of consensus in this community had frustrated attempts to obtain some needed major facilities in preceding surveys.

The panels began their technical work with essays submitted by individual panel members on what they identified as the most important issues or projects. After the essays were discussed, there were presentations by panel members or by invited outside experts on all the significant questions that were to be included within the text of the panel's report. A core group within each panel wrote the initial draft of the report, which was then iterated within the panel and then commented on by members of the survey committee.

The most intense discussions in the first nine months of the survey occurred within the panels. In order to ensure good communication between the panels and the survey committee, each member of the survey committee served as the vice-chair of one of the panels. This arrangement worked well, keeping the survey committee apprised of ideas as they developed and enabling each panel to understand the goals and procedures of the full survey.

Because of their special responsibilities, two of the panels operated differently from the others. The beautiful non-technical chapters on "Science Opportunities" and on "Astronomy as a National Asset" were written almost entirely by the relevant panel chairs (Alan Lightman and Virginia Trimble, *see* Table 2), with advice and comments from their panel members. We were fortunate to have in charge of these activities accomplished research astronomers who are also outstanding writers.

The survey committee avoided many potential problems by deciding that the panel reports would be advisory, rather than part of the findings of the survey, and that the reports would not be refereed by either the survey committee or by the NRC. The recommendations of the panels were not binding on the survey committee, but the panel reports contain important technical information, as well as detailed arguments advocating specific initiatives. The reports of the panels were published separately from, but simultaneously with, the full survey report by the National Academy Press under the title *Working Papers: Astronomy and Astrophysics Panel Reports.*

DEVELOPING A CONSENSUS

I believe that it was essential, in forming a consensus, to involve the community as much as possible. The survey was organized so that every astronomer who had something to say had an opportunity to be heard. Open discussions were held at AAS meetings and at several other professional society meetings. In January 1990, at the Washington, D.C. meeting of the AAS, nearly 1000 astronomers participated in open sessions that involved all 15 of the panels. The names of the survey committee members and of the chairs of the panels were published in the AAS *Newsletter*, along with remarks encouraging individual astronomers to present their ideas directly to survey committee members, panel chairs, or panel members.

Establishing the recommendations of the survey took 14 months, about a year less than was projected. The committee worked efficiently because we were busy scientists eager to get back to our research, because we had effective leadership and support from the NRC (Robert L. Riemer) and from the Executive Secretary of the survey (Chas Beichmann), and because we were the first decade survey to be able to rely on fax and e-mail communications for many of our discussions and iterations of texts. The survey committee also held six meetings at astronomical centers throughout the country.

I was surprised by one thing. Veterans of similar activities assured me that there would be a difficult and tense period of bargaining before we agreed on the final recommendations. This never happened. I believe the reason is that the committee judged the initiatives on the basis of scientific potential, without regard to political considerations.

The list of priorities was established by a gradual process that was much easier than any of us anticipated. The committee took straw ballots on three occasions during our regularly scheduled meetings, using as background material the preliminary reports of the advisory panels. The straw ballots focused the discussion on projects that were most likely to be considered important in the final deliberations. As preparation for the final ballot, the committee heard advocacy presentations from the panel chairs. The chairs also participated in discussions of the relative merits of all the initiatives, although the final recommendations were formulated by the survey committee in executive session.

Two strategic decisions helped the committee reach a consensus quickly and smoothly. First, the committee decided that if we failed to reach agreement in July 1990 at the pleasant facilities of the National Academy, within reach of cool Pacific breezes in Irvine, California, then we would meet a month later in the least desirable place in the middle of summer that we could think of, namely, Washington, D.C.

Second, several committee members proposed that I draw up, on the evening before the final voting, a draft list of recommended initiatives in order of priority. They suggested that the committee alter by consensus the draft set of recommendations in order to arrive at the final list of priorities. The proposers hoped that, by this process, the committee could avoid having "winners or losers." I was skeptical of the chances for success when the idea was proposed, but I agreed to try.

Having drawn up a handwritten list of priorities the night before our formal voting, I was surprised the next day at how rapidly we reached a consensus. We began with those equipment categories concerning which we were most in agreement and then worked our way to the more difficult choices. We went around the table, everyone stating their views about what change, if any, needed to be made in the ordered list that we were considering. By the time we had all spoken, the consensus was obvious and we adopted unanimously our priorities in each category.

In times of budgetary crisis, good citizenship also requires fiscal restraint. The survey committee studied approximately ten times as many initiatives as were endorsed, recommending that funding agencies invest in astronomical initiatives according to the scientific priorities established in the survey report.

THE SURVEY REPORT

The 180-page book presenting the recommendations was written in about three months. NRC reports are reviewed carefully. They must meet high standards of logic, of evidence, and of objectivity. In our case, the NRC selected 18 formal referees, in addition to a report review committee. The reviewers were anonymous NAS members and other qualified scientists, in physics, in astronomy, and in other related disciplines. The formal review process was painful, but I answered each review comment, even rhetorical questions, with a specific written response in order that we could complete the review quickly. The 18 referees helped to sharpen our arguments and to clarify our logic, but they did not suggest revisions of our priorities.

Ours was the fourth in a series of decade surveys by astronomers, led by A. Whitford, J. Greenstein, and G. Field, respectively. The highest priority initiatives in each survey were successfully undertaken, encouraging astronomers to submerge parochial interests and focus on the most important initiatives. Would another committee of astronomical experts have recommended a similar set of priorities? I think so, provided that they had also spent a year learning about and comparing all the proposed initiatives in this country and abroad. The report was published under the title *The Decade of Discovery in Astronomy and Astrophysics* by the National Academy Press (1991). It is still available and, I believe, still good reading.

CATEGORIES OF RECOMMENDATIONS

How many categories of recommendations should we have? Should we make separate recommendations for space missions and for ground based projects? Should we have recommendations that prioritized projects independently of the potential funding agency? These were the most hotly debated issues we faced in the survey.

In preliminary discussions, most agency personnel opposed absolute rankings that combined ground and space initiatives, worrying that their top priorities might be adversely affected by ineffectiveness at some other agency. We decided not to yield to these worries and instead created an overall prioritization independent of agency or of technique, because we believed that good citizenship required us to use our scientific expertise to provide the maximum possible guidance to those responsible for making budgetary decisions. We also provided separate recommendations within the categories of space-based projects and ground-based projects. In addition, we decided on a common-sense division of recommendations into Large, Medium, and Small, based upon the financial resources required to achieve the projects.

I believe that our decision to provide an overall prioritization was correct and increased the credibility of the survey report in Congress and in the Executive Branch, particularly at the Office of Management and Budget. Some high ranking agency officials predicted dire consequences for programs under their responsibility if we insisted on prioritizing across the space (NASA) and ground based (NSF, DOE) categories. They feared that their favorite programs would be held hostage to ineffectiveness or budgetary constraints at other agencies. As far as I know, the predicted difficulties did not occur. Recommended programs were not delayed inappropriately because of the competition for higher prioritization between ground-based and space-based projects.

OUR RECOMMENDATIONS AND HOW THEY FARED

What did we recommend? What was achieved? The committee assigned its highest priority for ground-based astronomy to the revitalization of the infrastructure for research, both equipment and people. It is difficult to assess quantitatively the effect of this recommendation for infrastructure support. Unlike new projects which are either funded or not (see Tables 3–5), the support actually achieved for infrastructure has to be judged against what that support would have been in the absence of our recommendation. We can never really know how bad the situation would have been in the absence of a strong statement by the survey committee. Our strong endorsement of infrastructure support has often been cited in discussions within NSF committees and with congressional staffers. Enthusiastic and energetic senior staff members at NSF and NASA, as well as our colleagues on the NRC Astronomy and Astrophysics Committee, have repeatedly used the high priority assigned to infrastructure support in the Decade Survey to argue for the maximum possible resources being directed to astronomy for individual grants and for maintenance of existing equipment.

TABLE 3. *Large Programs.*

Program	Status
Space Infrared Telescope Facility (SIRTF)	√
Infrared-optimized 8-m telescope	√
Millimeter Array (MMA)	+
Southern 8-m telescope	√

My own assessment is that our recommendation for infrastructure support for people and existing equipment was wonderfully successful with NASA (which has become the principal supporter of astronomical sciences in the 1990s) and only modestly successful at NSF. The freedom to redirect resources at NSF was limited in part by the large capital investments for the LIGO (gravity wave detector) and Gemini (northern and southern 8-m telescopes) programs.

Continuing to develop a space program with an improved balance between large and small projects, with emphasis on quicker and more efficient missions, was the

TABLE 4. *Moderate Programs.*

Program	Status
Adaptive optics	√
Dedicated spacecraft for FUSE	√
SOFIA	√
Delta-class Explorer acceleration (SMEX, MIDEX)	√
Optical and infrared interferometers	√
Several shared 4-m telescopes (private)	√
Astrometric Interferometry Mission (AIM)	+
High Resolution Fly's Eye	√
Large Earth-based Solar Telescope (LEST)	0
VLA extension	0

committee's highest priority for space research. This recommendation resonated with the views of the current NASA administrator (Dan Goldin) and has become a theme of the NASA astrophysics program.

I now want to review informally the fate of our priority recommendations for individual projects.

We recommended four Large Programs, which are shown in Table 3. All four of these programs are being developed! In addition, the AXAF observatory, recommended by the previous Decade Survey and strongly supported in our report, is nearing completion. SIRTF is NASA's next premier astrophysical observatory (concentrating on the infrared wavelengths) and has become an important part of the agency-wide Origins program. The two Gemini telescopes, the infrared-optimized 8-m northern telescope and the southern 8-m telescope, are funded through an international collaboration with important leadership provided by the NSF. At the time of this writing, it seems likely that the millimeter array (the MMA) will be included in the president's budget (for 1998) for a three year study leading to construction (provided no insuperable obstacles are encountered). The current status of each of the two Gemini 8-m telescopes is denoted by a check mark to represent the fact that these observatories are in an advanced stage of construction. I have denoted by a plus mark the status of the MMA to indicate that this major facility is currently in the development stage.

Our top six Moderate Programs, shown in Table 4, have all been successfully begun and the status of each one is indicated by a check mark. Our highest priority, adaptive optics, was largely declassified, and we now have access to important developments initiated in connection with national security activities. The civilian agencies have collaborated with the national security agencies in enabling this technology to be developed efficiently for astronomical purposes. We have a dedicated spacecraft for the

TABLE 5. *Illustrative Small Programs.*

Program	Status
Two-micron survey (2μSS)	√
Infrared instruments	√
Cosmic background explorer (MAP, CBI)	√

FUSE ultraviolet mission, and the contractors have been selected to build and fly the SOFIA airborne infrared telescope facility. The ARC and WIYN telescopes (see shared 4-m telescopes in Table 4) are examples of the successful implementation of the recommendation for 4-m telescopes. The high-resolution upgrade for the Fly's Eye has been effectively achieved, and the marvelous extension to the highest energy cosmic rays, the AUGER project (not a mature proposal at the time of the Decade Survey), seems almost certain to occur. I am personally very excited about the astronomy and the physics that will be possible with AUGER.

The intermediate priority Moderate Programs listed in Table 4 have been pursued with significant success. For example, the Astrometric Interferometry Mission (AIM) has been adopted as an ambitious NASA initiative (SIM). Collaborations have been formed and further discussions are underway to establish shared private 4-m and larger telescope consortia. The two Moderate Programs at the lower end of our priority listing, LEST and the VLA extension, were casualties (very much regretted) of the budget stringencies.

I want to recount an illustrative anecdote about Table 4. In the months that followed the release of the Decade Survey, I gave many talks about our recommendations and the exciting science that the recommendations could make possible. I always showed the full versions from the report of Tables 3–5, which included estimates for the cost of each project. I asked the audience during each talk if they noticed anything unusual about Table 4. Almost no one noticed the feature that I found most revealing. But, when I gave a talk to the faculty and trustees of the Institute for Advanced Study, one emeritus professor immediately noticed what I found remarkable. George Kennan, former ambassador to the Soviet Union and a distinguished scholar of Russian Studies, raised his hand and said, "Your highest priority recommendation is by far the least expensive. From all my years in dealing with governments, I cannot remember another example of the least expensive recommendation being the highest ranked." We prioritized according to scientific importance.

The committee recommended that an increased emphasis be given in the astronomy research budget to small and moderate programs. The committee did not prioritize small programs, recognizing that the agencies could use peer review for small initiatives to respond quickly to new scientific or technological developments. However, all three of our Illustrative Small Programs (see Table 5) listed as high priority are under development.

The Microwave Anisotropy Probe (MAP) and the Cosmic Background Imager (CBI) are complementary instruments, one in space (MAP) and one ground-based (CBI), which together will observe anisotropy in the microwave background radiation over angular scales from a few arc minutes to many degrees. I am proud that the Decade Survey helped to facilitate these crucial experiments, which otherwise might have had particular difficulty in obtaining adequate funding.

These are the things that worked for us: enlisting as committee members active research scientists eager to finish the job and get back to their own work; recruiting an effective executive secretary; insisting that the NRC provide adequate budgeting and staff support; having a logical plan and a specific timetable for completing the report; listening to everyone who wanted to be heard; concentrating on issues within the committee's competence, in our case, scientific priorities; having a talented editor

(Susan Maurizi) who could sharpen the final report; and working with a community that believes it is better for astronomers to make imperfect judgments about priorities for astronomy than it is to leave the decisions to Washington administrators.

In the years that have followed the publication of the Decade Survey, I have made many visits to Washington to discuss specific projects with congressional staff and members of Congress, with people from OMB and OSTP, and with senior leaders at NSF, NASA, and DOE. I could get in to talk to these important decision makers and could expect a sympathetic reception because the Decade Survey had a favorable reputation for having set scientific priorities based upon a consensus within the astronomy community. These visits were, I believe, particularly useful in helping to make possible the SIRTF, SOFIA, MMA, and cosmic background explorer projects, to facilitate the declassification of prior DOD work, and to initiate new research on adaptive optics.

PERSONAL REMARKS

I very much enjoyed participating in the Decade Survey. I did not expect to be able to say this when I started, but it is true. I learned a great deal about science and people from the process. Many individuals selflessly pulled together to make the survey a success and I am grateful to each of them for the shared experience.

I was lucky that Jerry Ostriker was also in Princeton. Jerry had unique experience as a major participant in both the Greenstein and the Field Committee decade surveys; he also chaired the project initiation subcommittees that established the Field Committee and our survey. I was not involved in the previous surveys nor with other NRC committees, so it was immensely helpful to me that Jerry understood from the inside how the NRC and the NAS worked. Jerry shared generously his organizational skills and his scientific insights.

I am especially grateful to Chas Beichman, who served both as Executive Secretary and as a member of the survey committee. Chas took leave from his normal research job to become a member of the Institute for Advanced Study for the duration of the survey. The only argument I had with Frank Press during the entire activity of the Decade Survey regarded Chas's presence in Princeton. Frank's initial position was that, according to National Academy rules, the oversight of the survey had to be maintained in Washington within the purview of the NRC. I said if that was the case then I could not serve, because I needed a "second-in-command" in Princeton in order to work efficiently on the survey while continuing my own research. We compromised: Frank found a description of Chas's appointment that allowed him to be in Princeton.

Chas understood the big picture. In addition, he knew exactly what things had to get done, and he made sure that they got done on time. When it was necessary to get the job completed, Chas did whatever background research, writing, or editing that was required. I urge future survey chairs to try to make sure that they have similarly strong support.

I am proud of what the Decade Survey accomplished. We all worked together and our scientific programs were improved because of the collaborations. Our report was welcomed and adopted by the NSF and NASA. It was widely praised in Congress and within the Executive Branch. The media coverage was large and favorable. As a community, we are frequently held up as an example to other groups of what can be accomplished by forming a consensus about scientific priorities. The process and recommendations of our survey were sufficiently persuasive, that we have achieved a surprisingly high fraction of what we proposed (*see* Tables 3–5). And, very important for me, I made a lot of close friends with whom I hope to share many pleasant experiences in the future.

THE CHANGING RESEARCH ENVIRONMENT

Sidney Carne Wolff

INTRODUCTION

As we approach the 100th birthday of the American Astronomical Society (AAS), we have much to celebrate. But while celebration alone may be all that is required for an individual who has reached the century mark, an organization must look forward as well as backward. If the AAS is to complete a second hundred years, we must try to anticipate some of the challenges of the next century.

Astronomers are surely no better at foretelling the future than anyone else. Helen Wright in her biography of George Ellery Hale quotes Simon Newcomb as saying in 1888, "We are probably nearing the limit of all we can know about astronomy." And Hale himself insisted that the new organization that he helped found be named the "Astronomical and Astrophysical Society of America" to ensure that the then young field of astrophysics would not be overlooked. Little could he have anticipated the triumphs of astrophysics over the next century — ranging from the determination of the structure of the Sun from interior to surface in remarkable detail, to the beginnings of an understanding of the evolution of galaxies. Nor could he have imagined the powerful tools that we now use to explore the universe. It is not the large aperture of groundbased telescopes that would have surprised him. In fact, Hale might have thought that we were a little slow in moving to apertures larger than 5 meters, since after all he initiated the effort that led to the world's largest telescope on four separate occasions. What would have been unpredictable a hundred years ago would have been the contributions that have been made by observations outside the optical spectrum, from gamma rays to radio waves, the operation of observatories in Earth orbit, and the visits to other planets in our solar system.

Equally unpredictable would have been the changes in the way we do our science, with the heavy reliance on federal funding rather than nearly complete dependence on private philanthropy; the growth in the number of institutions with strong research and graduate programs in astronomy; the increasing prominence of women in the field; and the advent of electronic publication and dissemination of information.

But the pace of change is accelerating, not slowing. Indeed, many futurists believe that we are in a period of change as profound as the industrial revolution. In such circumstances, we can spend very little time celebrating past achievements. Rather we must understand what values undergird our science and have led to its strength, and try to understand how to maintain those values while incorporating revolutionary changes in the ways we carry out astronomy research. Our goal must be to leave as strong a legacy to those who follow us as Hale and his contemporaries left to us.

THE RESEARCH ENVIRONMENT

What is the role of the AAS in ensuring that we do indeed provide an enduring legacy? As the only astronomical organization that represents our entire community, the AAS has a special responsibility for ensuring that the core values that are the source of our strength as a community are not compromised by the great changes that are in progress. Rather those values must be the basis for defining what is appropriate and beneficial change.

What are those core values? One is the fact we have endeavored to ensure that there are world class facilities in every region of the spectrum that are open to all astronomers on a competitive basis. Indeed, the advent of national observatories has surely been the source of one of the biggest changes over the past one hundred years in the way we conduct research in astronomy — and in who has the opportunity to contribute to that research. Kitt Peak National Observatory will have its 40th anniversary in 1998 and the first groundbreaking at the National Radio Astronomy Observatory occurred a year earlier. The creation of national observatories — in space and on the ground, in all wavelength regions from gamma rays through the optical to the radio region of the spectrum — has made it possible for astronomers to pursue their research based primarily on the quality of their ideas and not on the wealth of the institutions with which they are associated. The fact that forefront astronomy can be pursued in a variety of institutional settings has, in turn, ensured that excellence in astronomy, and hence in astronomy and science teaching, including especially undergraduate teaching, is widely distributed across the country. This distributed excellence is a national asset and one that few other scientific disciplines have managed to emulate to such a strong degree.

A fundamental issue for the community, however, is the extent to which we can maintain merit-based access as facilities become more expensive and budgets tighten. How do we weigh the priorities, such as observing opportunities for a large and distributed astronomical community compared with access to truly state of the art facilities for a few? As Director of one of the national observatories, I wrestle with that issue daily. But what is the role of the AAS in dealing with this and other issues of similar significance that face our community? It seems fairly obvious that the AAS can (almost) never advocate individual projects, since in the constrained budget environment in which we find ourselves, advocacy of one project almost inevitably means lack of support for others, and the AAS must represent all of its members, not merely subsets of them.

Fortunately, astronomy has the well established mechanism of the decade survey committees to establish priorities across the discipline, and openness has also characterized that priority-setting effort. In another article in this volume, John Bahcall describes the process that led to the recommendations for the decade of the nineties by the Astronomy and Astrophysics Survey Committee. Hundreds of astronomers were directly involved in this process, and all AAS members were kept informed of the activities of the Survey Committee and were given an opportunity to provide input. And so in terms of priority-setting, the AAS has traditionally played two roles, providing a forum where issues can be debated and then being an effective advocate for the collective set of priorities that is ultimately recommended.

ISSUES

It is the members of the AAS working as individuals and in teams — not the Society as an organization — that determine research directions and initiatives. Therefore, the AAS has helped to facilitate discussion of the issues being addressed in the decade surveys and in other studies of scientific and public policy but has not directly led the priority-setting efforts. However, most of these studies have looked at *what* should be done but not at *how* the programs might best be carried out in order to ensure that the astronomical community remains strong, diverse, and vibrant. What the AAS itself can uniquely do is concern itself with the environment in which astronomers work and with developing community consensus about the values and goals that should shape that environment.

Over the past several years, the AAS has quite appropriately taken on a more aggressive effort to build better communications with the funding agencies and Congress. These outside groups have a number of questions about activities within the research community, as do we ourselves. Some of the issues that we must confront over the next several years are the following:

1. Do we need to change the nature of graduate education? And, what are we training graduate students for?

Given both the qualitative advance in scientific opportunities offered by the new facilities that will come on-line over the next decade and the fundamental nature of the questions that we ask, astronomy is extremely attractive to young scientists. The number of people wanting to work in the field dramatically exceeds the number of permanent positions available in traditional settings — universities, observatories, and national laboratories. We clearly have a system that provides superb training for research astronomers, and we must preserve that capability. But are we providing equally superb training for the many graduate students who will ultimately be working in non-traditional settings?

The AAS recently sponsored a series of workshops around the country to explore this question. At the session I attended, I was struck by the lack of consensus on what the nature and content of the graduate program should be. One conflict lies in the nature of support; a very large fraction of graduate students are supported by research assistantships that are made available through grants to principal investigators. The availability of support therefore depends on the quality of the research being done by the investigator, not on the quality of the education being provided to the student. To the extent that training in research is what we wish to provide, this system works well. But what if we believe that graduate students should acquire a diverse set of skills to prepare them to work effectively in a variety of non-traditional settings? Should the content of the curriculum then become a factor in deciding which students are supported by federal funds?

Also, what about the expectations concerning outcomes of graduate education? The students attending the AAS workshops seemed for the most part realistic about the job situation, and many were seeking ways to prepare themselves for alternate careers. However, many were receiving the same message I did. When I was a graduate student, I was told that if what I wanted to do was teach in a small college, which was then my goal, I was wasting the time of the faculty. All too many students still receive that message when they try to take time out for an internship in industry or to teach at a community college — that if they do that, they must not really be serious about astronomy. Are faculty being realistic about what their students will face?

What about time scales? As industry representatives at the workshops emphasized, product cycles are becoming ever shorter and the pace at which work must be completed to remain competitive is accelerating. At the same time, the length of time required to complete a Ph.D. is growing ever longer. Should we shorten the time in graduate school? How can that goal be reconciled with providing the diverse set of skills desired by business and industry?

2. How can the AAS support the continued involvement of astronomers who may not be following traditional career paths?

Up until now, AAS activities, including especially its publications and meetings, have been focused on serving professional astronomers. However, a large fraction of people who have received advanced degrees in astronomy are now working in positions where astronomical research may be only a minor part of their activities. At a recent AAS meeting, I had the pleasure of talking to someone working in industry who had used some of her vacation to attend. She was enthusiastically sharing her experiences with others at the meeting and surely opening up new options for students nearing graduation. What do we do to ensure that our meetings are so attractive that colleagues like this will want to attend, even if they have to take vacation time to do so?

According to the first definition in the dictionary, an "amateur" is one that has a marked liking, fondness, or taste. Throughout history, important astronomical research has been carried out by dedicated "amateurs." It is possible that we are on the brink of a new era in which serious research can be carried out at modest cost by people outside the research universities. With the publicly available data archives, including especially the HST archive, and widely available software tools, significant problems can be tackled with only a work station or even a personal computer. New technologies have made 1-m telescopes equipped with science-grade CCDs for precise photometry available at very reasonable cost. What can the AAS do to support the activities of people working in non-traditional settings and to enable the dissemination of their results? And how do we as a community weigh the priorities of supporting these astronomers as compared with, for example, training additional graduate students?

3. What is the right balance between providing observing opportunities for large numbers of astronomers and offering truly world class facilities to fewer researchers?

This question lies at the heart of the conflicting views of the role of the national observatories. For most of the 40 years of its history, NOAO tried to do both — provide access to enough facilities so that most astronomers with competitive ideas had a reasonable chance of obtaining observing time and also to offer facilities that were the best of their type. We can no longer do both, and that is at the root of the painful choices NOAO is being forced to make. I suggest, however, that the community as a whole may also have to make similar choices. At the same time, as we project little or no growth in federal support for astronomical research, the costs of that research have grown dramatically. We are adding large new telescopes at an unprecedented rate. The number of 6.5-m and larger telescopes being built in this decade exceeds the number of 3.5- to 5-m telescopes built over the past 50 years. And these new telescopes must be *active* in order to achieve the best possible image quality. The traditional passive performance of telescopes like the Hale 5-m and the NOAO 4-m telescopes simply cannot produce the ultimate in image quality. The new active telescopes require a higher level of technical support in order to maintain performance at the optimum level. Thus multimillion dollar instruments and adaptive optics systems will become standard.

How are we going to fund these new capabilities when a single instrument or laser guide star system for a single large telescope costs more than half of the annual NSF funding for astronomical instrumentation? Are we building more telescopes than we can afford to operate and instrument at levels that are competitive internationally? After all, the investments per telescope by several other countries in construction,

Figure 1. Members of the AURA Board examine the 4-meter mirror destined for KPNO. The photograph was taken on January 7, 1970. In the Cassegrain hole are (l to r) Albert Hiltner, then President of AURA, N. U. Mayall, and an Owens-Illinois representative. In the background are (l to r) an Owens-Illinois representative, Margaret Edmondson, A. Kieth Pierce, and on the right, the second and fourth figures are Frank Edmondson and Orren Mohler, talking with Owens-Illinois representatives. NOAO photograph, identifications courtesy Frank Edmondson, from his book *AURA and its US National Observatories* (Cambridge, 1997).

operations, and instrumentation are higher than our own. Are we going to have to rely increasingly on private support, thereby reverting to the situation that characterized the first half of this century when forefront astronomy was pursued at only a few wealthy institutions? Should we concentrate our investment in fewer facilities so that a smaller number of astronomers can have access to the best possible capabilities? Or is the science better served if a large number of different people with different ideas and approaches are supported, albeit with equipment that does not always represent the state of the art?

4. How can astronomy and astronomers contribute in a broad sense to improving the society in which we live?

Most of us became astronomers because of our passion for the subject, and we have been rewarded by being able to contribute to a scientific field where advances have been achieved at a truly remarkable rate. However, a rapid pace of change characterizes society as a whole. As citizens, many of us would like to have an impact that extends beyond the profession we have chosen. How can we do that? Education is one obvious role, and astronomy is an excellent vehicle for advancing science education at pre-college, as well as college levels, and also for encouraging scientific literacy. One of the priorities for the AAS during my presidency was to identify resources to enhance its activities in education and to begin to define a program that would help the members to contribute more effectively to education at a broad range of levels. These activities are continuing and being enhanced. One only needs to look at the large attendance at the education sessions at the annual meetings to see how astronomers are strongly committed to contributing to all levels of education. Are there other ways in which we can use our skills as professional astronomers? And what can the AAS do to identify those opportunities?

These are difficult and challenging questions. Where are the answers going to come from? In the final analysis, astronomers themselves must confront these issues. We know that the environment in which we work is changing dramatically, and the challenge is to control that change and our response to it in such a way that the astronomers of the next century have the same remarkable opportunities that characterized the first one hundred years of the AAS. The current period of rapid change presents both new challenges and new opportunities for the AAS as an organization. The Society must take upon itself the leadership role of ensuring that the questions listed above and others like them are confronted forthrightly and openly debated with the goal of forging a consensus about how best to work together to ensure the continued vitality of the whole of the astronomical commity.

OUR CHANGING SOCIETY

Frank H. Shu

The two years, 1995–1996, that I spent as AAS President were a period of great change for the Society. After over two decades on their jobs, both Peter Boyce, the Executive Officer of the Society, and Helmut Abt, the Managing Editor of *The Astrophysical Journal*, were stepping down. In addition, Roger Bell and Bob O'Dell announced their intention not to continue as the Secretary and the Treasurer of the Society once their current terms had run their course. In other words, including my own succession to the post of President, the senior leadership of the AAS would undergo a complete make over in only two years.

Complicating the situation, an initiative had been set into motion for the *ApJ*, and eventually all the AAS journals, to be published electronically. Since the AAS led all other scientific societies in taking this inevitable but still giant step, no one knew what sort of pricing schedule, distributed among page charges and institutional and individual subscription fees, would work. A miscalculation could quickly send the Society to financial ruin because the costs of publishing the journals are such a large percentage (approximately 80%) of the Society's annual budget. Thus, it would be crucial to find people to fill the positions of Executive Officer and Editor-in-Chief (as Helmut Abt's position would eventually be called), who would be able to effect a smooth transition to electronic publishing in an environment where no working model yet existed.

The search committee for Executive Officer, chaired by Sidney Wolff, consisted of the Executive Committee augmented, later, by the President-Elect, Andrea Dupree. An initial pool of applicants for the job was winnowed to six finalists, who were interviewed by the Search Committee in the Washington Office of the AAS in April 1995. From this process emerged the selection of the next Executive Officer of the Society, Bob Milkey, who was then working at the Space Telescope Science Institute in Baltimore. Among his many other organizational skills, Bob came highly recommended for his extensive financial and project management experience. This experience would prove invaluable in the reorganization of the Washington Office and the conversion to electronic publishing. The retention of Peter Boyce as a senior staff member working on electronic publishing and public policy issues ensured that the Washington Office continued to operate in two of its most critical functions without any serious interruptions.

The search committee for the Editor-in-Chief for the reorganized *ApJ*, co-chaired by Jim Hesser and Jim Liebert, had a harder job. Filling Helmut Abt's shoes was a daunting prospect, and several well-qualified candidates removed themselves from consideration in deference to the respect with which they held the incumbent editor. Thus, the choice boiled down to one between hard-earned experience and a proven track record versus a fresh vision and enthusiastic embrace of the possibilities of the age of electronic publishing. In the end, Helmut Abt was appointed as the first Editor-in-Chief, and will continue to edit the *ApJ* through the end of the century as his successor is being sought. To lighten Helmut's workload, six new members were added to the Board of Scientific Editors. This precaution proved prescient when Helmut suffered a heart attack in the midst of the transition period. Because of the reduced number of papers being sent to Tucson for processing, Scientific Editor Anne Cowley could step in and heroically substitute for Helmut during his illness while still handling the manuscripts directed to her office at Arizona State University.

In contrast to this near-traumatic experience, the tasks of replacing Roger Bell and Bob O'Dell went much smoother. A former Secretary of the Society, Arlo Landolt of Louisiana State University, and a former Treasurer of the Society, Len Kuhi of the University of Minnesota, agreed to be nominated for new terms, respectively, as Secretary and Treasurer. Their election, together with that of Andrea Dupree as President, meant that a highly experienced and savvy team would be in place when the older members of the Executive Committee stepped down. Moreover, even after his term as Treasurer officially ended, Bob O'Dell continued to help the Society in its complex efforts to settle the Neeseman bequest, in which a villa in the south of France had been left to the AAS in honor of the memory of Neeseman's father-in-law, Henri Chrétien.

The main new initiative during my tenure as President was an expansion of the educational activities of the Society. In an era of declining public scientific literacy and a shrinking job market in astronomical research, it was clear that the AAS should be doing more at all levels of public and professional science education. An Astronomy Education Policy Board (AEPB) had been established under the co-chairship of Suzan Edwards of Smith College and Steve Strom of the University of Massachusetts to look into the problem and to make recommendations to the Council. The first AEPB report was an ambitious and far-sighted document that recommended a comprehensive reform of the science curriculum from the K–12 levels through the undergraduate and graduate astronomy programs at community colleges, four-year colleges, and research universities. To achieve this reform and to engage the research community in an urgent task vital to the future economic and cultural health of North America, a change in the values of the community needed to occur. Teaching and research needed to be seen as equally valuable contributions, by no means mutually exclusive, of a successful career as a professional astronomer. To help effect this change of values, the AAS would serve as a clearing house, information conduit, and policy forum for discussion and implementation of astronomy education issues. The ability of the AAS to provide these additional services would depend on hiring a full-time paid Education Coordinator, who would report to a reconstituted Education Board and Education Officer. The Board would function in an advisory capacity in a similar way to how the Publications Board provides advice on issues relating to the Society's journals. To pay for the extra costs of these expanded activities, the AEPB, aided by the new Executive Officer Bob Milkey, generated a proposal to the Education Program Office of the National Science Foundation (*see* Fraknoi and Wentzel, this volume, page 194).

Unfortunately, the NSF rejected our proposal. Reviewers criticized the scope of the proposed activities as too broad, and felt that the AAS had minimal experience and a weak track record in education. The reviewers also questioned the commitment of the AAS since it was not devoting much of its own resources to educational issues. The AAS Council rose to the occasion and authorized the funding of a half-time Education Coordinator by increasing membership dues ten dollars per annum. A survey of the membership in 1988 had shown that most members were willing to pay increased dues to support an enhanced education program. The AEPB then narrowed the focus of its study for the first year. A high-level policy discussion on astronomy graduate education was organized for the 1996 winter meeting of the AAS featuring keynote addresses by Bruce Alberts, the President of the National Academy of Sciences, and Neal Lane, the Director of the National Science Foundation. The education policy forum was followed by a series of round-table discussions involving astronomy department chairs around the country. From these discussions emerged a clear consensus that astronomy graduate education in North America should be broadened, so that our graduates would have a fuller range of choices—in industry, in teaching, in science journalism, etc.—than available to them in the more traditional venues of academia, observatories and national laboratories. A formal report of the conclusions drawn from this study was submitted to Council by the AEPB at the 1997 summer meeting of the AAS. In the interim, Doug Duncan of the University of Chicago and Adler Planetarium was hired on a half-time basis as the AAS Education Coordinator and Bruce Partridge was elected as the new AAS Education Officer to replace the outgoing Mary Kay Hemenway. As a result of this effort, the NSF decided that the AAS was indeed serious about its education initiative, and funded the second education proposal submitted to it by Bob Milkey and the AEPB.

By coincidence, at the same AAS Meeting addressed by Bruce Alberts and Neal Lane, Dan Goldin, the Administrator of the National Aeronautics and Space Administration, unveiled his vision for a streamlined NASA. NASA's reorganization plans were driven not only by the new budget realities in Washington, but also by Goldin's vision for space missions motivated by well-defined science goals (for example, those emanating from the theme of astronomical and biological origins). The centerpieces of the space missions to follow those of the Great Observatories would be a new-generation space telescope devoted primarily to the search for primeval galaxies at high redshifts and a space-interferometry mission to find and characterize earthlike planets around other stars.

Generally speaking, the astronomical community has reacted enthusiastically to the new philosophy at NASA of letting the science drive the missions rather than the missions drive the science. This visionary approach comes as a breath of fresh air. Moreover, I believe all astronomers are equally agreed that the specific scientific goals singled out for highest priority in the origins theme—the search for primeval galaxies and extrasolar earthlike planets—are noble objectives that resonate with the deepest human yearnings to understand our own place in the grand scheme of all things. These goals have widespread public support, and they put astronomy and the overall scientific endeavor in a most favorable intellectual light.

Nevertheless, many astronomers, and I count myself among them, are troubled by the possibility of an undesirable side-effect from a too highly focused approach. In the enthusiasm to embrace popular and even lofty goals, we should be careful in our endorsement of what is important science and, by implication, what is not important science. For the overall health of the field, viable levels of research activity should be maintained in all branches of astronomical knowledge. If certain fields—such as high-energy astrophysics or solar physics or stellar astronomy—should receive dramatically lower levels of funding in order to achieve the highest rate of advance in, for instance, cosmology or star and planet formation, then future graduate students are sure to notice and decide not to enter the less fashionable subjects. Without fresh blood, the currently less fashionable fields will wither and die. Their decay can only weaken the fields that flourish because they will miss the all-important cross-fertilization that occurs in those wonderful moments in science when hard-won insights in other, often seemingly obscure, areas suddenly prove crucial for breakthroughs in another specialty. Indeed, I would go so far as to claim that the most important breakthroughs in science are often made by outsiders to a field.

Thus, in the coming years and decades ahead, as the budgetary pressures on the science enterprise continue to mount, I hope that thoughtful astronomers in the most popular areas will willingly forego the chance to maximize the research funding for their own disciplines to allow the survival—at healthy levels—of subjects other than their own. We must avoid the physicists' trap of proclaiming the overarching importance of certain disciplines at the expense of other disciplines. If we follow that elitist path, we will end by defining our subject so narrowly as to leave no ecologically viable niche for *any* astronomer. We must thus be wary of an increasing politicization of science, where opportunists seize the day for the pursuit of personal agendas. As a science, astronomy is still incredibly intellectually robust, with much unexplored territory along many frontiers. Our diverse interests in the great unsolved problems of this

Figure 1. (l to r) Harold Weaver, AAS Treasurer from 1978 to 1987, with Frank Shu, AAS President, 1994–1996. Photograph circa mid-1980s by A. Fraknoi.

immense, complicated, and majestic universe, shared by the general public, is our most enduring strength. We must celebrate and nurture the glory of that diversity and resist all attempts to define worthwhile astronomy as anything less than what it is.

Responsibilities of an American Astronomical Society

Andrea K. Dupree

Astronomy is facing critical, but exciting times. We have impressive scientific results, challenging problems, and a field that can capture the imagination of the public. Yet the environment for astronomy has changed: the political, social, and fiscal climates for the scientific enterprise are not the same as they were decades ago. The modern astronomer faces complex challenges not only in choosing relevant and solvable problems to attack, but finding the support to accomplish the job. One of the primary functions of a modern American Astronomical Society, therefore, is to provide both intellectual and political leadership, both to its members and to society, to address the complexities of modern scientific life. It must seek out the most effective means whereby the entire discipline of astronomy in America is well-served and secure as a vigorous and competitive contributor to human culture and its understanding of the universe.

The AAS remains the principal professional society for astronomers in the United States. It benefits from active participation by members in the Americas, largely Canada and Mexico, as well as a growing membership in Europe and the Far East. As compared with the first years of the Society, the activities of the modern AAS are enormously diverse. It now manages world-class journals, holds large and sophisticated meetings, supports effective employment services, maintains subdisciplinary scientific divisions and allied issue-oriented groups, oversees programs and committees for special activities, encourages education and public outreach, and, evermore critical on the national stage, identifies and promotes consensus on public policy issues relating to the health and future state of the astronomical profession. The Council and the Executive Committee, with the help of the Executive Office, have an enormous responsibility to keep these many efforts productive and well-focussed.

I would like to discuss the major activities of today's Society, from my perspective as the current President, and suggest how some of these activities should be enhanced to meet the current and predicted challenges that our members face. As the essays in this centennial volume attest, our Society has undergone profound change and must continue to change to meet the constant call for more diversification and for more services, especially those tuned to aiding individual professional careers.

OUR SIZE

It might not seem that way to many of us who have travelled around the Sun more than a few dozen times, but we are still a small Society even though our members represent a wide variety of professional responsibilities and we have grown by a factor of ten in the past fifty years. Much has changed since Joel Stebbins predicted in his 1947 essay, reprinted in this volume, that the Society, then 625 members strong, would grow by 10 new members per year. We now comprise about 6500 members, a factor of 5 larger than Stebbins' forecast. So much for predictions. Certainly our membership has increased, as has its diversity, but we are still very small when compared to other disciplines. For instance, the American Mathematical Society has 30,000 members, the American Physical Society has 40,000 members, and the American Chemical Society has 150,000 members. Compared to them, we are still a highly selective, well-defined group of professionals that can act with one clear coherent voice.

But our small size, lack of broad industrial support, and the fiscally conservative legacy of those who managed the Society in past and quieter times, means that the Society is limited in the scope of its activities. The Society must carefully choose its priorities—what it can do, and what it cannot do—from among many worthwhile possibilities. Our budgeting philosophy requires each activity to be self-supporting. We rely heavily on volunteers to lead and participate in committees, surveys, and provision of resources for our members where the wisdom of our Secretary, now Arlo Landolt, is needed to identify and encourage volunteers from our membership. But as the challenges increase in complexity, and the needs in certain areas increase (discussed below), we have to constantly re-evaluate our priorities and how we allocate resources. As the chapters by Attis and Boyce make clear, we can rely only so much on the energies of volunteers. The work has to be spread around among a number of us. Equally clearly, we will be demanding more of the Executive Office of the Society, and so will have to expect to pay for additional staff and services or find additional ways to increase our income. Here we rely on careful oversight and budgeting talents by the Executive Officer, currently Bob Milkey, in consultation with our Treasurer, Len Kuhi. As always, the budget and scope of activities will be decided by consensus, with the Executive Officer, the Executive Committee, and the remaining members of the Council taking the lead, and, of course, the heat!

While our financial resources are not deep, the small size of the Society has its advantages, among them that a real sense of community exists. Members generally know (or know of) one another through recognition from scientific publications, from scientific collaboration, or interaction at observatories or through serving on various committees of the community. That we still exist as a more or less coherent community is not an accident. As the chapters on the formation of the Society's divisions attest, the forces of balkanization are constantly at play. But there are other stronger forces keeping us together: the fact that the Society has been adaptable to change, and that the leaders of our discipline early on saw the need to organize a national voice to insure that astronomers continue to define the needs of the profession, and not let others do it for us. The best example of the latter is how the community comes together once a decade to set priorities for our field in the "Decadal Surveys," which were initiated by astronomers in the early 1960s and managed by the National Academy of Sciences/National Research Council. John Bahcall's essay in this volume is a ringing endorsement for continuing the practice.

Quite frankly, as Wentzel and Fraknoi demonstrate in this volume, the AAS has been slow to adjust to the educational needs of the profession, and of society. But this is changing. Recently, in a study led by the AAS with funding from the National

Figure 1. Andrea Dupree represented the Society at the 90th birthday party for Dorrit Hoffleit at Yale in March 1997. Hoffleit joined the Society in 1930. Photograph by the editor.

Science Foundation, we evaluated the process of educating astronomers and have taken a hard look at priorities for training good teachers, researchers and scientists. Our relatively small size again has been an asset, for we were able to canvass effectively a representative sample of the community to learn what works, and what needs fixing.

To sum up, the small size of our community is an advantage—not only for communication and (relative) similarity of outlook, but also because we are flexible, and can respond quickly to new situations, discoveries, and initiatives. The AAS must continue to carefully choose what it can do to make a difference, and must be ready to discard initiatives that prove to be ineffective.

PUBLICATIONS

The publications of the AAS, principally *The Astrophysical Journal* and *The Astronomical Journal*, are both a major responsibility and a major asset of the Society. In the past decade, we have made outstanding progress in electronic publication, from manuscript submission to electronic postings, while keeping the costs to astronomers and libraries at a minimum. The quality and presentation of the journals are consistently high. Peter Boyce, the immediate past Executive Officer, shepherded these efforts to completion; it is generally acknowledged that the AAS led the way in electronic scientific publication.

As the Society's journals grow, so do the demands upon Society members to manage this growth effectively. The volunteer Publication Board, chaired by Robert Hanisch, works closely with the Council and the Executive Office to maintain priorities and provide clear oversight. The selection of Editors and Scientific Editors is never a simple task, and it is becoming a more frequent activity as the responsibilities of the positions increase. This has become a critical problem because the positions of Editors and Scientific Editors for *The Astrophysical Journal* and *The Astronomical Journal*, together with their army of referees, are still collegial. They are in the majority volunteer activities for which the Society's members, and the profession, are deeply in their debt. Helmut Abt, Editor-in-Chief, A. Dalgarno, Letters Editor of *The Astrophysical Journal*, and Paul Hodge, Editor of *The Astronomical Journal*, have dedicated substantial fractions of their professional careers to running our journals. It is through their thoughtful and exceedingly responsible efforts that we have journals generally recognized to be among the best, if not the best, in the world.

Maintaining the high standards and recognition our journals enjoy requires enormous effort. Because the Council of the AAS assumes overall responsibility, it must also be ever aware of the need to engage our best scientists to maintain quality, and also to seek constantly the most effective means of disseminating our scholarly information. As 'journals of record' the *ApJ* and *AJ* are critical barometers of the health of our profession and so demand the closest attention from the Council.

MEETINGS

Our meetings are getting larger and, some fear, more impersonal. We can no longer meet on a quiet college campus, or in E. C. Pickering's salon. Shapley's garden parties are history, as are intimate boat rides and observatory site inspections. People attending our meetings come for a wide variety of reasons, but the fundamental purposes of the meetings have remained much the same: to confer with colleagues, to hear about, examine, and debate the latest scientific findings and to celebrate prize winners. But our meetings have also become opportunities to listen to the views of policy makers, from inside the Beltway as well as among our colleagues. We can now also learn from others about the latest teaching strategies, and the most effective means to seek the right job. And there are growing numbers of displays of new publications from scholarly presses, new electronic services and new technologies to improve research and teaching. The poster and display sessions have established common ground for Society members to engage in freewheeling debate and discussion. They have proven to be ingenious ways to regain a sense of personal contact between researchers and educators who are seeking exposure and enlightenment. The good coffee and fresh pastries, supplied by friendly sponsoring organizations, always lubricate conversation.

The dynamics of our meetings have changed in profound ways. Beyond parallel sessions, posters, invited talks and new thematic structures, there is a new energy, a new awareness that when you attend an AAS meeting, the world is watching. A remarkable feature of our meetings in recent years has been the intense media interest.

Science reporters, writers from major newspapers, local and national radio and television crews camp out. Some broadcast directly from the meeting site. Making this happen has been the foresight of the Council; such outreach is critical and should be fostered. Much of the credit for this media attention goes to our Press Officer, now Steve Maran, who deftly orchestrates newsworthy results and finds new and effective ways to sensitize scientists to the interests and needs of attending press. Results from astronomy are now frequently featured in newspapers, magazines, and television. It is not enough that people have a deep-seated interest in their universe, and that astronomy seems to fascinate and amaze people as much as it does practitioners. What has made the difference is that the Society has found an engaging and effective means to reach out to the wider world; we are lucky because we have many gifted communicators among our members who like to tell people about the good astronomy that is supported by their tax dollars.

Getting the word out is very important, to be sure. We have an intrinsic responsibility to society to inform, but we also have a responsibility to our own discipline to maintain its health. Workshops on teaching strategies and on employment are very valuable, and all of it will have larger impact when we are sensitive to the need to address issues of policy and strategy that will affect the whole community. Increasingly, our meetings have become venues for community discussion on broad policy issues affecting all of astronomy.

EDUCATION

Most recently the AAS has taken the lead in a year-long study, initiated by Past President Frank Shu and carried out under the direction of Suzanne Edwards and Steve Strom, to analyze the patterns and goals of graduate education in astronomy in the United States. Part of this activity included an assessment of the content of astronomy and astrophysics education programs at major universities and colleges to ensure that our graduates have the skills necessary for today's jobs. The study has now concluded and its recommendations have yet to be implemented fully by the AAS. We have added a part time Education Coordinator to the staff of the Executive Office. This person will coordinate the education activities of the Society, arrange programs for members at our meetings, and actively increase our educational efforts under the direction of the Education Officer of the Society, now Bruce Partridge. New initiatives are also taking shape, such as an annual meeting of department chairs to share ideas and formulate curriculum plans and to coordinate and develop introductory astronomy courses for both specialists and non-scientists.

Education takes many forms. It can be outreach to the community, helping our members to be better educators of new astronomers, or it can be outreach to the world, helping our members learn how to communicate better to non-astronomers. Every professional astronomer has to be a teacher at some level. Workshops organized and run by the AAS will make us better teachers and communicators of our science. Upgrading the status of teaching at all levels, not only among our own members, but to the population at large, is a critical necessity that societies like the AAS need to foster in meaningful ways. We must address these issues through educating our members at meetings and through a more aggressive plan for providing both research and teaching resources to members.

EMPLOYMENT ISSUES

Job prospects for astronomy Ph.D.s have changed dramatically over the past 25 years. In the 1960s, a new graduate, if interested in teaching, moved directly into a position as Assistant Professor; now, a new graduate generally moves through a series of 2 or even 3 postdoctoral positions for some 6 to 9 years before taking up a tenure track research and/or teaching position. Although the number of astronomers finally moving into full time teaching/research positions has always been less than half of the available Ph.D.s being produced, the recent dramatic increase in postdoctoral positions and a diminution of permanent positions has led to deep concerns within the community about the obstacles preventing many young astronomers from becoming professionals. Many solutions have been presented in the past: from performing triage on the graduate student population to finding new ways to increase tenure-track positions to looking for employment outside of academe.

Certainly we need to actively seek out a broader range of employment opportunities for all astronomers, both by increasing the number of traditional teaching/ research positions and identifying areas of science and technology where astronomical training provides competitive access to a good job. Our Job Register, now posted on an electronic web site, is an excellent start, but it can always be enlarged, and advertised to a larger universe of employers as well. At each meeting of the Society, the Committee on Employment, now led by Ed Guinan, arranges a program to explore and elucidate the job situation for astronomers: the Committee has invited speakers who have chosen various traditional and non-traditional careers, and has brought in professional career counselors who have given advice on effective ways to get a job. In this area, a new initiative in Society Career Services, supported by the Executive Office of the AAS, can have a maximum impact for our members. A full Web-site has been initiated with electronic links to find a wider range of job opportunities, including resources created by other professional societies. The Society must also seek out other means to encourage its members to make contact with astronomers and physicists working in different job settings and to establish a network of people with advice and experience from a perspective different from the traditional academic or research mold.

I believe the Society should also take a leadership role in developing policies within the profession. Statements by the Society can affect how astronomy is practiced, and can set norms for the field. About a decade ago, the AAS recommended a date for announcing postdoctoral awards and acceptances, to remove the pressure on our youngest members for an early (and yet hopefully informed) decision. In addition, the AAS recommended increasing the usual one- or two-year postdoctoral appointment to a three-year term to enable young workers to establish some continuity in their research and to establish a foothold without constantly worrying about where they will be moving next. Both recommendations have endured and have strengthened the community.

PUBLIC POLICY

AAS members principally reside in the United States and receive funding and infrastructure support for their research through their employer (a college, university, laboratory, or industry). Most researchers today must supplement local support with grants from a U.S. Government agency, such as the National Aeronautics and Space Administration (NASA) and the National Science Foundation (NSF). There are also private foundations that contribute significantly to astronomical research; these resources are sought out by individual members and groups, generally without AAS involvement. Competition is fierce. Good track records are important. But how can the AAS help?

The AAS is in a pivotal position to act in two ways. It must inform the Government and Congress about why the nation needs a strong astronomical community, and at the same time it must educate AAS members about policies and priorities in Congress that influence decisions about funding levels. The Cold War is over. Policies change. The Society must both inform and be proactive in what is a very new world.

Congress, of course, allocates funds to activities it deems important for the country, and often what is deemed important is the result of coalition building. With severe competition for funds, astronomers must establish and maintain a coherent and engaging voice, and make that voice heard to as wide a constituency as possible. Astronomers must act individually and collectively to communicate the importance of basic research and the centrality of astronomy to the intellectual health of the nation. They must seek out their representatives, and know who makes a difference. In the past, small groups of astronomers, focussed on achieving a particular scientific goal, have banded together to win approval of specific science projects. This activity required intense day-to-day attention, to follow proposals as they worked their way through Congress. These efforts will continue, but they have to be moderated, or at least coordinated, with a broader sense of mission.

The AAS must of necessity take a broad, long-term view. It must speak for the community, and always keep the needs of that community in mind. This is not to say that in the event of a specific crisis the Council or Executive Office of the AAS must remain silent. We certainly have campaigned for projects in the past, but the Society's position is greatly strengthened when it can appeal to a general coherent plan that has been created and endorsed by the community at large. Decisions and prioritization must still be made within a plan. Funds for research are limited; resources for one activity can threaten the resources for another. The Council of the AAS generally cannot assess scientific tradeoffs, and is most effective when speaking for the general research effort of the community.

In addition to the Decadal Surveys that are a widely recognized accomplishment of the American Astronomical community, a particularly good example of consensus building occurred in 1997. The AAS collaborated with a number of scientific societies, through a Steering Committee formed by the American Physical Society, to endorse the value of basic research in the United States. Representing over one million scientists and engineers, we called for a 7% increase in congressional appropriations for basic research. Many articles emerged in the press during the spring to endorse this initiative. They cited studies evaluating the impressive financial return from the government's investment in basic research. This collective effort was modestly successful. The NSF budget was increased by 5% (up $159 million); the NASA budget for Science, Aeronautics and Technology received a 4.3% increase over FY'97.

To continue the initiative for the next budget cycle and through the following decade, the American Chemical Society and its Public Policy Staff, in consultation with the AAS and others, formulated a statement calling for a doubling of the research budget of our country in a decade. Over 100 scientific societies endorsed these principles, including societies representing physical sciences, natural sciences, medicine, and engineering. More than 3 million professionals are represented. A bill has been introduced in the U.S. Senate, with bipartisan sponsorship, calling for a decadal commitment to basic research.

Although the long-term effects of such initiatives are not known, it is becoming very evident that scientists no longer can continue their research assuming that there will always be adequate funding. For many scientists, this requires almost a behavioral change. More scientists need to communicate their results to the general public, to speak in understandable terms, and to use these acquired skills to convince their elected representatives that science is important. Astronomers find they have a comparatively easy job doing this because astronomy captures the attention and excitement of the public more than other physical sciences; it does not need to be a "hard sell" to an elected representative. Astronomy is the most popular of the physical sciences in the undergraduate curriculum. We must keep the subject attractive not only to maintain public support and educate students in a scientific way of thinking, but also perhaps to favorably influence future representatives in Congress!

The AAS through its Committee on Astronomy and Public Policy (CAPP), now led by Bruce Carney, has tried to convince our members of the need to communicate, and the ways to communicate, with Congress. Through the AAS Newsletter, electronic announcements, and at meetings, CAPP and the Executive Office inform and teach our members to be more outspoken about the work that they do and the results and benefits of astronomical research.

In the post Cold War world, basic research is frequently perceived as a luxury, a specialist's "hobby shop." The Administration and Congress are calling for quick return "practical results." Although astronomical research projects are not usually directly applicable to practical spinoffs, the astronomers' practice represents a critical testing ground for developing new technologies. Sensitive luggage detectors at airports and at the entrances to Congress, as well as dental x-ray devices were developed along with astronomical x-ray detectors; algorithms for improving Hubble Space Telescope images are under study for automatic detection of possible tumor sites; the transmission, handling and access to large data sets and associated signal processing problems have been successfully addressed by astronomers. The most direct benefit astronomy offers our young people, however, is that it stimulates interest and enthusiasm among the brightest students, drawing them to science and technology. Some stay with astronomy, but most move on to other technical, scientific, or engineering fields. Thus, astronomy is a means to maintaining a technically educated and competitive workforce.

We cannot, however, expect astronomy to speak for itself. We must seek new ways to convey the excitement of what we are doing to the public and to our representatives.

More of us should keep our elected officials aware of what we are doing. Politics is local. Our representatives want to know from their constituents about the effect of federal funds spent in their districts. So if you secure a research grant from a government agency, or obtain telescope time at a national facility, send a letter to tell your Representative and Senators. At the same time, let them know what your future needs are and encourage their support of basic science, and astronomy in particular, in the Federal Budget. If an elected official graduated from a college or university where you work, a letter can have a special impact. I believe that the AAS should actively educate its members on the importance of communicating with Congress. But, as always, it is equally important to do so as competently and effectively as possible. Coordination of such efforts by the staff of the AAS Executive Office is required to maintain a consistent presence as well as an informed awareness of Congressional issues. We may believe that elected representatives want happy constituents and look for ways to meet their needs because the next election is always on the horizon. But Congress is more sophisticated than that, so we need eyes and ears in Washington to advise us on tactics as the winds constantly change.

CONCLUDING THOUGHTS

Looking forward from 1997, at a time when we see the national news media frequently featuring space and space science as cover stories that emphasize the fascination of astronomy, I am convinced that astronomy will continue to captivate people as we constantly find new and exciting ways to explore and interpret the universe. I have every hope and expectation that the next century will bring ever more fascinating and fundamental aspects of our universe into sharper focus. But I know that this will not happen if we become complacent and fail to meet the obligations and expectations of society. The AAS leadership must represent our profession with a consistently strong voice and inspire participation from its members in order to carry out its responsibilities of publication, meetings, and public service. Only in this way will it continue to be an integral part of the career of a professional astronomer and adequately contribute to our society.

REFERENCES

AAS Meetings Before There Was an AAS: The Pre-History of the Society

Donald E. Osterbrock

1. W. J. Hussey, PAASA **1**, 1–42 (1910); R. Berendzen, Phys. Today **27**, 32–39 (1974).
2. H. Wright, *Explorer of the Universe: A Biography of George Ellery Hale* (New York: Dutton, 1966); D. E. Osterbrock, *Pauper & Prince: Ritchey, Hale, & Big American Telescopes* (Tucson: University of Arizona, 1993). The newspaper reactions are from the *Chicago Tribune*, 12, 13, 14, 16 October, 1892, and *Chicago Daily News*, 13 October 1892.
3. J. C. Hamson to W. R. Harper (WRH), 12 January 1893; S. Newcomb (SN) to WRH, 6 March 6 1893; J. E. Keeler (JEK) to WRH, 6 March 1893, Letters of the Board of Trustees, Special Collections, Regenstein Library, University of Chicago. (RL/LBT).
4. W. U. Masters and W. Wotkyns to WRH, 18 January 1893; W. H. Knight to GEH, 19 January 1893, RL/LBT; GEH to W. H. Knight, 26 January 1893. Mount Wilson Observatory Collection, Henry Huntington Library (HHL/MWO); G. E. Hale, ApJ **5**, 164–180 (1897); D. E. Osterbrock, *Yerkes Observatory, 1892-1950; The Birth, Near Death, and Resurrection of a Scientific Research Institution* (Chicago: University of Chicago, 1997).
5. J. A. Parkhurst to Hale, 19 January 1893; W. F. Furbeck to WRH, 13 March, 23 March, 1893; S. I. Clover to WRH, 21 March 1893; W. Heckman to WRH, 23 March 1893. (RL/LBT).
6. GEH to WRH, 4, 15 January 1893, RL/LBT; WRH to GEH, 9 January 1893, Yerkes Observatory Archives (YOA); GEH to W. Warner and A. Swasey (W&S), 24 February 1893. (HHL/MWO).
7. W. H. Hammersley to WRH, 2 February 1893; J. Johnston (JJ) to WRH, 8, 24 February 1893. (RL/LBT).
8. G. C. Walker to WRH, 17 February 1893, RL/LBT; T. C. Chamberlin (TCC) to GEH, 31 January 1893. (YOA).
9. GEH to W&S, 21 March 1893, HHL/MWO; WRH and M. A. Ryerson to Board of Trustees, March 1893, RL/LBT; Ann Wolfmeyer and Mary Burns Gage, *Lake Geneva: Newport of the West, 1870-1920* (Lake Geneva: Lake Geneva Historical Society, 1976).
10. *Lake Geneva Herald*, 8 December 1893; S. W. Burnham (SWB) to GEH, 9 December 1893, 9 July 1894. (YOA).
11. E. E. Ayer to JJ, 30 October 1894; C. T. Yerkes (CTY) to T. W. Goodspeed, 3 April 1894; GEH to WRH, 26 February 1895. (RL/LBT).
12. *Williams Bay Observer*, **20**, 27 May 1897; GEH to CTY, 31 May 1897, GEH to WRH, 20 May 1897; GEH to H. A. Rust (HAR), 25 May 1897, YOA. On Barnard, See William Sheehan, *The Immortal Fire Within: The Life and Work of Edward Emerson Barnard* (Cambridge: Cambridge University Press, 1995).
13. CTY to WRH, 24 May 1897, University Presidents' Papers, 1889–1925, Special Collections, Regenstein Library, University of Chicago. (RL/UPP).
14. *Williams Bay Observer*, 3 June 1897; GEH to C. A. Young, 1 June 1897, GEH to JEK, 1 June 1897, CTY to GEH, 2 June 1897. (YOA).
15. WRH to GEH, 9 April 1897; GEH to JEK, 10 April 1897; GEH to W. W. Campbell, 9 August 1897. (YOA).
16. *Chicago Tribune*, 18–22 October 1897. The *Tribune* covered the dedication in depth and is the source for most of the descriptive material. See also *Chicago Daily News* and *Chicago Daily Inter Ocean* for the same week, *University of Chicago Weekly*, **6** (4), 1897, and *Lake Geneva Herald*, 22 October 1897.
17. GEH to J. M. Van Vleck, 13 October 1897; GEH to E. C. Pickering (ECP), 13 October 1897; GEH to F. W. Shepardson, 13 October 1897. (YOA).
18. *Williams Bay Observer*, 22 October 1897, gives these and many other details of the week's events.
19. G. E. Hale, ApJ **6**, 353–362 (1897), relates most of the happenings of the week.
20. W. W. Payne, Pop. Astr. **5**, 340–351 (1897).
21. *University Record* (Chicago) **2**, 235–236 (1897).
22. J. E. Keeler, ApJ **6**, 271–288 (1897); D. E. Osterbrock, *James E. Keeler, Pioneer American Astrophysicist and the Early Development of American Astrophysics* (Cambridge: Cambridge University, 1984).
23. *University Record* (Chicago) **2**, 246–250 (1897).
24. J. D. Butler (JDB) to GEH, 17 October 1897. (YOA); JDB to WRH, 4 November 1897. (RL/UPP).
25. *Chicago Tribune*, 22 October 1897.
26. W. S. Adams, Science **106**, 196–200 (1947).
27. S. Newcomb, N. Amer. Rev. **122**, 88–123 (1876); William Alvord, PASP **10**, 49–58 (1898). Albert Moyer, *A Scientist's Voice in American Culture* (California, 1992).
28. S. Newcomb, ApJ **6**, 289–309 (1897).
29. GEH to HAR, 26 October 1897. (YOA).
30. C. H. Rockwell to GEH, 26 October 1897; JEK to GEH, 1 November 1897; ECP to GEH, 8 November 1897. (YOA).
31. J. S. Ames (JSA) to GEH, 7 October 1897, 19

March 1898; TCC to GEH, 26 March 1898. (YOA).

32. ECP to GEH, 23 March 1898. (YOA).

33. GEH to ECP, 26 March, 3 May, 13 May 1898, YOA; G. E. H[ale, ed.], ApJ **8**, 54–55 (1898).

34. B. Z. Jones and L. G. Boyd, *The Harvard College Observatory: The First Four Directorships, 1839–1919* (Cambridge: Harvard University, 1971).

35. G. E. H[ale, ed.], ApJ **8**, 229–256 (1898); H. R. Donaghe, Pop. Astr. **6**, 481–487 (1898).

36. G. E. H[ale], ApJ **8**, 193–198 (1898); [W. J. Hussey], PAASA **1**, 43–44 (1910).

37. E. E. Barnard, Pop. Astr. **6**, 425–455 (1898).

38. [W. J. Hussey], PAASA **1**, vii–xiv (1910).

39. GEH to SN, 5 May 1898; GEH to SN, 5, 16 January 1899; JSA to GEH, 12 December 1898. (YOA).

40. D. E. Osterbrock, ApJ **438**, 1–7 (1995).

41. G. C. Comstock to GEH, 6, 13 October 1898. (YOA).

42. G. C. Comstock, ApJ **10**, 58 (1899); G. E. H[ale], ApJ **10**, 211–220 (1899).

43. List of ``Charter Members,'' PAASA **1**, x–xi (1910).

44. ECP to GEH, 30, 31 August 1899. (YOA).

45. [W. W. Payne], Pop. Astr. **7**, 444–446 (1899).

46. See references 35, 36.

47. J. Stebbins, Pop. Astr. **55**, 409–413, (1947). Reprinted in this volume, *see* page xxx.

The Pickering Years

David H. DeVorkin

1. Howard Plotkin, *Proceedings of the American Philosophical Society* **122**, 385–399 (1978).

2. Hale to Pickering, 28 August 1899, emphasis in original; G. C. Comstock to Pickering, 21 July 1899. E. C. Pickering Papers, Harvard University Archives, UA V 630.20.15. Hereinafter noted as ECP/HUA. Much of the activities of the pre-Pickering years have been gleaned from this file, unless otherwise noted.

3. ``Special Meeting of the Council, New York City, January 1900,'' American Astronomical Society, Minutes of the Council, Secretary's Copy, pp. 7–8; January 1903 meeting, p. 24. AIP microfilm. Hereinafter noted as (AAS/AIP).

4. Comstock letters 1903–1905, Secretary's files, (AAS/AIP).

5. ``7th Meeting, Columbia University, New York, December, 1905,'' p. 30. (AAS/AIP).

6. ``4th Meeting, Washington, December and January 1902–1903,'' p. 22. (AAS/AIP).

7. Comstock to Council, 8 March 1906. (ECP/HUA).

8. Pickering to Comstock, 12 August; Comstock to Pickering, 15 August 1908. (ECP/HUA).

9. Much of the information in this section was compiled from meeting reports in *Science* and in the *Publications of the American Astronomical Society*. Adapted from essays by Brant Sponberg and the author in *History of the AAS*, accessible from the Society's Web Page, www.aas.org. *See* also Berendzen, ref. 20.

10. Dorrit Hoffleit, *Astronomy at Yale 1701–1968* (New Haven: Connecticut Academy of Sciences, 1994), Chapter 13.

11. David DeVorkin, Isis **72**, 29–49 (1981); Howard Plotkin, Annals of Science **43**, 365–367 (1978).

12. John Lankford, *American Astronomy: Community, Careers and Power, 1859–1940* (Chicago: University of Chicago Press, 1997), p. 200, n. 20. DeVorkin, *Henry Norris Russell* (forthcoming).

13. Pickering to Hale, 18 January 1917. (ECP/HUA).

14. Russell to Hale, 18 September 1917. Reel 49, NRC files. George Ellery Hale Papers, Huntington Library, microfilm edition.

15. Howard Plotkin, Isis **69**, 44–57 (1978); Journal for the History of Astronomy **21**, 47–58 (1990). Robert E. Kohler, *Partners in Science, Foundations and Natural Scientists 1900–1945* (Chicago: U. Chicago Press, 1991). DeVorkin, *Henry Norris Russell* (forthcoming).

16. Adapted from Web essays by Brant Sponberg and the author, reference 9. *See* also Berendzen, ref. 20.

17. John Lankford, 1997, chapter 3.

18. Simon Newcomb, ``The Progress and Tendency of Astronomy.'' Address to the National Academy of Sciences (18 April 1901). Newcomb Collection, Manuscript Division, Library of Congress, 11–12.

19. Newcomb to George Ellery Hale, 30 November 1899, Newcomb Collection, Manuscript Division, Library of Congress.

20. Richard Berendzen, Phys. Today **27**, No. 12, 32–39 (1974).

21. Hale to Keeler, 11 September 1897. Hale microfilm. Trudy Bell, The Griffith Observer **42**, 2–10 (1978).

22. Newcomb to Hale, 24 December 1898, quoted in Berendzen, p. 37.

23. Stenographer's transcript, ``Tenth Annual Meeting of the A. & A. S. A, 21 August 1909.'' (AAS/AIP).

24. Campbell to Comstock, 5 March 1908. (AAS/AIP).

25. Stebbins, Pop. Astr. **55**, 404 (1947). Reprinted in this volume, *see* p. xxx.

26. *Ibid.*

27. Hussey to Campbell, 26 January 1914. (AAS/AIP).
28. Stenographers transcript, "Tenth Annual Meeting of the A. & A.S.A., 21 August 1909." (AAS/AIP).
29. Hussey to Campbell, 26 January 1914. (AAS/AIP).
30. "10th Meeting, Yerkes Observatory, August 1909," pp. 43–44. (AAS/AIP).
31. Campbell to Fox, 2 February 1914. (AAS/AIP).
32. *Ibid*.
33. Gathered from Society reports in the PAAS as well as from Council Minutes (AAS/AIP).
34. "Special Meeting of the Council, Washington, March 8, 1919," p. 113. (AAS/AIP). Resolution printed in PAAS **4**, 70 (1923).
35. "11th meeting, Harvard College Observatory, August 1910," p. 48. (AAS/AIP).
36. Stebbins, 408, (1947). Reprinted in this volume, *see* p. xxx.
37. "23rd Meeting, Ann Arbor, September 1919," p. 116. AAS Council Minutes, AAS Records, AIP. "Twenty-Third Meeting," PAAS **4**, 71–72 (1923).
38. "Twenty-Fourth Meeting, 1920," 136; "Twenty-Sixth meeting, 1921." PAAS **4** (1923). Council deliberations over the resumption of international relations began in August 1918 in response to an appeal from Hale, and continued through 1920. See, for instance, "Special Meeting of the Council, Washington, March 8, 1919," p. 112. (AAS/AIP).
39. "Twenty-Fourth Meeting," 133–135, quote from p. 135; "Twenty-Seventh Meeting," PAAS **4** (1923). Council Minutes, 27th through the 30th meetings. (AAS/AIP). On the Neighbors and the "generals" see Lankford, 1997, 204; and DeVorkin, *Henry Norris Russell*, (forthcoming).
40. "Twenty-Seventh Meeting," PAAS **4** (1923). Council Minutes, 27th through the 30th meetings. (AAS/AIP).
41. "88th Meeting, Amherst, Massachusetts, December 28–31, 1952," p. 164. (AAS/AIP).

The First West Coast Meeting of the AAS

Donald E. Osterbrock

1. W. W. Campbell (WWC) to E. C. Pickering (ECP), 23 August 1912. Mary Lea Shane Archives of the Lick Observatory, University of California, Santa Cruz (SLO); [P. Fox], PAASA **2**, 107–109 (1915).
2. WWC to ECP, 18 March 1914; R. H. Tucker to ECP, 23 April 1914; WWC to Frank Schlesinger, 30 March 1914; WWC to J. S. Barr, 20 February 1915; P. Fox to WWC, 6 May 1915. (SLO).
3. W. W. Campbell, Science **42**, 227–238 (1915).
4. ECP to WWC, 4 December 1914; WWC to ECP, 2 February 1915, 23 April 1915, 29 June 1915. SLO.
5. G. E. Hale, PASP **27**, 161–178 (1915).
6. [J. Stebbins], PAAS **3**, 107–111 (1918); [R. G. Aitken], PASP **27**, 195–201 (1915).
7. H. D. Curtis, PASP **27**, 105–109 (1915).

Amateurs and the Society During the Formative Years

Marc Rothenberg and Thomas R. Williams

1. This chapter re-examines issues first considered in Marc Rothenberg, Social Studies of Science **11**, 305–325 (1981).
2. Konrad H. Jarausch, *The Unfree Professions: German Lawyers, Teachers and Engineers, 1900–1950* (New York: Oxford University Press, 1990), pp. 5–7; Margali S. Larson, *The Rise of Professionalism* (Berkeley: University of California Press, 1977); Eliot Freidson, *Professionalism Reborn* (Chicago: University of Chicago Press, 1994), p. 16; Robert A. Stebbins, *Amateurs, Professionals, and Serious Leisure* (Montreal and Kingston: McGill-Queen's University Press, 1992); Elliott A. Krause, *Death of the Guilds: Professions, States and the Advance of Capitalism, 1930 to the Present* (New Haven: Yale University Press, 1996).
3. Nathan Reingold, in *The Pursuit of Knowledge in the Early American Republic*, A. Oleson and S. C. Brown, eds. (Baltimore: Johns Hopkins University Press, 1976), pp. 33–69; Robert V. Bruce, *The Launching of Modern American Science 1846–1876* (New York: Alfred A. Knopf, 1987); Nathan O. Hatch, in *The Professions in American History*, Nathan O. Hatch, ed. (Notre Dame: University of Notre Dame Press, 1988); Daniel J. Kevles in *ibid.*, pp. 107–125; Bruce A. Kimball, *The "True Professional Ideal" in America, a History* (Cambridge: Blackwell Publishers, 1992); John Lankford, *American Astronomy, Community, Careers, and Power, 1859–1940* (Chicago: University of Chicago Press, 1997).
4. Bulletin of the Geological Society **1**, 571 (1890); C. A. Browne and M. E. Weeks, *A History of the American Chemical Society: Seventy-five Eventful Years* (Washington, D.C.: American Chemical Society, 1952), pp. 205–206; Toby A. Appel, in Gerald L. Geison, ed., *Physiology in the American Context, 1850–1940* (Baltimore: American Physiological Society, 1987), pp. 155–176, see p. 165.

5. Jack Meadows and Tim Fisher, New Scientist, 752–753 (September 14, 1978).
6. For the education of American astronomers, see Lankford (1997), p. 76; and on the contributions of amateurs to astronomy, see Thomas R. Williams, Sky & Telescope **76** (5), 484–486 (1986).
7. Science **10**, 786 (1899).
8. Charter members are listed in Publications of the Astronomical and Astrophysical Society of America (PAASA), **1**, x–xi (1910).
9. J. A. Parkhurst, Pop. Astr. **16**, 231–239 (1908).
10. PAASA **1**, xvii (1910).
11. Richard Berendzen, Phys. Today **27**, no. 12, 32–39 (December 1974).
12. PAASA **1**, passim (1910).
13. See the discussion in Rothenberg, (1981), 322.
14. E. C. Pickering to William J. Hussey, 19 January 1909 (AAS/AIP).
15. E. D. Roe to William J. Hussey, 29 January 1909 (AAS/AIP).
16. See the discussion in Rothenberg (1981), 322.
17. PAASA **2**, passim (1915), and PAAS **3**, 1–148, (1918).
18. Frederick C. Leonard, Pop. Astr. **19**, 455–456 (1911).
19. Leonard, *ibid.*; Leonard to Pickering, 14 April 1911. UAV 630.17.5, Harvard College Observatory, Harvard University Archives (hereafter, ECP/HUA). John Mellish, working with Toronto attorney Albert Richard-Hassard, had attempted to form a similar organization of amateurs in 1909. Their letter campaign garnered at least 21 members in the United States and Canada but was never formalized or publicized. Mellish to A. R. Hassard, 20 February 1909. RASC Archives.
20. P. R. Heyl to Pickering, 14 July 1885; 17 August 1885. UAV 630.19 (ECP/HUA); Pop. Astr. **19**, 520–522 (1911); William Tyler Olcott, *ibid.*, 129–142.
21. Parkhurst to Pickering, 10 December 1887. UAV 630.17.5 (ECP/HUA).
22. Herbert C. Wilson to Pickering, 11 September 1911, Popular Astronomy folder. UAV 630.17.5 (ECP/HUA).
23. Frederick C. Leonard, Pop. Astr. **19**, 455–457 (1911). [Wilson] Pop. Astr. **19**, 456–157 (1911).
24. Pickering to Wilson, 7 September 1911. UAV 630.16 (ECP/HUA). Portions of Pickering's letter were published in Pop. Astr. **19**, 520–521 (1911).
25. Robert A. Stebbins, International Journal of Comparative Sociology **21**, 34–48 (1980).
26. Pickering to William T. Olcott, 2 October 1911. UAV 630.16 (ECP/HUA)
27. David Todd to Pickering, 4 October 1911 UAV 630.17.5; Pickering to Todd, 5 October 1911. UAV 630.16 (ECP/HUA).
28. Pickering to Olcott, 7 October 1911. UAV 630.16; Olcott to Pickering, 9 October 1911. UAV 630.17.5 (ECP/HUA).
29. Pop. Astr. **19**, 655–656 (1911); R. Newton Mayall, Review of Pop. Astr. **55**, No. 513, 4–9 (September-October 1961) and No. 514, 8–12 (November-December 1961). For evidence of Pickering's control, see Pickering-Olcott correspondence in UAV 630.17.5 (ECP/HUA).
30. PAAS **3**, 355–362 (1918); Olcott to Philip Fox, 5 September 1914; Fox to Olcott, 8 September 1914. (AAS/AIP).
31. George B. Comstock to Pickering, 1 October 1908. UAV 630.17.5 (ECP/HUA); PAAS **3**, 258; 354 (1918).
32. Fox to Pickering, 30 June 1914; Pickering to Fox, 6 July 1914. (AAS/AIP).
33. For the role of women in astronomy during this era, see Lankford (1997), pp. 287–359.
34. PAAS **3**, 187 (1918).
35. Nathan Reingold (1976), pp. 33–69; Stebbins (1980), 34–48.
36. Frank Schlesinger to Members of the Committee on Associate Membership, 22 November 1916, Schlesinger Papers, Allegheny Observatory Records, Archives of Industrial Society, University of Pittsburgh (hereafter, FS/UP).
37. Schlesinger to Members of the Committee on Associate Membership, 9 December 1916. (FS/UP).
38. Schlesinger to Members of the Committee on Associate Membership, 22 November 1916. (FS/UP).
39. [E. C. Pickering] to Schlesinger, 20 December 1916. (AAS/AIP).
40. Schlesinger to Members of the Committee on Associate Membership, 9 December 1916. (FS/UP).
41. "Minutes of the Council," American Astronomical Society, 30 August 1917. (FS/UP).
42. "Minutes of the Council," American Astronomical Society, 29 August 1917. (FS/UP).

Honorary American Astronomers: Canada and the American Astronomical Society

Richard A. Jarrell

1. Richard A. Jarrell, *The Cold Light of Dawn. A History of Canadian Astronomy* (Toronto: University of Toronto Press, 1988).
2. Box 1 Supplement, Folder 1, American Astronomical Society Papers, American Institute of Physics, hereafter cited as (AAS/AIP).

3. Box 1 Supplement, Folder 3, "Constitution and By-Laws of the Astronomical and Astrophysical Society of America with List of Members, January 1903," and "Astronomical and Astrophysical Society of America Constitution, By-Laws and List of Members, April 1911." (AAS/AIP).

4. Richard A. Jarrell, J. R. Astron. Soc. Canada **71**, 221–233 (1977).

5. C. A. Chant, J. R. Astron. Soc. Canada **1**, 67–68 (1907).

6. Richard A. Jarrell, Trans. R. Soc. Canada (Ser. IV) **20**, 633–647 (1982).

7. Box 7 Supplement, Folder 10. R. Curtiss to J. Stebbins, 10 July 1911. (AAS/AIP).

8. C. A. Chant, J. R. Astron. Soc. Canada **5**, 327–338 (1911).

9. Box 8 Additional, Minutebook 1899–1917, Minutes for 1911. (AAS/AIP).

10. Box 1 Supplement, Folder 3, "American Astromical Society Constitution, By-Laws and List of Members" (March 1918). (AAS/AIP).

11. Ralph E. De Lury, J. R. Astron. Soc. Canada **12**, 381–391 (1918).

12. Ralph E. De Lury, J. R. Astron. Soc. Canada **23**, 243–248 (1929).

13. Box 5 Supplement, Folder 13, AAS Council Minutes 1921–36. (AAS/AIP).

14. J.F. Heard, J. R. Astron. Soc. Canada **29**, 313–315 (1935), from 314.

15. Box 8 Additional. Minutes of Council/Secretary's Copy, Vol III, 1933–44. (AAS/AIP).

16. C. A. Chant, J. R. Astron. Soc. Canada **43**, 138–141 (1949).

17. Box 4 Additional, Programs to 1968. (AAS/AIP).

18. J. R. Astron. Soc. Canada **53**, 245–248 (1959).

19. R. M. Petrie, J. R. Astron. Soc. Canada **46**, 129–132 (1952).

20. Box 6 Additional, AAS Council Minutes 1957–1962, File "Officers, Committees." (AAS/AIP).

21. Box 4 Additional, Programs to 1968. (AAS/AIP).

22. Astron. J. **73**, S161–S210 (1968).

23. BAAS **7**, 503–571 (1975).

24. BAAS **12**, 759–881 (1980).

25. 189th Meeting, American Astronomical Society, 12–16 January 1997. (AAS, Washington, DC, 1996).

26. R. Peter Broughton, *Looking Up. A History of the Royal Astronomical Society of Canada* (Toronto: Dundurn Press, 1993).

27. Yves Gingras, *Physics and the Rise of Scientific Research in Canada* (Kingston/Montreal: McGill-Queen's University Press, 1991).

28. *American Astronomical Society, 1997 Membership Directory* (Washington, DC: AAS, 1996).

29. *Canadian Astronomical Society, Membership Directory 1996.*

30. K. O. Wright, J. R. Astron. Soc. Canada, **42**, 201–208 (1948), on 208.

A Century of Astronomy in México: Collaboration with American Astronomers

Silvia Torres-Peimbert

1. Moreno Corral in *Historia de la Astronomía en México,* edited by M. A. Moreno (México: UNAM, 1983), p. 215; E. Piña Garza, and L. Dagdug Lima, *Ciencia* **47**, 293 (1996).

2. J. Gallo, *El Observatorio Astronómico Nacional en su Quincuagésimo Aniversario* (Tacubaya: OAN, 1924).

3. W. W. Morgan, P. C. Keenan, and E. Kellman, *An Atlas of Stellar Spectra* (Chicago: Univ. of Chicago Press, 1943).

4. B. J. Bok, Sky & Telescope **1** (2), 3 (1941); **4** (6), 3 (1945); in *Historia de la Astronomía en México*, edited by M. A. Moreno (México: UNAM, 1983), p. 267; N. U. Mayall, *PASP* **54**, 117 (1942); D. H. Menzel, Sky & Telescope **1** (6), 3 (1942); P. Pishmish, in *Historia de la Astronomía en México*, p. 281; H. N. Russell, Sci. Am. **166**, 230 (1942).

5. N. U. Mayall, PASP **54**, 117 (1942). Halley Mogey was a son of the telescope maker William Mogey. *See* Peter A. Serrada, Rittenhouse **3**, 141–144 (1989).

6. D. H. Menzel, Sky & Telescope **1** (6), 3 (1942).

7. N. U. Mayall, PASP **54**, 117 (1942).

8. C. H. Payne-Gaposchkin, Sky & Telescope **1** (6), 11 (1942); H. N. Russell, Sci. Am. **166**, 230 (1942).

9. D. H. Menzel, Sky & Telescope **1** (6), 3 (1942). The talks include: Walter S. Adams, interstellar lines; Joel Stebbins, absorbing clouds in the galactic plane; Henrietta Swope, the faint variable stars in Ophiuchus and Sagittarius; Otto Struve, the relation of stars to nebulosity; Fred L. Whipple, interstellar dust clouds as the mode of origin of stars; Sergei Gaposchkin, classification of variable stars; H. N. Russell, the probable life history of a star with mass equal to that of our sun; F. Recillas, W UMa stars; C. Payne-Gaposchkin, novae; Bart Bok, the spectroscopic and photometric survey of the region of Carina; R. H. Baker, observations in the region of Aquila; J. Gallo, star counts on the astrographic plates; J. A. Pearce, rotation of the galaxy; N. U. Mayall, the velocities of 53 globular clusters; H. Shapley, galactic studies from the survey of the whole sky; P. Pishmish, revision of important magnitude standards; C. Graef, a technique for the measurement of stellar colors; W. W.

Morgan, the presentation of a new spectral classification scheme; A. N. Vyssotsky, the extension to fainter magnitudes of spectral classification; R. W. Wood, spectral classification with large objective gratings; D. H. Menzel, variable phenomena on the sun; R. R. McMath, solar prominences; R. D. Evans, on the age of the solar system; C. T. Elvey, problems of the night sky; Manuel Sandoval Vallarta, the emission of charged particles by the sun; C. Graef, Lifshitz, Martínez and A. Baños, paths of the cosmic rays in the earth's field; G. D. Birkhoff, the mathematical concept of time.

10. C. Allen, J. de la Herrán and H. Johnson, Sky & Telescope **60** (4) 270 (1980).
11. A. Serrano, Rev. Mex. A.A. Ser. Conf. **4**, 67 (1996); L. Carrasco private communication, 1997.
12. F. Valle, *Anuario del Observatorio Astronómico Nacional de Tacubaya para 1891* (Tacubaya: OAN), p. 131; J. Gallo Sarlat, in *Historia de la Astronomía en México*, p. 245.
13. B. J. Bok, Sky & Telescope **1** (2), 3 (1941).
14. G. Haro, Proc. Nat. Acad. Sci. **30**, 247 (1944).
15. M. Alvarez and E. López, in *Historia de la Astronomía en México*, p. 311.
16. C. A. Federer Jr., Sky & Telescope **20** (4), 184 (1960).

Personal Reminiscences of Being AAS Treasurer and Other Stories

Frank K. Edmondson

1. D. B. McLaughlin, Pop. Astr. **41**, 419–420 (1933).
2. PASP **46**, 312 (1934).
3. Bok to Edmondson, n.d., AAS Treasurer Files. Edmondson Files, Indiana University Archives.

Recollections after Fifty Years: Haverford AAS Meeting, December 1950

Vera C. Rubin

1. AJ **58**, 30 (1953).
2. Frank Kerr, in *The World of Galaxies*, eds. H. G. Corwin, Jr. and L. Bottinelli. (New York: Springer-Verlag, 1989), p. 452.
3. Owen Gingerich, Phys. Today **47**, 34 (December 1994).

The AAS as a Network

Arlo U. Landolt

1. E. C. Pickering, PAASA **1**, 262 (1906).
2. L. Spitzer, AJ **61**, 194 (1956).

3. Adriaan Blaauw, *History of the IAU* (Dordrecht: Kluwer Academic Publishers, 1994), p. 1.
4. Alfred A. Fowler, ed., *Transactions of the International Astronomical Union* **1**, 219 (1922).
5. Blaauw (1994), p. 172.
6. PAAS **7**, 208 (1933); **8**, 1 (1934).
7. "Council Minutes, Harvard Faculty Club, Cambridge, Massachusetts, June 8, 1945," p. 431. Council Minutes. (AAS/AIP).
8. "89th Meeting, Boulder, Colorado, August 26–30, 1953," pp. 589; 591; "90th Meeting, Nashville, Tennessee, December 27–30, 1953," p. 606. Council Minutes. (AAS/AIP).
9. Council Minutes, pp. 1732; 1818. (AAS/AIP).
10. Council Minutes, pp. 2770; 3070; 3080. (AAS/AIP).
11. Council Minutes, pp. 4267; 4337. (AAS/AIP).

The Post-war Society: Responding to New Patterns of Patronage

David H. DeVorkin

1. Bart Bok oral history, 14 June 1978, (AIP); Peggy Aldrich Kidwell, in Margaret W. Rossiter and Clark A. Elliott, eds., *Science at Harvard University*; D. H. DeVorkin, Minerva **18**, 595 (1980).
2. Dean B. McLaughlin, "Council Minutes" for the 65th, 66th, and 67th meetings (December 1940; September 1941; December 1941), 369; 373–374; 387. (AAS/AIP).
3. Otto Struve, Pop. Astr. **51**, 474 (1943).
4. *Ibid.*
5. Harlow Shapley to Isaiah Bowman, 6 November 1946, quoted in Daniel Kevles, *The Physicists: The History of a Scientific Community in Modern America* (New York: Alfred A. Knopf, 1978), p. 355.
6. Leo Goldberg oral history, 17 May 1978, p. 79. (AIP).
7. E. R. Piore, *The Impact of ONR Support on Universities*, 27 December 1947, p. 11. Institutions, Associations, Individuals folder. (NRC/CF).
8. E. R. Piore, *Ibid.*
9. Gerard Kuiper to S. Chandrasekhar, 5 August 1943. Box 19.21. (SC/UCL).
10. Kuiper to Chandrasekhar, 19 September 1943. Box 19.21. (SC/UCL).
11. Paul F. Lee to Detlev Bronk, 3 December 1947. (NRC/CF). There is a large literature on the post-war reconstruction of American science by governmental funding. See, among many sources, an article by S. S. Schweber on the ONR, in E. Mendelsohn, M. R. Smith and P. Weingart,. eds., *Science, Technology and the Military* (Dordrecht: Kluwer Academic Publishers, 1988); J. Merton

England, *A Patron for Pure Science: The National Science Foundation's Formative Years, 1945–1957* (Washington, D.C.: National Science Foundation, 1982); and S. W. Leslie, *The Cold War and American Science* (Stanford: Stanford University Press, 1993).

12. "Memorandum on the Support of Astronomical Research by the Office of Naval Research," n.d. (1947). (DHM/HUA).

13. "To the Members of the American Astronomical Society," 16 February 1948. (JGP/CITA). R. C. Gibbs, "Minutes of meeting of the NRC Committee on Astronomy, Advisory to ONR," 20 March 1948; Otto Struve, "Memorandum on the Work of the Committee on Astronomy Advisory to the Office of Naval Research," 21 April 1948. (NRC/CF).

14. Otto Struve, "Memorandum on the Work of the Committee on Astronomy Advisory to the Office of Naval Research," 21 April 1948. (NRC/CF).

15. "Committee Activities, 1949–1950," 22 May 1950. NRC Division of Mathematics and Physical Sciences (M&PS). (NRC/CF).

16. A. T. Waterman to F. B. Jewett, 7 January 1947; "Minutes, Executive Board: Committee on Geophysics: Advisory to ONR," 8 January 1948; Gibbs to Bronk "Committee on Astronomy, Advisory to ONR," 23 August 1949. (NRC/CF).

17. Gibbs to Bronk, 22 March 1948. M&PS, (NRC/CF).

18. Lyman Spitzer, "Normal Pre-War Astronomical Expenditures in the United States," 26 April 1948. (CDS/LA). The annual expenditure for new equipment, upgrades of old telescopes, and the costs of mounting eclipse expeditions and special devices, came to some $400 thousand per year. Without the 200-inch, the average expenditure for equipment and expeditions came to only $140 thousand per year.

19. On Lawrence, see Robert Seidel, in *Pions to Quarks: Particle Physics in the 1950s*, edited by Laurie M. Brown, Max Dresden, and Lillian Hoddeson (New York: Cambridge University Press, 1989), p. 498.

20. Gibbs, "Minutes," Second meeting of the Committee on Astronomy, Advisory to ONR, 7 January 1949, 16 February 1949. (NRC/CF).

21. Goldberg to Shane, 23 February 1950. (CDS/LA).

22. Bowen to Gibbs, 2 February 1948. (ISB/HL).

23. Greenstein was an outspoken critic of the parochial insularity of graduate training at observatories. See Greenstein to Spitzer, 27 April 1946. (JGP/CITA).

24. Bok to Committee, 24 March 1949; reply quoted from Spitzer to Bok, 29 March 1949. (ISB/HL).

25. Whitford to Bok, 30 March 1949. (ISB/HL).

26. Shane quoted in "Preliminary Proposals for Support of Astronomy by the National Science Foundation," Box 6 Folder S IV, (JGP/CITA). See also "Council Minutes of the American Astronomical Society V" (1948–1950), p. 505. Mimeograph copy. (AAS/AIP).

27. "Preliminary Proposals for Support of Astronomy by the National Science Foundation," p. 5. Box 6 Folder S IV. (JGP/CITA).

28. Greenstein to Menzel, 17 February 1950. (JGP/CITA).

29. Brouwer to Joy, 21 February 1950; Joy to Shane, 16 February 1950; Stebbins to Shane (n.d.), circa 25 February 1950. (CDS/LA).

30. Whipple to Shane, 13 July 1950. (CDS/LA).

31. *Ibid.*

32. Shane to NSF Committee and Council, 6 July 1950. (CDS/LA).

33. On the deliberations, see J. Merton England, *A Patron for Pure Science* (Washington, D.C.: National Science Foundation, 1982).

34. Kevles (1978), p. 358.

35. Gibbs to W. W. Ruby, 12 September 1952. (NRC/CF). Transfers of funds from the other military service agencies were expected as well.

36. Greenstein to Spitzer, 7 January; 17 April 1952. Box 6, (JGP/CITA).

37. R. C. Gibbs, "Report on Recommendations by NRC Committee on Astronomy, Advisory to ONR to Office of Naval Research...," 2 February 1953; R. C. Gibbs and John S. Coleman, "Report on Recommendations by NRC Committee on Astronomy, Advisory to ONR to Office of Naval Research...," 19 February 1955; John S. Coleman "Report on Recommendations by NRC Committee on Astronomy, Advisory to ONR to Office of Naval Research...," 24 February 1956. (NRC/CF).

38. Baum to F. J. Weyl, 3 December 1959. (NRC/CF). Leo Goldberg oral history, 17 May 1978, p. 79. (AIP).

39. Alan T. Waterman Diary entry, 17 March 1954, noted in England (1982), p. 255. England shows that by this time at least Waterman was carefully selecting various disciplines as targets that were ripe for "larger and sometimes collaborative programs." England (1982), *Ibid.*, and chaps. 13 and 14.

40. Otto Struve to Whipple, Goldberg, Whitford, Mayall, and Kuiper, 19 January 1955: draft of "The General Needs of Astronomy," p. 11. Struve/NSF folder. (BA/BUA).

41. A. E. Whitford, "The Plan for a New American Observatory," draft dated 10 November 1955, p. 5. "Astronomy Folder," (NSF). On the role of physicists in establishing the National Radio Astronomy Observatory, see Allan A. Needell, Osiris **3**, 261–288 (1987); and Needell, Journal for the History of Astronomy **22**, 55–67 (1991).

42. Whitford, *Ibid.*, pp. 6–7.

The Modern Society: Changes in Demographics

David DeVorkin and Paul Routly

1. "87th meeting, Victoria, June 24, 1952," Council Minutes, AAS Records, AIP. Hereinafter (AAS/AIP).

2. "105th meeting, Pittsburgh, 18 April 1960," p. 130 (running pagination, p. 847). (AAS/AIP).

3. "92nd meeting, Princeton: 3–6 April 1955," p. 209. (AAS/AIP).

4. John Lankford, *American Astronomy: Community, Careers and Power, 1859–1940* (Chicago: University of Chicago Press, 1997).

5. "97th Meeting, Cambridge, Massachusetts, May 1957," p. 299 (running page 718). (AAS/AIP).

6. "103rd meeting, Toronto, August 1959," pp. 810–814 (running pagination). (AAS/AIP).

7. "105th meeting, Pittsburgh, 18 April 1960," p. 126 (running pagination, p. 843). (AAS/AIP).

8. "106th meeting, Mexico City, 21 August 1960," pp. 138–139 (running pagination, 855–856). (AAS/AIP).

9. "87th meeting, Victoria, June 24, 1952." (AAS/AIP).

10. "89th meeting, Boulder, 26–30 August 1953," pp. 168ff. (AAS/AIP)

11. William A. Baum oral history, 14 January 1997, p. 10rd. (AIP/NASM).

12. "90th Meeting Nashville, 27–30 December 1953;" "91st Meeting Ann Arbor, 20–23 June 1954." (AAS/AIP).

13. Baum oral history, p. 2rd. (AIP/NASM).

14. Baum oral history, p. 11rd. (AIP/NASM).

15. Baum oral history, p. 12rd. (AIP/NASM).

16. "92nd meeting, Princeton: 3–6 April 1955," pp. 206; 210–211. AAS. (AAS/AIP).

17. "93rd meeting, Troy, New York, November 9–12, 1955," pp. 220; 222; 234. (AAS/AIP).

18. Program brochures for meetings. U. S. Naval Observatory Library.

19. See, for instance, meeting reports from Madison and Wellesley: BAAS **10**, n. 2, 460, 1978; BAAS **11**, n. 2, 405, 1979.

20. Program brochure for the Tampa meeting, December 1970, p. 5. U. S. Naval Observatory Library.

21. Richard Lee Walker oral history, 13 January 1997, pp. 16–18rd. (AIP/NASM). Program, 115th meeting, Georgetown University. December 1963. U. S. Naval Observatory Library.

22. Baum oral history, p. 15rd. (AIP/NASM).

23. Walker oral history, p. 22rd. (AIP/NASM).

24. Walker oral history, p. 27rd. (AIP/NASM).

The Origins of the Executive Office at the American Astronomical Society, 1959–64

David A. Attis

1. Lyman Spitzer to Paul M. Routly, 29 November 1961. Box 25, Folder 7. Lyman Spitzer Papers, Manuscript Division, Department of Rare Books and Special Collections, Princeton University Library. (LSP/PUL). Published with permission of the Princeton University Library. I would like to thank Lyman Spitzer for discussions and comments on this chapter and David DeVorkin for additional information and advice. Paul Routly kindly commented on an earlier draft.

2. R. Berendzen and M. T. Moslen, in Berendzen, ed., *Education in and History of Modern Astronomy* (New York Academy of Sciences, 1972). See also Ronald E. Doel, *Solar System Astronomy in America: Communities, Patronage, and Interdisciplinary Science, 1920–1960* (New York: Cambridge University Press, 1996), p. 189.

3. Sky & Telescope, **20** 183 (1960).

4. "Meeting of Council, A.A.S., 2 P.M., Dec. 27, 1960." Box 25, Folder 8. (LSP/PUL).

5. "Memo from L. Spitzer (President) to the Executive Committee, Subject: Proposed Position of Executive Officer, August 20, 1961." Box 25, Folder 7. (LSP/PUL).

6. Spitzer to William Hinckly, 1 February 1962. Box 25, Folder 7. (LSP/PUL).

7. Spitzer to Carl Borgmann, 14 February 1962. Box 25, Folder 7. (LSP/PUL).

8. Routly to C. S. Beals, 3 December 1962; Routly to E. Wilson Lyon (President of Pomona), 14 December 1962. Box 25, Folder 7. (LSP/PUL).

9. C. S. Beals to Routly, 7 December 1962. Box 25, Folder 7. (LSP/PUL).

10. G. C. McVittie to Routly, 7 December 1962. Box 25, Folder 7. (LSP/PUL).

11. Spitzer to Routly, 19 November 1962. Box 25, Folder 7. (LSP/PUL).

Moving the AAS Executive Office to Washington

Peter B. Boyce

1. In the early 1980s, Ralph Alpher of the Dudley Observatory Board of Trustees consulted the author as part of their process to find an effective role for a small private observatory in the present era of large telescopes, space missions and multi-wavelength observations. He was so impressed with the AAS program that he opted to close the Dudley Observatory as a research institution and to establish, instead, the Dudley research awards.
2. "Meeting of AAS Council, January 11, 1981," Albuquerque, NM. AAS Council Minutes p. 2562. AAS files.
3. "Council Minutes," p. 2446. AAS files.
4. AAS Newsletter **1** p. 1. AAS files.

A Brief History of *The Astronomical Journal*

Paul W. Hodge

1. Dieter Herrmann, J. Hist. Astron. **2**, 98–108 (1971).
2. Seth Chandler, AJ **18**, 33–34 (1896). For a more nuanced analysis of Gould's character and relationship to the Dudley Observatory, see James, reference 10.
3. Benjamin Gould, AJ **1**, 1 (1849).
4. Benjamin Gould, AJ **6**, ii (1859).
5. G. M. Clemence and L. F. Jenkins, *General Index to the First Fifty Volumes, Astronomical Journal* (New Haven: AAS, 1948).
6. Donald Osterbrock, ApJ **438**, 1–7 (1995). There is a growing literature on the emergence of astrophysics in America. See: John Lankford and Ricky Slavings, *American Astronomy: Community, Careers and Power, 1859–1940* (Chicago: University of Chicago Press, 1997).
7. Edwin P. Hubble, AJ **29**, 168 (1916).
8. Seth B. Nicholson and Harlow Shapley, AJ **30**, 127–128 (1917).
9. Seth B. Nicholson and Harlow Shapley, AJ **30**, 129 (1917).
10. Mary Ann James, *Elites in Conflict*. (New Brunswick: Rutgers U. Press, 1987).
11. Benjamin Boss, *History of the Dudley Observatory, 1852–1956* (Albany: Dudley Obs., 1968), p. 69.
12. "60th Meeting, Ann Arbor, Michigan, Sept. 1938", p. 143. Council Minutes, AAS Records, AIP.
13. "70th Meeting, Cambridge, Mass., May, 1943," p. 409. Council Minutes, AAS Records, AIP.
14. "67th Meeting, Cleveland, Ohio, December, 1941," p. 387. Council Minutes, AAS Records, AIP.
15. "68th Meeting, New Haven, Conn., June, 1942," p. 392. Council Minutes, AAS Records, AIP.
16. P. Hodge (Editor), *Astronomical Journal General Index, 1976–1996* (Woodbury, NY: AIP, 1997).
17. N. H. Baker, AJ **89**, iii (1984).
18. "71st Meeting, Cincinnati, Ohio, November, 1943," p. 417. Council Minutes, AAS Records, AIP.
19. E. E. Barnard, AJ **24**, 40 (1915).
20. "190th Meeting, Winston Salem, North Carolina, June 1997." Council Minutes, Hodge Papers.

The American Astronomical Society and *The Astrophysical Journal*

Helmut A. Abt

1. H. Abt, ApJ **455**, 407 (1995).
2. Peter B. Boyce and Heather Dalterio, Phys. Today **49**, 42 (1996); Computers in Phys. **10**, 216 (1996).
3. These were listed in H. Abt, ApJ **357**, 1 (1990).
4. H. H. Barschall, Phys. Today **39**, 34 (1986).

Committee on the Status of Women in Astronomy

Susan Simkin

1. BAAS **6**, 412 (1974). Deborah Jean Warner, "Women Astronomers," Natural History, 12–26 (May 1979).
2. BAAS **6**, 413 (1974).
3. Margaret Burbidge, Ann. Rev. Ast. and Ap., **32**, 1 (1994).
4. A. Cowley, private communication.
5. S. Wolff, private communication.
6. D. Osterbrock, private communication.
7. BAAS **6**, 412 (1974).
8. BAAS **12**, 624 (1980).
9. STATUS, **1** (1986).
10. BAAS **27**, 1031 (1995).
11. BAAS **27**, 1049 (1995).

Astronomy Education and the American Astronomical Society

Andrew Fraknoi and Donat Wentzel

1. J. Bishop, Griffith Observer, March 1980, p. 2.
2. PAASA **1**, 210 (1910).

3. S. F. Whiting, PAAS **2**, 145 (1915).
4. K. Bracher, Mercury **14**, no. 5, 1 (1989).
5. J. Pitman, Pop. Astr. **49**, 531 (1941).
6. M. Williams, Pop. Astr. **50**, 65 (1942).
7. D. B. McLaughlin, Pop. Astr. **52**, 313 (1944).
8. F. Miller, private communication.
9. "92nd Meeting, April 1955," pp. 629ff. AAS Council minutes, American Astronomical Society Papers, American Institute of Physics, hereinafter (AAS/AIP).
10. "94th Meeting, March 1956," p. 657. (AAS/AIP).
11. "100th Meeting, June 1958," Appendix 4, p. 779; "103rd Meeting, August/September, 1959," "Annual report of the CEA," p. 829. (AAS/AIP).
12. "106th Meeting, August 1960," p. 877. (AAS/AIP).
13. "107th Meeting, December 1960," pp. 893ff. (AAS/AIP).
14. J. M. Chamberlain, AJ **68**, 215 (1963).
15. G. Abell, BAAS **2**, 254 (1970).
16. BAAS **2**, 254ff (1970).
17. S. Ross, Sky & Telescope (November 1969), 304.
18. R. Berendzen, Annals of the N.Y. Academy of Sciences **198**, 5ff (1972).
19. G. Abell, Annals of the N.Y. Academy of Sciences **198**, 8 (1972).
20. "135th Meeting, August 1971," p. 1583; quote from "136th Meeting, December, 1971," pp. 1647ff.
21. C. Tolbert, BAAS **20**, 770 (1988).
22. V. Trimble, Sky & Telescope (November 1991), 485.
23. Report of the Edwards Committee, June 1994.

The American Astronomical Society and the News Media

Stephen P. Maran

1. Anonymous, "Put Width of Universe At Million Light-Years," *The New York Times* (September 3, 1921).
2. Anonymous, "Seek Einstein Data in Coming Eclipses," *The New York Times* (September 4, 1921).
3. Joel Stebbins, "Minutes of the Council, American Astronomical Society," Vassar College (December 26, 1923).
4. Anonymous, "Another Solar System Is Found 36 Trillion Miles From the Sun," *The New York Times* (April 19, 1963).
5. Stephen Strauss, "Something to be said for pack journalism," *Globe & Mail* (Toronto, January 20, 1997).

6. Charles Petit, "A Roomful of Reporters had Stars in their Eyes at Astronomy Conference," ScienceWriters **43**, No. 4, 1 (1996).

The Origin of the Divisions of the American Astronomical Society and the History of the High Energy Astrophysics Division

Virginia Trimble

1. Martin Schwarzschild to Virginia Trimble. 16 Dec. 1996. Additions in square brackets.
2. Communications to the author from Parker, Kraushaar, Schmidt, Woltjer, and Giacconi.
3. L. Gratton, *High Energy Astrophysics*, (New York: Academic Press, 1966), p. 2.
4. HEAD bylaws. BAAS **10**, 493 (1978).
5. Material courtesy William Kraushaar.
6. HEAD Newsletter No. 5, December, 1971.
7. Material courtesy William Kraushaar.
8. C. de Jager and A. Jappel, eds., *Proceedings of the Fourteenth General Assembly, Brighton 1970*, (Dordrecht, Holland: D. Reidel, 1971), p. 302. Modified from the original listing by the inclusion of first names.
9. V. Trimble, *Visit to a Small Universe*, (New York: AIP Press, 1992), p. 28.
10. *See* Division annual reports in the BAAS, and material courtesy William Kraushaar.
11. HEAD Newsletter, 1996.
12. Records courtesy HEAD Secretary-Tresurer.

The Solar Physics Division

John H. Thomas

1. J. W. Firor, "Notes on the early history of the SPD," 8 May 1995.
2. "Minutes of the Solar Physics Subcommittee of the NASA Space Sciences Steering Committee, April 1965." Quoted in K. Hufbauer, *Exploring the Sun* (Baltimore: Johns Hopkins Univ. Press, 1991).
3. L. Goldberg to J. Firor, 11 May 1965. Leo Goldberg papers, Harvard University Archives (henceforth LG/HUA).
4. R. Noyes to L. Goldberg, 26 July 1965. (LG/HUA).
5. J. Firor to L. Goldberg, 16 July 1965, SPD archives, Niels Bohr Library, Center for History of Physics (henceforth SPD/NBL).
6. L. Goldberg to J. Firor, 30 September 1965. (LG/HUA).
7. G. C. McVittie to A. K. Pierce, 2 February 1968. (SPD/NBL).
8. J. W. Firor to G. C. McVittie, 4 March 1968. (SPD/NBL).
9. A. E. Whitford to AAS members, 10 July 1968. (SPD/NBL).

10. "Report of the AAS Council, August 1969." AAS archives, Niels Bohr Library.
11. M. Schwarzschild to J. Firor, 23 November 1968. (SPD/NBL).
12. R. G. Athay to J. Firor, 12 May 1970. (SPD/NBL).

The Beginnings of the Division for Planetary Sciences of the American Astronomical Society

Dale P. Cruikshank and Joseph W. Chamberlain

1. R. E. Doel, *Solar System Astronomy in America* (Cambridge: Cambridge University Press, 1996).
2. J. N. Tatarewicz, *Space Technology and Planetary Astronomy* (Bloomington: Indiana University Press, 1990).
3. G. P. Kuiper, in *The Atmospheres of the Earth and Planets* (Chicago: Univ. of Chicago Press, 2nd edition, 1952), p. v.
4. G. P. Kuiper, ed., *The Atmospheres of the Earth and Planets* (Chicago: Univ. of Chicago Press, 2nd edition, 1952).
5. D. P. Cruikshank, *Biographical Memoirs of the National Academy of Sciences* **62**, 259–295, 1993.
6. G. P. Kuiper, Communications of the Lunar and Planetary Laboratory **9**, 183, 403–407, 1973.
7. H. C. Urey, *The Planets, Their Origin and Development* (New Haven: Yale Univ. Press, 1952).
8. G. P. Kuiper, ed., *The Sun* (Chicago: Univ. of Chicago Press, 1953).
9. G. P. Kuiper, ed., *The Earth as a Planet* (Chicago: Univ. of Chicago Press, 1954).
10. A. Danjon, in *The Earth as a Planet* (Chicago Univ. of Chicago Press, 1953), pp. 726–738.
11. J. W. Chamberlain, BAAS **21**, 891–895 (1989).
12. First Arizona Conference on Planetary Atmospheres, published in *The Atmospheres of Venus and Mars*, J. C. Brandt and M. B. McElroy, eds. (New York: Gordon and Breach Science Publ., Inc., 1968).
13. "Second Arizona Conference on Planetary Atmospheres," J. Atm. Sci. **25** (4), 533–671, 1968.
14. "Third Arizona Conference on Planetary Atmospheres," J. Atm. Sci. **26** (5), 795–1001, 1969.
15. "Fourth Arizona Conference on Planetary Atmospheres," Earth and Extraterrestrial Sciences **1**, 171–184, 1970, and J. Atm. Sci. **27**, 523–560, 1970.
16. "Fifth Arizona Conference on Planetary Atmospheres," J. Atm. Sci. **28**, 833–1086, 1971.
17. *Planetary Astronomy, An Appraisal of Ground-Based Opportunities*, Publication 1688, (National Academy of Sciences, 1968). The panel consisted of John S. Hall (Chair), J. W. Chamberlain, W. C. DeMarcus, R. Hide, G. P. Kuiper, B. Mason, C. H. Mayer, B. C. Murray, W. A. Noyes, Jr., J. Oro, T. C. Owen, G. H. Petengill, D. H. Rank, E. Roemer, and R. L. Wildey. W. E. Brunk and Urner Liddell were contributors from NASA, and N. W. Hinners served as a consultant.
18. Owen to Chamberlain, 16 August 1985.
19. Sagan and Owen memo, 1 February 1968. The memo was distributed to Edward Anders, Joseph W. Chamberlain, Frank D. Drake, George B. Field, John S. Hall, Seymour L. Hess, Norman Horowitz, Arvydas Kliore, Gerard P. Kuiper, Guido Münch, John (Juan) Oro, Tobias Owen, Gordon H. Pettengill, Carl Sagan, Eugene M. Shoemaker, Harlan J. Smith, Rupert Wildt, and Albert G. Wilson. These individuals appeared on the "Tentative List of Members of Organizing Committee."
20. Draft letter to Whitford from Sagan and Owen, 1 February 1968.
21. Anders to Sagan, 8 February 1968.
22. Owen and Sagan to Whitford, 18 March 1968.
23. Sagan and Owen cover letter, 21 March 1968.
24. Whitford to Owen, 12 April 1968.
25. Smith to Owen, 16 April 1968. Bracketed words in original.
26. Owen and Sagan memo to distribution, 18 May 1968. Sent to people listed above under (19).
27. Smith to Owen, 16 May 1968.
28. McVittie to Chamberlain, 16 September 1968, with copies to Edward Anders, Lewis Branscomb, Richard Goody, John S. Hall, Arvydas Kliore, Michael McElroy, Tobias Owen, Gordon H. Pettengill, Carl Sagan, and Harlan J. Smith.
29. Whitford to Chamberlain, approximately late 1985.
30. Chamberlain to Organizing Committee, 17 September 1968.
31. Chamberlain to long list of scientists, 1 October 1968.
32. Anders to Chamberlain, 4 November 1968.
33. Nominees for the Committee were R. Goody, G. Kuiper, M. McElroy, B. Murray, G. Pettengill, C. Sagan, I. Shapiro, H. Smith, and F. Whipple, Chamberlain to the Organizing Committee, 30 December 1968.
34. Chamberlain to Organizing Committee, 30 December 1968.
35. Chamberlain to Schwarzschild, 20 January 1969.
36. Schwarzschild to Chamberlain, 19 February 1969.

37. Chamberlain to Schwarzschild, 26 February 1969.
38. Anders to Chamberlain, 11 March 1969.
39. Anders to Chamberlain, 29 April 1969.
40. Chamberlain to Organizing Committee, 24 April 1969.
41. Chamberlain memorandum of invitation to join the DPS, 16 May 1969.
42. Minutes of the first DPS Business meeting, by Owen, January, 1970.
43. Chamberlain to Anders, 25 November 1969.
44. Anders to Chamberlain, 1 December 1969.
45. D. M. Hunten to Cruikshank, quoting from his notes made in 1977, 15 May 1997.
46. Eberhart to Sagan, 2 April 1975.
47. BAAS **28**, 1175–1177, 1996.

The Founding of the Division on Dynamical Astronomy—A Few Recollections

R. L. Duncombe

1. Schwarzschild to Herrick, 18 October 1968. Author's files.
2. *Ibid*.
3. *Ibid*.
4. *Ibid*., p. 3.
5. *Ibid*., p. 4.
6. *Ibid*., p. 5.
7. Victor Szebehely to Martin Schwarzschild, 27 November 1968. Author's files.
8. *Ibid*., p. 3.
9. Schwarzschild to Danby, *et al.*, 4 March 1969. Author's files.

The Historical Astronomy Division

Katherine Bracher

1. J. S. Eddy to K. Bracher, 30 July 1996.
2. K. Brecher to L. W. Fredrick, 22 January 1979.
3. O. Gingerich to K. Bracher, 24 July 1996.
4. K. Brecher to L. W. Fredrick, 27 May 1979.
5. O. Gingerich to L. W. Fredrick, 3 November 1979.
6. L. Doggett, in HAD Newsletter No. 26, 6, February 1993.
7. D. Diadevaia to Bracher, 1997, private communication.
8. J. Lankford, in HAD Newsletter No. 24, 1992.
9. These papers were published as a special edition of the *Journal for the History of Astronomy*, guest-edited by Robert McCutcheon, Ron Doel, LeRoy Doggett and David DeVorkin, JHA **26**, pt. 4 (November 1995).
10. "National Observatories" also appeared as a special issue in JHA **22**, pt. 1 (February 1991).
11. J. Lankford, BAAS **16**, 560–564, 1984.
12. The papers were published as a special issue in JHA **21**, pt. 1 (February 1990).

Prioritizing Science: A Story of the Decade Survey for the 1990s

John N. Bahcall

1. This article is based upon a shorter report published in Science **251**, 1412 (1991). *See* Popular Papers at http://www.sns.ias.edu/~jnb

GLOSSARY

AAAS - American Association for the Advancement of Science
A&A - *Astronomy and Astrophysics*
AAS - American Astronomical Society
AG - Astronomische Gesellschaft
AGU - American Geophysical Union
AIM - Astrometric Interferometry Mission
AJ - *The Astronomical Journal*
ANS - Astronomical Netherlands Satellite
ApJ - *The Astrophysical Journal*
APS - American Physical Society
ARC - NASA-Ames Research Center for Astrophysical Research Consortium
ASCA - Advanced Satellite for Cosmology and Astrophysics
ASP - The Astronomical Society of the Pacific
AUGER - Cosmic-Ray Program
AURA - Association of Universities for Research in Astronomy
AXAF - Advanced X-Ray Astronomy Facility
BAAS - *Bulletin of the American Astronomical Society*
BATSE - Detector on Compton Gamma Ray Observatory
CBI - Cosmic Background Imager
CCD - Charged Coupled Device
CfA - Harvard-Smithsonian Center for Astrophysics
CGRO - Compton Gamma Ray Observatory Satellite
COBE - Cosmic Background Explorer
COS-B - Celestial Gamma Ray satellite
CSWA - Committee on the Status of Women in Astronomy
DCP - Division of Cosmic Physics
DOD - Department of Defense
DOE - Department of Energy
EGRET - Detector on Compton Gamma Ray Observatory
FUSE - Far Ultraviolet Explorer
GONG - Global Oscillations Network Group
HAO - High Altitude Observatory
HEAO - High Energy Astrophysics Observatory
HST - Hubble Space Telescope
IRAS - Infra Red Astronomy Satellite
ISM - Interstellar Medium
IUE - International Ultraviolet Explorer Satellite
JRASC - *Journal of the Royal Astronomical Society of Canada*
LEST - Large Earth-based Solar Telescope
LIGO - Laser Interferometric Gravitational Wave Observatory
MAP - Microwave Anisotropy Probe

MIDEX - (NASA) Mid-Class Explorer
MMA - Millimeter Array
MNRAS - *Monthly Notices of the Royal Astronomical Society*
NASA - National Aeronautics and Space Administration
NCAR - National Center for Atmospheric Research
NOAA - National Oceanographic and Atmospheric Administration
NOAO - National Optical Astronomy Observatories
NRAO - National Radio Astronomy Observatories
NSF - National Science Foundation
NSO - National Solar Observatory
OAO - Orbiting Astronomical Observatory
OMB - Office of Management and Budget
OSTP - Office of Science and Technology Policy
OSO - Orbiting Solar Observatory
PAAS - *Publications of the American Astronomical Society*
PAASA - *Publications of the Astronomical and Astrophysical Society of America*
PASP - *Publications of the Astronomical Society of the Pacific*
PhysToday - *Physics Today*
Pop. Astr. - *Popular Astronomy*
RAS - Royal Astronomical Society of London
RASC - Royal Astronomical Society of Canada
ROSAT - Roentgen Satellite - European x-ray satellite
RXTE - Rossi X-Ray Timing Explorer
SAS - Small Astronomy Satellite
SIRTF - Space Infrared Telescope Facility
SMEX - Small Explorer
SNR - Supernova Remnant
SOFIA - Stratospheric Observatory for Infrared Astronomy
SoHo - Solar and Heliospheric Observatory
SPD - Solar Physics Division
STScI - Space Telescope Science Institute
VLA - Very Large Array radio telescope
WIYN - Wisconsin-Indiana-Yale-National Optical Astronomy Observatories (NOAO) Consortium
XRB - X-Ray Background
Yohkoh - Japanese word for "Sunbeam" - a solar satellite observatory

AUTHOR BIOGRAPHIES

Helmut A. Abt has been the Managing Editor and first Editor-in-Chief of the *ApJ* from 1971-1998, only the sixth person to hold that position (after Hale, Frost, Struve, Morgan, and Chandrasekhar). His background includes degrees at Northwestern University and Caltech, and positions at the Lick, Yerkes (1953–59), and Kitt Peak National Observatories (1959–97). He did most of the field work for the selection of KPNO. His research has been on stellar duplicity, rotation, classification, and evolution, and on astrosociology.

David A. Attis studied physics as an undergraduate at the University of Chicago where he first encountered the history of science. From there he gained a master's degree in history and philosophy of science at the University of Cambridge and is now working on his dissertation on the history of nineteenth century mathematics and physics in Ireland, under Norton Wise at Princeton University. In preparing his chapter he enjoyed the advice and counsel of Lyman Spitzer, who commented on drafts and offered personal insights.

John Norris Bahcall is Professor of Natural Sciences at the Institute for Advanced Study, Princeton. He trained in physics at Berkeley (1956) and Harvard (1961), and was on the faculty of the California Institute of Technology. His interests include models of the Galaxy, dark matter, atomic and nuclear physics applied to astronomical systems, stellar evolution, and quasar emission and absorption lines. He has garnered numerous awards for his research on quasars and on solar neutrinos, most recently the Hans Bethe Prize (1998). He was President of the American Astronomical Society from 1990–1992 and Chair of the National Academy Decade Survey Committee for Astronomy and Astrophysics in the 1990s.

Peter Bradford Boyce is immediate past Executive Officer of the AAS. He graduated from Harvard and then received a Ph.D. in astronomy from the University of Michigan in 1963. He has been a staff member at the Lowell Observatory, adjunct Professor at Ohio State University, and then came to Washington to serve as Program Director of the Astronomy Division at NSF. He was a Congressional Fellow in 1977–1978 before becoming the third AAS Executive Officer. His interests include public science policy and federal funding for astronomy, photoelectric spectra, instrumentation and SETI.

Katherine Bracher is Professor Emeritus of Astronomy at Whitman College in Walla Walla, Washington, where she had been on the faculty since 1967. She received her A.B. degree in astronomy from Mount Holyoke College, and the A.M. and Ph.D. from Indiana University. With interests in the history of astronomy, she has served as Chair (1989–1991) of the Historical Astronomy Division of the American Astronomical Society and as a member of the ASP's History Committee. In 1989, she received Whitman's Lange Award for Distinguished Science Teaching.

E. Margaret Burbidge, emeritus Professor in the Center for Astrophysics and Space Science at the University of California, Irvine, trained at the University of London. She has won countless awards and prizes for her work and has held many distinguished positions in astronomy, including President of the AAS (1976–1978) and the AAAS (1982); Director, Royal Greenwich Observatory (1972–1973); member of the NAS Space Science Board (1971–1974). She is a Fellow of the Royal Society. Her interests include astronomical spectroscopy, nucleosynthesis, and extragalactic astronomy and cosmology.

Joseph W. Chamberlain, emeritus Professor in the Department of Space Physics and Astronomy at Rice University, was educated at the Universities of Missouri and Michigan. He was project scientist at the U.S. Air Force Cambridge Research Center (1951–1953) and was a staff member at the Yerkes Observatory from 1953 to 1962. He then was associate Director of the planetary science division of KPNO from 1962 to 1970. In 1971, he became adjunct professor at Rice and from 1971 to 1973 was Director of the Lunar Science Institute. His specialties include planetary atmospheres, aurora and airglow, as well as atmospheric pollution and climate.

Dale P. Cruikshank is a planetary scientist at NASA's Ames Research Center. He received his B.S. from Iowa State University in 1961 and his Ph.D. from the University of Arizona in 1968. He has worked in Moscow and the Crimea, spent one more year at the Lunar and Planetary Laboratory, and in 1970 joined the faculty of the University of Hawaii. His specialty is asteroids and the small bodies of the outer Solar System. He is particularly interested in the organic material on small bodies, and the connections of such material with the organic matter and ices in the interstellar medium. He also studies the infrared spectra of asteroids, with the specific goal of tracing certain kinds of meteorites to their asteroidal parent bodies.

David H. DeVorkin trained in astronomy at UCLA, San Diego State and Yale, and holds a Ph.D. in the history of science from the University of Leicester (1978). He is curator of the history of astronomy and the space sciences at the National Air and Space Museum, Smithsonian Institution. His specialties are 20th century American astrophysics and space science. During the process of editing this centennial book, he was Chair of the Historical Astronomy Division (1997–1998) of the AAS.

Raynor L. Duncombe, professor of aerospace science, the University of Texas at Austin since 1976, has degrees from Wesleyan University and the University of Iowa. He held the position of Astronomer at the U.S. Naval Observatory from 1942 to 1975 and was Director of the Nautical Almanac Office from 1963 to 1975. His specialties include theories of the principal planets and minor planets, astronomical constants and astrometry. He is a member of the astrometry team of the Hubble Space Telescope and is a charter member of the Division of Dynamical Astronomy.

Andrea K. Dupree, a senior scientist at the Smithsonian Astrophysical Observatory (part of the Harvard-Smithsonian Center for Astrophysics), specializes in ultraviolet astronomy and was President of the American Astronomical Society from 1996–1998. A graduate of Wellesley College, Dupree received her doctorate in astrophysics from Harvard University. She has been a lecturer in the Harvard Astronomy department, and served as Director of the Solar and Stellar Physics Division of the Center for Astrophysics from 1980 to 1987. Her research centers on stars, their atmospheres, structure, and evolution using spectroscopic methods.

Frank K. Edmondson is Professor Emeritus of Astronomy at Indiana University. Following graduation from I.U. in 1933, he was at the Lowell Observatory for two years, and returned to I.U. as Instructor after he received his Ph.D. from Harvard in 1937. He was Treasurer of the AAS for twenty-one years (1954–1975), and also served as Secretary of Section D of the AAAS (1950–1958) and President (1962). Other positions include: Chairman of the U.S. National Committee of the International Astronomical Union (1958–1964), NSF Program Director for Astronomy (1956–1957), Member of the AURA Board of Directors (1957–1983), Vice President (1957–1961), and President (1962–1965). He was appointed AURA Consultant/Historian at the time of his retirement in 1989.

Andrew Fraknoi is Chair of the Astronomy Department at Foothill College and an Educational Consultant for the ASP. He was the ASP Executive Director for 14 years and edited *Mercury* magazine and *The Universe in the Classroom* newsletter. Currently, he is the Director of Project ASTRO, a program to link professional and amateur astronomers with 4th through 9th grade classrooms around the country. He is author or co-author of 13 books on astronomy and astronomy education and appears regularly on local and national radio programs. He is the recipient of the AAS Annenberg Foundation Prize and the ASP's Klumpke-Roberts Award; Asteroid 4859 has been named Asteroid Fraknoi to recognize his work in education and public outreach.

Laurence W. Fredrick is emeritus Professor of Astronomy at the University of Virginia. He trained at Swarthmore and received his Ph.D. from the University of Pennsylvania and has worked at the Sproul and Lowell Observatories. He was Secretary of the AAS from 1969 to 1980. His interests include binary stars, infrared spectroscopy, image tubes, and astrometry.

Paul Hodge has been the Editor of the *The Astronomical Journal* since 1984. He also serves as a Professor of Astronomy at the University of Washington, where he has been on the faculty since 1965. His research work has been concentrated on stars, star clusters, stellar evolution, and interstellar matter in nearby galaxies.

Richard A. Jarrell is Professor of Science & Technology Studies in the Faculty of Pure and Applied Science at York University. He is a graduate of Indiana University and holds a Ph.D. in the history of science from the University of Toronto. He has published widely in the history of Canadian and Irish science, especially history of astronomy. His *Cold Light of Dawn* was the first full-length treatment of Canadian astronomy.

Steve Maran, AAS Press Officer since 1985, is Assistant Director of Space Sciences at NASA's Goddard Space Flight Center in Greenbelt, MD. A Co-Investigator on the Hubble Space Telescope Imaging Spectrograph and the Goddard High Resolution Spectrograph, he is the Editor of *The Astronomy and Astrophysics Encyclopedia,* among other works. He began dealing with the news media in 1957 as the press representative of the New York Moonwatch Team, which tracked Sputniks from a rooftop at Rockefeller Center. He holds the B.S. in Physics from Brooklyn College and the M.A. and Ph.D. in Astronomy from the University of Michigan.

Donald E. Osterbrock is a research astronomer who attended his first AAS meeting in 1950 and joined the Society in 1952, the year he received his Ph.D. degree. He was the Director of Lick Observatory from 1973 to 1981, President of the American Astronomical Society from 1988 to 1990, and Chair of its Centennial Committee since its formation in 1995. He was not present at the founding of the AAS, but became a historian in his later years, and has published numerous papers and four books on the history of American astronomy and astrophysics in the big-telescope era.

Marc Rothenberg is Editor, Joseph Henry Papers Project, Office of Smithsonian Institution Archives. He specializes in the history of American physical science, including astronomy, from the War of 1812 to World War I. He is most concerned with issues of education and patronage.

Paul M. Routly was trained at McGill University and received a Ph.D. in astrophysics from Princeton in 1951. He has held positions at Caltech, Pomona College and at the U.S. Naval Observatory. He was the Society's first Executive Officer, serving from 1962 to 1969. He has had research interests in astrometry, molecular spectroscopy and atomic transition probabilities. He has been a volunteer researcher in the Division of Space History at the National Air and Space Museum for almost a decade.

Vera C. Rubin is an observational astronomer who specializes in the study of motions of gas and stars in galaxies and motions of galaxies in the universe. She is a graduate of Vassar College (B.A.), Cornell University (M.A.) and Georgetown University (Ph.D.); George Gamow was her thesis advisor. She is a member of the U.S. National Academy of Sciences and a staff member of the Carnegie Institution of Washington, Department of Terrestrial Magnetism. President Clinton awarded her the National Medal of Science in 1993. In 1996, she received the Gold Medal of the Royal Astronomical Society (London); the first woman to be awarded the Medal since Caroline Herschel in 1828.

Susan M. Simkin has been a Professor of Physics and Astronomy at Michigan State University since 1983. She received her B.A. from Earlham College (Richmond, Indiana) in 1962 and Ph.D. in astronomy from the University of Wisconsin (Madison) in 1967. Prior to 1983, she held a succession of research and teaching positions at Columbia University, the Kapteyn Institute, and Mt. Stromlo Observatory. She has served on numerous committees for the AAS, AAAS and NRAO. Her research interests include the study of active galaxies (both optical and radio) and the development of observational measurement techniques.

John H. Thomas is Professor of Mechanical and Aerospace Sciences and of Astronomy at the University of Rochester, where he has also served as University Dean of Graduate Studies. He is an original member of the Solar Physics Division and served as Chair of the Division during 1995–97. His research in solar physics has included theoretical and observational studies of dynamical phenomena in sunspots, helioseismology, and theoretical studies of the solar dynamo. He is a Scientific Editor of *The Astrophysical Journal* and an Affiliate Scientist at the High Altitude Observatory, and he has held visiting positions at Sacramento Peak Observatory, the Max-Planck-Institute for Astrophysics, and the universities of Cambridge, Oxford, and Sydney.

Silvia Torres-Peimbert was born in Mexico City and did undergraduate study at the National University of Mexico and graduate study at the University of California, Berkeley. She has been on the staff of the Institute of Astronomy of the National University of Mexico since 1969. Her main interests are in abundance determinations in planetary nebulae and HII regions. In addition, she is editor of *Revista Méxicana de Astronoma y Astrofísica*.

Virginia Trimble oscillates between the University of California, Irvine, and the University of Maryland at roughly 30 nHz. She was one of the less successful Chairs of the High Energy Astrophysics Division and is currently one of the Vice Presidents of the American Astronomical Society and is Vice Chair of the Historical Astronomy Division. Her astronomical interests include the structure and evolution of stars and galaxies, cosmology, and life in the universe.

Donat G. Wentzel is Professor Emeritus, Department of Astronomy, University of Maryland College Park. His research interests include the plasma physics of cosmic rays and the magnetohydrodynamics and plasma physics of the Sun, and a long-time commitment to educational activities. He has developed curricula which portray frontier science as a human activity involving judgment of data and interpretations, an emphasis widely copied and today known as "science awareness." He helped start the Task Group on Education in Astronomy for the AAS, and for the IAU he helped to organize several International Schools for Young Astronomers (most recently in Iran) and supervised the Visiting Lecturers Program and the project Teaching for Astronomy Development (mostly Vietnam and Central America).

Thomas R. Williams retired after a career in industry, and is now a graduate student at Rice University. His historical interests include the contributions of amateurs to astronomy, and observatories as institutions in nineteenth and early twentieth-century America. Tom's interests as an amateur astronomer include variable stars and comets.

Sidney Carne Wolff is Director, National Optical Astronomy Observatories. She holds a B.A. from Carleton College, Minnesota, 1962 (honorary Doctor of Science, 1985); Ph.D. University of California, Berkeley, 1966 and was President of the AAS (1992–94). Her research interests include: stellar atmospheres and the evolution, formation and composition of stars. She has authored over 75 professional articles, one book, and co-authored four college astronomy texts.

INDEX